Great Jews

in the

Performing Arts

Great Jews

in the

Performing
Arts

Darryl Lyman

JD | JONATHAN DAVID PUBLISHERS, INC.
Middle Village, New York 11379

GREAT JEWS
IN THE
PERFORMING ARTS

Copyright © 1999

by Darryl Lyman

Jonathan David Publishers, Inc.
68-22 Eliot Avenue
Middle Village, New York 11379

www.jdbooks.com

2 4 6 8 10 9 7 5 3 1

Library of Congress Cataloging-in-Publication Data

Lyman, Darryl, 1944
    Great Jews in the Performing Arts / by Darryl Lyman
         p.   cm.
    Includes Index.
    ISBN 0-8246-0419-9
    1.   Jewish entertainers—United States Biography Dictionaries.
    I.   Title.
    PN1583.L93 1999
    791' .089' 924073—dc21   99-28219
    [B]   CIP

Designed and composed by John Reinhardt Book Design

Printed in the United States of America

Contents

THUMBNAIL SKETCHES

CONTENTS

Acknowledgments

Thanks are due to the following for their help in acquiring the photographs reproduced in this book: the bookstores Larry Edmunds Bookshop (Hollywood) and Eddie Brandt's Saturday Matinee (North Hollywood), Jerry Ohlinger's Movie Material Store (New York), Movie Time News (New York); the film studios Columbia, Metro-Goldwyn-Mayer, Orion, Paramount, Republic, Twentieth Century-Fox, United Artists, Universal, and Warner Bros.; the television networks ABC, CBS, NBC, and PBS; the magazines *International Musician* and *Musical America*; the staffs of the American Jewish Archives, Herbert Breslin, Inc. ICM Artists, Ltd. and the William Morris Agency; and the individuals Jaacov Agor, Clarence S. Bull, Coburn, Shimon Finkel, Roman Freulich, Brian Hamill, Gene Kornman, Dennis Lyman, Newey, Joyce Rudolph, Jack Scagnetti, Barbra Streisand, and Joe Walters.

Introduction

Great Jews in the Performing Arts presents more than one hundred detailed biographies and two hundred brief biological sketched of Jewish actors, actresses, comedians, and dancers. (Well-known musicians are profiled in my work, *Great Jews in Music*.) This book is not intended to be an encyclopedic reference book about Jewish performers. Its purpose is to show the vast range of contributions that Jews of diverse nationalities and from different eras made to all types of popular, classical, and traditional entertainment, from musical comedies to ballet to Hebrew theater. Thus, while this book contains more than three hundred entries, it is not all-inclusive—readers may have favorite performers who do not appear here.

Jews have participated in the performing arts for almost two thousand years, and this book includes accounts of a number of Jewish performers who lived in previous centuries. The following brief historical overview of Jews in the performing arts should help clarify the circumstances and events that affected how those performers lived and worked.

Ancient Theater

In ancient times pious Jews rejected all stage activity, and no Jewish theater was created in Palestine. However, during the first century B.C.E., gentile theaters were established there, and many Jews attended the pagan theaters. By the first century of the Christian era, Jews were even performing on the pagan stage. In Rome the Jewish actor Aliturus was among Emperor Nero's favorites, and a man named Menophilus appears to have been a Jewish comedian. The third-century rabbinical scholar Resh Lakish earned his living as a circus strongman.

During that time, however, most gentile shows were dominated by coarse, ribald comedy that often ridiculed Jews and their customs. As Jews became increasingly unpopular, they tended to conceal their origin. Consequently, for several centuries Jewish theatrical activity was obscured.

Jewish Theater, Middle Ages to 1900

In medieval European ghettos, Jews routinely hired Jewish clowns to appear at social events and at wedding celebrations. In fact, the earliest, and for a long time the only, professional Yiddish-speaking theatrical performers were clowns. As late as the nineteenth century, some Hasidic rabbis employed jesters.

From the late medieval period until the late nineteenth century, Yiddish theater was limited primarily to plays that celebrated religious holidays, like Purim. Clowning was a principal element of the elaborate Purim plays. The celebration would begin with a procession led by all sorts of clowns. The clown-hero of the day was the crazy Purim King, a fat, Bacchus-like character holding a wineglass and riding on a wine cask pulled by schoolboys. Accompanying him were assorted fools and clowns, such as one holding—and wearing—kitchen utensils and another dressed as a servant girl. Following the clowns came people dressed like characters from the Bible, tradespeople, musicians, and others—all proceeding through the ghetto streets to the location where the play was being held. Purim plays were based on Bible stories, but they always included slapstick clowning between serious plot elements.

Jews in Gentile Theater, Middle Ages to 1900

In the Middle Ages, troupes of gentile clowns, mimes, and acrobats roamed Europe. Among those performers were nearly always some Jews. They told jokes, acted in skits, and performed feats of physical dexterity in marketplaces, in princely courts, and in Christian mystery plays (religious dramas based on biblical texts).

Otherwise, Jews were seldom allowed to appear on the gentile stage until the mid-1800s. Jewish actors, few in number, faced prejudice and, often, abuse. For example, Jews were forced to play clowns and buffoons in front of gentile audiences, and in medieval Italy, Jews were compelled to participate in carnival shows as mounts for the gentile public. Many Jewish characters were created by gentile playwrights, but they were nearly always villainous (such as Shylock in Shakespeare's *The Merchant of Venice)* and were played by non-Jews.

The Jewish emancipation and assimilation movements of the nineteenth century opened doors for Jews on the stage. Near the end of the 1800s, Jews finally began to gain recognition in the gentile theater. Among the prominent Jewish actors of the time were Rudolf Schildkraut in Germany and David Warfield in the United States.

Modern Yiddish Theater

The late nineteenth century also saw the rise of the modern Yiddish theater—a secular, commercial theatrical movement that sprang from the tradition of the old Purim plays, especially through the efforts of Abraham Goldfaden, a playwright, composer, producer, manager, and impresario. Goldfaden started his career as a Purim player, performed in some early Yiddish secular plays, and, in Romania in 1876, began to stage his own

secular shows modeled on his experience in the Purim entertainments. The movement soon spread throughout Europe and the United States. A strong Yiddish theater thrived for many years in New York City, where the stars included the dramatic actor Jacob Adler and the comedian Sigmund Mogulesko.

However, a decline set in between World Wars I and II, as more and more American Jews grew up without Yiddish. In the popular Jewish theater, performers began to combine English and Yiddish into a form sometimes called "potato Yiddish." Inevitably, many Yiddish-speaking actors and actresses tried to switch to the English-language stage. Among the most successful were Paul Muni and Molly Picon. After World War II the Yiddish theater virtually died out, though as late as the 1980's Yiddish players were still staging brief seasons in New York City. By the 1990s Yiddish productions were reduced to an occasional show, such as Avi Hoffman's music revue *Too Jewish?* (1995).

Jews in Modern Vernacular Performing Arts

The earliest significant influx of Jews into the modern vernacular performing arts occurred in the realm of light entertainment. From the Middle Ages on, Jews had excelled as clowns, mimes, singers, dancers, jugglers, acrobats, storytellers, and wild-animal tamers. From their traditions emerged innumerable early-twentieth-century revue, burlesque, vaudeville, music-hall, and musical-comedy stars. Some of the best known performers included the escape artist Harry Houdini; the burlesque clown Bert Lahr; the revue and musical-comedy performers Fanny Brice, Eddie Cantor, and Al Jolson; and the comedian-actors Jack Benny, George Burns, and Ed Wynn.

Eventually, Jews succeeded in all types of performing-arts venues, including Broadway, nightclubs, the borscht belt (the theaters and nightclubs associated with the Jewish summer camps and resort hotels of the Catskill Mountains), comedy clubs, radio, TV, and films. Among the film giants of Jewish heritage are Woody Allen, Lauren Bacall, Tony Curtis, Kirk Douglas, Harrison Ford, John Garfield, Dustin Hoffman, Jerry Lewis, the Marx Brothers, Edward G. Robinson, Peter Sellers, and Barbra Streisand. Jewish television stars include Beatrice Arthur, Edward Asner, Milton Berle, Sid Caesar, Peter Falk, Jack Klugman, Hal Linden, Leonard Nimoy, William Shatner, Dinah Shore, and Henry Winkler.

Definition of a Jew

Who is a Jew? *Great Jews in the Performing Arts* follows this definition: a Jew is anyone who was born of a Jewish mother (the Orthodox definition of a Jew), who converted to Judaism, or who, regardless of which parent was Jewish, identified as a Jew or was widely perceived as such by contemporaries (this category is necessary to cover cases, especially from the premodern era, where details of parentage are not available in published sources). People fitting the definition according to Jewish law (that is, the first category above) are included even if they rejected their Jewish identity or converted to another religion.

Excluded are most performers born of a Jewish father and non-Jewish mother. For example, Paulette Goddard, originally Pauline Marian Levy or Levee, had a Jewish father and Catholic mother, as did Douglas Fairbanks, Sr., originally Douglas Elton Ulman. This group also includes Don Adams, Melvyn Douglas, Carrie Fisher, John Houseman, Michael Landon, Paul Newman, and Simone Signoret.

Notes on Style

Abbreviations

The following abbreviations are sometimes used in this text:

Fr. = France
G.B. = Great Britain
Ger. = Germany
It. = Italy
Pol. = Poland
U.S. = United States
Yid. = Yiddish

Dates

Film dates, unless otherwise noted, are years of general release, as distinct from years of productions, copyright, or limited release.

Selected Performances

In the "Selected Performances" lists, television appearances are limited to shows in which the person had a continuing role in a series.

Major
Biographies

Luther Adler

Distinguished Stage, Film, and Television Actor

Luther Adler learned the craft of acting in the American Yiddish theater before turning to the English-language stage, where he became an important leading man on Broadway. Later he had a substantial career as a character actor in films and on TV.

L uther (originally, Lutha) Adler was born in New York City, New York, on May 4, 1903, into a family of famous actors and actresses. He began acting at the age of five, appearing in plays with his father's Yiddish theater company until 1921. He then entered the English-language theater, working in New York City in *The Hand of the Potter* (1921) and touring in *Sonya* (1922).

Adler made his Broadway debut in 1923, playing Leon Kantor, a young violinist with a self-sacrificing mother, in *Humoresque*. Throughout the rest of the 1920s, he worked steadily on the English-language stage. In 1929 he replaced Horace Braham as Samuel Kaplan, the law student, in *Street Scene*.

Adler returned to the Yiddish stage in 1930 and 1931, then joined the Group Theater, where he began with a minor role in *Night over Taos* (1932). Over the next several years, he gave a number of outstanding performances, which earned him the reputation of being one of the most distinguished stage actors of his time. He played the ambitious, vicious Sam Ginsburg in *Success Story* (1932), the radical professor Julian Vardaman in *Alien Corn* (1933), the steadfast physician Dr. Gordon in *Men in White* (1933), and the crippled war veteran Moe Axelrod in *Awake and Sing!* (1935). He also played

Joe Bonaparte (perhaps the most important role of his career) in *Golden Boy* (1937), Charleston in *Thunder Rock* (1939), Mr. Robinson in *Jane Eyre* (1943), which he also directed, and the title character in *Uncle Harry* (1944).

The Holocaust prompted Adler and others to participate in stage works that focused the general public's attention on the plight of Jews. In 1943 he appeared in Ben Hecht's pageant *We Will Never Die*. The program consisted of three parts: "The Roll Call," a recitation of names of great Jews in the arts and sciences from ancient times to the modern era, "Jews in the War," a dramatization of the contributions of American Jewish war heroes, and "Remember Us," a presentation of reports about the slaughters in Nazi Europe. In 1946 Adler directed Hecht's drama-pageant *A Flat Is Born*, which was produced to aid and explain the cause of Zionism. Among the performers whom Adler directed in the play were Paul Muni, Celia Adler (his half sister), and the young non-Jew Marlon Brando.

Adler devoted the late 1940s and early 1950s primarily to film work. (He had made his movie debut in 1937 in *Lancer Spy*, but it wasn't until 1949, when he played a belligerent Dutch tycoon in *Wake of the Red Witch*, that he became firmly established as an important movie character actor.) His heavy features often led filmmakers to cast him as a villain. He played a crime boss in *D.O.A.* (1950), Adolph Hitler in *The Desert Fox* (1951), and Janus the Great, a vaudeville star who kills, and then impersonates, Hitler, in *The Magic Face* (1951).

From the early 1950s until his death in 1984, he divided his time among stage, TV, and movie

he had a regular role in the series *The Psychiatrist.*

Adler had minor roles in the films *The Girl in the Red Velvet Swing* (1955) and *The Last Angry Man* (1959). In *Cast a Giant Shadow* (1966), a story about the Arab-Israeli War of 1948, he played Jacob Zion. In *The Man in the Glass Booth* (1975), he was the judge in the trial of a Jew who claims that he is a Nazi war criminal and who becomes obsessed with the idea that he can absorb Nazi guilt and Israeli hatred. Adler's later films included *Voyage of the Damned* (1976) and *Absence of Malice* (1981). It is interesting to note that Adler was never fully appreciated in Hollywood, and his acting was frequently much better than the poor movies in which he was often cast.

Adler married twice. In 1938 he wedded the actress Sylvia Sidney. She appeared with him in *We Will Never Die.* They had a son, Jacob, before they divorced in the late 1940s. In 1959 he married Julia Hadley Roche.

Adler died at his home in Kutztown, Pennsylvania, on December 8, 1984.

Luther Adler

projects. His stage roles included Shylock in *The Merchant of Venice* (1953), Eddie Carbone in *A View from the Bridge* (1957), Willy Loman in *Death of a Salesman* (1960), Henry Drummond in *Inherit the Wind* (1961), Chebutykin in *The Three Sisters* (1964), and, as a replacement for Zero Mostel, Tevye in *Fiddler on the Roof* (1965).

Adler contributed fine performances to a number of live productions during TV's Golden Age. Among the plays that he appeared in were "Hedda Gabler," on *The U.S. Steel Hour* (1954), "Man with a Vengeance," on *General Electric Theater* (1955), and "The Plot to Kill Stalin," on *Playhouse 90* (1958). He later guest-starred on many TV dramatic series, including *Twilight Zone* (1965), *Ben Casey* (1965), and *Hawaii Five-O* (1972). In 1971

SELECTED PERFORMANCES:

STAGE

The Hand of the Potter (1921)
Sonya (1922)
Humoresque (1923)
The Monkey Talks (1925)
Monkey Business (1926)
We Americans (1926)
John (1927)
Red Rust (1929)
Street Scene (1929)
Millions (1930)
The Wild Man (1930)
Night over Taos (1932)
Success Story (1932)

Alien Corn (1933)
Men in White (1933)
Gold Eagle Guy (1934)
Awake and Sing! (1935)
Waiting for Lefty (1935)
Paradise Lost (1935)
The Case of Clyde Griffiths (1936)
Johnny Johnson (1936)
Golden Boy (1937)
Rocket to the Moon (1938)
Thunder Rock (1939)
Two on an Island (1940)
No Time for Comedy (1940)
Accent on Youth (1941)
The Russian People (1942)
Jane Eyre (1943)
Uncle Harry (1944)
Common Ground (1945)
The Beggars Are Coming to Town (1945)
Dunnigan's Daughter (1945)
Tovarich (1952)
The Play's the Thing (1952)
The Merchant of Venice (1953)
The Time of the Cuckoo (1954)
Angel Street (1955)
A Month in the Country (1956)
Reclining Figure (1956)
A View from the Bridge (1957)
Death of a Salesman (1960)
Inherit the Wind (1961)
The Happy Time (1962)
Anna Christie (1962)
Tchin-Tchin (1963)
Brecht on Brecht (1963)
The Passion of Josef D. (1964)
The Three Sisters (1964)
Fiddler on the Roof (1965)
The Tenth Man (1966)

Lancer Spy (1937)
Cornered (1945)
Saigon (1948)
The Loves of Carmen (1948)
Wake of the Red Witch (1949)
House of Strangers (1949)
South Sea Sinner (1950)
Under My Skin (1950)
D.O.A. (1950)
Kiss Tomorrow Goodbye (1950)
M (1951)
The Magic Face (1951)
The Desert Fox (1951)
Hoodlum Empire (1952)
The Tall Texan (1953)
The Miami Story (1954)
Crashout (1955)
The Girl in the Red Velvet Swing (1955)
Hot Blood (1956)
The Last Angry Man (1959)
Cast a Giant Shadow (1966)
The Brotherhood (1968)
The Sunshine Patriot (TV, 1968)
The Psychiatrist: God Bless the Children (TV, 1970)
Crazy Joe (1974)
The Man in the Glass Booth (1975)
Murph the Surf (1975)
Voyage of the Damned (1976)
The Three Sisters (1977)
Absence of Malice (1981)

TV

The Psychiatrist (1971)

Woody Allen

Sage of Anxiety

W. H. Auden, in his poem *The Age of Anxiety*, gave a serious voice to mankind's feelings about the tensions and complexities of modern life. The richest comic expression of those feelings lies in the work of Woody Allen. As a stand-up comedian, actor, and filmmaker, he creates unforgettable comic neurotic characters.

Allen fashions his fictional personae by blend ing elements from his two favorite comedians, Bob Hope (representing traditional humor) and Mort Sahl (representing the counterculture). Into that mix Allen pours the classic characteristics of the Jewish schlemiel (loser), with his insecurities, self-deprecation, and fear of everyday objects ("My toaster hates me"). The characters are deepened through his pondering of the modern existential crisis and his constant debating with himself about spiritual-material conflicts (often expressed as paradoxes, as when he describes his parents' values as "God and carpeting").

Woody Allen was born of Orthodox Jewish parents in New York City, on December 1, 1935. His original name was Allan Stewart Konigsberg. While growing up in the Flatbush section of Brooklyn, he spent as little time as possible at schoolwork, preferring to play sports (especially baseball), watch stage shows, and perform magic tricks.

After graduating from Midwood High School in Brooklyn, he was pressured by his parents into going to college. He briefly attended New York University and then City College of the City University of New York, both of which expelled him within a few months because of his low marks and poor attendance.

Meanwhile, however, Allen had been pursuing his true calling in life—comedy. In his early teens he began to sell gags to newspapers. Later, still in his teens, he wrote material for radio and TV performers, including Sid Caesar. By then he had taken the name Woody Allen. After he left school, he was able to earn a good living as a TV comedy writer. His material was used on *The Tonight Show*, *The Garry Moore Show*, and other programs.

In the late 1950s and early 1960s, his personal life and career took sharp turns. His marriage to Harlene Rosen, whom he had wed in 1954, ended in 1960. He also decided during this period to become a performer, beginning as a stand-up comic in Greenwich Village nightclubs.

A shy man, he found performing to be difficult at first. After a while, however, he soon felt more comfortable on the stage and became a tremendous success after he created his now most well-known fictional persona: an intelligent contemporary urban man struggling feebly against the alienation and anxieties of the cold, mechanized modern world—in comic terms, a klutzy neurotic. By 1963 Allen, through nightclub dates and TV appearances, had established a national reputation.

In 1964 Allen was asked to write and costar in his first film, *What's New, Pussycat?* (1965), a broad,

Woody Allen

episodic sex farce. In *Casino Royale* (1967) he played Jimmy Bond, a spoof of the he-man spy James Bond. Allen wrote, but did not appear in, the light comedy play *Don't Drink the Water*, which was staged in 1966 and released as a film in 1969. He both wrote and starred in *Play It Again, Sam*, staged in 1969 and released as a film in 1972. The story centers on a neurotic film critic trying to recover from the defection of his wife. He drifts back and forth between the worlds of reality and fantasy, conferring with the ghost of the macho Humphrey Bogart.

Allen drew some of the subject matter of *Play It Again, Sam* from his personal experience. In 1966 Allen married the actress Louise Lasser, who had appeared in *What's New, Pussycat?* Within a few years, however, that marriage, too, ended in divorce.

Allen and Lasser appeared together in several films, even after they split up. Among them were *Take the Money and Run* (1969), *Bananas* (1971), and *Everything You Always Wanted to Know about Sex* (*but Were Afraid to Ask)* (1972). Besides starring in those films, Allen directed them and helped write the screenplays. *Take the Money and Run* is a mock documentary of a young man who aspires to become Public Enemy Number One but who fails to make even the top ten. *Bananas* parodies Latin American revolutions, while *Everything You Always Wanted to Know about Sex* spoofs the popular sex manual of that name.

Allen coscripted, directed, and starred in *Sleeper* (1973). This film is generally regarded as the first of Allen's truly great motion pictures, in which a witty script blends with a visual complexity and continuity to create a rich comic-film artistry. Set two hundred years in the future, the film satirizes sophisticated modern life. Allen also played clarinet (at which he is very proficient) in the jazz background score for the movie.

Next, Allen starred in *Love and Death* (1975), a mock epic set in czarist Russia during the Napoleonic wars, in which the protagonist (Allen) is a self-professed "militant coward." Allen also wrote and directed the film, which may be viewed as a spoof of nineteenth-century Russian novels. He then starred in *The Front* (1976), a film about the evils of blacklisting during the McCarthy era. With *Annie Hall* (1977) he returned to his triple role as coscriptwriter, director, and star. While telling the tender, introspective story of the breakup of a love affair, the film provides subtle insight into modern relationships. Diane Keaton, who played the title role, won an Academy Award for her performance.

After writing and directing, but not appearing in, the movie *Interiors* (1978), Allen made *Manhattan* (1979), a romanticized paean to his beloved city. Besides cowriting and directing the film, he starred as Isaac Davis, a successful comedy writer who quits his TV job to write a novel. Though imbued with much humor, the story is also a serious study of selling out, both personally and artistically. Allen then wrote, directed, and starred (as Sandy Bates, a comedy-film director) in *Stardust Memories* (1980). In it, he directs acid humor at both himself and overly serious movie fans.

Allen's mature writing has extended beyond films. Besides writing pieces for major periodicals, including *Playboy* and the *New Yorker*, he has published the books *Getting Even* (1971), *Without Feathers* (1975), and *Side Effects* (1980). He also wrote the play *The Floating Light Bulb*, which was staged in 1981.

A Midsummer Night's Sex Comedy (1982), which Allen wrote, directed, and starred in, was his next film. In *Zelig* (1983) Allen spliced images of himself into newsreel clips from the 1920s and 1930s. Besides playing the role of the human chameleon in the picture, Allen wrote and directed this "mockumentary." He then wrote, directed, and starred in *Broadway Danny Rose* (1984), the story of a small-time talent agent who falls in love with the girlfriend of a second-rate nightclub singer, the agent's own client.

Allen wrote and directed, but did not appear in, *The Purple Rose of Cairo* (1985), a fantasy about a housewife and her movie hero, who walks off the screen and into her gray life. In *Hannah and Her Sisters* (1986), which Allen wrote, directed, and starred in, he dealt with some of his familiar topics: adultery, upscale New York City life, and the modern existential crisis. But he also incorporated new elements: the celebrating of family and the finding of love.

Allen continued to work occasionally as an actor in other filmmakers' productions. He was cast in *King Lear* (1988), *Scenes from a Mall* (1991), and *The Sunshine Boys* (TV, 1997). He also appeared as himself in *Wild Man Blues* (1998), a documentary (directed by Barbara Kopple) about the 1996 European tour of Woody Allen's New Orleans-style jazz band.

Allen wrote, directed, and narrated (but did not appear in) *Radio Days* (1987), a nostalgic story about radio's golden age. His *September* (1987), and *Another Woman* (1988), both of which he wrote and directed are dramatic films, the first being an homage to the Swedish filmmaker Ingmar Bergman. Allen also wrote (or cowrote) and directed *Alice* (1990), *Bullets over Broadway* (1994), and *Celebrity* (1998).

As a writer (or cowriter), director, and actor, he created *Oedipus Wrecks*, one of three short films constituting *New York Stories* (1989); *Crimes and Misdemeanors* (1989); *Husbands and Wives* (1992); *Shadows and Fog* (1992); *Manhattan Murder Mystery* (1993); *Don't Drink the Water* (TV, 1994), based on his 1966 stage play; *Mighty Aphrodite* (1995); *Everyone Says I Love You* (1996), an homage to 1930s Hollywood musicals; and *Deconstructing Harry* (1997). *Oedipus Wrecks*, vintage Allen, is about a young man whose mother tries to sabotage his love life. In *Mighty Aphrodite*, one of Allen's funniest films, a sportswriter adopts a baby boy and then tracks down the child's mother, a prostitute with whom he becomes involved. At the end the writer and the prostitute discover that they are each unknowingly the parent of the other's child. Throughout the film a Greek chorus looks on and comments. *Deconstructing Harry* concerns an author who writes a best-seller about his best friends, who now become his worst enemies. Allen's character in this movie, Harry Block, is not his usual lovable schlemiel but rather an abrasive person who is at a crisis point in his life and describes himself as "spiritually bankrupt."

Allen's personal life has been the focus of much media attention. During his years of work with Diane Keaton, Allen became personally involved with the actress. He later developed an intimate relationship with Mia Farrow who, like Keaton, starred in several Allen films. The Farrow-Allen romance abruptly ended when she discovered that he was having an affair with Soon-Yi Previn, Farrow's adopted daughter. He then lost a well-publicized custody battle with her for their son, Satchel, and their adopted boy, Moses, and girl, Dylan. In late December 1997, the sixty-two-year-old Allen married Previn, aged twenty-seven.

In his work as a stand-up comedian and especially in his films, Woody Allen has created an urban Everyman who is the most important "little guy" in motion pictures since Charlie Chaplin and the most perfect comic embodiment of Auden's *Age of Anxiety*.

Diane Keaton spars with Woody in a scene from Annie Hall.

SELECTED PERFORMANCES:

STAGE

Play It Again, Sam (1969)

FILMS

What's New, Pussycat? (1965)
Casino Royale (1967)
Take the Money and Run (1969)
Bananas (1971)
Play It Again, Sam (1972)
Everything You Always Wanted to Know about Sex*
    (*but Were Afraid to Ask) (1972)
Sleeper (1973)
Love and Death (1975)
The Front (1976)
Annie Hall (1977)
Manhattan (1979)
Stardust Memories (1980)
A Midsummer Night's Sex Comedy (1982)
Zelig (1983)
Broadway Danny Rose (1984)
Hannah and Her Sisters (1986)
Radio Days (narrator, 1987)
King Lear (1988)
Oedipus Wrecks (in *New York Stories*, 1989)

Crimes and Misdemeanors (1989)
Scenes from a Mall (1991)
Shadows and Fog (1992)
Husbands and Wives (1992)
Manhattan Murder Mystery (1993)
Don't Drink the Water (TV, 1994)
Mighty Aphrodite (1995)
Everyone Says I Love You (1996)
Deconstructing Harry (1997)
The Sunshine Boys (produced 1995; TV, 1997)
Wild Man Blues (documentary, 1998)
Antz (animated, voice only, 1998)

TV

Hot Dog (1970–71)

Robert A. Alper

Rabbi-Comic

Rabbi Robert A. Alper bills himself as "the world's only practicing clergyman doing stand-up comedy . . . intentionally." Since 1986 he has simultaneously served as a rabbi and performed as a professional comic.

Robert Abelson Alper was born in Providence, Rhode Island, on January 29, 1945. Coming from a Reform Jewish home, wanting a people-oriented career, and having a rabbi uncle as a role model, he chose to enter the field of rabbinics. He graduated from Lehigh University (1966), was ordained at Hebrew Union College (1972), and became the first Jew to earn a Doctor of Ministry degree at Princeton Theological Seminary (1984). After serving as a full-time assistant and associate rabbi at Temple Beth Zion in Buffalo, New York (1972–78), Alper was a full-time rabbi at Congregation Beth Or in Spring House, Pennsylvania (1978–86).

Since childhood Alper had always had a gift for making people laugh. As a rabbi he used humor effectively in his preaching, teaching, and counseling, and he looked forward to making announcements at services so that he could improvise funny lines. In 1986 he entered a contest for the Jewish Comic of the Year in Philadelphia and took third place out of more than a hundred entrants. Hooked on humor, he switched to a part-time rabbi position at Temple Micah in Glenside, Pennsylvania, officiating at monthly services and on High Holy Days, and began his career as a stand-up comedian.

At first, Alper received little support. Some nights he bombed. "Some colleagues," he says, "I'm sure, were judgmental (what? a rabbi judgmental?) until they saw the act." It was not easy to win over an audience while at the same time distancing himself from the off-color humor that characterizes much of the comedy industry. Many of his colleagues were also skeptical until they watched him perform. But by the early 1990s, Alper was a solid success. He performed on radio; on TV, including *Entertainment Tonight* and *Good Morning, America*; and at comedy clubs, synagogues, conventions, and Jewish community centers.

Alper developed a clean, gentle style modeled after the styles of such comedians as Jerry Seinfeld and Bob Newhart. He also played on his facial resemblance to Steve Martin (Alper's publicity photograph shows him holding a picture of the other comedian). Alper refuses to use profanity or suggestive material or to tell jokes about circumcision, Jewish mothers, Jewish American Princesses, or other topics that do not present a positive Jewish image.

He does, however, glory in the Jewish milieu. Many of his jokes focus on his role as a rabbi. Here is one of his gems: "A woman whose husband had just died called, asking, 'Rabbi, how long after the funeral must I wait before I can start dating?' Suddenly my other phone rang. 'Just a minute,' I said. 'Thank you,' she said and hung up." Another example: "We follow Jewish tradition in my family. When our son was born, we named him after my grandfather. We call him 'Grandpa.'" And: "We have a Jew-

Robert A. Alper

ish cable news network. Every hour a guy meanders across the screen and says, 'You don't want to know about it.'"

Alper believes in the notion that laughter can be therapeutic. Sick people, for example, have told him that after listening to his comedy tapes, their conditions have improved. He also feels that his jobs as comedian and rabbi often overlap, explaining that "while there always was lots of humor in my rabbinate, I've discovered that there's a lot of rabbi in my humor."

Alper has carved out a unique place for himself as the world's only rabbi-comic. Alper shares his life and success with his wife, Sherri, who is a social worker, and their two children, Zack and Jessie.

Alan Arkin

Versatile Actor

Alan Arkin is one of America's most versatile film, TV, and stage actors. He is a respected and durable comic actor, and he has played a wide range of serious roles, including a thug, a deaf-mute, and a Nazi prisoner.

Alan Wolf Arkin was born in New York City, New York, on March 26, 1934. He became interested in entertaining others at a young age. For example, as a child he was overheard telling his friends, "Let's play circus. I'll be everything."

When Arkin was a teenager, he moved with his parents to the Highland Park section of Los Angeles, California, where he attended Benjamin Franklin High School. There, he won a talent contest by imitating another versatile performer, Danny Kaye.

After graduating from high school in 1951, Arkin studied drama at Los Angeles City College and Los Angeles State College. In 1953 he enrolled at Bennington College, having received a special drama scholarship that the all-women's school created so that men would be available for male roles in school plays. In 1955 he left Bennington without a degree.

Arkin settled in New York City and began a career as a songwriter and folk singer. In the late 1950s, he sang in nightclubs in the United States and Europe with a folk trio called the Tarriers.

During this time Arkin was also pursuing his acting career. In 1958 he had a small part in the off-Broadway play *Heloise*. He then joined an improvisational group in Saint Louis, returned briefly to New York City, and joined Second City, a Chicago improvisational group.

It was in Chicago that Arkin finally found himself as an actor. Through the improvisational method, he learned how to mold characters and shape scenes. With Second City, Arkin made his Broadway debut in a revue entitled *From the Second City* (1961). He then appeared in *Man Out Loud, Girl Quiet* (1962), for which he also composed the music.

Arkin's career took off after he was cast as a Jewish adolescent in the Broadway farce *Enter Laughing* (1963). Originally listed as a minor supporting actor, he gave such a brilliant performance as the stagestruck Bronx delivery boy that he stole the show and was soon given star billing. After playing a role in another Broadway comedy, *Luv* (1964), Arkin got his first part in a movie. In the film, the hilarious comedy *The Russians Are Coming, the Russians Are Coming* (1966), he played the wacky leader of a landing party of Russian sailors whose submarine is grounded on a New England island.

Arkin refused to be typecast after his spectacular film debut and subsequently accepted only movie roles that allowed him to exercise his versatility. In *Wait Until Dark* (1967), he played a diabolic thug. In *The Heart Is a Lonely Hunter* (1968), he starred as a deaf-mute who loses, one by one, the few connections he has with the rest of the world and finally commits suicide.

Returning to comedy, Arkin starred in *Inspector Clouseau* (1968) as the bumbling French detective previously (and subsequently) played by Peter Sellers. In *Popi* (1969) Arkin was cast as a

Alan Arkin

played a dentist unsupectingly dragged into a trail of comic mayhem, while for *The Last Unicorn* (1982), an animated children's film, he skillfully recorded the voice of Schmendrick the Magician. In the fact-based *A Deadly Business* (TV, 1986) he played Harold Kaufman, a man who goes undercover for the FBI to expose organized crime's involvement in illegal toxic-waste dumping.

In *Escape from Sobibor* (TV, 1987), another fact-based film, Arkin had one of his most powerful roles, as Leon Feldhendler, leader of the most daring and successful mass escape from a Nazi death camp during World War II. In the spring of 1987 he starred in the TV comedy series *Harry*, as Harry Porschak, a schemer working in a hospital purchasing department.

In the 1990s Arkin was exceptionally active, appearing in a number of theatrical and made-for-TV movies. His wide-ranging dramas and comedies included *Edward Scissorhands* (1990), *Glengarry Glen Ross* (1992), *Doomsday Gun* (TV, 1994), *Heck's Way Home* (TV, 1996), *Grosse Pointe Blank* (1997), *Gattaca* (1997), *Four Days in September* (1997), and *Slums of Beverly Hills* (1998). In 1998 he directed and starred with Elaine May in a New York City production of *Power Plays*, a set of three one-act plays, one of which he also wrote.

Arkin's versatility has been evident in other areas of his career as well. Besides performing as a folk singer, he has been involved in children's music. He composed "Cuddle Bug," "That's Me," and other children's songs, and he recorded children's albums, including *The Babysitters* (1958) and *The Family Album* (1965). He has also directed

Puerto Rican father. In *Catch-22* (1970) he played Yossarian, who loses control of his life and mind when he is trapped in the madness of wartime military service.

Arkin had the title role in *The Defection of Simas Kudirka* (TV, 1978), based on the true story of a Lithuanian seaman who leaped from a Russian ship to the deck of an American Coast Guard cutter in an abortive bid for freedom in 1970. In *The In-Laws* (1979), a spoof of international crime dramas he

films and plays. In addition, he is a gifted writer, having published the children's books *Tony's Hard Work Day* (1972) and *The Learning Condition* (1976) and the adult book *Halfway through the Door* (1979), an account of his experiences with yoga.

Arkin married the actress Barbara Dana in 1964. They had met the previous year when she was his leading lady in *Enter Laughing*. Later they costarred together in a series of spots for the children's TV series *Sesame Street* and in the comedy series *Harry*. They had a son, Anthony. From a previous marriage, to a woman he met at Bennington, Arkin had two sons: Adam and Matthew. All three boys have become actors and have appeared with their father. Examples include, Alan and Adam in *Chu Chu and the Philly Flash* (1981) and Alan and Matthew in *North* (1994).

SELECTED PERFORMANCES:

STAGE

Heloise (1958)
From the Second City (1961)
Man Out Loud, Girl Quiet (1962)
Enter Laughing (1963)
Luv (1964)
The White House Murder Case (1970)
The Opening (1972)
Power Plays (1998)

FILMS

The Russians Are Coming, the Russians Are Coming (1966)
Wait Until Dark (1967)
Woman Times Seven (1967)
The Heart Is a Lonely Hunter (1968)
Inspector Clouseau (1968)
The Monitors (1969)

Popi (1969)
Catch-22 (1970)
Little Murders (1971)
Last of the Red Hot Lovers (1972)
Freebie and the Bean (1974)
Hearts of the West (1975)
Rafferty and the Gold Dust Twins (1975)
The Seven-Per-Cent Solution (1976)
The Other Side of Hell (TV, 1978)
The Defection of Simas Kudirka (TV, 1978)
The In-Laws (1979)
The Magician of Lubin (1979)
Simon (1980)
Improper Channels (1981)
Chu Chu and the Philly Flash (1981)
The Last Unicorn (1982)
Joshua Then and Now (1985)
Bad Medicine (1985)
Big Trouble (1986)
A Deadly Business (TV, 1986)
Escape from Sobibor (TV, 1987)
Edward Scissorhands (1990)
Glengarry Glen Ross (1992)
So I Married an Axe Murderer (1993)
Indian Summer (1993)
Taking the Heat (TV, 1993)
North (1994)
Doomsday Gun (TV, 1994)
Steal Big, Steal Little (1995)
Mother Night (1996)
Heck's Way Home (TV, 1996)
Grosse Pointe Blank (1997)
Four Days in September (1997)
Gattaca (1997)
Slums of Beverly Hills (1998)

TV

Harry (1987)

Beatrice Arthur

Maude and Dorothy

Beatrice ("Bea") Arthur specializes in portraying comic characters of the commanding, acerbic type. She won national fame as the cause-conscious heroine of the TV sitcom *Maude* (1972–78), and from 1985 to 1992 she played the no-nonsense Dorothy in the popular comedy series *The Golden Girls*.

Beatrice Arthur was born in New York City, New York, on May 13, 1926. Her original name was Bernice Frankel. As a youngster, she moved with her family to Cambridge, Maryland. While attending Cambridge High School, she amused her friends with imitations of Mae West. She graduated from Linden Hall High School in Liberty, Pennsylvania, and studied for two years at Blackstone College, a junior college in Virginia. After earning a degree as a medical-lab technician at the Franklin Institute of Science and Arts and working for a short time at a hospital in Cambridge, she decided to go into show business.

A 5-foot 9½-inch-tall standout with a deep, distinctive voice, Beatrice Arthur moved to New York City. There, along with fellow students Marlon Brando and Gene Saks, she studied acting for two years under Erwin Piscator at the Dramatic Workshop of the New School for Social Research. In 1947 she made her first stage appearance in the title role of the Dramatic Workshop's production of *Lysistrata* (1947).

Later in 1947, at the Cherry Lane Theater in Greenwich Village, she made her professional debut, as a member of the speaking chorus in *The Dog beneath the Skin*. Over the next couple of years, at the same theater, she played many important roles, including Inez in *No Exit* (1948), Kate in *The Taming of the Shrew* (1948), and Hesione in *Heartbreak House* (1949).

Also at Cherry Lane was Gene Saks, whom Arthur married in 1950. It was largely because of her encouragement that Saks later turned to directing, at which he became very successful. They adopted two sons, Matthew and Daniel, before they divorced.

In 1951 Arthur joined the stock company at Atlantic City's Circle Theater, where she appeared in several productions, including *The Voice of the Turtle* (1951). In 1953 she worked as the resident comedienne at the Tamiment Theater in Pennsylvania. She played Lucy Brown in the off-Broadway production of Kurt Weill's *The Threepenny Opera* (1954). In 1955 she was a comedienne in *Shoestring Revue*. And in 1957 she appeared in her first Broadway comedy, *Nature's Way*.

Early in her career, when her theater work was sporadic, Arthur occasionally sang in major New York City nightclubs, such as the Blue Angel and Number One Fifth Avenue. She sometimes took parts on TV programs. In 1948 she sang in a TV production of *Once upon a Time*. And in the 1950s, she had bit parts on TV variety series hosted by Steve Allen, Sid Caesar, Ed Sullivan, and others. In 1959 Norman Lear, who had been a fan of Arthur's since he saw her in *Shoestring Revue*, asked her to join the cast of *George Gobel*, a television show of which Lear was the producer-director. Arthur went to Hollywood for the show, but after making two episodes, she returned to New York City.

Beatrice Arthur

In the early 1960s, Arthur went into semiretirement from the theater. She appeared in *Gay Divorce* (1960) and *A Matter of Position* (1962), but she spent much of her time encouraging her husband, who had recently begun his career as a director. In 1964 she returned to the stage in the role of Yente the Matchmaker in *Fiddler on the Roof.* She then won her greatest acclaim as a Broadway actress with her performance in *Mame* (1966), as Vera Charles, Aunt Mame's friend and severest critic. Arthur's husband, Gene Saks, directed the show.

In the late 1960s, Arthur went into semiretirement again. This time her purpose was simply to enjoy the country home forty miles outside Manhattan that she and Saks had purchased. In the early 1970s, Lear tried to induce her to appear on the new TV series *All in the Family.* Arthur was reluctant, partly because she did not want to travel to Hollywood and partly because she was simply not attracted to TV.

Finally she agreed to do a guest part in *All in the Family.* Her performance, aired in late 1971, was electric. The series was dominated by the character Archie Bunker (played by Carroll O'Connor, with whom Arthur had appeared in the 1958 play *Ulysses in Nighttown*), a reactionary, bigoted loudmouth. Arthur created the new character Maude, cousin of Archie's wife, Edith (played by Jean Stapleton). Maude, an outspoken liberal, proved to be more than a match for Archie and gave him his long-overdue comeuppance.

Arthur's performance was so well received that the following year she was given her own TV comedy series, *Maude*, which ran until 1978. The character Maude, an aggressive libertarian and women's libber, made the country laugh at her own human foibles as she tackled such controversial topics as abortion, race relations, and pornography. Maude remains the role by which Arthur is most popularly identified.

Arthur has been in only a few movies. Her first film appearance was a small part in *That Kind of Woman* (1959). She also had roles in the filmed

Bea Arthur

version of *Mame* (1974) and in Mel Brooks's comedy *History of the World, Part I* (1981).

From 1985 to 1992 Arthur had the role of Dorothy, another forceful character given to making caustic comments, in the hit TV sitcom *The Golden Girls.* Living with her octogenarian mother and two middle-aged women, Dorothy was the long-suffering anchor of the household, coping with the quirks of the others. When her mother decided to spend the night with an eighty-five-year-old man, Dorothy, in a role reversal, commanded, "Ma, you're not spending the night at Rocco's. Listen, you live under our roof—you live by *our* rules!"

Since *The Golden Girls* ended, Arthur has not been visible enough for her many fans. She appeared in the film *For Better or Worse* (TV, 1996), and in 1998 she returned to her first love, the stage, performing in the comedy *After-Play* at a theater in Beverly Hills, California.

Beatrice Arthur became a household name when she starred in Maude *with Bill Macy.*

SELECTED PERFORMANCES:

STAGE

The Dog beneath the Skin (1947)
Gas (1947)
Yerma (1947)
No Exit (1948)
The Taming of the Shrew (1948)
Six Characters in Search of an Author (1948)
The Owl and the Pussycat (1948)
Yes Is for a Very Young Man (1949)
The Creditors (1949)
Heartbreak House (1949)
Personal Appearance (1951)
Candle Light (1951)
Love or Money (1951)
The Voice of the Turtle (1951)
The New Moon (1953)
Gentlemen Prefer Blondes (1953)
The Threepenny Opera (1954)
Shoestring Revue (1955)
Seventh Heaven (1955)
What's the Rush? (1956)

Mistress of the Inn (1957)
Nature's Way (1957)
Ulysses in Nighttown (1958)
Gay Divorce (1960)
A Matter of Position (1962)
Fiddler on the Roof (1964)
Mame (1966)
A Mother's Kisses (1968)
The Floating Light Bulb (1981)
After-Play (1998)

FILMS

That Kind of Woman (1959)
Lovers and Other Strangers (1970)
Mame (1974)
History of the World, Part I (1981)
For Better or Worse (TV, 1996)

TV

Maude (1972–78)
Amanda's (1983)
The Golden Girls (1985–92)

Edward Asner

Lou Grant

Edward ("Ed") Asner became nationally famous with his role as the gruff but lovable Lou Grant on the TV series *The Mary Tyler Moore Show* (1970–77) and *Lou Grant* (1977–82). He also played similar roles on other TV series and became a respected dramatic and comedic character actor in many films.

Edward Asner was born of Russian immigrant parents in Kansas City, Missouri, on November 15, 1929. While in his teens, he performed on a local radio station as part of a class that he took at Wyandotte High School. He attended the University of Chicago, where he was active in the drama program.

After two years of college (1947–49), he dropped out and began to do odd jobs. In 1951 he was drafted into the army and sent to Europe. There he managed a highly rated army basketball team.

Released from the military in 1953, Asner was invited to join the Playwrights Theater Club in Chicago, where he performed in plays for two years. In 1955 he moved to New York City and began to act in off-Broadway productions, the most notable of which was the Brecht-Weill musical *The Threepenny Opera* (1956). In 1957 he had a regular role as a police sergeant in the TV crime-drama series *Decoy*. Returning to the stage, he performed numerous Shakespearean roles, such as Bardolph in *The Merry Wives of Windsor* (1959) and the Duke of Exeter in *Henry V* (1960).

In 1959 Asner married the literary agent Nancy Lou Sykes, an Episcopalian. They had delayed the marriage for two years for fear that an intermarriage would anger his Orthodox parents. The wedding ceremony was civil, and their four children—Matthew, Liza, Kathryn, and Charles—were raised in the Jewish faith.

In the early 1960s Asner moved to Los Angeles, where he played a police lieutenant on the popular TV crime-drama series *Naked City* (1960–63). From 1964 to 1965 he was a regular on the dramatic series *Slattery's People*. Over the next several years he acted in a number of movies and TV dramas, often as a policeman or a criminal.

Asner's big break came in 1970 when he became a regular member of the cast on the new TV comedy series *The Mary Tyler Moore Show*. Though he had had very little experience in comedy, he auditioned for, and won, the role of Lou Grant, the irascible but lovable boss of the fictitious WJM-TV newsroom in Minneapolis. For seven seasons (1970–77) the show was one of the most popular series on TV.

During the run of *The Mary Tyler Moore Show*, Asner frequently used his free time to continue his career as a dramatic actor, especially in made-for-TV movies. For example, in *Hey, I'm Alive!* (TV, 1975) he played an airplane pilot who crashes in a frozen Yukon forest and, with his female passenger, somehow finds the physical and psychological strength to survive the forty-nine days until they are rescued. In *Rich Man, Poor Man* (TV, 1976) he was the patriarch of the Jordache family. In *Roots* (TV, 1977) he was a captain of a slave ship. In the biopic *The Life and Assassination of the Kingfish* (TV, 1977) he portrayed Huey Long, Louisiana's Depression-era governor and United States senator.

When *The Mary Tyler Moore Show* went off the air in 1977, Asner's role became the basis for a dramatic series, *Lou Grant* (1977–82). In that show he played the hard-hitting but compassionate city editor of a Los Angeles newspaper.

The Lou Grant character closely resembled Asner himself. Like Grant, Asner became identified with important public issues about which he had strong opinions. That identification became a source of great controversy during his term as the elected president of the Screen Actors Guild (1981–85). He used his visibility to voice his liberal viewpoint on a number of political and social issues, such as American involvement in El Salvador, which he opposed. When the *Lou Grant* series was canceled, it was widely assumed that the reason for the cancellation was Asner's controversial opinions about that issue.

Asner also lent his name to a wide variety of Jewish causes. In 1979, for example, he hosted a PBS series on Jewish holidays. In early 1985 he received a medal from the Jewish Theological Seminary of America for his service in promoting "human rights and interfaith understanding."

Meanwhile, Asner's acting career continued. In *Anatomy of an Illness* (TV, 1984) he portrayed Norman Cousins in the true story of the latter's efforts to cure himself of a debilitating spinal disorder after the medical community had given up hope. Asner also narrated the TV documentary *Battered Wives, Shattered Lives* (1985).

In the late 1980s Asner returned to the television format and portrayed characters clearly in the Lou Grant gruff-but-lovable mold. He played Joe

Edward Asner

Danzig, the principal of an inner-city high school, in *The Bronx Zoo* (1987–88) and Gil Jones, the owner of a garage, in *Thunder Alley* (1994–95).

During this period Asner continued to appear as a character actor in numerous theatrical and made-for-TV movies. They included *Kate's Secret* (TV, 1986), *Moon over Parador* (1988), *JFK* (1991), *Cruel Doubt* (TV, 1992), *Gone in the Night* (TV, 1996), and *Payback* (TV, 1997). He also participated in the documentary films *Tell the Truth and Run: George Seldes and the American Press* (1997), as the voice of Seldes, and *The Long Way Home* (1997), about the birth of modern Israel.

SELECTED PERFORMANCES:

STAGE

Venice Preserv'd (1955)
The Threepenny Opera (1956)
Romeo and Juliet (1959)
The Merry Wives of Windsor (1959)
All's Well That Ends Well (1959)
Legend of Lovers (1959)
The Tempest (1959)
Henry V (1960)
Face of a Hero (1960)
Born Yesterday (1989)

FILMS

The Satan Bug (1965)
The Slender Thread (1965)
The Doomsday Flight (TV, 1966)
El Dorado (1967)
Gunn (1967)
The Venetian Affair (1967)
Change of Habit (1969)
Daughter of the Mind (TV, 1969)
The House on Greenapple Road (TV, 1970)
The Old Man Who Cried Wolf! (TV, 1970)
Halls of Anger (1970)
They Call Me MISTER Tibbs (1970)
The Last Child (TV, 1971)
They Call It Murder (TV, 1971)
Skin Game (1971)
Haunts of the Very Rich (TV, 1972)
The Police Story (TV, 1973)
The Girl Most Likely to ... (TV, 1973)
The Impostor (TV, 1975)
Death Scream (TV, 1975)
Hey, I'm Alive! (TV, 1975)
Rich Man, Poor Man (TV, 1976)
Gus (1976)
Roots (TV, 1977)
The Life and Assassination of the Kingfish
  (TV, 1977)

The Gathering (TV, 1977)
Family Man (TV, 1979)
A Small Killing (TV, 1981)
Fort Apache, the Bronx (1981)
Daniel (1983)
Anatomy of an Illness (TV, 1984)
Kate's Secret (TV, 1986)
The Christmas Star (TV, 1986)
Cracked Up (TV, 1987)
Moon over Parador (1988)
Good Cops, Bad Cops (TV, 1990)
JFK (1991)
Switched at Birth (TV, 1991)
Silent Motive (TV, 1991)
Cruel Doubt (TV, 1992)
Happily Ever After (1993)
Gypsy (TV, 1993)
Heads (TV, 1994)
Gone in the Night (TV, 1996)
The Story of Santa Claus (TV, 1996)
Dog's Best Friend (TV, 1997)
Payback (TV, 1997)
A Christmas Carol (1997)
*Tell the Truth and Run: George Seldes and the
  American Press* (documentary, 1997)
The Long Way Home (documentary, 1997)
Hard Rain (1998)

TV

Decoy (1957)
Naked City (1960–63)
Slattery's People (1964–65)
The Mary Tyler Moore Show (1970–77)
Lou Grant (1977–82)
Off the Rack (1985)
The Bronx Zoo (1987–88)
The Trials of Rosie O'Neill (1991–92)
Fish Police (animated, voice only, 1992)
Hearts Afire (1992–93)
Thunder Alley (1994–95)

Lauren Bacall

Elegant Lady

--◄○►--

One of the truly great movie legends in film history, Lauren Bacall is the epitome of effortless elegance. A powerful on-screen presence, Bacall has attained her legendary stature by working hard, absorbing the lessons of life, and focusing on her career. Her screen roles have included just about everything from a twenty-year-old sexpot in *To Have and Have Not* (1944) to a haughty mother-figure in *The Mirror Has Two Faces* (1996).

--◄○►--

Lauren Bacall was born Betty Joan Perske in New York City, New York, on September 16, 1924. Her mother had been born in Romania with the surname Weinstein-Bacal ("Weinstein" is German, and "Bacal" Romanian, for "wineglass"). When the Weinstein-Bacals arrived in the United States, immigration officials dropped the second half of the hyphenated name and the family became simply the Weinsteins.

Natalie Weinstein married William Perske, a native New Yorker. When Bacall was six years old, her parents split up. After the divorce her mother took the name Bacal. Lauren Bacall, then, grew up as Betty Bacal.

At an early age, Bacall made up her mind to become a Hollywood actress. As a preteenager she did some modeling, and while attending Manhattan's Julia Richman High School, she took Saturday-morning drama lessons at the New York School of the Theater. After graduating from high school in 1940, Bacall studied at the American Academy of Dramatic Arts in New York City for one year. She then worked as a model and a theater usher.

Bacall made her professional acting debut in the Broadway show *Johnny 2 x 4* (1942), in which she had a walk-on part. At about that time, she added another *l* to her surname to avoid such mispronunciations as "Backle." Later that year she was given a speaking role in the Broadway play *Franklin Street*, but it closed out of town.

Bacall got her big break when her picture appeared on the cover of the March 1943 issue of *Harper's Bazaar* magazine. The photo was seen by the movie director Howard Hawks, and soon Bacall was on her way to Hollywood. Hawks changed her first name to Lauren and gave her an important role opposite Humphrey Bogart in *To Have and Have Not* (1944). In this film she created what came to be called The Look, a pose with her chin down and her eyes insinuatingly up. She has said that the pose originated merely as a way of controlling her nerves in her earliest scenes with her famous costar.

Bacall soon began a romance with Bogart. They married in 1945 and appeared together in *The Big Sleep* (1946), *Dark Passage* (1947), and *Key Largo* (1948). Bogart and Bacall also worked together in the radio series *Bold Venture* (1950–51). They had a son, Stephen and a daughter, Leslie.

Bacall made a tremendous impact in her early movies, usually cast as a tough, sultry woman of the world. Later, her roles widened, as in *How to Marry a Millionaire* (1953), in which she played one of three models (with Betty Grable and Marilyn Monroe) in search of rich husbands. The

Lauren Bacall

part allowed her to show her great talent as a comedienne.

In 1957 Bogart died. Bacall, devastated, had difficulty at first redefining herself. Nevertheless, she continued to work, returning in 1959 to the Broadway stage in *Goodbye, Charlie*, in which she played a callous philanderer whose punishment after death is to be sent back to earth as a woman.

In 1961 Bacall married actor Jason Robards, Jr. They had a son, Sam, before divorcing in 1969.

During the 1960s and 1970s, Bacall appeared in several movies, including *Sex and the Single Girl* (1964), *Harper* (1966), *Murder on the Orient Express* (1974), and *Perfect Gentlemen* (TV, 1978). In 1965 she stole the show in the Broadway comedy *Cactus Flower*, as a dentist's secretary who wins her boss after posing as his wife to get him out of a sticky situation with a younger woman. And in the 1970 Broadway show *Applause*, a musical version of the famous movie *All about Eve*, Bacall gave an electric performance in her portrayal of a fading film star.

In 1981 Bacall hit the New York City stage as a high-powered newscaster in the musical *Woman of the Year*. In the movie *The Fan* (1981) she played a high-strung Broadway star preparing for her first musical and becoming a homicidal maniac's object of attention. From 1983 to 1984 she toured with *Woman of the Year*, and in 1985 she starred in a London production of *Sweet Bird of Youth*, which moved to Los Angeles in 1987.

Returning to films in the late 1980s, Bacall appeared in *Appointment with Death* (1988), *Innocent Victim* (1990), the British TV movie *A Foreign Field* (TV, 1993), and *Ready to Wear* (1994). In *The Mirror Has Two Faces* (1996) she played the vain mother of Barbra Streisand's character, and in *My Fellow Americans* (1996) Bacall was the wife of an ex-president of the United States. In December 1997 Bacall was awarded the prestigious Kennedy Center Honor for her lifetime achievement in the performing arts.

In her autobiographies, *By Myself* (1979) and *Now* (1994), Bacall shows her real-life qualities of humor, perception, and straightforwardness. Those qualities also characterize her work. Even during her early years she exuded a rare kind of elegance in her performances. With added years she has refined and enriched her stage and screen presence, so that she now virtually dominates every project that she touches.

SELECTED PERFORMANCES:

STAGE

Johnny 2 x 4 (1942)
Franklin Street (1942)
Goodbye, Charlie (1959)
Cactus Flower (1965)
Applause (1970)
Woman of the Year (1981, 1983–84)
Sweet Bird of Youth (1985, 1987)

FILMS

To Have and Have Not (1944)
Confidential Agent (1945)
The Big Sleep (1946)
Dark Passage (1947)
Key Largo (1948)
Young Man with a Horn (1950)
Bright Leaf (1950)
How to Marry a Millionaire (1953)
Woman's World (1954)
The Cobweb (1955)
Blood Alley (1955)
Written on the Wind (1956)
Designing Woman (1957)
The Gift of Love (1958)
Flame over India (1960)
Sex and the Single Girl (1964)
Shock Treatment (1964)
Harper (1966)
Murder on the Orient Express (1974)
The Shootist (1976)
Perfect Gentlemen (TV, 1978)
The Fan (1981)
Health (1982)
Appointment with Death (1988)
Mr. North (1988)
Dinner at Eight (TV, 1989)
Innocent Victim (1990)
Misery (1990)
All I Want for Christmas (1991)
The Portrait (TV, 1993)
A Foreign Field (G.B., TV, 1993)
Ready to Wear (1994)
From the Mixed-up Files of Mrs. Basil E. Frankweiler (TV, 1995)
The Mirror Has Two Faces (1996)
My Fellow Americans (1996)

RADIO

Bold Venture (1950–51)

Lauren Bacall

Martin Balsam

Archie Bunker's Partner

Martin Balsam was a highly respected character actor for over fifty years. Highlights of his career included performing three roles in the play *You Know I Can't Hear You When the Water's Running* (1967); having key roles in such film classics as *Twelve Angry Men* (1957), *Psycho* (1960), *A Thousand Clowns* (1965), and *Raid on Entebbe* (TV, 1977); and serving as a Jewish comic foil for a WASP bigot in the TV sitcom *Archie Bunker's Place* (1979–81).

Martin Henry Balsam was born in New York City, New York, on November 4, 1919. He made his stage debut by appearing as a villain in an amateur production of *Pot Boiler* (1935). After graduating from DeWitt Clinton High School in 1937, he worked at odd jobs for a few years.

In 1941 Balsam made his professional acting debut by portraying Johann in a Locust Valley, New York, production of *The Play's the Thing*. He made his New York City acting debut later that year, as Mr. Blow in *Ghost for Sale*.

From 1941 to 1945, Balsam was in the military, first with the army and then, from 1943 on, with the air force. Returning to civilian life, he studied acting under Erwin Piscator at the Dramatic Workshop of the New School for Social Research from 1946 to 1948. In 1948 he became a member of the famed Actors Studio of New York City.

Balsam returned to the stage in 1947, playing Sizzi in *Lamp at Midnight*. Over the next several years, he demonstrated his ability as a versatile character actor in a variety of plays, including *Macbeth* (1948), *Home of the Brave* (1949), *The Rose Tattoo* (1951), *Camino Real* (1953), and *Detective Story* (1953). He also began to make guest appearances on television. His early TV credits included the comedy series *The Goldbergs* and *Mr. Peepers*, the drama series *Inner Sanctum*, and the anthology series *Playhouse 90*.

As a result of his successful performances on the stage and on TV, Balsam began to get film offers. He received critical acclaim for his portrayal of a crime investigator in *On the Waterfront* (1954). In *Twelve Angry Men* (1957), he played the foreman of the jury. He was the private investigator who was attacked by a madman with a knife in a classic scene from the Hitchcock masterpiece *Psycho* (1960). Balsam also played the presidential press secretary in *Seven Days in May* (1964).

In one of his finest performances, Balsam portrayed Arnold Burns, the conventional brother of an offbeat New Yorker (played by Jason Robards, Jr.), in *A Thousand Clowns* (1965). In the black comedy *Catch-22* (1970), he played the ridiculous Colonel Cathcart. Balsam also gave an excellent performance as a son who misjudges his father, (portrayed by Edward G. Robinson) in *The Old Man Who Cried Wolf!* (TV, 1970). In *The Taking of Pelham One Two Three* (1974), Balsam played a member of a gang of subway-train hijackers.

In 1977 Balsam played a Jewish airplane passenger in the TV movie *Raid on Entebbe*, a recounting of the true story of a planeload of people who were kidnapped by terrorists, held at the Entebbe Airport in Uganda, and finally rescued in a daring raid by Israeli commandos. In *The House on*

Martin Balsam

From 1979 to 1981, Balsam had a regular role, as Murray Klein, on the TV comedy series *Archie Bunker's Place*. He played the liberal, Jewish business partner of the reactionary, super-WASP bigot Archie Bunker.

Balsam was married three times. In 1952 he wedded actress Pearl L. Somner, whom he divorced in 1954. In 1959 he married actress Joyce Van Patten, with whom he had a daughter, Talia, before obtaining a divorce in 1962. He married Irene Miller, a TV production assistant, in 1963, and with her he had a son, Adam, and a daughter, Zoe. This marriage, too, ended in divorce. Talia Balsam became an actress, appearing in numerous films, including one film, *The Millionaire* (TV, 1978), in which her father also appeared.

Martin Balsam was found dead of natural causes in his Rome, Italy, hotel room on the morning of February 13, 1996.

SELECTED PERFORMANCES:

STAGE

The Play's the Thing (1941)
Ghost for Sale (1941)
Lamp at Midnight (1947)
The Wanhope Building (1947)

Garibaldi Street (TV, 1979), he portrayed Isser Harel, the author of the book serving as the basis for the film, which tells the story of the capture of the real-life Nazi war criminal Adolf Eichmann by Israeli agents in Argentina in 1960. Balsam's later movies included *Little Gloria—Happy at Last* (TV, 1982), *I Want to Live!* (TV, 1983), *The Delta Force* (1986), and *Cape Fear* (1991).

While Balsam was pursuing his film career, he also continued to appear in plays. He received favorable reviews for his performance in *You Know I Can't Hear You When the Water's Running* (1967). His later stage work included *Death of a Salesman* (1974) and *Cold Storage* (1977).

Macbeth (1948)
Sundown Beach (1948)
The Closing Door (1949)
Three Men on a Horse (1949)
Home of the Brave (1949)
A Letter from Harry (1949)
The Rose Tattoo (1951)
Camino Real (1953)
The Country Girl (1953)
Detective Story (1953)
Thirteen Clocks (1954)
Wedding Breakfast (1955)
Middle of the Night (1956)
With Respect to Joey (1957)

A View from the Bridge (1958)
The Iceman Cometh (1961)
Nowhere to Go but Up (1962)
The Porcelain Year (1965)
*You Know I Can't Hear You When the Water's
    Running* (1967)
Death of a Salesman (1974)
Cold Storage (1977)

FILMS

On the Waterfront (1954)
Twelve Angry Men (1957)
Time Limit (1957)
Marjorie Morningstar (1958)
Al Capone (1959)
Middle of the Night (1959)
Psycho (1960)
Ada (1961)
Breakfast at Tiffany's (1961)
Cape Fear (1962)
Everybody Go Home! (1962)
Who's Been Sleeping in My Bed? (1963)
The Carpetbaggers (1964)
Seven Days in May (1964)
The Bedford Incident (1965)
Conquered City (1965)
Harlow (1965)
A Thousand Clowns (1965)
After the Fox (1966)
Hombre (1967)
The Good Guys and the Bad Guys (1969)
Me, Natalie (1969)
Trilogy (1969)
Catch-22 (1970)
Little Big Man (1970)
Tora! Tora! Tora! (1970)
Hunters Are for Killing (TV, 1970)
The Old Man Who Cried Wolf! (TV, 1970)
The Anderson Tapes (1971)
Night of Terror (TV, 1972)
The Man (1972)

The Stone Killer (1973)
Summer Wishes, Winter Dreams (1973)
A Brand New Life (TV, 1973)
The Six-Million-Dollar Man (TV, 1973)
Trapped beneath the Sea (TV, 1974)
Confessions of a Police Captain (1974)
The Taking of Pelham One Two Three (1974)
Murder on the Orient Express (1974)
Mitchell (1975)
Miles to Go before I Sleep (TV, 1975)
Death among Friends (TV, 1975)
The Lindberg Kidnapping Case (TV, 1976)
All the President's Men (1976)
Two Minute Warning (1976)
The Sentinel (1977)
Raid on Entebbe (TV, 1977)
Contract on Cherry Street (TV, 1977)
The Storyteller (TV, 1977)
Siege (TV, 1978)
Rainbow (TV, 1978)
The Millionaire (TV, 1978)
The Silver Bears (1978)
Cuba (1979)
The Seeding of Sarah Burns (TV, 1979)
The House on Garibaldi Street (TV, 1979)
Aunt Mary (TV, 1979)
The Love Tapes (TV, 1980)
The People vs. Jean Harris (TV, 1981)
Little Gloria... Happy at Last (TV, 1982)
I Want to Live! (TV, 1983)
Space (TV, 1985)
St. Elmo's Fire (1985)
The Delta Force (1986)
Second Serve (TV, 1986)
Queenie (TV, 1987)
Two Evil Eyes (1990)
Cape Fear (1991)
The Silence of the Hams (1995)

TV

All in the Family (1979–81)

Roseanne Barr

Domestic Goddess

Roseanne Barr is arguably the most popular female comedienne of our times. Her comedy is about "married couples that love each other and yet can't stand each other." In order to lampoon family life most effectively, she has adopted the stage persona of an embattled housewife, or as she puts it, a "domestic goddess." "My husband," Barr complains in one of her typical nightclub routines, "comes home and says 'Roseanne, don't you think we should talk about our sexual problems?' Like I'm going to turn off *Wheel of Fortune* for that!" From 1988 to 1997, she starred in the hit TV sitcom *Roseanne*, an extension of her club act, which in turn is an extension of her life.

Roseanne Barr was born in Salt Lake City, Utah, on November 3, 1952. Barr, her brother, and her two sisters faced anti-Semitism in the predominately Mormon city and were frequently beaten by other children. Her rough childhood made her tough minded but insecure.

In her adolescence Barr became rebellious. She would, for example, repeatedly wander down the middle of busy highways, forcing cars to swerve around her. At the age of sixteen, she was finally hit by a car and seriously hurt. She spent the next eight months in a Utah state hospital, where her doctors were principally concerned about her mental health.

Shortly after her release from the hospital, she dropped out of high school and moved to Colorado. There, she married Bill Pentland, a truck driver and later a postal worker, had three children (Jessica, Jennifer, and Jake), became a traditional suburban housewife, and struggled for years to make ends meet financially.

Debts finally forced her to take a job as a cocktail waitress in Denver. To get the job, she had to lose 95 pounds, from 200 down to 105. ("I've since gained it all back," she later admitted.) Her first public jokes were caustic replies that she made to the suggestive comments of male customers.

With comedy fever rising in her blood, she visited a Denver comedy club in 1981. Angered by the sexism of the male comics, she quickly wrote a five-minute rebuttal, which the manager allowed her to deliver. Her little act was a hit, and soon she was on the road as a touring comic in Missouri, Arizona, Oklahoma, and Texas.

In 1985 Barr appeared at the Comedy Store in Los Angeles. Her act impressed scouts from *The Tonight Show*. After performing several times on that show, she found herself in demand at major venues, such as Caesar's Palace in Las Vegas. In the summer of 1986, she toured with Julio Iglesias, and in 1987 she starred in her own HBO special.

Her routines depicted domestic life as a kind of war of wills. "My husband asked me if we have any cheese puffs," she said in one routine. "Like he can't go and lift that couch cushion up himself." And, "My husband wanted more space, so I locked him out of the house." The children, too, participated in the battles: "My kids have a game they play on family vacations. They like to count how many Dairy Queens we pass before I grab the wheel and force the car off the road."

Barr's stage and TV appearances were so successful that in 1988 she was offered her own TV sitcom, *Roseanne*. She portrayed a factory worker who constantly berated her seldom-working husband and barked impatiently at her three children. Troubled by the fact that most TV families are dominated by the father character Barr wanted *Roseanne* to address the real-life hardships and accomplishments of women. In one early episode, her character learned that a married couple she knew had divorced. "They shoulda stuck it out in the trenches," she responded sarcastically, "dodgin' that shrapnel with the rest of us that believe in true love."

Barr acknowledged being influenced by many other comedians, such as Jack Benny, Carol Burnett, Totie Fields, Richard Pryor, and Steve Martin. "But most of all," she said, "above anyone on earth, I adore Jackie Gleason. That's what I want my series to be—*The Honeymooners*, only I'm Ralph."

As the series progressed, the Roseanne character quit her factory job to run a luncheonette. Later she became a millionaire by winning a lottery. Throughout these changes, however, the show remained focused on the struggles of Middle America. After a successful nine-season run the series ended in 1997.

During her *Roseanne* years, Barr went through many changes in her personal life. In 1990 she divorced her first husband and married Tom Arnold, her TV costar. For the next several years she billed herself as Roseanne Arnold. In 1994 she divorced Arnold, and early the following year, she married Ben Thomas, her former driver and bodyguard. She then called herself, simply, Roseanne. In 1998 her third marriage ended in divorce.

While working on her TV series, Barr also appeared in theatrical films and made-for-TV movies. She acted in *She-Devil* (1989), *Freddy's Dead: The Final Nightmare* (1991), *The Woman Who Loved Elvis* (TV, 1993), *Meet Wally Sparks* (1997), and other movies.

In September 1998 she began hosting *The Roseanne Show*, a daytime TV talk show. As one of the biggest stars in show business today, Roseanne Barr has future options in live comedy performances, on TV, and in films.

Roseanne Barr

SELECTED PERFORMANCES:

FILMS

She-Devil (1989)
Look Who's Talking Too (voice only, 1990)
Backfield in Motion (TV, 1991)
Freddy's Dead: The Final Nightmare (1991)
The Woman Who Loved Elvis (TV, 1993)
Even Cowgirls Get the Blues (1994)
Unzipped (1995)
Blue in the Face (1995)
Meet Wally Sparks (1997)

TV

Roseanne (1988–97)
The Roseanne Show (1998–   )

Gene Barry

Debonair TV Star

Gene Barry has had an exceptionally successful career as a television actor. During the 1950s and 1960s he starred in several popular series, notably *Bat Masterson* (1958–61) and *Burke's Law* (1963–65). Later he had leading roles in many made-for-TV movies, including *Aspen* (TV, 1977) and *The Gambler Returns: The Luck of the Draw* (TV, 1991).

Gene Barry was born in New York City, New York, on June 4, 1922. His original name was Eugene Klass. While attending New Utrecht High School in Brooklyn, he participated in school theatrical productions and studied music.

Soon after leaving high school, Barry began to appear in professional productions. In 1942 he made his Broadway debut, performing in the musical *The New Moon*. He also sang in revivals of classic operettas, such as *The Merry Widow* (1943).

In 1944 Barry married Betty Claire Kalb. They had three children: Michael, Fredric, and Liza.

In the early 1950s Barry made his first movies, beginning with *The Atomic City* (1952). In the science-fiction picture *The War of the Worlds* (1953) he starred as a scientist. He acted in a number of other films in the 1950s, including the western musical *Red Garters* (1954).

But it was on TV that Barry had his greatest success. In the revised format of the *Our Miss Brooks* (1955–56) comedy series, he played the elementary-school gym instructor Gene Talbot, a suitor to the English teacher Connie Brooks (played by Eve Arden).

Barry got the biggest break of his career when he was chosen to play the title role in the TV western series *Bat Masterson* (1958–61). As Bat Masterson, famed real-life lawman of the Old West, Barry was finally able to apply his dignified, debonair manner—which distinguishes all of his best work—to a character of great popular appeal.

After *Bat Masterson* was cancelled, Barry starred in several other TV series. In *Burke's Law* (1963–65) he was a Los Angeles police captain. That series spun off a sequel, *Amos Burke, Secret Agent* (1965–66). He also starred in the crime drama *The Name of the Game* (1968–71) and the adventure series *The Adventurer* (1972).

Barry has also acted in many TV movies. In *Prescription: Murder* (TV, 1968) his character became the first killer to be captured by Lieutenant Columbo (played by Peter Falk), later the principal character in the now legendary TV series *Columbo*. Other movies featuring Barry included *The Devil and Miss Sarah* (TV, 1971), *Aspen* (TV, 1977), and *The Adventures of Nellie Bly* (TV, 1981).

In 1983 Barry starred in the New York City stage production of the musical *La Cage aux Folles*, as the owner of a homosexual nightclub. In early 1986 he gave a striking performance in an episode of the TV series *Crazy like a Fox*, as an aging but flamboyant actor whose eccentric behavior prompts his daughter to seek a competency hearing against him.

In 1991 Barry returned to the New York City stage to appear in an off-Broadway production of the musical *Give My Regards to Broadway*. During the 1994–95 TV season he starred in yet another

Gene Barry

reincarnation of Amos Burke in a new series called *Burke's Law*. Barry also continues to perform a song-and-dance act in nightclubs.

SELECTED PERFORMANCES:

STAGE

The New Moon (1942)
Rosalinda (1942)
The Merry Widow (1943)
Catherine Was Great (1944)
The Would-Be Gentleman (1946)
Bless You All (1950)
The Perfect Setup (1962)
La Cage aux Folles (1983)
Give My Regards to Broadway (1991)

FILMS

The Atomic City (1952)
The Girls of Pleasure Island (1953)
The War of the Worlds (1953)
Those Redheads from Seattle (1953)
Alaska Seas (1954)
Red Garters (1954)
Naked Alibi (1954)
Soldier of Fortune (1955)
The Purple Mask (1955)
Back from Eternity (1956)
China Gate (1957)
Thunder Road (1958)
Maroc 7 (1966)
Subterfuge (1968)
Prescription: Murder (TV, 1968)
Istanbul Express (TV, 1968)
Do You Take This Stranger? (TV, 1971)
The Devil and Miss Sarah (TV, 1971)
Ransom for Alice! (TV, 1977)
Aspen (TV, 1977)
Guyana, Cult of the Damned (1980)
A Cry for Love (TV, 1980)
The Girl, the Gold Watch, and Dynamite (TV, 1981)
The Adventures of Nellie Bly (TV, 1981)
Perry Mason: The Case of the Lost Love (TV, 1987)

Gene Barry

Turn Back the Clock (TV, 1989)
The Gambler Returns: The Luck of the Draw (TV, 1991)

TV

Our Miss Brooks (1955–56)
Bat Masterson (1958–61)
Burke's Law (1963–65)
Amos Burke, Secret Agent (1965–66)
The Name of the Game (1968–71)
The Adventurer (1972)
Burke's Law (1994–95)

Richard Benjamin

Mild-Mannered Actor

Richard Benjamin, noted for his film portrayals of mild-mannered characters, played such roles in several important black comedies of the early 1970s, including *Catch-22* (1970), and later in light comedies, such as *The Last Married Couple in America* (1980).

Richard Benjamin was born in New York City, New York, on May 22, 1938. He was educated at the High School of Performing Arts in New York City and at Northwestern University's drama school in Evanston, Illinois. As a teenager he played some bit parts in movies such as *Thunder over the Plains* (1953). But it was on the New York City stage that he first made a name for himself. He appeared in a number of plays, including Shakespeare's *As You Like It* (1963), before making his Broadway debut in *The Star-Spangled Girl* (1966).

During the 1967–68 TV season he costarred with his wife, Paula Prentiss (whom he had married in 1961), in the comedy series *He and She*. He then played an aimless Jewish youth in the film *Goodbye, Columbus* (1969).

In the early 1970s Benjamin gained fame for his performances in several black comedies. In these films his boyish image, pleasant manner, and clean-cut appearance sharply contrasted with the weird inner natures of his characters. In *Catch-22* (1970) he portrayed Major Danby, who cheerfully accepts the madness and slaughter going on around him in World War II and does his job in a pleasant, businesslike fashion. In *Portnoy's Complaint* (1972) he played a model Jewish youth who seethes within. Benjamin also gave fine performances during those years in *Diary of a Mad Housewife* (1970) and *The Marriage of a Young Stockbroker* (1971).

From the mid-1970s to the early 1980s, Benjamin played supporting roles in light comedies. His films included *The Sunshine Boys* (1975), *House Calls* (1978), and *The Last Married Couple in America* (1980). In the back-to-nature comedy *Packin' It In* (TV, 1983), he costarred with Paula Prentiss.

Benjamin then virtually gave up acting to devote himself to directing. In 1969 he directed his wife in two New York City plays, and he won acclaim for his direction of such films as *My Favorite Year* (1982), *City Heat* (1984), *The Money Pit* (1986), *Milk Money* (1994), and *Mrs. Winterbourne* (1996).

Benjamin returned to acting in Woody Allen's film *Deconstructing Harry* (1997), performing a role remarkably similar to the ones he played when he became famous as a film actor in the 1960s and 1970s: an emotionally and sexually immature modern Jewish male. In 1998 Benjamin and his wife, Paula Prentiss, replaced Alan Arkin and Elaine May in a New York City production of *Power Plays*.

SELECTED PERFORMANCES:

STAGE

As You Like It (1963)
The Star-Spangled Girl (1966)
The Little Black Book (1972)
The Norman Conquests (1975)
Power Plays (1998)

Richard Benjamin

Richard Benjamin

FILMS

Thunder over the Plains (1953)
Crime Wave (1954)
Goodbye, Columbus (1969)
Catch-22 (1970)
Diary of a Mad Housewife (1970)
The Marriage of a Young Stockbroker (1971)
The Steagle (1971)
Portnoy's Complaint (1972)
The Last of Sheila (1973)
Westworld (1973)
The Sunshine Boys (1975)

House Calls (1978)
Scavenger Hunt (1979)
The Last Married Couple in America (1980)
How to Beat the High Cost of Living (1980)
First Family (1980)
Saturday the Fourteenth (1982)
Packin' It In (TV, 1983)
Deconstructing Harry (1997)

TV

He and She (1967–68)
Quark (1978)

Jack Benny

Trailblazing Comedian

Most American stage comedians in the early twentieth century created humor through slapstick, pomposity, exaggerated dialects, or isolated jokes. The first performer to rise to a higher level of comedy was Jack Benny, whose more sophisticated techniques, especially his use of a consistent, rounded character, proved to be much more enduring.

The character Benny played in his act was gentle, low-key, and self-effacing. Benny did not tell jokes; he built comic scenes. The pace was deliciously slow, and his timing, particularly his use of silence, was incredible.

For example, when a thief bellowed out, "Your money or your life!" Benny's character did not respond. When the thief repeated his command, his character, (who was notoriously miserly) replied, "I'm thinking it over!" The character became so well known that Benny could, and did, walk out onto a Las Vegas stage, fold his arms, and look silently at the audience for almost a full minute while they roared with laughter. His first line was "What are you laughing at?"

Jack Benny was born in Chicago, Illinois, on February 14, 1894. His original name was Benjamin (Benny) Kubelsky. He was raised in Waukegan, Illinois, where he began to take violin lessons at the age of six. Later he studied at the Chicago School of Music. When he was fourteen, he began to play in local dance bands and theater orchestras. He also played in the Waukegan Town-

ship High School Orchestra until he flunked out of school after his second term.

Benny never went back to school. Having little formal education profoundly affected him later in life. He became an avid reader and made a conscious effort to learn the ways of the world.

After leaving school, Benny got a job playing the violin at a local vaudeville house. In 1911 the Marx Brothers performed their popular vaudeville act there. The boys' mother liked Benny's playing and offered him a job as their musical accompanist. Benny's parents refused to let the seventeen year old travel with the brothers on the vaudeville circuit, but the episode gave him confidence and allowed him to meet Zeppo Marx, who became a good friend of Benny's.

When Benny turned eighteen, he decided to seriously pursue a career in show business. He formed a musical duo with the pianist Cora Salisbury and they played classical and popular pieces on vaudeville stages. Soon, the established violinist Jan Kubelik complained to officials of the vaudeville circuit that the value of his name was being jeopardized by the young upstart's use of the name Kubelsky. After futilely arguing that his name really was Kubelsky, the teenager adopted the stage name Ben K. Benny. In 1913 he changed the spelling to Ben K. Bennie ("I thought it looked much classier," he later explained) and began playing with a pianist named Lyman Woods.

In 1917 the act broke up, and Benny enlisted in the navy. There, he played the violin at regular Saturday-night shows put on by and for the sailors. One night the audience started booing him. In desperation, he began, haltingly at first, to ad-

Jack Benny

Jack Benny

lib a navy joke: "You see, I claim the Swiss navy is bigger than the Irish navy . . . but that the *Jewish* navy is bigger than both of them put together." It was the first time that he had ever talked onstage, and he brought the house down. Later, he had a comic part in a service revue.

In late 1918 Benny left the navy. The following year he returned to the vaudeville circuit, as Ben K. Benny. He told jokes, performed comic bits on the violin, and even sang a little. Again, however, someone complained about Benny's stage name (this time it was the vaudeville star Ben Bernie). In January 1921 the future great entertainer adopted the stage name Jack (after the vaudeville comic Jack Osterman) Benny (after his own original first name).

Over the next several years, Benny became a star vaudevillian. Also during that time, he had a four-year love affair with Mary Kelly, a vaudeville dancer. They planned to marry, but in early 1926 she called off the engagement because her strongly Catholic family, objecting to Benny's being Jewish, threatened to disown her if she married him.

In early 1927 he married Sadie Marks. They had first met in Vancouver, Canada, in 1922, when her parents invited the Marx Brothers to Passover dinner, and Zeppo Marx showed up not with his brothers but with Jack Benny. Sadie was only twelve at the time. In 1926 they met again, when her family was living in Los Angeles and Benny was appearing there at the Orpheum Theater.

Benny invited his wife to help him in his vaudeville act. Later, they also worked together on radio, in movies, and on TV. For her professional work, she changed her name to Marie Marsh and then to Mary Livingstone. The Bennys had no children of their own. In 1934 they adopted a baby girl, Joan.

During the late 1920s and early 1930s, Benny continued to be a vaudeville star, notably at New York City's Palace Theater (1927-29, 1931). When Benny got married, he was working in the revue *The Great Temptations*. He later appeared in the revue *Earl Carroll Vanities of 1930*. In 1934 he acted in the play *Bring On the Girls*, a political satire.

Benny also began making films during this period, including *The Hollywood Revue* (1929) and *Chasing Rainbows* (1930). He later appeared in such light film fare as *The Big Broadcast of 1937* (1936), *Artists and Models* (1937), and *Buck Benny Rides Again* (1940). In *Charley's Aunt* (1941) Benny, cast in the title role, had audiences rolling with laugh-ter in the aisles. Benny's finest screen work was in *To Be or Not to Be* (1942), as a Shakespearean actor who dresses up as a Nazi and outwits the Gestapo. He also gave fine comedy performances in *George Washington Slept Here* (1942) and *The Horn Blows at Midnight* (1945).

However, Benny gained his greatest fame through the medium of radio. *The Jack Benny Program* was phenomenally successful for over twenty years (1932–55). The basis for his long-lived popularity was that ordinary people could identify with him. He portrayed a consistent, realistic character involved in simple but carefully planned comedic situations; he was not just a voice telling a string of unrelated jokes. Moreover, he allowed himself to be the target of most of the humor, especially through the themes of his being "the world's worst violin player" and "the stingiest man in show business." (In reality he was a fine violinist and a gentle, generous person.) In Jack Benny's radio character, audiences found a forgivably fallible average guy confidently making plans only to have them explode in his face.

Benny was renowned for his comic timing. But it was not instinctive; he had to work to develop it. The classic example of this aspect of his artistry was his response to insulting remarks directed at him by another character: he would pause, then come out with a perfectly timed "Well!"

The famous "feud" between Benny and comedian Fred Allen started in 1937, when Allen, on his own radio show, poked fun at Benny's violin playing. Thereafter, they took turns hurling insults at each other. Allen, for example, on Benny: "When Jack Benny plays the violin, it sounds as if the strings are still back in the cat." Benny, for example, on Allen: "Listening to Fred Allen is like listening to two Abbots and no Costello." Actually, Benny and Allen were close friends who deeply admired each other's work.

Benny's radio show made his theme song, "Love in Bloom," one of the most familiar songs in America. In the early 1930s, he was in a supper club, when the orchestra asked him to join them on the violin in the next number. By chance, the song was "Love in Bloom." A writer mentioned the performance in a newspaper column, and soon so many others began to associate him with this song that he decided to adopt it as his theme. The same melody introduced each episode of his TV series, which ran from 1950 to 1965.

The TV programs were immensely popular and followed the same basic format as the radio shows. After the series went off the air, he returned to TV for many specials. In his later years, he also played small roles in a number of motion pictures, including *Gypsy* (1962); *It's a Mad, Mad, Mad, Mad World* (1963); and *A Guide for the Married Man* (1967). He also continued to give live performances at hotels and elsewhere.

Benny was ready to begin filming *The Sunshine Boys* (the role was later taken by George Burns, one of Benny's closest friends), when it was discovered that he had terminal cancer of the pancreas. Benny died at his home in Beverly Hills, California, on December 26, 1974. He was universally mourned as the most beloved comedian of his time. One of the provisions in his will was that one red rose be delivered to his wife, Mary, every day for the rest of her life. Mary, with Hilliard Marks (her brother) and Marcia Borie, wrote *Jack Benny* (1978), the definitive book on the great entertainer.

SELECTED PERFORMANCES:

STAGE

The Great Temptations (1926)
Earl Carroll Vanities of 1930 (1930)
Bring On the Girls (1934)
Jack Benny (1963)

FILMS

The Hollywood Revue (1929)
Chasing Rainbows (1930)
The Medicine Man (1930)
Transatlantic Merry-Go-Round (1934)
Broadway Melody of 1936 (1935)
It's in the Air (1935)
The Big Broadcast of 1937 (1936)
College Holiday (1936)
Artists and Models (1937)
Artists and Models Abroad (1938)
Man about Town (1939)
Buck Benny Rides Again (1940)
Love Thy Neighbor (1940)
Charley's Aunt (1941)
To Be or Not to Be (1942)
George Washington Slept Here (1942)
The Meanest Man in the World (1943)
Hollywood Canteen (1944)
The Horn Blows at Midnight (1945)
It's in the Bag (1945)
Somebody Loves Me (1952)
Gypsy (1962)
Its' a Mad, Mad, Mad, Mad World (1963)
A Guide for the Married Man (1967)

RADIO

The Jack Benny Program (1932–55)

TV

The Jack Benny Program (1950–65)

Milton Berle

Mr. Television

Many early commercial TV programs were variety shows, much in the tradition of vaudeville. The most popular variety series in TV history, and the medium's first major success, was *Texaco Star Theater* (1948–53), hosted by the acknowledged master of the variety form, Milton Berle. Many American families bought their first TV sets specifically to see him. Known affectionately as Uncle Miltie and respectfully as Mr. Television, he was the small screen's first superstar.

Milton Berle was born in New York City, New York, on July 12, 1908. His original name was Milton Berlinger. When he was five years old, he won a Charles Chaplin contest. Soon his mother was able to get parts for him in silent movies, beginning with an episode in the serial *The Perils of Pauline* (1914). He went on to play juvenile parts in many films, both in the New York-New Jersey area and in California. Among the movies that he appeared in were *Tillie's Punctured Romance* (1914), with Charles Chaplin; *Rebecca of Sunnybrook Farm* (1917), with Mary Pickford; and *The Mark of Zorro* (1920), with Douglas Fairbanks, Sr.

After playing in some vaudeville kid acts in Philadelphia, he returned to New York City to appear in the Broadway musical *Florodora* (1920). Then he changed his stage name to Milton Berle and began to do comic routines in adult vaudeville shows. Meanwhile, he finished his formal education through the Professional Children's School, doing his homework on the road and

mailing it in. In 1931 he added nightclubs to his schedule.

The major break in his career came when he was asked to act as master of ceremonies at vaudeville's famous Palace Theater in New York City early in 1932. Later that year he was a star comedian in the Broadway revue *Earl Carroll Vanities*. He returned to Broadway in several more shows, including *See My Lawyer* (1939) and *Ziegfeld Follies of 1943* (1943).

In the late 1930s Berle began to act in movies again. His early films as an adult actor included *New Faces of 1937* (1937), *Sun Valley Serenade* (1941), and *Always Leave Them Laughing* (1949).

He also entered radio during this time, hosting several different shows from 1939 to 1949. But his essentially visual brand of humor did not fare well on radio, though he was personally pleased with his final radio variety series, *Texaco Star Theater* (1948–49).

Television, however, was a different matter. Berle was among the first to perform on TV, with appearances in experimental broadcasts in 1929 and 1933. When he was offered the job of hosting the TV version of *Texaco Star Theater* in 1948, shortly after the radio version was established, he jumped at the opportunity because he was convinced that his comedy style would do well on the small screen.

Berle opened each show with his own routine and then introduced the other acts, in which he often participated. The program was telecast live, and he had no cue cards. When he muffed a line, he actually became funnier by ad-libbing, drawing on his years of experience on vaudeville and

Milton Berle

and his struggling for years in the rough world of show business.

After *Texaco Star Theater* went off the air in 1953, he hosted several other TV shows, but with decreasing popular success. Among them were *The Buick Berle Show* (1953–55) and *The Kraft Music Hall* (1958–59).

After he left his regular TV series, Berle continued to return to the small screen for numerous specials. He also acted in *Last of the Red Hot Lovers* (1970), *The Sunshine Boys* (1976), and other plays. And he appeared in many movies, including *It's a Mad, Mad, Mad, Mad World* (1963); *The Oscar* (1966); *Lepke* (1975); and *Broadway Danny Rose* (1984). He surprised most observers by showing a remarkable talent for straight dramatic acting, notably in the movies *Seven in Darkness* (TV, 1969) and *Family Business* (TV, 1983).

In 1984 Berle was among the first seven people inducted into the Television Academy Hall of Fame. In June 1985 he had quadruple bypass heart surgery. The operation was a success, and soon he was making public appearances again. Since then he has appeared in two films, *Side by Side* (TV, 1988) and *Driving Me Crazy* (1991) and the stage production *Charles Busch's Dressing Up* (1994).

Berle has been married four times. His first wife was the showgirl Joyce Mathews, with whom he had two marriages, both ending in divorce. They adopted a baby girl, Victoria. In 1953 he married the film publicist Ruth Cosgrove, with whom he adopted a son, William. Ruth died in 1989, and in 1991 he married the clothing designer Lorna Adams. From that marriage he has a stepdaughter, Susan. In 1997 Lorna began to publish *Milton*, a "luxury gambling magazine" (gambling is one of Berle's great interests).

Milton Berle

nightclub stages. His humor was fast paced, and much of it was physical—pure slapstick and buffoonery, such as wearing outlandish women's clothing. His verbal style was aggressive, flippant, and sometimes insulting ("What is this, an audience or an oil painting?"). In later years he admitted that his onstage abrasiveness reflected to a large degree his offstage personality, which had been affected by his lack of a normal childhood

Like his wife, Berle has a strong literary bent. He wrote two remarkably candid memoirs, *Milton Berle: An Autobiography* (with Haskell Frankel, 1974) and *B.S. I Love You: Sixty Funny Years with the Famous and the Infamous* (1988). He also published two books (1989 and 1993) filled with thousands of his best gags, anecdotes, and one-liners. What's more, Berle, during his more than eighty years in show business, has collected vast quantities of American humor. He has willed to the Library of Congress his file of over five million jokes, which he has catalogued and cross-indexed by subject, by who told the jokes first and where, and by comics who used the material later. The catalog will be an important lasting treasure, just as he himself has been a living comedy treasure for so many years.

Milton Berle celebrated his ninetieth birthday at a large charity event in Los Angeles on July 12, 1998.

SELECTED PERFORMANCES:

STAGE

Florodora (1920)
Earl Carroll Vanities of 1932 (1932)
Saluta (1934)
Lost Paradise (1934)
See My Lawyer (1939)
Ziegfeld Follies of 1943 (1943)
The Goodbye People (1968)
Last of the Red Hot Lovers (1970)
Two by Two (1971)
Norman, Is That You? (1973)
The Sunshine Boys (1976)
Charles Busch's Dressing Up (1994)

FILMS

New Faces of 1937 (1937)
Radio City Revels (1938)
Tall, Dark, and Handsome (1941)
Sun Valley Serenade (1941)
Rise and Shine (1941)
A Gentleman at Heart (1942)
Whispering Ghosts (1942)
Over My Dead Body (1942)
Margin for Error (1943)
Always Leave Them Laughing (1949)
Let's Make Love (1960)
The Bellboy (1960)
It's a Mad, Mad, Mad, Mad World (1963)
The Sound of Laughter (1963)
The Loved One (1965)
The Oscar (1966)
The Happening (1967)
Who's Minding the Mint? (1967)
For Singles Only (1968)
Seven in Darkness (TV, 1969)
Can Heironymus Merkin Ever Forget Mercy Humppe and Find True Happiness? (1969)
Evil Roy Slade (TV, 1972)
The Legend of Valentino (TV, 1975)
Lepke (1975)
The Muppet Movie (1979)
Cracking Up (1983, originally released as *Smorgasbord*)
Family Business (TV, 1983)
Broadway Danny Rose (1984)
Side by Side (TV, 1988)
Driving Me Crazy (1991)

RADIO

Texaco Star Theater (1948–49)

TV

Texaco Star Theater (or *The Milton Berle Show*, 1948–53)
The Buick Berle Show (1953–55)
The Milton Berle Show (1955–56)
The Kraft Music Hall (1958–59)
Jackpot Bowling (1960–61)
The Milton Berle Show (1966–67)

Theodore Bikel

"General Practitioner" Actor

Theodore Bikel has had a long career as a respected character actor on stage and screen. Known especially for the great variety in his roles, he has called himself a "general practitioner" actor.

Theodore Bikel was born in Vienna, Austria, on May 2, 1924. He learned Hebrew and Yiddish in his parents' home, and German in the Vienna public schools.

After Nazi Germany took over Austria in 1938, the family fled to Palestine. There, young Bikel attended agricultural college for one year and worked as a laborer on a collective farm, or kibbutz. But he also studied linguistics and showed a flair for the theater. Consequently, he was reassigned to direct the staging of pageants for his community.

After several years on the kibbutz, he went to Tel Aviv to become an apprentice actor at the Habimah, the Hebrew national theater. He left Habimah and helped to found the Tel Aviv Chamber Theater (1944), where he acted in plays for two years.

In 1946 Bikel left Palestine to study acting at the Royal Academy of Dramatic Art in London, from which he graduated in 1948. He soon began to appear in plays on the London stage, debuting in *You Can't Take It with You* (1948). The following year he played Pablo Gonzales in *A Streetcar Named Desire*, and in 1950 he toured as Harold Mitchell in the same play.

Bikel moved to the United States in 1954 and became a naturalized American citizen in 1961. He made his American stage debut in New York City with his performance as Inspector Massoubre in *Tonight in Samarkand* (1955). He got his first great leading role, as Captain Georg Von Trapp in the original Broadway production of the Rodgers and Hammerstein musical *The Sound of Music*, in 1959.

In the late fifties, Bikel started acting on TV, giving powerful performances on TV anthology series, as in "The Bridge of San Luis Rey" (1958) for *The Du Pont Show of the Month* and "The Dybbuk" (1960) for *The Play of the Week*. He also wrote and performed material for *The Eternal Light* and *Look Up and Live*, spiritually oriented TV programs. Later, he guest-starred in many TV series, such as *All in the Family, Cannon*, and *Twilight Zone*.

Bikel made his movie debut in the American film *The African Queen* (1951), as a German soldier. He played supporting roles in numerous British and American films throughout the 1950s and 1960s, including roles as a humane Southern sheriff in *The Defiant Ones* (1958) and a Russian in *The Russians are Coming, the Russians are Coming* (1966). In *Victory at Entebbe* (TV, 1976), which was based on a true story, he played one of the Jews captured by terrorists, imprisoned at Uganda's Entebbe Airport, and then rescued by a daring Israeli raid on July 4, 1976.

Bikel appeared in many films, but he never became a movie star. He preferred to remain a character actor in supporting roles to avoid being stereotyped. Often overlooked by critics and audiences, Bikel nevertheless impressed careful observers with his dependability, no matter how much his characters varied in age, nationality, or personality. Comparing actors with doctors, he said he preferred to be not a specialist but a "general practitioner" so that he could acquire a wide range of experiences.

Meanwhile, his career expanded beyond just acting. Since 1955 he has been a folksinger, accompanying himself on the guitar, in annual concert tours throughout the United States, Canada, and Europe. From 1958 to 1963, he had his own radio music show, *At Home with Theodore Bikel*. His albums include *Israeli Folk Songs* (1955), *Jewish Folk Songs* (1958), *Bravo Bikel* (1959), *Folk Songs from Just about Everywhere* (1959), *From Bondage to Freedom* (1961), *The Best of Bikel* (1962), and *Theodore Bikel Is Tevye* (1968). His album *Silent No More* (1972) consists of songs that were illegal to perform in Soviet Russia. Bikel also collected folksongs from a variety of cultures and published some of them with comments in the book *Folksongs and Footnotes* (1960).

In recent years the stage has been Bikel's principal working place. Since 1967 he has starred many times as Tevye in the Bock and Harnick musical *Fiddler on the Roof*, a story about Jews in a 1905 Russian village. His other stage appearances included roles in *The Rothschilds* (1972), *Zorba* (1976), and *The Threepenny Opera* (1983 and 1998). In 1999 he made a triumphant return to the New York stage playing a Holocaust survivor in the Jewish Repertory Theater's production of *The Gathering*.

Bikel also continues to return periodically to film work. Among the movies in which he appeared were *Dark Tower* (1989), *Shattered* (1991), *Benefit of the Doubt* (1993), and *Shadow Conspiracy* (1997).

In 1967 Bikel married Rita Weinberg. They have two sons. Some years earlier he had been married for a time to Ofra Ichilov, an Israeli.

Theodore Bikel

Bikel has long been active in politics and Jewish affairs. He founded the arts chapter of the American Jewish Congress in 1961. In 1968 he was a delegate to the Democratic National Convention. And from 1973 to 1982, he served as president of the Actors' Equity Association. In December 1984 Bikel, along with two other leaders of the American Jewish Congress, was arrested at the South African Embassy in Washington, D.C., while protesting South Africa's policy of racial segregation.

SELECTED PERFORMANCES:

STAGE

Tevye the Milkman (1943)
Charley's Aunt (1945)
You Can't Take It with You (1948)
A Streetcar Named Desire (1950)
The Love of Four Colonels (1951)
Dear Charles (1954)
Tonight in Samarkand (1955)
The Lark (1955)
The Rope Dancers (1957)
The Sound of Music (1959)
Brecht on Brecht (1962)
Café Crown (1964)
Pousse-Café (1966)
Fiddler on the Roof (1967 and many times since then)
The Rothschilds (1972)
The Sunshine Boys (1973)
The Good Doctor (1975)
Zorba (1976)
The Inspector General (1978)

The Threepenny Opera (1983, 1998)
The Gathering (1999)

FILMS

The African Queen (1951)
Never Let Me Go (1953)
Melba (1953)
Desperate Moment (1953)
The Little Kidnappers (1954)
Chance Meeting (1955)
The Vintage (1957)
The Pride and the Passion (1957)
The Defiant Ones (1958)
Woman Obsessed (1959)
The Angry Hills (1959)
A Dog of Flanders (1960)
My Fair Lady (1964)
Sands of the Kalahari (1965)
The Russians are Coming, the Russians are Coming (1966)
Festival (1967)
The Desperate Ones (1968)
Sweet November (1968)
My Side of the Mountain (1969)
Darker Than Amber (1970)
Killer by Night (TV, 1972)
Murder on Flight 502 (TV, 1975)
Victory at Entebbe (TV, 1976)
Testimony of Two Men (TV, 1977)
Loose Change (TV, 1978)
Dark Tower (1989)
See You in the Morning (1989)
Shattered (1991)
The Assassination Game (1993)
Benefit of the Doubt (1993)
Shadow Conspiracy (1997)

Claire Bloom

Outstanding Dramatic Actress

Claire Bloom is one of the great dramatic actresses of her time. She has won renown for her stage, film, and TV performances of Shakespearean roles. Her performances in plays by Christopher Fry, Henrik Ibsen, and Tennessee Williams have also been well received. Bloom's popularity among general audiences is based largely on her roles in such movies as *Limelight* (1952), *Look Back in Anger* (1959), and *Charly* (1968). Though possessing great physical beauty, she has never relied on that for getting by with soft roles. On the contrary, she has deliberately sought the most arduous roles available and interpreted them with rare depth and intensity.

Claire Bloom was born in North Finchley, a suburb of London, England, on February 15, 1931. Her original name was Patricia Claire Blume. She had early acting ambitions, which were encouraged by the well-known actress Mary Grew, Claire's mother's sister.

In 1941 Claire, her brother, and her mother moved to the United States to get away from World War II. While in America, Claire took dancing lessons and began to sing and act on both the stage and on radio. The family traveled to Portugal in 1943 and moved back to England in early 1944. Claire soon began to take dancing and acting lessons in London, first at the Cone School and then at the Guildhall School of Music and Drama (1944–45) and the Central School of Speech Training and Dramatic Art (1945–46), the latter being

the training ground for players at London's famed Old Vic theater.

In 1946 she began her professional career by performing in plays with the British Broadcasting Corporation (BBC) radio repertory. She made her stage debut with the Oxford Repertory Theater in *It Depends What You Mean* (1946). In 1947 she made her London stage debut when she appeared as a walk-on in *The White Devil*. She also made her first movie that year, *The Blind Goddess* (released 1948).

Bloom then spent a season performing Shakespearean roles in Stratford-upon-Avon, including Ophelia in *Hamlet* (1948). Returning to London, she proved herself in modern plays, such as Christopher Fry's *The Lady's Not for Burning* (1949) and Jean Anouilh's *Ring round the Moon* (1950).

In 1952 Bloom costarred with Charles Chaplin in his last great film, *Limelight*. As the struggling, wistful young ballet dancer in the movie, Bloom made a tremendous impression. Overnight she became an international film star.

During the same year, she hit her stride as a stage actress by making her debut at the Old Vic, as Juliet in Shakespeare's *Romeo and Juliet*. Many critics regarded Bloom as the greatest Juliet of her time. She continued to play Shakespearean roles at the Old Vic through the 1953 to 1954 season. In 1956 she gave her first New York City performances, again in Shakespearean roles with the Old Vic company.

From the 1950s on, Bloom continually alternated her film and stage work between England and the United States. Her early movies included *Richard III* (1955), *The Brothers Karamazov* (1958), and *Look Back in Anger* (1959). She acted in many

Claire Bloom

Shakespearean plays, as well as in a New York City production of *Rashomon* (1959).

Her costar in *Rashomon* was Rod Steiger. They married in 1959 and sometimes acted together, as in the film *The Illustrated Man* (1969). They had one child, Anna, before divorcing in 1969. In that year she also began an unsuccessful marriage to the producer-director Hillard Elkins, whom she divorced in 1974.

In the 1960s Bloom turned increasingly away from plays and toward films so that she could spend as much time as possible with her daughter. Among her movies during that time were *The Haunting* (1963), in which she played a bohemian with lesbian leanings and ESP powers; *The Spy Who Came in from the Cold* (1965), in which she played a mild-mannered Communist librarian; and *Charly* (1968), in which she was cast as a scientist who falls in love with a man who is the object of her experiments.

In 1971 Bloom returned to the stage and was highly praised for her performances as Nora in a New York City production of Ibsen's *A Doll's House* and as the title character in *Hedda Gabler*. In 1974 she played Blanche DuBois (her favorite role) in a London production of Tennessee Williams's *A Streetcar Named Desire*. From 1981 to 1982, she toured the United States in *These Are Women*, a portrait of Shakespeare's heroines. From the 1970s to the 1990s, she often appeared in one-woman stage performances, and in the 1998–99 Broadway season she won acclaim for her portrayal of Clytemnestra in Sophocles' *Electra*.

After her return to the stage in the early 1970s, she continued to appear in films. They included *A Doll's House* (1973), *Islands in the Stream* (1977), *Clash of the Titans* (1981), *Déjà Vu* (1985), *Crimes and Misdemeanors* (1989), and *Shameless* (1996).

Bloom has appeared frequently on TV, in both England and America, since the early 1950s. Among her many performances for American TV anthologies were those as Roxanne in "Cyrano de Bergerac" (1956) on *Producers' Showcase* and as Queen Anne in "Soldier in Love" (1967) on *Hallmark Hall of Fame*. She was a member of the cast in the BBC-TV series *The Legacy* (1975) and *Brideshead Revisited* (1981). And she gave extraordinarily rich and mature performances in the BBC-TV series of productions based on Shakespearean plays, including her roles as Katharine in *Henry VIII* (TV, 1979), Gertrude in *Hamlet* (TV, 1980),

and Constance in *King John* (TV, 1983). Her other TV movies included *Anastasia: The Mystery of Anna* (TV, 1986), *Queenie* (TV, 1987), and *It's Nothing Personal* (TV, 1993).

In 1990 Bloom married the writer Philip Roth, with whom she had lived since the 1970s. They separated in 1993, and their divorce became final in 1995.

Bloom is the author of the autobiographical books *Limelight and After: The Education of an Actress* (1982) and *Leaving a Doll's House: A Memoir* (1996).

SELECTED PERFORMANCES:

STAGE

It Depends What You Mean (1946)
The White Devil (1947)
He Who Gets Slapped (1947)
The Wanderer (1947)
King John (1948)
Hamlet (1948)
The Winter's Tale (1948)
The Damask Cheek (1949)
The Lady's Not for Burning (1949)
Ring round the Moon (1950)
Romeo and Juliet (1952)
The Merchant of Venice (1953)
Hamlet (1953)
Coriolanus (1954)
Twelfth Night (1954)
The Tempest (1954)
King Lear (1955)
Richard II (1956)
Romeo and Juliet (1956)
Duel of Angels (1958)
Rashomon (1959)
Altona (1961)
The Trojan Women (1963)
Ivanov (1965)
A Doll's House (1971)
Hedda Gabler (1971)
Vivat! Vivat Regina! (1972)
A Streetcar Named Desire (1974)
The Innocents (1976)
Rosmersholm (1977)
The Cherry Orchard (1981)
These Are Women (1981)
When We Dead Awaken (1990)
Electra (1998)

FILMS

The Blind Goddess (1948)
Limelight (1952)
The Man Between (1953)
Richard III (1955)
Alexander the Great (1956)
The Brothers Karamazov
  (1958)
The Buccaneer (1958)
Look Back in Anger (1959)
Brainwashed (1961)
The Chapman Report (1962)
*The Wonderful World of the
  Brothers Grimm* (1962)
The Haunting (1963)
The Outrage (1964)
*The Spy Who Came In From
  the Cold* (1965)
Charly (1968)
The Illustrated Man (1969)
Three into Two Won't Go
  (1969)
A Severed Head (1971)
Red Sky at Morning (1971)
A Doll's House (1973)
Islands in the Stream (1977)
Backstairs at the White House
  (TV, 1979)
Henry VIII (TV, 1979)
Hamlet (TV, 1980)
Clash of the Titans (1981)
King John (TV, 1983)
Déjà Vu (1985)
Promises to Keep (TV, 1985)
Liberty (TV, 1986)
Anastasia: The Mystery of Anna (TV, 1986)
Queenie (TV, 1987)
Crimes and Misdemeanors (1989)
It's Nothing Personal (TV, 1993)
The Princess and the Goblin (1994)
Mighty Aphrodite (1995)

Claire Bloom

Shameless (1996)
Daylight (1996)

TV

The Legacy (1975)
Brideshead Revisited (1981)

Victor Borge

Unmelancholy Dane

Victor Borge is a unique figure in the world of entertainment. Equally adept at performing comic monologues, sight gags, pure silliness (as in his "phonetic punctuation"), and musical humor, he has created an act of unparalleled hilarity and sophistication.

Victor Borge was born in Copenhagen, Denmark, on January 3, 1909. His original name was Börg Rosenbaum. Borge's father was a violinist in the Royal Danish Opera Orchestra and his mother was an accomplished pianist. Borge began playing the piano at an early age, and he gave his first public recital when he was only eight years old. As an adolescent and a young man, Borge performed professionally and studied music at the Royal Danish Music Conservatory, at the Vienna Music Conservatory, and then privately in Berlin. At the age of twenty-three, he returned to Copenhagen, where he continued to pursue his career as a concert pianist.

To relieve his nervous tension at concerts, Borge began to talk lightheartedly to his audience during performances. His humor was so effective that he was invited to perform in theatrical revues, where he developed a music-and-comedy act that led to engagements at nightclubs and elsewhere. Soon, he dropped concertizing altogether. By 1937 he was one of Denmark's most famous comic entertainers, performing successfully in stage, radio, and film productions.

During this time he publicly derided Hitler and the Nazis. When Denmark and Germany signed a nonaggression pact, he commented, "Now the good German citizens can sleep peacefully in their beds, secure from the threat of Danish aggression."

In April 1940 the Germans invaded Denmark. Borge happened to be in Stockholm, Sweden, with a touring revue at the time. Later that year he arrived in the United States to join his wife, the former Elsie Chilton, an American citizen who had already fled from Denmark to America.

After learning English by reading newspapers and watching films, Borge transferred his humor into the new language and obtained work performing at hotels and nightclubs, and on the radio. He got his big break when he landed a regular spot on the radio series *The Kraft Music Hall*, hosted by Bing Crosby. Borge performed on the show over fifty times from 1942 to 1943. He had a brief career as a Hollywood actor, appearing as a British crook in *Higher and Higher* (1943). He hosted his own radio show during the summer of 1945 and again from 1946 to 1947.

Feeling artistically restricted by the rigid time limits imposed on him at hotels, in nightclubs, and on radio programs, Borge began performing in concert halls and auditoriums, where he could determine the appropriate length of his performances on the basis of his interaction with audience members. He called his act *Concert with Comedy*.

In 1953 he took his act to Broadway. His show, renamed *Comedy in Music*, ran for 849 performances, still the record for the longest-running one-person show in theatrical history.

In 1956 Borge took *Comedy in Music* back on

Victor Borge

to move four times while he wrote it." "I have played all over the world—piano, of course." He frequently ends his concerts with this classic quip: "I want to thank my parents for making this possible—and I want to thank my children for making it necessary."

Borge's sight gags include slamming the piano lid on his fingers and playing sheet music that has been placed upside down on his music desk (resulting in music that moves consistently in the wrong direction). To keep from falling off the piano bench, he ties himself down with seat belts.

Borge's famous "phonetic punctuation" consists of distinct vocalizations to indicate commas, dashes, periods, and other punctuation marks. Incorporated into a spoken sentence, these zany sounds produce some of his most sidesplitting moments.

His musical humor centers on his sly, unexpected shifting from one melody to another in midstream. The connection is usually a short motif that is similar in both pieces, and the humor is often intensified when the shift is made from a classical piece to a light popular tune. Sometimes, he deliberately plays a piece incorrectly, either hitting the wrong notes or adding his own bizarre extensions of the composer's melody. Borge has also been known to pull out a pair of scissors and quite literally cut out and paste together parts of different works.

Borge takes a philosophical approach to his profession. "I see humor as a mode of living," he has said. "Man is obviously not perfect, and the void between our mistakes and perfection or attempted perfection, provides us with material for true comedy."

These views reflect the intellectual, humanitarian essence of Borge the private man. He constantly reads to enrich his mind and spirit, has involved himself with the international organization CARE, and helped to found the Thanks to Scandinavia Foundation, which has offered scholarships to Scandinavian students in recognition of the Scandinavian people's efforts to save Jews during the Holocaust. He is also known for being a kind and sensitive man.

the road. Over the next several decades, he toured in the United States, Europe, and Asia; continued to work in radio; and became one of the highest-paid entertainers on TV, making many guest appearances and starring in special programs. Beginning in his sixties, he also conducted, and performed as a soloist with, major symphony orchestras. Well into his seventies, he was still giving over two hundred comedy concerts a year. In 1993 he issued the first in a series of comedy videos, *Victor Borge: Then and Now.*

Over the years Borge has carefully built up a large catalog of comedy bits from which he creates a routine. His accent, deadpan understatement, and stop-start speaking cadence characterize his monologues. "Did you know that Mozart had no arms and no legs?" Borge asks, for example. "I've seen statues of him on people's pianos." "This concerto was written in four flats, because Rachmaninoff had

Borge (second from left) played a ladies' man in Higher and Higher.

Borge shares his public success and private happiness with his second wife, the former Sarabel Sanna Scraper, whom he married in 1953. They are often visited by his six children from his two marriages as well as by his many grandchildren.

Beloved the world over, Victor Borge always shows sensitivity to the feelings of others. "A smile," he says, is the shortest distance between two people."

SELECTED PERFORMANCES:

STAGE

Comedy in Music (1953–56)

FILMS

Higher and Higher (1943)
The Daydreamer (1966)
The King of Comedy (1983)

RADIO

The Kraft Music Hall (1942–43)
The Victor Borge Show (1945–47)

Fanny Brice

Queen of Theater Comedy

Fanny Brice was America's premier comedienne associated with burlesque, vaudeville, and Broadway. As a comic singer and an actress-clown, she created an enormous body of humor.

Fanny Brice was born in New York City, New York, on October 29, 1891. Her original name was Fannie Borach. At an early age, she began to develop skills as an entertainer. Her parents were saloon owners, and as a young child, she was encouraged by her father, Charles Borach (a happy-go-lucky gambler known as Pinochle Charlie), to sing for his customers.

Brice honed her acting talents by engaging in numerous childhood pranks. For example, she and one of her siblings often went to Coney Island, where they would stop passersby and tearfully pretend to be stranded far from home. That ploy nearly always induced the strangers to offer carfare, which the youngsters spent on hot dogs and amusement-park rides.

Brice, determined to make a career in show business, quit school before she turned fourteen. She entered many amateur-night contests as a singer, and soon she was averaging thirty dollars a week in prize money. It was during that period that she changed her last name to Brice, after John Brice, a friend of her mother's (she later changed the spelling of her first name to Fanny). The young entertainer made the change because she was tired of having her name punned by friends, as in "More-Ache" and "Bore-Act."

At fifteen Brice was hired as a chorus girl for a Broadway revue, George M. Cohan's *The Talk of New York*. Cohan fired her during rehearsals when he found out that she could not dance. Soon, however, she got a job in a touring show called *A Royal Slave*, in which she played the part of an alligator.

After a few years of struggling, Brice got a big break as a singer in the touring show *Transatlantic Burlesque* (1910). She also toured that year with the burlesque show *The College Girl*. While on that tour, she impulsively married Frank White, a Springfield, Massachusetts, barber. The marriage was soon annulled on the grounds that she was underage.

Brice's comic performances in *The College Girl* attracted the attention of the great Broadway producer Florenz Ziegfeld, who quickly signed her for the 1910 season of his *Follies* revue. Brice subsequently appeared in many of the annual *Ziegfeld Follies* productions throughout the 1910s and early 1920s, specializing in humorous songs and skits in which she made a virtue of her plainness.

In 1918 Brice married Jules W. ("Nick") Arnstein (also known by several other names). She remained loyal to him through his imprisonment in Sing Sing for fraud (1915–17) and in Leavenworth for theft (1924–25), but she finally divorced him in 1927 for infidelity. Their two children, Frances and William, were raised by servants while Brice worked. Her own parents had separated when she was a child, and she learned from her mother, who went into the real-estate business, how to be a strong, independent woman. Yet Brice missed having a family life. "If a woman has a career," she said, "she misses an awful lot."

Fanny Brice

Meanwhile, however, Brice's career was flourishing. Besides appearing in seven seasons of Ziegfeld's *Follies* from 1910 through 1923, she worked in other shows, including the Broadway musical comedy *The Honeymoon Express* (1913). She headlined at the Palace Theater, New York City's prestigious vaudeville house, in 1923, and appeared in *The Music Box Revue* in 1924.

From 1925 to 1926, Brice toured on the vaudeville circuit. By this point in her career, Brice had assembled a large, varied repertory, both as a singer and as an actress. Her vocal techniques included her satiric "concert-room vocalizing," her broadly humorous specialities (such as "I'm an Indian"), and her comic, Yiddish-accented renditions of songs (such as "Sadie Salome, Go Home"). But she could also make her audiences weep by singing sad ballads, notably "My Man," whose lyrics echoed the story of Brice's unhappy marriage to Arnstein. On November 21, 1927, in her first public appearance after her divorce from Arnstein, she stood silent for fifteen minutes onstage in the Palace Theater, refusing audience demands for the song.

As an actress-clown, Brice was a pioneer in proving that women could create brilliant comedy without exploiting their sexuality and without relying on homemaking topics. She was famed for her lampoons of fan dancers, tap dancers, lady evangelists, and silent-screen vamps (her vamp skits ended with the wonderful line, "I may be a bad woman, but I'm awful good company"). Her comic performances of *The Dying Swan* ballet and of modern dance were hilarious, as were her burlesque of *Camille* (with W.C. Fields as the maid) and her Yiddish-dialect monologues. But she was never cruel; she always poked fun with sensitivity and human understanding Brice explained her approach to humor: "You must set up your audience for the laugh you are working for. So you go along and everything is fine, like any other art, and then—boom! You give it to them. Like there is a beautiful painting of a woman and you paint a mustache on her."

In 1926 Brice took her first serious dramatic role, a part in David Belasco's production of Willard Mack's *Fanny* (1926), a play unrelated to the story of the star's own life. Her performance left much to be desired; wisely, she thereafter returned to comedy, appearing in the musical *Fioretta* in 1929.

In 1929 Brice married the Broadway producer Billy Rose (originally William Samuel Rosenberg).

She was featured in two of his shows: *Sweet and Low* (1930) and *Crazy Quilt* (1931). In 1938 she divorced Rose for infidelity.

In the late 1920s, Brice started appearing in movies, beginning with *My Man* (1928), in which she played a poor girl who becomes a star. She portrayed herself in *The Great Ziegfeld* (1936) and performed, with a heavy Yiddish accent, in the comic skit "A Sweepstakes Ticket" in *Ziegfeld Follies* (1946). But she was never really comfortable around cameras: "Making pictures is like making love in public," she said. "You can't be at ease when somebody is watching." Her wild ethnic humor was more appropriate in the raucous burlesque and vaudeville theaters than in the comparatively bland movies of the time.

She did, however, influence the films of others. Twentieth-Century Fox, without her permission, based the 1939 movie *Rose of Washington Square* on her life. Brice brought a $750,000 defamation suit against the studio. The suit was settled out of court, Brice receiving $30,000 in December 1940. Many years later Barbra Streisand sensitively portrayed Brice in the Broadway musical *Funny Girl* (1964) and in its movie adaptation in 1968, as well as in a film sequel, *Funny Lady* (1974).

Radio proved to be a good medium for Brice's talents. In 1932 she performed as a straight singer with George Olsen's orchestra in a short-lived radio series. But she became best known to millions of listeners for her creation of the impish little-girl character Baby Snooks. Brice had invented the character, modeled after the real-life child star Baby Peggy, as part of her vaudeville act in 1912. At a party in 1921, Brice revived the character to perform the burlesque song "Poor Pauline" as a six-year-old child might sing it. Baby Snooks then appeared on the stage in *Sweet and Low* in 1930, as well as in the 1934 and 1936 productions of the *Ziegfeld Follies*. The precocious brat was introduced to radio listeners in 1936 on *The Ziegfeld Follies of the Air*. She then made regular appearances on *Good News* (the name of the program was changed to *Maxwell House Coffee Time* in 1940) from 1937 to the early forties. In 1944 the enfant terrible (who constantly badgered her father with the question, "Why-y-y, Daddy?") was given her own radio series, *The Baby Snooks Show*, which remained on the air for the rest of Brice's life.

As the Baby Snooks character became increasingly well known, Brice almost completely abandoned her natural voice in public, preferring to speak in Snooks's mischievous-little-girl tones. In interviews, Brice often referred to "Schnooks" as if the character were a real person.

In her private life, Brice was interested in far more than just show business. She was an art collector, an oil painter, a dress designer (she designed the costumes for *Crazy Quilt*), and a gifted interior decorator (she decorated the homes of Eddie Cantor, Ira Gershwin, Dinah Shore, and others).

At the age of fifty-nine, she suffered a massive cerebral hemorrhage at her home in Beverly Hills, California. She died five days later, on May 29, 1951. Brice left the bulk of her $2 million estate to her two children.

Fanny Brice

SELECTED PERFORMANCES:

STAGE

Follies of 1910 (1910)
Ziegfeld Follies of 1911 (1911)
The Honeymoon Express (1913)
Nobody Home (1915)
Ziegfeld Follies of 1916 (1916)
Ziegfeld Follies of 1917 (1917)
Ziegfeld Follies of 1920 (1920)
Ziegfeld Follies of 1921 (1921)
Ziegfeld Follies of 1923 (1923)
The Music Box Revue (1924)
Fanny (1926)
Fioretta (1929)
Sweet and Low (1930)
Crazy Quilt (1931)
Ziegfeld Follies of 1934 (1934)
Ziegfeld Follies of 1936 (1936)

FILMS

My Man (1928)

Night Club (1929)
Be Yourself! (1930)
The Great Ziegfeld (1936)
Everybody Sing (1938)
Ziegfeld Follies (1946)

RADIO

The Ziegfeld Follies of the Air (1932, 1936)
Good News (1937–40)
Maxwell House Coffee Time (1940–44)
The Baby Snooks Show (1944–51)

Albert Brooks

Hollywood Brat Who Made Good

Among Hollywood insiders and a small group of comedy devotees, Albert Brooks is considered one of the best writers and directors of comedic films in America. His movies are cynical yet optimistic: they acknowledge the pain of existence yet also point out that much of the pain is needlessly self-inflicted. He sees the world as being full of absurdities created by the ridiculous side of human nature. Accordingly, Brook's philosophy of creating effective comedy is a simple one: "Since I find reality funny, the better I can mirror it, the funnier the movie will be."

Albert Brooks was born in Los Angeles, California, on July 22, 1947. His father, the radio comedian Harry Einstein (known professionally as Parkyakarkus), tested the boy's sense of humor by naming him Albert, knowing that the youngster would face years of teasing comparisons with the legendary scientist Albert Einstein. Brooks passed the test and soon became the class clown at school. After graduating in 1965 from Beverly Hills High School (where his schoolmates included Rob Reiner and Richard Dreyfuss), he studied for three years in the drama department at Pittsburgh's Carnegie Tech, intending to become a serious actor. Convinced by his friends that comedy was his true forte, Brooks left college, changed his surname, and began his career as a comedian.

In 1968 he performed an inept-ventriloquist act on Steve Allen's TV show. Soon, he was invited to perform the same routine on shows hosted by Merv Griffin and Ed Sullivan. In 1969 Brooks was a regular on the TV musical-variety series *Dean Martin Presents the Golddiggers*.

In the early seventies, Brooks abandoned his ventriloquist act and began performing as a stand-up comedian. He made a successful appearance on *The Tonight Show* in 1972 and returned dozens of times. He also appeared frequently on other TV talk and variety shows, took his act on the road, and made the albums *Comedy Minus One* (1973) and *A Star Is Bought* (1975).

Brooks's appreciation for the absurd was evident in his act. In one routine he played a mime who described his every action with a French accent: "Now I am walking down ze stairs. Now I am petting ze dog." He was also a shadow artist whose broken hand reduced him to such impressions as "a bunny hiding behind a rock." Brooks was a riot as an elephant trainer who had to replace his ailing pachyderm with a frog. "Find the nut, boy," the trainer commanded as the "blindfolded" frog, covered by a blanket, hopped about the stage.

Soon, however, Brooks felt bored and stifled doing the same routines again and again. Consequently, he decided to start making and acting in films. For the TV series *Saturday Night Live* (1975–76), he created several short comedy films, including an interview with a blind cabdriver and a parody of TV network promos for new series. In the theatrical film drama *Taxi Driver* (1976), he played a campaign worker.

Brooks cowrote, directed, and starred in *Real Life* (1979). The film is about an obnoxious documentary filmmaker (played by Brooks) who, while filming a "typical American family," manipulates and distorts the events in their lives. The movie is a devastating illustration of how the mass media have dominated and nearly destroyed family life in America.

Brooks then had a small but effective role in the comedy *Private Benjamin* (1980). He played Yale Goodman, a high-pressure businessman who dies while making love on the bathroom floor on his wedding night. In *Modern Romance* (1981), which he cowrote, directed, and starred in, Brooks took the role of a neurotic film editor who struggles to find happiness with his girlfriend. The movie insightfully explores many of the realistic difficulties in maintaining a love relationship in the modern world.

After acting in the films *Twilight Zone: The Movie* (1983) and *Unfaithfully Yours* (1984), he cowrote, directed, and starred in *Lost in America* (1985). The film is about two yuppies, a man (Brooks) and his wife, who become fed up with the fast life, buy a motor home, hit the road in a voyage of self-discovery, and then repent their decision. The movie is a satire on the values of American baby boomers, who want simplicity yet also want luxury, and who want freedom yet also want the security of belonging to a corporate structure.

Brooks received plaudits for his role in the comedy *Broadcast News* (1987). He portrayed a brilliant TV reporter who longs to be an anchorman but, given the chance, flops.

Next, Brooks wrote, directed, and starred in *Defending Your Life* (1991). It was his first film with a big budget (about $20 million) and his first with a major costar, Meryl Streep. The film is about a man (Brooks) who dies in a car crash and is tried in an afterlife court to determine if he can go on to the next phase of existence or if he must be sent back to Earth in another incarnation to try again.

In the mid and later 1990s, Brooks has acted in several films, including *I'll Do Anything* (1994), *The Scout* (1994) (which he also cowrote), *Critical Care* (1997), and *Out of Sight* (1998).

As a writer-director-actor, Brooks's most successful film to date is *Mother* (1996). In this film he plays a twice-divorced man who believes that his problems with women result from his strained relationship with his mother, played by Debbie Reynolds. To resolve this issue within himself, he moves in with his mother, with disastrous—and hilarious—consequences.

In 1997, Brooks married Kimberly Shlain, a multimedia producer. In 1998 they had a son, Jacob Eli.

Albert Brooks

Brooks's intelligence shines through in all his films. Hence, he has struggled to win acceptance at big studios and from mass audiences. But among Hollywood insiders and a small cult of comedy fans, Albert Brooks is regarded as one of the funniest in the business.

SELECTED PERFORMANCES:

FILMS

Taxi Driver (1976)
Real Life (1978)
Private Benjamin (1980)
Modern Romance (1981)
Twilight Zone: The Movie (1983)
Unfaithfully Yours (1984)
Lost in America (1985)
Broadcast News (1987)
Defending Your Life (1991)
I'll Do Anything (1994)
The Scout (1994)
Mother (1996)
Critical Care (1997)
Out of Sight (1998)

TV

The Steve Allen Show (1968)
Dean Martin Presents the Golddiggers (1969)
Hot Wheels (animated, voice only, 1969–71)

Mel Brooks

Wild Parodist

A parody is an artistic work that imitates the style of another work. The effect of the parody is often comic, and the purpose may be either to ridicule or to pay tribute to the original. The man who raised film parody to an art form is Mel Brooks.

Mel Brooks was born in New York City, New York, on June 28, 1926. His original name was Melvyn Kaminsky.

When Brooks had just passed his second birthday, his father died, leaving the boy with a permanent sense of loss, outrage, and fear of death. "I'm sure a lot of my comedy is based on anger and hostility," the adult Brooks has admitted. "I learned to clothe [my anger] in comedy to spare myself problems—like a punch in the face." Another factor in his makeup was his feeling that as a Jew and as a person he did not fit into mainstream American society.

Fortunately, Brook's mother was able to serve as a positive role model for the young boy. "My mother had this exuberant joy of living, and she infected me with that," he has said. "She really was responsible for the growth of my imagination."

In his teens Brooks earned money by playing the drums after school and during summer vacations. After graduating from high school in 1943, he attended Brooklyn College of the City University of New York for one year. He then went into the army, where he was trained as a combat engineer whose specialty was to deactivate land mines. His first action was in the Battle of the Bulge in December 1944.

After leaving the army in 1946, he became a professional musician, playing drums in nightclubs and on the borscht circuit. He began as Mel Kaminsky, but he soon changed his name to Mel Brooks (after his mother's maiden name, Brookman) to avoid confusion with the well-known jazz trumpeter Max Kaminsky. Gradually, Brooks turned to comedy—he made his first appearance as a comedian when he filled in for an ailing comic at a small Catskills hotel.

While working on the borscht circuit, Brooks became friends with Sid Caesar. In 1949 Caesar asked Brooks to help write comic sketches for Caesar's TV series *The Admiral Broadway Revue*. A year later Brooks joined Caesar, Carl Reiner, Imogene Coca, and others in writing for the extremely successful TV variety series *Your Show of Shows*. Brooks occasionally appeared on the program as a performer. When that show went off the air in 1954, he continued to work with Caesar, notably in *Caesar's Hour* (1954–57). Later, he helped to create the TV spy-spoof series *Get Smart* (1965) and the comedy series *When Things Were Rotten* (1975).

Brooks also worked on several Broadway shows. He wrote and acted in the sketch "Of Fathers and Sons," a parody of *Death of a Salesman*, for the revue *New Faces of 1952* (1952). He also worked on the books for the musical comedies *Shinbone Alley* (1957) and *All American* (1962).

In 1960 Brooks made the first of a series of comedy records with Carl Reiner, in which Brooks played a two-thousand-year-old man with a Yid-

Mel Brooks

dish accent. The old man had seen everything but been impressed by nothing. The series culminated in a three-disc album entitled *The Incomplete Works of Carl Reiner and Mel Brooks* (1973).

Brooks reached the peak of his success when he turned to filmmaking. From the beginning of his film career, Brooks's principal technique has been to parody established film genres, with such knowledge of, and obvious affection for, the originals that the spoofs can quite accurately be called homages. A talented producer, writer, director, and actor, Brooks is often involved in his films on more than one level.

Brooks's first major film was *The Producers* (1967), which he wrote and directed. It parodies the old putting-on-the-show musical films popular in the 1930s. Here, however, the show is called *Springtime for Hitler*, which surprisingly becomes a camp hit.

After playing a bit part in *Putney Swope* (1979), Brooks wrote and directed *The Twelve Chairs* (1970), a comedy about greed in early Communist Russia. A highlight of the film is Brooks's performance as Tikon, an ex-serf who yearns for his former master's beatings.

With *Blazing Saddles* (1974), a parody of Hollywood Westerns, Brooks reached his full stride as a filmmaker and simultaneously became a cult hero to many of his fans. Besides coscripting and directing the movie, he played a villainous governor and a Yiddish-speaking Indian chief.

In *Young Frankenstein* (1974), a takeoff on 1930s horror movies, Brooks served as cowriter and director. He coscripted, directed, and starred in *Silent Movie* (1976), an affectionate spoof about a director trying to make a present-day silent picture. In *High Anxiety* (1977), a parody of Alfred Hitchcock's thrillers, Brooks played Dr. Richard H. Thorndyke, a Nobel Prize–winning psychiatrist who suffers from "high anxiety." He also coscripted, produced, and directed the film.

After making a cameo appearance in *The Muppet Movie* (1979), Brooks wrote, produced, and directed *History of the World, Part I* (1981). He played several roles in the film, including that of Moses. Brooks then produced and starred in a remake of the classic 1942 comedy *To Be or Not to Be* (1984), in which a troupe of actors outwits the Nazis. His next film was *Spaceballs* (1987), a spoof of space epics, which he cowrote, directed, and starred in.

After lending his voice to the film *Look Who's Talking Too* (1990), Brooks cowrote, directed, and starred in *Life Stinks* (1991). It parodies those films, like *Sullivan's Travels* (1941), in which a wealthy or successful person feigns poverty and homelessness for a time. Brooks's next film as a writer-director-actor was *Robin Hood: Men in Tights* (1993), a comic version of the famous 1938 movie *The Adventures of Robin Hood*. Brooks had a cameo role in *The Little Rascals* (1994) and then cowrote, directed, and starred in *Dracula: Dead and Loving It* (1995), a takeoff on the well-known Dracula horror movies.

Through the years Brooks has developed close associations with a number of actors and actresses who have appeared regularly in his works. Those performers include Dom DeLuise (*The Twelve Chairs; Blazing Saddles; Silent Movie; History of the World, Part I*), Marty Feldman (*Young Frankenstein, Silent Movie*), Madeline Kahn (*Blazing Saddles; Young Frankenstein; High Anxiety; History of the World, Part I*), Harvey Korman (*Blazing Saddles; High Anxiety; History of the World, Part I*), Cloris Leachman (*Young Frankenstein; High Anxiety; History of the World, Part I*), and Gene Wilder (*The Producers, Blazing Saddles, Young Frankenstein*).

Brooks established a film production company, Brooksfilms. It has produced several of his movies, including *History of the World, Part I* and *To Be or Not to Be*. It has also produced some serious dramatic films, notably *The Elephant Man* (1980).

Brooks is married to actress Anne Bancroft, whom he wed in 1964. They had one child, Maximilian. From an earlier marriage, to Florence Baum, he had three children: Stefanie, Nick, and Edward. Bancroft appeared with Brooks in *Silent Movie* and *To Be or Not to Be* and was featured in *The Elephant Man*.

In 1997 Brooks joined forces with Carl Reiner to record a CD (he once again played the two-thousand-year-old man). Meanwhile, film buffs await more movies from Mel Brooks, who has secured a firm place for himself in movie history as the unrivaled king of parody.

SELECTED PERFORMANCES:

STAGE

New Faces of 1952 (1952)

FILMS

Putney Swope (1969)
The Twelve Chairs (1970)
Blazing Saddles (1974)
Silent Movie (1976)
High Anxiety (1977)
The Muppet Movie (1979)
History of the World, Part I (1981)
To Be or Not to Be (1984)
Spaceballs (1987)
Look Who's Talking Too (voice only, 1990)
Life Stinks (1991)
Robin Hood: Men in Tights (1993)
The Little Rascals (1994)
Dracula: Dead and Loving It (1995)

Lenny Bruce

Pioneer "Sick" Comedian

Lenny Bruce revolutionized American humor. He was the first major comedian to employ raw, controversial language and imagery in an attempt to expose and destroy the prejudices and repressions of middle-class America.

All my humor is based on destruction and despair," Bruce said. Believing that everyone had occasional dark or selfish thoughts and feelings, he used obscenity and unconventional subject matter as a kind of psychological dynamite to blow away his own and his audience's inhibitions and to lay bare the secret layers of the human mind. He developed a reputation as a "sick" comedian because of his vulgar language and his controversial jokes involving such topics as toilets, vibrators, amputees, and religion (he attacked organized religion and became one of the first entertainers to publicly confront the problem of being Jewish in a gentile world).

Lenny Bruce was born in Mineola, Long Island, New York, on October 13, 1925. His original name was Leonard Alfred Schneider. When he was small, his parents divorced, and he was passed back and forth between them. His stormy childhood affected his outlook on life and influenced his style as a comedian.

In 1942 Bruce quit high school to enlist in the navy, serving on the *USS Brooklyn* during the Italian campaign in World War II. After the war he settled in New York City and began to develop a comedy act. He began by imitating the unsophis-

ticated comedy routines of his mother, a vaudeville comedienne.

Soon, however, he came under the influence of other experienced people in show business. His most important mentor was Joe Ancis, a talented but professionally unsuccessful comic. Ancis taught Bruce the art of avant-garde improvisational comedy.

In 1948 Bruce won a talent contest on the radio program *Arthur Godfrey's Talent Scouts*. For the next several years, he worked in small nightclubs in the New York City area and on the borscht circuit of the Catskill Mountains. During that period, he married the striptease performer Honey Harlowe. They had one child, Kitty.

In 1953 Bruce and his wife moved to the West Coast. For the next few years, he worked primarily as the master of ceremonies and comedian at the burlesque theaters where his wife performed. In 1956 she was convicted of drug charges and sentenced to two years in prison. The following year they were divorced and he was awarded custody of their child.

In the late 1950s and early 1960s Bruce rose to the peak of his popularity by appearing at the Hungry I and other bistros in San Francisco. The city was the center of the beatnik movement, and Bruce led the comedy wing. He usually presented his routines as largely improvised surrealistic dramatic skits in which he spoke all the parts. Only a minority of people at the time understood that his purpose in using dirty words and bizarre imagery was to provide his audience members with a kind of catharsis, shocking them beyond the surface of things.

Bruce was arrested many times for obscenity

and for the possession of narcotics. The obscenity charges never stuck, but in 1965 he was convicted on a drug charge and given probation. The arrests and trials had a profound effect on him. He began to devote much of his time to studying the law, and his performances suffered by his rambling on and on about his being persecuted. Indeed, the repeated arrests effectively deprived him of his livelihood, and in October 1965 he went bankrupt. On August 3, 1966, he died of a drug overdose in Los Angeles, California.

"Satire," Bruce once observed, "is tragedy plus time." Bruce himself did not have enough time to witness the social liberalizations that he and others were calling for—or enough time to look back and see his own tragedy as a fleeting satiric reflection of the period in which he lived. But his rage against censorship, prejudice, and hypocrisy made him a cult figure among many after his death, and he is still regarded as the most famous exponent of "sick" comedy.

Lenny Bruce

George Burns

Show-Biz Methuselah

George Burns held a unique place in show business history, not only because of his longevity, but also because of the way he used his age as a comedy asset. Well into his nineties, he was still making public appearances as a comedian. "Thanks for the standing ovation," he would say. "I'm at the point now where I get a standing ovation just for standing."

George Burns was born in New York City, New York, on January 20, 1896. His original name was Nathan Birnbaum.

When Burns was seven, his father died. The boy immediately went to work at part-time odd jobs. While he worked, the young entertainer would perform in various ways. For example, he would sing as he walked up and down the streets of his neighborhood selling crackers.

A few years later, he quit school and organized himself and three other children into a singing quartet. The boys sang wherever they found a crowd of people, passing a hat to collect whatever they could.

Striking out on his own, Burns developed a variety of routines, including trick roller-skating, and in his early teens he began to perform on the vaudeville stage. When he was fourteen, he had a case of stage fright that led him to search for a prop that he could hold on to for security; he chose the cheapest thing he could think of—a cigar.

Meanwhile, Burns changed his name in two stages. First, he became Nathan Burns, having acquired the new surname from neighbors who knew that he regularly stole coal from the Burns Brothers coal company. Later, he adopted the first name of George because it was the nickname of one of his older brothers, Isadore, whom Burns admired.

Even after Burns changed his name, he often performed under a variety of pseudonyms. According to Burns, he frequently used false names because his early acts were so bad that he feared he would not be able to get jobs if managers knew who he really was.

Burns also went through a succession of partners, including a trained seal. He then teamed up with Hannah Siegal, and the two performed a Latin dance act. After working for a while in the New York City area, they were offered a contract for a long tour. But Siegal's parents refused to let her go unless Burns married her. The youngsters married, toured for thirty-six weeks together, and then, returning to New York City, amicably divorced.

Burns continued to labor in small-time vaudeville for several more years. He has since admitted that his problem was that he could not deliver material as well as he could create it. That problem was solved in 1923, when he met Gracie Allen. She was a young, unemployed Irish-American Catholic trying to break into show business. Hearing that Burns was looking for a partner for his new comedy act, she asked for the job and got it. At first she played the straight part, while Burns told the jokes. But audiences tended to laugh at her questions more than at his jokes. Burns and Allen switched roles and soon became a hit act.

George Burns

In 1926 they married. Later that year they hit the big time by signing with the B. F. Keith chain of theaters. In 1929 they began to make one-reel movies. A few years later, they started acting in feature-films. In all, they appeared in more than a dozen pictures together, including *College Humor* (1933), *The Big Broadcast of 1936* (1935), and *Honolulu* (1939).

The duo had their greatest success, however, in radio. After making guest appearances on radio programs for a while, they got their own show. *The George Burns and Gracie Allen Show* (1932–50) was one of the most popular in radio history. At first they drew from their episodic vaudeville routines. But in 1942 they changed the format to a situation comedy, with a sustained story line in each program.

In 1950 they switched over to the new medium of television. Their series, *The George Burns and Gracie Allen Show* (1950–58), was a domestic situation comedy in which Burns played a professional entertainer and Allen played his scatterbrained wife. The show concerned itself primarily with their home life and with the simple situations that she somehow managed to make unbelievably complex. Burns, the only character aware of the audience, would make explanations and comments to viewers between scenes.

Burns credited Allen with being the principal figure in their success. She had an uncanny genius for delivering non sequiturs, malapropisms, and other zany remarks with absolute believability. Also a fine and intelligent dramatic actress, Allen sometimes tired of playing the fool, but she went along with it because the team was so successful.

Burns and Allen had no children of their own. But they adopted a daughter (Sandra) and a son (Ronald), both of whom appeared on the Burns and Allen TV show.

In 1958 Allen retired. Burns continued to appear on TV (in his own series) for another season. In 1960, at the age of sixty-four, he launched a new career for himself by developing a solo nightclub act, consisting of songs and patter (often based on recollections). His trademarks were his cigar, his unfinished songs (actually performed as a low murmuring), and his self-deprecation. After Allen's death, in 1964, Burns added another element to his act: his preoccupation with being around very young women.

From 1964 to 1965, Burns was a regular on the TV series *Wendy and Me*. Over the next decade, he continued to perform his nightclub act. By the mid-seventies, however, Burns was not in great demand, and it appeared as if his career was on the decline. But in 1974, Burns's career was resurrected when he was offered an important movie role. Reluctant at first to take the job because it had originally been offered to his best friend, Jack Benny, who had died earlier that year, Burns was finally convinced by Benny's agent that the late comedian would have wanted Burns to play the role.

The part was that of Al Lewis in *The Sunshine Boys* (1975). Lewis and Willie Clark (played by Walter Matthau) are retired entertainers who used to form a great vaudeville comedy team but who have not spoken to each other in twelve years. Brought together for a one-shot TV special, they resume old battles and open old wounds. In *The Sunshine Boys*, Burns surprised both filmmakers and audiences with his acting skills, which had never really been tested in his routines with Allen or in his solo nightclub acts.

Burns went on to make a number of movies. The best known is the satirical fantasy *Oh, God!* (1977), in which Burns played the title role. Others include *Sgt. Pepper's Lonely Hearts Club Band* (1978); *Just You and Me, Kid* (1979); and *Oh, God! Book II* (1980). In *Two of a Kind* (TV, 1982), he starred as a senior citizen who becomes lethargic after he is put into a nursing home by his son, but then becomes interested in life again when he is visited by his retarded grandson. In *Oh, God! You Devil* (1984), he played both the Deity and the Prince of Darkness. Among his later films were *Wisecracks* (1992) and *Radioland Murders* (1994).

During the years that Burns was acting in films, he continued to give live performances. In 1983, for example, he worked at New York City's Palace Theater, where he had first performed in 1924. He also appeared regularly on TV specials, talk shows, comedy series, and commercials. In 1985 he hosted *George Burns Comedy Week*, an anthology. In 1991 he was guest of honor on a TV special celebrating his ninety-fifth birthday. In 1993 he guest-starred in an episode of the sitcom *The Golden Palace*. Burns continued to participate in various TV programs until 1995.

He also branched out into making recordings and writing books. His albums included *George Burns in Nashville* (1981) and *Gracie: A Love Story*

George Burns

(1990). Among his many well-received books were *Living It Up; or, They Still Love Me in Altoona!* (1976); *The Third Time Around* (1980); *How to Live to Be One Hundred—or More: The Ultimate Diet, Sex and Exercise Book* (*At My Age, Sex Gets Second Billing)* (1983); *Dr. Burns's Prescription for Happiness* (1984); *Dear George: Advice and Answers from America's Leading Expert on Everything from A to B* (1985); *Gracie: A Love Story* (1988); and *One Hundred Years, One Hundred Stories* (1996).

In July 1994 Burns accidentally fell in his bathtub and injured his head. That September he had successful surgery to remove fluid from his brain. By January 1995 he felt well enough to make a public appearance on his ninety-ninth birthday. However, when he turned one hundred years old, on January 20, 1996, he was too ill to appear. He died in his Beverly Hills, California, home forty-nine days later, on March 9, 1996, the acknowledged Methuselah of show business.

SELECTED PERFORMANCES:

FILMS

International House (1933)
College Humor (1933)
Six of a Kind (1934)
We're Not Dressing (1934)
Many Happy Returns (1934)

Love in Bloom (1935)
The Big Broadcast of 1936 (1935)
Here Comes Cookie (1935)
The Big Broadcast of 1937 (1936)
College Holiday (1936)
A Damsel in Distress (1937)
College Swing (1938)
Honolulu (1939)
The Sunshine Boys (1975)
Oh, God! (1977)
Sgt. Pepper's Lonely Hearts Club Band (1978)
The Comedy Company (TV, 1978)
Just You and Me, Kid (1979)
Going in Style (1979)
Oh, God! Book II (1980)
Two of a Kind (TV, 1982)
Oh, God! You Devil (1984)
Eighteen Again! (1988)
Wisecracks (1992)
Radioland Murders (1994)

RADIO

The George Burns and Gracie Allen Show (1932–50)

TV

The George Burns and Gracie Allen Show (1950–58)
The George Burns Show (1958–59)
Wendy and Me (1964–65)
George Burns Comedy Week (1985)

Red Buttons

Little Guy with Troubles

Red Buttons has had a successful dual career, as a fine dramatic actor and as a comedian. His humor stems from his comedy persona as, he says, "a little guy and his troubles."

R ed Buttons was born in New York City, New York, on February 5, 1919. His original name was Aaron Chwatt. He grew up on the Lower East Side of Manhattan and the Bronx.

At the age of twelve, Buttons won an amateur-night contest, under the name Little Skippy, by singing "Sweet Jennie Lee." In 1935 he became a bellboy and singer at Dinty Moore's tavern in the Bronx. Because he had red hair and his bell-boy uniform was loaded with buttons, customers nicknamed him Red Buttons. That year he also gave his first performances on the borscht circuit.

Buttons graduated from the Bronx's Evander Childs High School in 1937. In 1938 he worked on the borscht circuit again. The next year he became a burlesque comic.

In 1941 Buttons was offered a part in the movie *The Admiral Takes a Wife*, a musical comedy about peacetime naval life in Hawaii. He accepted the role, moving to Hollywood during the filming. Unfortunately, the Japanese attack on Pearl Harbor occurred just three days before the scheduled release of the film and the movie was shelved.

In 1942 Buttons, back in New York City, performed in the stage farce *Vickie*. After he left the show, he worked for a few months in vaudeville and burlesque theaters.

In 1943 Buttons was drafted into the army and cast in the service play *Winged Victory* (1943), which was staged for the Army Emergency Relief. After a long run in New York City, the play, with Buttons, was filmed (1944). He then toured with the show. In 1945 Buttons was transferred to another entertainment unit, which performed at the Potsdam Conference.

Following his discharge from the army in 1946, Buttons had a one-word part in the movie *13 Rue Madeline* (1946) and appeared in the New York City stage musicals *Barefoot Boy with Cheek* (1947) and *Hold It!* (1948). Through his stage performances, he began to develop a wide reputation as a comic, and he was invited to perform as a guest on TV shows, including Milton Berle's.

In 1947 Buttons married a burlesque performer known as Roxanne. Their marriage was short-lived, and in 1949 he married Helayne McNorton. In 1963 they divorced, and the following year he married Alicia Pratt.

Buttons finally attained stardom when he was given his own TV series, *The Red Buttons Show*, in 1952. At first it was a musical-variety show, featuring short comic sketches in which Buttons played several recurring characters, such as Buttons the Bellboy, Muggsy (a juvenile delinquent), and Rocky Buttons (a punch-drunk prizefighter). His low-key humor was much appreciated by audiences, and the show became very popular. However, by the end of the 1953 to 1954 season, it had become a situation comedy and its ratings began to drop. The show went off the air in 1955.

The next two years were difficult for Buttons.

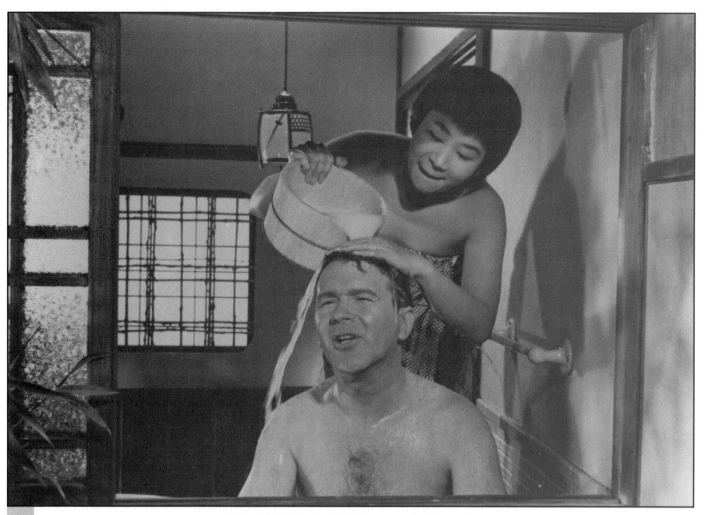

Miyoshi Umeki gives Red Buttons a dousing in Sayonara.

He worked very little, chiefly in nightclubs. A highlight of that period was his portrayal of Bottom in Shakespeare's *A Midsummer Night's Dream* in the summer of 1956.

Then came a great turning point in his career: he was given an important role in the movie *Sayonara* (1957). Buttons played Sergeant Joe Kelly, an American serviceman based in post–World War II Japan. Kelly and his Japanese bride, relentlessly harassed by people objecting to mixed marriages, commit double suicide. For his sensitive tragicomic portrayal of Kelly, Buttons won universal praise.

After his success in *Sayonara* Buttons began to work steadily as a character actor in films, often in serious dramatic roles. His early movies included *The Big Circus* (1959); *The Longest Day* (1962); *Stagecoach* (1966); *They Shoot Horses, Don't They?* (1969); and *The Poseidon Adventure* (1972).

However, Buttons did not abandon comedy. He starred in the short-lived TV situation-comedy series *The Double Life of Henry Phyfe* (1966), and he still performs as a nightclub comic.

Buttons's later films included *Pete's Dragon* (1977), *The Dream Merchants* (TV, 1980), and *Reunion at Fairborough* (TV, 1985). In *Alice in Wonderland* (TV, 1985), he played the White Rabbit.

During the 1987 to 1988 TV season, Buttons had a recurring role on the dramatic series *Knots Landing*, and for many years he has appeared as a guest on other TV programs, such as the sitcom *Roseanne*. His other work in the 1990s included roles in the films *The Ambulance* (1993) and *It Could Happen to You* (1994).

Marlon Brando (left) is confronted by Buttons in Sayonara.

SELECTED PERFORMANCES:

STAGE

Vickie (1942)
Winged Victory (1943)
Barefoot Boy with Cheek (1947)
Hold It! (1948)
A Midsummer Night's Dream (1956)

FILMS

Winged Victory (1944)
13 Rue Madeleine (1946)
Sayonara (1957)
Imitation General (1958)
The Big Circus (1959)
One, Two, Three (1961)
Five Weeks in a Balloon (1962)
Gay Purr-ee (1962)
Hatari! (1962)
The Longest Day (1962)
A Ticklish Affair (1963)
Your Cheatin' Heart (1964)
Harlow (1965)
Up from the Beach (1965)
Stagecoach (1966)
They Shoot Horses, Don't They? (1969)

Breakout (TV, 1970)
The Poseidon Adventure (1972)
The New, Original Wonder Woman (TV, 1975)
Louis Armstrong—Chicago Style (TV, 1976)
Gable and Lombard (1976)
Viva Knievel (1977)
Pete's Dragon (1977)
Telethon (TV, 1977)
Vega$ (TV, 1978)
The Users (TV, 1978)
Movie Movie (1978)
When Time Ran Out (1980)
Power (TV, 1980)
The Dream Merchants (TV, 1980)
Leave 'Em Laughing (TV, 1981)
Side Show (TV, 1981)
Reunion at Fairborough (TV, 1985)
Alice in Wonderland (TV, 1985)
Eighteen Again! (1988)
The Ambulance (1993)
It Could Happen to You (1994)

TV

The Red Buttons Show (1952–55)
The Double Life of Henry Phyfe (1966)
Knots Landing (1987–88)

James Caan

Dynamic Actor

◄○►

James Caan has one of the most dynamic acting styles among contemporary actors. Whether he plays a doomed football player, a vicious gangster, or a soft-hearted sailor, he creates a lasting impression through the energy he brings to his roles.

◄○►

James Caan was born in New York City, New York, on March 26, 1939. In his youth he was interested mostly in sports. After graduating from Manhattan's Rhodes School at the age of sixteen, he enrolled at Michigan State University so that he could be part of its celebrated football team. When he failed to make the team, he transferred to Hofstra University in Hempstead, New York. But the academic life did not suit him, and he soon dropped out.

After working odd jobs for a while, Caan enrolled at the Neighborhood Playhouse in New York City, where he studied acting for one year. He then studied for two years under the drama coach Wynn Handman. In 1960, billed as Jimmy Caan, he appeared in an off-Broadway production of the play *La Ronde*. After serving as an understudy in a Broadway play the following year, he moved to California. There, he soon found work as a guest performer on *Route 66, Ben Casey,* and other TV drama series.

In the mid-sixties, Caan began acting in films. In his first movie, *Lady in a Cage* (1964), he played the leader of a trio of violent hoodlums. He then gave a well-received performance in *The Glory Guys* (1965). He got his first starring role in the movie

Red Line 7000 (1965), in which he played a racing-car driver. Over the next several years, he acted in a number of films, including *The Rain People* (1969), in which he played a gentle, brain-damaged ex-football player.

Caan finally attained stardom when he played the wisecracking, fun-loving football player Brian Piccolo in the movie *Brian's Song* (TV, 1971). The film recounts the true story of the young running back's rivalry and friendship with Gale Sayers. Caan movingly portrayed Piccolo's last days before the latter's early death from cancer.

In *The Godfather* (1972) Caan gave an outstanding performance as a volatile young gangster. Though he was surrounded by major talents in that movie, including Marlon Brando, Caan, with his characteristic dynamism, held his own.

To avoid being typecast as a violent criminal, Caan began to select roles that would allow him to show his versatility. In *Slither* (1973), for example, he played an offbeat comedy role. In *Cinderella Liberty* (1973) he was a sailor who becomes involved with a prostitute and her child. In *The Gambler* (1974) he portrayed a compulsive gambler.

Caan's later films included *Rollerball* (1975), *Thief* (1981), and *Gardens of Stone* (1987). In the 1990s he starred in *Dick Tracy* (1990), *Flesh and Bone* (1993), and *Bulletproof* (1996).

Caan has been married four times. In 1961 he married Dee Jay Mattis (also reported as DeeJay Mathis), then the lead dancer on the *Sing Along with Mitch* TV series. They had a daughter, Tara, before divorcing in 1966. In 1976 he married the model Sheila Ryan, with whom he had a son, Scott, before divorcing again. Scott became an actor and appeared with his father in the film *A Boy Called Hate* (1996). Caan's third marriage, to Ingrid Hajek in 1990, produced another son, Alexander, before it, too, ended in divorce. In 1995 he married Linda O'Gara (also reported as Linda Stokes), with whom he had a son, James.

SELECTED PERFOR-MANCES:

STAGE

La Ronde (1960)

FILMS

Lady in a Cage (1964)
The Glory Guys (1965)
Red Line 7000 (1965)
El Dorado (1967)
Games (1967)
Countdown (1968)
Journey to Shiloh (1968)
The Rain People (1969)
Submarine X-1 (1969)
Rabbit, Run (1970)
Brian's Song (TV, 1971)
T.R. Baskin (1971)
The Godfather (1972)
Slither (1973)
Cinderella Liberty (1973)
Freebie and the Bean (1974)
The Gambler (1974)
The Godfather, Part II (1974)
Funny Lady (1975)
Rollerball (1975)
The Killer Elite (1975)
Harry and Walter Go to New York (1976)
Silent Movie (1976)
A Bridge Too Far (1977)
Another Man, Another Chance (1977)
Comes a Horseman (1978)
Chapter Two (1979)

James Caan

Hide in Plain Sight (1980)
Thief (1981)
Bolero (1982)
Kiss Me Goodbye (1982)
Gardens of Stone (1987)
Alien Nation (1988)
Dick Tracy (1990)
Honeymoon in Vegas (1992)
The Program (1993)
Flesh and Bone (1993)
A Boy Called Hate (1996)
Bottle Rocket (1996)
Erasure (1996)
Bulletproof (1996)
North Star (1996)

Sid Caesar

Comedian of Many Faces

Sid Caesar remains best known as the star of the highly regarded early TV comedy-variety series *Your Show of Shows* (1950–54). His unmatched ability to ape many languages, create sound effects, and imitate people put him into a class of his own.

Sid Caesar (full name, Isaac Sidney Caesar) was born in Yonkers, New York, on September 8, 1922. His father owned a luncheonette, and Caesar learned to mimic the languages of the Italian, Russian, Hungarian, Polish, French, and Spanish customers.

While attending Hawthorne Junior High School, Caesar earned money by playing the saxophone in a band at dances and weddings. During his years at Yonkers High School, he played in a band at school events and in restaurants and bars.

After graduating from high school in 1939, he moved to New York City, where he soon found work as a theater usher and doorman. Meanwhile, he studied to become a professional musician, taking saxophone lessons from Frank Chase of NBC Symphony Orchestra and auditing music theory courses at the Julliard School of Music. In 1940, to earn money, he began to play in dance bands at hotels and casinos. He rapidly became known as an excellent musician.

Simultaneously, Caesar was performing in comic sketches on the borscht circuit. His reputation as a comic grew as fast as his reputation as a saxophonist. In the summer of 1941, he worked as a comic in Monticello, New York, and in the fall of

that year, he returned to New York City to work as a musician.

In the summer of 1942, Caesar performed as a comic at the Avon Lodge in the Catskills. He married the owner's niece, Florence Levy, in 1943. They had three children: Michele, Rick, and Karen.

Late in 1942, Caesar entered the Coast Guard. He helped to stage revues for the service personnel and performed in the revue *Tars and Spars*, which toured many American cities. In *Tars and Spars*, Caesar performed his now famous warmovie routine, a monologue in which he played several characters and created many sound effects. The tour culminated in Los Angeles, where the show was made into a movie that was released in early 1946.

Meanwhile, World War II had ended and Caesar had left the Coast Guard. He stayed in Los Angeles and appeared in another movie, *The Guilt of Janet Ames* (1947), in which he played a nightclub comic. Then, he went back to New York City, performing in nightclubs and in the Broadway revue *Make Mine Manhattan* (1948).

In 1949 Caesar hosted his first television show, *The Admiral Broadway Revue*. He then was the host of *Your Show of Shows* (1950–54), *Caesar's Hour* (1954–57), and *Sid Caesar Invites You* (1958). Unlike many other early TV comedy-variety shows, which featured stand-up comedy or slapstick vaudeville routines, Caesar's show featured well-rounded sketches created by some of the best comedy writers of the time (including Woody Allen, Mel Brooks, and Neil Simon). In these sketches Caesar played a variety of zany characters, his most famous being the Professor, a character who pretended to know everything but actually knew nothing. Caesar also did a monologue as a fly, including sound effects, and performed skits that parodied specific movies, TV shows, and operas. He revealed a genuine comic genius in his version of the opera *Pagliacci*, making the audience alternately laugh and cry.

Sid Caesar the comedian was brash and aggressive. But Sid Caesar the person was intellectual, shy, and highly sensitive. Therefore, when his TV series was canceled in 1958, he fell apart. In his autobiography, *Where Have I Been?* (with Bill Davidson, 1982), Caesar confessed that between 1958 and 1978, his feelings of insecurity and the pressures of success caused him to become dependent on alcohol and pills. He experienced periods of despair alternating with periods of rage and violence. "I worked," he wrote in his autobiography, "and I was there, but I really wasn't there." He was still effective in the Broadway musical *Little Me* (1962), in which he played seven roles. But, as he admitted, he was working with "residual" capabilities.

Through the rest of the 1960s and most of the 1970s, he continued going through the motions of performing in nightclubs, on TV, on the stage, and in films, such as *The Busy Body* (1967) and *Silent Movie* (1976). In 1978 he finally hit rock bottom and began to turn his life around. By the early 1980s, he felt fully recovered in body and spirit.

In 1981 Caesar toured in the stage production *A Touch of Burlesque*, which was filmed and shown on cable TV in 1982. Thereafter, he continued to be healthy and active on the stage, in films, and on television. He appeared in the stage productions *Sid Caesar and Company: Does Anybody Know What*

Sis Caesar and Janet Blair

I'm Talking About? (1989) and *Together Again* (1990). His films of that period include *Over the Brooklyn Bridge* (1984), *Alice in Wonderland* (TV, 1985), *Side by Side* (TV, 1988), and *Vegas Vacation* (1997). In 1986 he portrayed a Scrooge-like landlord in the television production of *Christmas Show*, and in 1997 he guest-starred as Uncle Harold in the "Citizen Buchman" episode of the TV sitcom *Mad about You.*

Sid Caesar

SELECTED PERFORMANCES:

STAGE

Make Mine Manhattan (1948)
Little Me (1962)
Last of the Red Hot Lovers (1972)
The Prisoner of Second Avenue (1973)
A Touch of Burlesque (1981)
*Sid Caesar and Company: Does Anybody Know
  What I'm Talking About?* (1989)
Together Again (1990)

FILMS

Tars and Spars (1946)
The Guilt of Janet Ames (1947)
It's a Mad, Mad, Mad, Mad World (1963)
The Busy Body (1976)
A Guide for the Married Man (1967)
The Spirit Is Willing (1967)
Flight to Holocaust (TV, 1973)
Airport 1975 (1974)
Silent Movie (1976)

Curse of the Black Widow (TV, 1977)
Grease (1978)
The Cheap Detective (1978)
The Fiendish Plot of Dr. Fu Manchu (1980)
The Munsters' Revenge (TV, 1981)
History of the World, Part I (1981)
Grease II (1982)
Found Money (TV, 1983)
Over the Brooklyn Bridge (1984)
Love Is Never Silent (TV, 1985)
Alice in Wonderland (TV, 1985)
The Emperor's New Clothes (1987)
Freedom Fighter (TV, 1988)
Side by Side (TV, 1988)
Vegas Vacation (1997)

TV

The Admiral Broadway Revue (1949)
Your Show of Shows (1950–54)
Caesar's Hour (1954–57)
Sid Caesar Invites You (1958)
The Sid Caesar Show (1963–64)

Dyan Cannon

Versatile Actress

A talented and beautiful actress, Dyan Cannon was at one time in danger of being typecast as a floozy. Since the late 1970s, however, she has carefully chosen her roles in order to show her versatility.

D yan Cannon was born in Tacoma, Washington, on January 4, 1937. Her original name was Samille Diane Friesen. She is the daughter of a Baptist father and Jewish mother.

After briefly attending the University of Washington, she moved to Los Angeles and worked as a model. In the late 1950s, she began to find some acting jobs. She made guest appearances on TV series, such as *Playhouse Ninety* and *Bat Masterson*, and had a minor role in the movie *The Rise and Fall of Legs Diamond* (1960).

From 1960 to 1961, Cannon had a regular part in the TV soap opera *Full Circle*. She then studied acting in New York City with Sanford Meisner and appeared in the Broadway plays *The Fun Couple* (1962) and *The Ninety-Day Mistress* (1967).

In the early 1960s, Cannon lived with actor Cary Grant. They married in 1965 and had one child, Jennifer, before divorcing in 1968.

Cannon then resumed her film career, taking a role in *Bob and Carol and Ted and Alice* (1969). Among her movies over the next few years were *Doctors' Wives* (1971), *Such Good Friends* (1971), and *Death Scream* (TV, 1975).

After trying her hand at directing with the movie *Number One* (1976), Cannon then returned to acting, giving outstanding performances in *Lady of the House* (TV, 1978) and *Heaven Can Wait* (1978). In the former film, which is based on fact, she played an ex-madam who, despite opposition, served as mayor of Sausalito, California. In the comedy *Heaven Can Wait*, Cannon portrayed a scheming would-be murderess.

In the 1980s Cannon appeared in the films *Honeysuckle Rose* (1980), *Author! Author!* (1982), and *Master of the Game* (TV, 1984). In 1985 she had the title role in the well-publicized two-part TV movie *Jenny's War*, as an American woman searching for her son in Nazi Germany just before World War II. That same year Cannon married the attorney Stanley Finberg.

In the 1990s Cannon acted in a number of made-for-TV movies and theatrical films. Her TV movies included *Based on an Untrue Story* (TV, 1993) and *The Rockford Files: If the Frame Fits* (TV, 1996). She appeared on the big screen in *The End of Innocence* (1991) and in the popular comedy *Out to Sea* (1997).

SELECTED PERFORMANCES:

STAGE

The Fun Couple (1962)
The Ninety-Day Mistress (1967)

FILMS

The Rise and Fall of Legs Diamond (1960)
Bob and Carol and Ted and Alice (1969)
Doctors' Wives (1971)
The Anderson Tapes (1971)
Such Good Friends (1971)

Dyan Cannon

The Love Machine (1971)
The Burglars (1972)
Shamus (1973)
The Last of Sheila (1973)
Death Scream (TV, 1975)
Lady of the House (TV, 1978)
Heaven Can Wait (1978)
Revenge of the Pink Panther (1978)
Honeysuckle Rose (1980)
Coast to Coast (1980)
Having It All (TV, 1982)
Deathtrap (1982)
Author! Author! (1982)
Master of the Game (TV, 1984)
Jenny's War (TV, 1985)

Caddyshack II (1988)
Jailbirds (TV, 1991)
The End of Innocence (1991)
Christmas in Connecticut (TV, 1992)
Based on an Untrue Story (TV, 1993)
The Pickle (1993)
A Perry Mason Mystery: The Case of the Jealous Jokester (TV, 1995)
The Rockford Files: If the Frame Fits (TV, 1996)
Eight Heads in a Duffel Bag (1997)
That Darn Cat (1997)
Out to Sea (1997)

TV

Full Circle (1960–61)

Eddie Cantor

Banjo Eyes

Eddie Cantor's performances as a comic singer and actor were marked by energy and cheerfulness. In the 1919 *Ziegfeld Follies*, he was billed as the "Apostle of Pep," and at the age of sixty, he was described as looking like forty and acting like twenty. But his enormous popularity during his lifetime was primarily the result of his dignified yet boyish charm and his sincere warmth. He was nicknamed "Banjo Eyes" because of his wide, expressive eyes.

E ddie Cantor was born in New York City, New York, on January 31, 1892. His Russian immigrant parents died when he was a toddler, and the orphan (originally named Isidore Itzkowitz), was raised on Manhattan's Lower East Side by his maternal grandmother, Esther Kantrowitz, a warmhearted woman who greatly influenced the future entertainer's gentle, kindly character.

Esther was also partially responsible (inadvertently) for her grandson's name change. When she was enrolling the six year old in school, she mistakenly began to give the registrar her own name, Kantrowitz, but never finished it. The registrar wrote down "Isidore Kanter." Later, the boy changed the spelling of his new surname to Cantor. Still later he changed his first name to Eddie because his girlfriend, Ida Tobias, liked the name.

Cantor's grandmother also influenced his choice of career. An excellent mimic, she gave Cantor the idea of performing for others. He often sang and performed comic impersonations for his friends, sometimes combining the two skills, as when he pretended to be Anna Held singing "I Just Can't Make My Eyes Behave."

Soon after leaving school at the age of thirteen, Cantor teamed up with a friend to perform a variety act at weddings and other events. In 1907 they made their first appearance on a public stage, at the Clinton Music Hall, but the act fell flat because they spoke in English, not realizing that they were in a Yiddish theater.

Cantor then got a job with a touring burlesque show. When the tour folded four weeks later, he became a singing waiter in a Coney Island saloon. The pianist at the saloon, Jimmy Durante, became Cantor's lifelong friend.

In 1909 Cantor was hired to perform as a comedian on a small vaudeville circuit. There, he quickly became identified by his large, expressive eyes and well known for his ability to repeat the same act in various ethnic accents and in blackface. He continued to perform in blackface from 1910 to 1912, working as an assistant to the comedy juggling team of Bedini and Arthur. The trio parodied the famous stars of the day. During this period he developed what would later become his trademark gestures—skipping back and forth on the stage, clapping and gyrating his hands, and rolling his eyes as he sang—originally his way of hiding his stagefright.

From 1912 to 1914, Cantor toured with Gus Edwards's *Kid Kabaret* revue. There, he met George Jessel, who, like Durante, became a lifelong friend and a well-known entertainer.

In 1914 Cantor married Ida Tobias. He had met her in 1905, and she encouraged him during the

Eddie Cantor

Eddie Cantor

his first musical: a Los Angeles production of *Canary Cottage*. He next worked for twenty-seven weeks at Florenz Ziegfeld's New York City supper club, the Midnight Frolic. That engagement led to Cantor's Broadway debut in the *Ziegfeld Follies of 1917* (he was also in the 1918 and 1919 productions of the show).

Cantor next appeared in the revues *The Midnight Rounders* (1920) and *Make It Snappy* (1922). In a famous skit in the latter show, he played Max, a mousy tailor whose customer demanded a coat with a belt in the back; the "belt" he received was not the type he expected. He also starred in the musical comedy *Kid Boots* (1923), which was one of his biggest hits. He headlined in the *Ziegfeld Follies of 1927* and performed in the musical comedy *Whoopee* (1928). In 1941 he appeared on the stage for the last time, starring in a show titled after his nickname, *Banjo Eyes*.

In his stage appearances, Cantor performed some of his routines in blackface. Like other white entertainers of the time, such as Al Jolson and Sophie Tucker, Cantor did not use blackface to mock black people. The use of blackface was a theatrical convention that helped performers overcome inhibitions. After they gained confidence, they could come out from behind the "mask" and perform without the black makeup.

The development of sound movies in the late 1920s doomed vaudeville and hurt the live theater in general. Cantor quickly adapted himself to the new medium. He made his first film appearance in a silent-movie version of *Kid Boots* (1926). Among his musical talkies were *Glorifying the American Girl* (1929), based on the stage musical *Whoopee* (1930); *Palmy Days* (1931); *Roman Scandals* (1933); *Ali Baba Goes to Town* (1937); *Thank Your Lucky Stars* (1943); and *If You Knew Susie* (1948). Cantor had a nonmusical comedic role in *Forty Little Mothers* (1940). He appeared briefly in, and sang for the music track of, the biopic *The Eddie Cantor Story* (1953), in which he was portrayed by Keefe Brasselle.

early years of his career. Their marriage was widely regarded as one of the most harmonious in show business. It also became one of the best-known marriages because Cantor later incorporated numerous anecdotes about his wife and five daughters (Marjorie, Natalie, Edna, Marilyn, and Janet) in his routines. He adopted "Ida, Sweet As Apple Cider" as his theme song.

The Cantors honeymooned in London. While there, he appeared in the revue *Not Likely*, in which he achieved his first major success. Until then he had relied on imitations and dialects. In *Not Likely* he sang and performed comedy routines as himself.

Cantor soon returned to the United States and to his vaudeville work as a blackface comedian and singer. Breaking blackface tradition, however, he performed without speaking in a dialect and without comedy clothes. In 1916 he appeared in

However, it was through radio that Cantor reached the peak of his popularity. He made some guest appearances on radio shows during the 1920s, then made a very successful appearance on Rudy Vallee's *Fleischmann Hour* in February 1931. In September of that year, Cantor took over as host of *The Chase and Sanborn Hour*, soon also known as *The Eddie Cantor Show*. He hosted radio variety shows almost continuously for the next two decades, pioneering the use of live-audience response on radio and introducing new talents such as Harry Einstein, Deanna Durbin, Dinah Shore, and Eddie Fisher.

In 1950, at Cantor's suggestion, NBC established the TV series *The Colgate Comedy Hour*, in which Cantor and several other comedians rotated in hosting their own variety programs. *The Eddie Cantor Show* (1950–54) was part of that series. In 1955 he hosted and occasionally starred in *The Eddie Cantor Comedy Theater*, a series of variety programs and comedy plays. Later, he made guest appearances on many TV programs. In 1956 he won critical acclaim for a dramatic role in "Seidman and Son" on the *Playhouse Ninety* TV anthology series.

Cantor was extremely active in raising funds for many causes. In 1920 he began to give benefit performances for Surprise Lake Camp, a camp for underprivileged youngsters. This project meant a great deal to Cantor because he had attended and enjoyed the camp as a child. In the late 1930s, he helped to raise money for a program that sent children to Palestine whose parents had been killed or interned by the Nazis. He raised hundreds of millions of dollars for other causes, including hospitals, veterans programs, Catholic and Protestant projects, and the United Jewish Appeal. Many of his projects benefitted Israel, where he was affectionately referred to in Yiddish as the "Schnorrer" (beggar). He also named and helped organize the March of Dimes.

Cantor wrote several books, including the autobiographical *My Life Is in Your Hands* (with David Freeman, 1928) and *Take My Life* (with Jane Kesner Ardmore, 1957). In 1963 he published a book of recollections, *As I Remember Them*.

After he suffered a heart attack in 1952, Cantor was forced into semiretirement. In 1962 his life changed even more drastically with the death of his beloved Ida. Cantor died in Los Angeles, California, on October 10, 1964.

SELECTED PERFORMANCES:

STAGE

Kid Kabaret (1912)
Not Likely (1914)
Canary Cottage (1916)
Ziegfeld Follies of 1917 (1917)
Ziegfeld Follies of 1918 (1918)
Ziegfeld Follies of 1919 (1919)
The Midnight Rounders (1920)
Broadway Brevities of 1920 (1920)
Make It Snappy (1922)
Kid Boots (1923)
Ziegfeld Follies of 1923 (1923)
Ziegfeld Follies of 1927 (1927)
Whoopee (1928)
Banjo Eyes (1941)

FILMS

Kid Boots (1926)
Special Delivery (1927)
Glorifying the American Girl (1929)
Whoopee (1930)
Palmy Days (1931)
The Kid from Spain (1932)
Roman Scandals (1933)
Kid Millions (1934)
Strike Me Pink (1936)
Ali Baba Goes to Town (1937)
Forty Little Mothers (1940)
Thank Your Lucky Stars (1943)
Hollywood Canteen (1944)
Show Business (1944)
If You Knew Susie (1948)
The Story of Will Rogers (1952)
The Eddie Cantor Story (1953)

RADIO

The Eddie Cantor Show (also known as *The Chase and Sanborn Hour*, 1931–34; *The Eddie Cantor Pabst Blue Ribbon Show*, 1935–39; and *Time to Smile*, 1940–49).

TV

The Eddie Cantor Show (1950–54, part of *The Colgate Comedy Hour*)
The Eddie Cantor Comedy Theater (1955)

Morris Carnovsky

Distinguished Shakespearean Actor

◄○►

Morris Carnovsky was a renowned Shakespearean actor who gave especially memorable performances in the title role of *King Lear* and as Shylock in *The Merchant of Venice*. He was widely admired, especially by those knowledgeable about the theater, for the range of his character-acting skills. He was particularly effective portraying troubled, thoughtful men.

◄○►

Morris Carnovsky was born in Saint Louis, Missouri, on September 5, 1897. He made his stage debut by performing the title role in a high school production of *Disraeli* (1914). Later, he appeared in more plays in Saint Louis, earned a B.A. degree (1920) at Washington University, and then performed with stock companies in Boston. He studied acting under Emanuel Reacher in 1922 and Michael Chekhov in 1935.

Carnovsky made his New York City debut by taking the role of Reb Aaron in *The God of Vengeance* in 1922. From 1924 to 1930, he was a member of the Theater Guild. Among the roles he played during this period were those of Kublai the Great Khan in *Marco Millions* (1928), the title role in *Uncle Vanya* (1929), and Francis Bacon in *Elizabeth the Queen* (1930). He continued to perform important roles after he left the Guild, including those of Dr. Levine, the unhappy physician, in *Men in White* (1933); Jacob, the self-sacrificing grandfather, in *Awake and Sing!* (1935); Mr. Bonaparte, the father whose son becomes a boxer instead of a violinist, in *Golden Boy* (1937); and

Ben Stark, the dentist with a shrewish wife, in *Rocket to the Moon* (1938).

Carnovsky made his film debut by portraying the author Anatole France in *The Life of Émile Zola* (1937). Throughout the 1940s and early 1950s, Carnovsky appeared in numerous movies. In *Rhapsody in Blue* (1945), he played George Gershwin's father. In *Cyrano de Bergerac* (1950), he was the hero's friend, Le Bret. Among his other films were *Edge of Darkness* (1943), *Our Vines Have Tender Grapes* (1945), and *Dead Reckoning* (1947).

Carnovsky's life took a dramatic turn in the early 1950s, when he was blacklisted in Hollywood for his refusal to cooperate with the House Committee on Un-American Activities. His stage career continued to flourish however. He played Aaron Katz and the Presiding Angel in both the stage (1953) and television (1961) version of *The World of Sholom Aleichem*. In 1954 Carnovsky played Tzaddik in *Dybbuk*, and beginning in 1956, frequently appeared at the American Shakespeare Festival in Stratford, Connecticut. He became one of the most distinguished Shakespearean actors of his time.

Carnovsky's affinity for Shakespeare stemmed at least in part from his love of language. "I began by adoring words," he said in 1970. "I've always liked to learn words, and as an actor I've learned how to use them for all their juiciness and malleability."

While Carnovsky was deeply committed to Shakespearean theater, he by no means abandoned contemporary theater. In 1961 he played the part of the Logician in *Rhinoceros* and of Mr. Baker in *Come Blow Your Horn*. He was highly praised for two portrayals of the scientist Galileo, in *Galileo* (1966) and in *Lamp at Midnight* (1969).

Carnovsky eventually returned to film acting, appearing in *A View from the Bridge* (1962) and *The Gambler* (1974), and narrating *The City* (1977). He also had a major role in the British TV movie *The Chicago Eight Conspiracy Trial* (TV, 1970).

In 1941 Carnovsky married the actress Phoebe Brand, with whom he had a son. His first marriage, to Florence Lasersohn, lasted from 1922 to 1933.

Carnovsky died in Easton, Connecticut, on September 1, 1992.

Morris Carnovsky

SELECTED PERFORMANCES:

STAGE

The God of Vengeance (1922)
The Failures (1923)
Saint Joan (1923)
The Creaking Chair (1926)
Juarez and Maximilian (1926)
The Brothers Karamazov (1927)
The Doctor's Dilemma (1927)
Marco Millions (1928)
Volpone (1928)
Uncle Vanya (1929)
Hotel Universe (1930)
Elizabeth the Queen (1930)
Night over Taos (1932)
Men in White (1933)
Awake and Sing! (1935)
Paradise Lost (1935)
The Case of Clyde Griffiths (1936)
Johnny Johnson (1936)
Golden Boy (1937)
Rocket to the Moon (1938)
Thunder Rock (1939)
Night Music (1940)
My Sister Eileen (1940)
Café Crown (1942)
An Enemy of the People (1950)
The World of Sholom Aleichem (1953)
The Dybbuk (1954)
The Three Sisters (1955)
King John (1956)
Measure for Measure (1956)

The Taming of the Shrew (1956)
The Merchant of Venice (1957 and several times thereafter)
Hamlet (1958)
Romeo and Juliet (1959)
The Merry Wives of Windsor (1959)
Twelfth Night (1960, 1961)
The Tempest (1960)
Antony and Cleopatra (1960)
Rhinoceros (1961)
Come Blow Your Horn (1961)
Richard III (1961)
A Family Affair (1962)
The Caucasian Chalk Circle (1962)
King Lear (1963 and several times thereafter)
Galileo (1966)
Antigone (1967)
Lamp at Midnight (1969)

Hamlet (1969)
A Swan Song (1972)
Awake and Sing! (1976)

FILMS

The Life of Emile Zola (1937)
Tovarich (1937)
Edge of Darkness (1943)
Address Unknown (1944)
The Master Race (1944)
Rhapsody in Blue (1945)
Our Vines Have Tender Grapes (1945)
Cornered (1945)
Miss Susie Slagle's (1946)

Dead Reckoning (1947)
Dishonored Lady (1947)
Saigon (1948)
Siren of Atlantis (1949)
Thieves' Highway (1949)
Gun Crazy (1950)
Cyrano de Bergerac (1950)
The Second Woman (1951)
A View from the Bridge (1962)
The Chicago Eight Conspiracy Trial (G.B., TV, 1970)
The Gambler (1974)
The City (narrator, 1977)

Jeff Chandler

Action Hero

Jeff Chandler was one of the great action heros in films of the 1950s. He is remembered for his performances in westerns, war movies, and other types of adventure films.

Jeff Chandler was born in New York City, New York, on December 15, 1918. His original name was Ira Grossel. His parents separated when he was very young, and he was raised by his mother.

As a boy, Chandler acted in school plays. After graduating from Erasmus Hall High School, he studied art for one year, then went to work as a layout artist. He soon realized, however, that what he really wanted to do was to act. He studied acting at a New York City drama school for a brief period, then joined a Long Island stock company. In the summer of 1941, he and a friend started their own stock company, called the Shady Lane Playhouse, in Illinois.

When World War II started, Chandler entered the army. He fought as an infantryman in the Pacific theater and rose from the rank of private to that of first lieutenant.

Released from the army in 1946, Chandler soon began to get parts on radio programs. Over the next several years, he became a popular radio performer, playing the title roles in the medical-drama series *The Private Practice of Dr. Dana* (1947–48) and the private-detective series *Michael Shayne* (1948). He was also in the original radio version of the series *Our Miss Brooks* (1948–49), playing the bashful biology teacher Philip Boynton (a rare comedy role for him).

Chandler's success as a radio actor led to offers for film work. His first movie role was a bit part as a surly gambler in *Johnny O'Clock* (1947). In *Sword in the Desert* (1949), he played an underground leader of Jews fighting the British in Palestine. His performance in that film convinced many that he was ready to be a leading man.

Chandler's rise to stardom really began when he was cast as Cochise, a chief of the Chiricahua Indians in the American Southwest, in the western *Broken Arrow* (1950). He played the same character in *The Battle at Apache Pass* (1952). For the next decade, he played the hero in westerns and other action dramas. Because of his prematurely gray hair and gaunt features, he was frequently given parts (like his Cochise roles) actually designed for men older than he.

In *Two Flags West* (1950), Chandler portrayed a tough cavalry commandant. In *Deported* (1950), he played a gangster sent from the United States back to his native Italy, where he becomes reformed through love. In *Away All Boats* (1956), he starred as the captain of a ship carrying American troops to the Pacific theater during World War II. In *Jeanne Eagels* (1957) he was a carnival barker.

Chandler gave a particularly strong performance as a lawman in the western *Man with a Shadow* (1958). That same year, he starred in *Raw Wind in Eden* (1958), an adventure story set on a Mediterranean island. In the war drama *Merrill's Marauders* (1962), he played Brigadier General Frank Merrill, the courageous, inspirational leader of an American unit that went behind Japanese lines during World War II.

In 1956 Chandler and his agent, Meyer Mishkin, established a film production company, Earlmar Productions. Chandler also owned a recording company, Chandler Music, which published his songs (he was both a songwriter and singer).

Chandler was an active supporter of Israel. As a result, in 1960 his films were banned from all Arab countries.

Chandler married the former actress Marjorie Hoshelle in 1946. They separated in 1954, later reunited, separated again in 1957, and finally divorced in 1960. They had two daughters, Jamie and Dana.

On June 17, 1961, Chandler died in Culver City, California, of complications, specifically blood poisoning, following spinal surgery. He was only forty-two.

SELECTED PERFORMANCES:

FILMS

Johnny O'Clock (1947)
The Invisible Wall (1947)
Roses Are Red (1947)
Sword in the Desert (1949)
Abandoned Woman (1949)
Broken Arrow (1950)
Two Flags West (1950)
Deported (1950)
Bird of Paradise (1951)
Smuggler's Island (1951)
Iron Man (1951)
Flame of Araby (1951)
The Battle at Apache Pass (1952)
Red Ball Express (1952)
Because of You (1952)
East of Sumatra (1953)
The Great Sioux Uprising (1953)
Yankee Pasha (1954)
Sign of the Pagan (1955)
Foxfire (1955)
Female on the Beach (1955)
The Spoilers (1955)
Toy Tiger (1956)
Away All Boats (1956)
Pillars of the Sky (1956)
The Tattered Dress (1957)
Jeanne Eagels (1957)
Man with a Shadow (1958)

Jeff Chandler (foreground) in a scene from Sword in the Desert.

The Lady Takes a Flyer (1958)
Raw Wind in Eden (1958)
Stranger in My Arms (1959)
Thunder in the Sun (1959)
Ten Seconds to Hell (1959)
Return to Peyton Place (1961)
Merrill's Marauders (1962)

RADIO

The Private Practice of Dr. Dana (1947–48)
Michael Shayne (1948)
Our Miss Brooks (1948–49)

Jill Clayburgh

Conveyer of Emotional Complexity

Jill Clayburgh is renowned for her ability to effectively convey complex emotions through her acting. She excels at portraying intelligent, vulnerable women and is adept at communicating subtle emotional changes.

J ill Clayburgh was born in New York City, New York, on April 30, 1944. She came from an affluent, cultured Upper East Side family, and she was educated at the exclusive Brearley School. She attended Sarah Lawrence College, where she studied philosophy, religion, and literature.

Clayburgh was introduced to the theater during one of her college summer vacations. Persuaded by a friend to work as an apprentice at the Williamsburg Theater Festival in Massachusetts, she painted scenery, had a one-line part in Shaw's *Man and Superman*, and became hooked on acting. Soon afterwards, while still in college, she got a role in the movie *The Wedding Party* (which was released several years later, in 1969).

After graduating from college, Clayburgh studied acting in Manhattan with Uta Hagen and John Lehne, from whom she learned a modified form of the Method technique. She became a member of the Charles Playhouse in Boston, where she met the young actor Al Pacino.

Clayburgh and Pacino became romantically involved, and they moved back to New York City together. There, she appeared in off-Broadway plays, including *Calling In Crazy* (1969), in which she played a half-hearted nonconformist. During that time she also acted in TV shows, such as *N.Y.P.D.* and *Search for Tomorrow*.

Clayburgh made her Broadway debut in 1970, as the beautiful, spirited Hannah Cohen in the musical *The Rothschilds* (1970). The following year she appeared in a Los Angeles production of *Othello*. She then played the role of Naomi in the film *Portnoy's Complaint* (1972). She also had small parts in the movies *The Thief Who Came to Dinner* (1973) and *The Terminal Man* (1974).

In 1975 Clayburgh played a prostitute in the film *Hustling* (TV, 1975). Her performance was so well-received that she began to be offered leading roles. In *Griffin and Phoenix* (TV, 1976) she played a terminally ill woman who has a last love affair. In *Gable and Lombard* (1976), she portrayed the actress Carole Lombard. In *An Unmarried Woman* (1978), she played a woman traumatized by her husband's sudden leavetaking after many years of marriage. In the Italian-made movie *La Luna* (1979, *Luna* in the United States), she was a self-centered mother with an unhealthy attachment to her son.

In 1979 Clayburgh appeared in a Long Beach, California, production of the play *In the Boom Boom Room*, portraying a vulnerable, morally wounded go-go dancer. That year she also married the play's author, David Rabe, with whom she had a daughter, Lily.

Clayburgh then returned to her film work, playing an edgy career woman living with a man who resents her success in *I'm Dancing As Fast As I Can* (1982). In *Hanna K.* (1983) she portrayed a lawyer defending an Arab in a land dispute. In *Miles to Go* (TV, 1986), she was a woman dying of cancer

Jill Clayburgh

The Nest (1970)
The Devil's Disciple (1970)
The Rothschilds (1970)
Othello (1971)
Pippin (1972)
Jumpers (1974)
In the Boom Boom Room (1979)
Design of Living (1984)

FILMS

The Wedding Party (1969)
Portnoy's Complaint (1972)
The Snoop Sisters (TV, 1972)
The Thief Who Came to Dinner (1973)
The Terminal Man (1974)
Hustling (TV, 1975)
The Art of Crime (TV, 1975)
Griffin and Phoenix (TV, 1976)
Gable and Lombard (1976)
Silver Streak (1976)
Semi-Tough (1977)
An Unmarried Woman (1978)
La Luna (1979, It.; U.S., *Luna*)
Starting Over (1979)
It's My Turn (1980)
First Monday in October (1981)
I'm Dancing As Fast As I Can (1982)
Hanna K. (1983)
Miles to Go (TV, 1986)
Shy People (1987)
Reason for Living: The Jill Ireland Story (TV, 1991)
Whispers in the Dark (1992)
Trial: The Price of Passion (TV, 1992)
Rich in Love (1993)
Firestorm: Seventy-two Hours in Oakland (TV, 1993)
Naked in New York (1994)
For the Love of Nancy (TV, 1994)
Honor Thy Father and Mother: The True Story of the Menendez Murders (TV, 1994)
The Face on the Milk Carton (TV, 1995)
Going All the Way (1997)
Fools Rush In (1997)
Crowned and Dangerous (TV, 1997)
Sins of the Mind (TV, 1997)
When Innocence Is Lost (TV, 1997)

and worrying about how her death would affect her husband's and children's lives.

In the 1990s Clayburgh's work reflected her growing maturity and wisdom and her performances took on an increased depth. She produced stunning performances in numerous films, namely, *Reason for Living: The Jill Ireland Story* (TV, 1991), *Whispers in the Dark* (1992), *Naked in New York* (1994), *The Face on the Milk Carton* (TV, 1995), *Fools Rush In* (1997), and *When Innocence Is Lost* (TV, 1997).

SELECTED PERFORMANCES:

STAGE

It's Called the Sugar Plum (1968)
The Sudden and Accidental Re-education of Horse Johnson (1968)
Calling In Crazy (1969)

Lee J. Cobb

Gravel-Voiced Actor

Lee J. Cobb was one of America's busiest and best character actors. Few performers could match the incredibly wide range of roles that he played, from the heartbreakingly defeated Willy Loman in the stage production of *Death of a Salesman* (1949) to the brutal criminal Johnny Friendly in the film *On the Waterfront* (1954). Many critics agreed that Cobb's gravel-voiced performances enhanced, even salvaged, countless films.

Lee J. Cobb was born in New York City, New York, on December 8, 1911. His original name was Leo Jacoby.

After a wrist injury ended his early dreams of becoming a concert violinist, he turned to acting. After graduating from high school in New York City, he went to California, where he became associated with the Pasadena Playhouse in 1929. He soon returned to New York City, then moved back to California in 1931 and worked as an actor-director at the Pasadena Playhouse for two years.

Returning once again to New York, Cobb made his Broadway debut in 1935, playing Koch and the Saloon Keeper in *Crime and Punishment*. That year he also became a member of the famed Group Theater. He performed a number of roles with the group, including those of Mr. Carp in *Golden Boy* (1937) and Lammanawitsz in *The Gentle People* (1939).

In 1939 Cobb appeared in the movie version of *Golden Boy*. For the next several years, he alternately worked in Hollywood films and on the New York City stage.

From 1943 to 1945, Cobb served in the United States Air Force, acting in the stage show *Winged Victory* (1943). He also appeared in the filmed version (1944).

After his discharge, Cobb returned to Hollywood and continued his career as a character actor. In *Anna and the King of Siam* (1946), he played a Siamese prime minister; in *Boomerang* (1947), a police chief; in *Captain from Castile* (1947), a Spanish buccaneer; in *Call Northside 777* (1948), a newspaper editor; and in *The Dark Past* (1948), a scientist.

Cobb finally gained widespread renown as an actor when he played Willy Loman in Arthur Miller's *Death of a Salesman* (1949) on Broadway. Afterwards, he appeared in several plays, including a revival of *Golden Boy* (1952). He also made guest appearances in numerous TV series, such as *Playhouse Ninety*, *Studio One*, and *Zane Grey Theater*. In the long-running TV western series *The Virginian* (1962–70), he played Judge Henry Garth, and in the courtroom drama *The Young Lawyers* (1970–71), he played David Barrett.

Cobb spent most of his mature years making movies. His most famous part was that of the vicious gangster Johnny Friendly in the film *On the Waterfront* (1954). He also played a Chinese warlord in *The Left Hand of God* (1955) and a country judge in *The Man in the Gray Flannel Suit* (1956).

In the mid-1950s Cobb testified before the House Committee on Un-American Activities. He admitted that he had briefly been a member of the Communist party in the 1930s. Shortly after his testimony, he suffered a massive heart attack that nearly killed him.

Cobb soon returned to work, giving outstand-

ing performances as a hard-line jurist in *Twelve Angry Men* (1957) and, in one of his most memorable roles, as the father in *The Brothers Karamazov* (1958). In *Exodus* (1960), a film about the events leading up to the liberation of Israel in 1948, he played a Jewish conservative.

Among Cobb's later movies were *Come Blow Your Horn* (1963), *Mackenna's Gold* (1969), and *The Exorcist* (1973). Near the end of his life, he also starred in several TV movies. For example, in *Dr. Max* (TV, 1974), which was based on the same story as that used in the 1959 movie *The Last Angry Man* (starring Paul Muni), Cobb played a curmudgeonly big-city doctor who has a genuine concern for his poverty-stricken patients.

Cobb was married twice. In 1940 he wedded the actress Helen Beverly, with whom he had two children, Vincent and Julie. They divorced in

1952, and in 1957 he married Mary Hirsch, a Los Angeles schoolteacher. They raised two children, one from her previous marriage and one of their own.

Cobb died in Los Angeles, California, on February 11, 1976.

SELECTED PERFORMANCES:

STAGE

Crime and Punishment (1935)
Waiting for Lefty (1935)
Till the Day I Die (1935)
The Mother (1935)
Bitter Stream (1936)
Happy Valley, Limited (1936)
Golden Boy (1937)
The Gentle People (1939)
Thunder Rock (1939)
The Fifth Column (1940)
Clash by Night (1941)
Winged Victory (1943)
Death of a Salesman (1949)
Golden Boy (1952)
The Emperor's Clothes (1953)
King Lear (1968)

FILMS

Golden Boy (1939)
This Thing Called Love (1941)
Men of Boys Town (1941)
Paris Calling (1942)
The Moon Is Down (1943)
Tonight We Raid Calais (1943)
The Song of Bernadette (1943)
Winged Victory (1944)
Anna and the King of Siam (1946)
Boomerang (1947)
Johnny O'Clock (1947)
Captain from Castile (1947)
Call Northside 777 (1948)
The Miracle of the Bells (1948)
The Luck of the Irish (1948)
The Dark Past (1948)
Thieves' Highway (1949)
The Man Who Cheated Himself (1951)
Sirocco (1951)
The Fighter (1952)
The Tall Texan (1953)

Lee J. Cobb

Yankee Pasha (1954)
Gorilla at Large (1954)
On the Waterfront (1954)
The Racers (1955)
The Left Hand of God (1955)

The Man in the Gray Flannel Suit (1956)
Twelve Angry Men (1957)
The Garment Jungle (1957)
The Three Faces of Eve (1957)
The Brothers Karamazov (1958)
Man of the West (1958)
Party Girl (1958)
The Trap (1959)
Green Mansions (1959)
But Not for Me (1959)
Exodus (1960)
The Four Horsemen of the Apocalypse (1962)
Come Blow Your Horn (1963)
How the West Was Won (1963)
Our Man Flint (1966)
In Like Flint (1967)
Coogan's Bluff (1968)
Mackenna's Gold (1969)
The Liberation of L. B. Jones (1970)
Macho Callahan (1970)
Lawman (1971)
Heat of Anger (TV, 1972)
Double Indemnity (TV, 1973)
The Man Who Loved Cat Dancing (1973)
The Exorcist (1973)
Dr. Max (TV, 1974)
Trapped beneath the Sea (TV, 1974)
The Great Ice Rip-off (TV, 1974)
That Lucky Touch (1975)

TV

The Virginian (1962–70)
The Young Lawyers (1970–71)

Billy Crystal

"Mahvelous" Mimic

Billy Crystal is one of the most popular comedians of our time. Not only is he a talented stand-up performer, but he is also an accomplished film and TV actor. More concerned with moving his audience than making them laugh, Crystal describes his comedy style as "bittersweet." His hilarious yet poignant impressions and warm, gentle style has endeared him to fans of all ages.

Billy (originally William) Crystal was born in Long Beach, New York, on March 14, 1947 (some sources give the birthplace as Manhattan and the year as 1948). In his autobiography, *Absolutely Mahvelous* (1986), Crystal describes the influence of his early surroundings on his later career. His paternal grandfather was a Yiddish actor. His mother loved the theater and performed in shows at the synagogue. One of his uncles, Milt Gabler, founded Commodore Records, which specialized in jazz. Crystal's father, who managed Gabler's shop in Manhattan, often invited jazz musicians to the Crystal family home, where Billy Crystal met Billie Holiday, W. C. Handy, and other jazz greats. He imitated the musicians' jive talk and performed for his family by mimicking the televised and recorded routines of professional comedians. "We had swinging seders," he later recalled.

Crystal majored in theater at Nassau Community College and then studied TV and film direction under Martin Scorsese at New York University, earning a B.F.A. degree there in 1970. That same year he married Janice Goldfinger, with whom he had two children, Jennifer and Lindsey.

While he was still a student, Crystal co-founded a three-person improvisational comedy troupe called successively We the People, Comedy Jam, and Three's Company. For several years the trio performed at Greenwich Village clubs, small Eastern colleges, and trade shows. Crystal then went solo. He struggled for a couple of years, performing in clubs and making occasional TV appearances.

Crystal then relocated to Los Angeles, hoping the move would further his career. He was performing one night at the Comedy Store, when he was spotted by the TV producer Norman Lear. Soon, Crystal had a guest role in Lear's sitcom *All in the Family*. Then, the producer cast him as Jodie Dallas, the first openly homosexual character in the history of television, in the sitcom *Soap*, a spoof of soap operas.

During his four seasons as a member of the *Soap* cast (1977–81), Crystal also appeared in several movies. In *Rabbit Test* (1978) he played the world's first pregnant man. His other films included *Breaking Up Is Hard to Do* (TV, 1979) and *Enola Gay: The Men, the Mission, the Atomic Bomb* (TV, 1980).

When Crystal was not working on episodes of *Soap* or acting in movies, he was busy performing as a stand-up comedian. Feeling, as he has said, "at home in other bodies," he worked not as a traditional joketeller but as a mimic, humorously imitating real people and creating imaginary characters. He mimicked, for example, Sammy Davis, Jr., singing "We Are the World" with Yiddish asides. Crystal also did impressions of Muhammad

Billy Crystal

Billy Crystal

Ali, Jewish relatives, and old jazz musicians. Among his fictional characters were Penny Lane, a transvestite; Rabbit, an octogenarian veteran of the old Negro Baseball League; and an unnamed elderly punch-drunk boxer who boasted that he broke his nose seventy-seven times in one fight. The comedian's most famous character was Fernando, inspired by, but only loosely based on, the late actor Fernando Lamas. Fernando's expression "You look maaaaaavelous" became a national catchphrase.

In 1982 Crystal hosted a short-lived TV series, *The Billy Crystal Comedy Hour*. During the 1984 to 1985 television season, he rejuvenated the slumping comedy series *Saturday Night Live* with his gallery of impersonations. It was on this show that Crystal introduced the Fernando character. In 1985 he issued the comedy album *Mahvelous*.

After Crystal left *Saturday Night Live* , he rapidly achieved megastardom by appearing in a string of hit movies and hosting nationally televised awards shows. He hosted the Grammy Awards for three consecutive years (1987–89), then hosted the Academy Awards throughout most of the 1990s (1990–93, 1997–98). He cowrote and acted in the film *Memories of Me* (1988); provided the story idea and starred in *City Slickers* (1991); and cowrote, starred in, and directed both *Mr. Saturday Night* (1992) and *Forget Paris* (1995), which he also acted in and directed. He also starred in *Father's Day* (1997); Woody Allen's *Deconstructing Harry* (1997); and *Analyze This*, with Robert DeNiro (1999).

FILMS

SST—Death Flight (TV, 1977)
Human Feelings (TV, 1978)
Rabbit Test (1978)
Breaking Up Is Hard to Do (TV, 1979)
Enola Gay: The Men, the Mission, the Atomic Bomb (TV, 1980)
This Is Spinal Tap (1984)
Running Scared (1986)
The Princess Bride (1987)
Throw Momma from the Train (1987)
Memories of Me (1988)
When Harry Met Sally (1989)
City Slickers (1991)
Mr. Saturday Night (1992)
Voice of America: In Search of Dr. Seuss (TV, 1994)
City Slickers II: The Legend of Curly's Gold (1994)
Forget Paris (1995)
Hamlet (1996)
Father's Day (1997)
Deconstructing Harry (1997)
My Giant (1998)
Analyze This (1999)

TV

Soap (1977–81)
The Billy Crystal Comedy Hour (1982)
Saturday Night Live (1984–85)

Tony Curtis

Popular Leading Man

Tony Curtis was one of the most popular leading men in films of the 1950s and 1960s. In more recent years, he has demonstrated his ability as a character actor.

Tony Curtis was born in New York City, New York, on June 3, 1925. His original name was Bernard Schwartz.

Curtis's father had been an actor in Hungary. But after immigrating to the United States, he found English to be difficult and became a tailor.

Curtis grew up in a tough neighborhood, faced anti-Semitism, and became a gang member. A truant officer took the boy to the Jones Memorial Settlement House, where he developed an interest in acting in plays.

Before finishing high school, Curtis ran away from home (his mother was abusive) and joined the navy. After being discharged he went back to high school, graduating in 1946. He then studied for one year at the Dramatic Workshop of the New School for Social Research in New York City. Next, he toured the borscht circuit with a stock company, then began to make stage appearances in the New York City area, notably as the lead role in *Golden Boy* with the Cherry Lane Players in Greenwich Village. He was seen by a talent scout and signed to a Hollywood film contract.

In Curtis's early days at Universal-International Pictures, he changed his name (first to Anthony Curtis, later to Tony) and began to take courses in voice, dramatics, gymnastics, horsemanship, and pantomime. Meanwhile, he performed bit parts in several movies, including *City across the River* (1949) and *Francis* (1950). His first leading role was in *The Prince Who Was a Thief* (1951). He soon became enormously popular with audiences for his athleticism, good looks, and genial personality.

Critics, however, remained cool toward Curtis for many years. In 1953 he began psychoanalysis, which he claimed helped him both as a person and as an actor. In the late 1950s, Curtis finally began to win critical acceptance as a serious actor. He gave a series of excellent performances, appearing in such classic films as *Sweet Smell of Success* (1957), as an overly ambitious publicist; *Kings Go Forth* (1958), as a spoiled rich youth; *The Defiant Ones* (1958), as an embittered escaped convict; and *Some Like It Hot* (1959), as a bogus female saxophonist and phony millionaire.

In the 1960s and 1970s, he continued to expand his range as a leading man. He portrayed a stereotyped hero and daredevil in the comedy *The Great Race* (1965), a homicidal maniac in the mystery *The Boston Strangler* (1968), and a gangster in *Lepke* (1975). Curtis was widely praised for his performance as David O. Selznick in *Moviola: The Scarlett O'Hara War* (TV, 1980), a film about the legendary producer's search for a leading lady for his 1939 movie *Gone with the Wind*.

By the early 1980s Curtis had become increasingly incapacitated as a result of a longtime addiction to alcohol and drugs. In 1984 he entered the Betty Ford Center in Rancho Mirage, California, where he received help in overcoming his addictions.

Curtis then campaigned for, and won, the role

Tony Curtis

Tony Curtis

Black Shield of Falworth (1954), *The Perfect Furlough* (1959), and *Who Was That Lady?* (1960). They had two daughters, Kelly and Jamie Lee (who later became a well-known actress), before divorcing in the early 1960s. In 1963 Curtis married the actress Christine Kaufmann, with whom he appeared in *Taras Bulba* (1962) and *Wild and Wonderful* (1964). They had two daughters, Alexandra and Allegra, before divorcing in 1967. The following year he married Leslie Allen, with whom he had two sons, Nicholas and Benjamin, before that marriage, too, ended in divorce. In 1993 he married Lisa Deutsch.

SELECTED PERFORMANCES:

STAGE

I Ought to Be in Pictures (1980)

FILMS

Criss Cross (1949)
City across the River (1949)
The Lady Gambles (1949)
Johnny Stool Pigeon (1949)
Francis (1950)
I Was a Shoplifter (1950)
Winchester '73 (1950)
Sierra (1950)
Kansas Raiders (1951)
The Prince Who Was a Thief (1951)
Flesh and Fury (1952)
The Vikings (1952)
No Room for the Groom (1952)
Son of Ali Baba (1952)
Houdini (1953)
Forbidden (1954)
Beachhead (1954)
Johnny Dark (1954)
The Black Shield of Falworth (1954)
Six Bridges to Cross (1955)
So This Is Paris (1955)
The Purple Mask (1955)
The Square Jungle (1955)
Trapeze (1956)
The Rawhide Years (1956)
Mister Cory (1957)
Sweet Smell of Success (1957)
The Midnight Story (1957)

of the crime boss Salvatore ("Sam") Giancana in the fact-based movie *Mafia Princess* (TV, 1986). He gave a powerful performance and rejuvenated his career. In *Murder in Three Acts* (TV, 1986), he played a retired film star surrounded by memorabilia of better days; Curtis shipped many of his own photos, awards, and other objects from his Palm Springs, California, home to Acapulco, Mexico, for location shooting. His later films included *Prime Target* (1991), *A Perry Mason Mystery: The Case of the Grimacing Governor* (TV, 1994), and *The Immortals* (1996).

Curtis has had four marriages. In 1951 he married the actress Janet Leigh, with whom he appeared in the films *The Vikings* (1952), *Houdini, The*

Kings Go Forth (1958)
The Defiant Ones (1958)
The Perfect Furlough (1959)
Some Like It Hot (1959)
Operation Petticoat (1959)
Who Was That Lady? (1960)
The Rat Race (1960)
Spartacus (1960)
The Great Impostor (1961)
The Outsider (1961)
Taras Bulba (1962)
Captain Newman, M.D. (1963)
Forty Pounds of Trouble (1963)
The List of Adrian Messenger (1963)
Goodbye Charlie (1964)
Paris When It Sizzles (1964)
Sex and the Single Girl (1964)
Wild and Wonderful (1964)
Boeing Boeing (1965)
The Great Race (1965)
Arrivederci, Baby! (1966)
Chamber of Horrors (1966)
Not with My Wife, You Don't! (1966)
Don't Make Waves (1967)
The Boston Strangler (1968)
Rosemary's Baby (1968)
On My Way to the Crusades, I Met a Girl Who. . .
   (1969)
Those Daring Young Men in Their Jaunty Jalopies
   (1969)
Suppose They Gave a War and Nobody Came
   (1970)
You Can't Win 'Em All (1970)
The Third Girl from the Left (TV, 1973)
The Count of Monte Cristo (TV, 1975)
The Big Ripoff (TV, 1975)

Lepke (1975)
The Last Tycoon (1976)
The Manitou (1978)
The Bad News Bears Go to Japan (1978)
Vega$ (TV, 1978)
The Users (TV, 1978)
Sextette (1979)
Title Shot (1979)
Little Miss Marker (1980)
The Mirror Crack'd (1980)
Moviola: The Scarlett O'Hara War (TV, 1980)
Inmates: A Love Story (TV, 1981)
The Million Dollar Face (TV, 1981)
Portrait of a Showgirl (TV, 1982)
Where Is Parsifal? (1984)
Insignificance (1985)
Mafia Princess (TV, 1986)
Club Life (1986)
Murder in Three Acts (TV, 1986)
Welcome to Germany (1988)
Thanksgiving Day (TV, 1990)
Prime Target (1991)
Christmas in Connecticut (TV, 1992)
Center of the Web (1992)
Beauty and the Bandit (TV, 1994)
*A Perry Mason Mystery: The Case of the Grimacing
   Governor* (TV, 1994)
Naked in New York (1994)
The Immortals (1996)
The Celluloid Closet (1996)

TV

The Persuaders (1971–72)
McCoy (1975–76)
Vega$ (1978–81)

Rodney Dangerfield

Comedian Who Gets No Respect

Rodney Dangerfield's success is the result of his creation of a unique comedic appearance and personality. His plaintive, bugging eyes have been likened to fried eggs, and his brow-wiping, neck-craning, tie-adjusting, and shoulder-twitching suggest a thoroughly modern neurotic. The basis of his verbal humor is best expressed in his trademark appeal for sympathy: "I don't get no respect." "My mother never breast fed me," he says. "She told me she liked me as a friend. Life has been going downhill ever since then. My psychiatrist told me I was going crazy. I said, 'If you don't mind, I'd like a second opinion.' He said, 'Okay. You're ugly, too.'"

Rodney Dangerfield was born in Babylon, New York, on November 22, 1921. His original name was Jacob Cohen.

Dangerfield struggled through many difficulties as a child. His father, at one time a vaudeville pantomime comic, ran out on the family when Rodney was just a baby. Later, his mother moved the family to a neighborhood in Queens where the cost of living was beyond their means. The boy faced not only poverty but also the embarrassment of having a job that required him to deliver groceries to the homes of the well-to-do children with whom he went to school. He also encountered anti-Semitism, even among his teachers.

At fifteen Dangerfield began to write jokes as a way of escaping reality. "Comedy is a camouflage for depression," he would later admit. The first joke he ever wrote already showed that he viewed himself as a loser: "When I played hide-and-seek, they wouldn't even look for me." Soon, he was working in the Catskills as a stand-up comedian under the name Jack Roy (Roy was his father's stage name). For the next nine years, he struggled as a comic and a singing waiter. He already showed signs of being a good comedy writer, but he lacked a distinct stage character.

When Dangerfield was twenty-eight, he left show business. For the next dozen years he ran his own business, selling house paint and siding. During those years he continued to write jokes, and he sold some of them to Jackie Mason and Joan Rivers.

When Dangerfield was in his early forties, he decided to return to the stage and got a booking at a Brooklyn nightclub where he had worked years before. To avoid embarrassment, he asked the club's owner, George McFadden, to bill him under a new name. McFadden chose the name Rodney Dangerfield, which the would-be comedian permanently adopted.

By this point Dangerfield had developed a clearly defined stage personality: the loser who keeps trying. His act was extremely successful, and his career soon received tremendous boosts from TV appearances on *The Ed Sullivan Show* and *The Tonight Show*. In 1969 he opened his own nightclub, Dangerfield's, in New York City, so that he could spend more time with his children, Brian and Melanie, whom he had with his first wife, the former Joyce Indig. Later, Joyce died, and in the mid-1990s Dangerfield married Joan Child.

Meanwhile, his career was moving forward at a

rapid pace. TV remained an important vehicle for him. During the 1972 to 1973 television season, he was a regular on *The Dean Martin Show*, a musical-variety series. Later, he often appeared on *The Tonight Show* and frequently guest-hosted *Saturday Night Live*. In the late 1980s, he increased his exposure through his TV commercials for Miller Lite beer. He appeared in the commercials with a number of former athletes, from whom he consistently got no respect.

Dangerfield recorded several comedy albums, such as *The Loser* (1967) and *Rappin' Rodney* (1983). He also wrote books, including *I Don't Get No Respect* (1973), and performed on the New York City stage in *Rodney Dangerfield on Broadway!* (1988).

Dangerfield has appeared in only a small number of films—too few from his fans' point of view. In the fantasy *The Projectionist* (1971), he played a dual role as a theater manager and as a villain. In *Caddyshack* (1980) he was the loudmouth Al Czervik, a nouveau-riche boor. In *Easy Money* (1983) he portrayed a cheerful reprobate who, to collect a multimillion-dollar inheritance, must give up his high-living ways. In *Back to School* (1986), he was a clothing-store tycoon who returns to college. He wrote the screenplay, and supplied a voice, for the animated film *Rover Dangerfield* (1992). His other movies include *Moving* (1988), *Ladybugs* (1992), *Casper* (1995), and *Casper: A Spirited Beginning* (1997).

Rodney Dangerfield

SELECTED PERFORMANCES:

STAGE

Rodney Dangerfield on Broadway! (1988)

FILMS

The Projectionist (1971)
Caddyshack (1980)
Easy Money (1983)
Back to School (1986)
Benny and Barney: Las Vegas Undercover (TV, 1987)
Moving (1988)
Ladybugs (1992)
Rover Dangerfield (animated, voice only 1992)
Natural Born Killers (1994)
Casper (1995)
Casper: A Spirited Beginning (1997)
Meet Wally Sparks (1997)

TV

The Dean Martin Show (1972–73)

Howard da Silva

Tough-Looking Actor

Known for his rugged features and tough-guy roles, Howard da Silva was actually one of America's most versatile character actors. He could send chills up the spines of viewers watching him play a murderer in the film *They Live by Night* (1948), but he could also convincingly play Benjamin Franklin in the stage musical *1776* (1969).

Howard da Silva was born in Cleveland, Ohio, on May 4, 1909. His original name was Harold Silverblatt. He grew up in the Bronx, New York.

When da Silva was a young man, he moved to Pittsburgh, where he attended the Carnegie Institute of Technology, financing his education by working in steel mills. Then, in 1928, he joined Eva La Gallienne's Civic Repertory Company in New York City. For the next decade, he was extremely active as a character actor on the stage. Among his roles were those of Schumann in *Siegfried* (1930), a stationmaster in *The Cherry Orchard* (1931), the Cook and the White Knight in *Alice in Wonderland* (1932), Thorvald in *A Doll's House* (1933), Hansy McCulloh in *Black Pit* (1935), Lewis in *Golden Boy* (1937), and Jack Armstrong in *Abe Lincoln in Illinois* (1938).

Da Silva repeated his role as Jack Armstrong in the filmed version of *Abe Lincoln in Illinois* (1940). Throughout the 1940s and early 1950s, he spent most of his time making movies. He also appeared on TV. His most important stage appearance during that period was as Jud Fry in the Rodgers and Hammerstein musical *Oklahoma!* (1943).

At first, da Silva was offered only bit parts in films, but he gradually began to receive more substantial roles. He was often cast as a heavy because of his tough-looking facial features. He gave a powerful performance as one of the murderous escaped convicts in *They Live by Night* (1948). Among his other films were *The Sea Wolf* (1941), *Sergeant York* (1941), *Keeper of the Flame* (1943), *The Lost Weekend* (1945), *The Blue Dahlia* (1946), *Two Years before the Mast* (1946), and *M* (1951).

In the early fifties, da Silva appeared as an unfriendly witness before the House Un-American Activities Committee and fell victim to the McCarthy-era blacklisting of liberal-leaning entertainers. For the next decade, he was barred from movies and TV. As a result, he returned full time to the stage, increasing his theatrical reputation by producing, directing, and acting in plays at theaters all over America. His character-acting abilities were displayed in such works as *The World of Sholom Aleichem* (1953), *Mister Roberts* (1954), *The Adding Machine* (1956), *Volpone* (1957), and *Fiorello!* (1959).

Beginning in the early 1960s, da Silva was again allowed to work in films and on TV. He gave a beautiful performance as Dr. Alan Swinford, a gentle, understanding psychiatrist for disturbed youngsters, in the movie *David and Lisa* (1962). And he began to make guest appearances on such TV series as *Ben Casey, The Defenders, The Man from U.N.C.L.E.,* and *Outer Limits.* In 1965 he had a regular role, as a district attorney, in the series *For the People.*

The highlight of da Silva's work in the late 1960s was his role as Benjamin Franklin in the musical *1776* (1969). He performed the work at the White

Howard da Silva

Howard da Silva

House by special invitation of President Richard M. Nixon (an ironic turn of events, considering Nixon's strong support for, and leadership in, the witch-hunting that had caused da Silva to be black-listed in the 1950s). Da Silva repeated his role in the filmed version of *1776* (1972).

From the mid-seventies to the early eighties, da Silva was active in theater, film, and TV. In 1974 he played Nikita Khrushchev in the TV docudrama *The Missiles of October*. Da Silva was highly praised for his supporting-role performance in the TV drama "Verna: USO Girl" (1978) on *Great Performances*. In 1981 he portrayed the film tycoon Louis B. Mayer in the movie *Mommie Dearest*.

Da Silva married Marjorie Nelson in 1950. They divorced in 1960, and the following year he wedded the actress Nancy Nutter. His marriages produced two sons (Peter and Daniel) and three daughters (Rachel, Judith, and Margaret).

SELECTED PERFORMANCES:

STAGE

The Would-Be Gentleman (1929)
Romeo and Juliet (1930)
Siegfried (1930)
Alison's House (1930)
Camille (1931)
The Cherry Orchard (1931)
Liliom (1932)
The Three Sisters (1932)
Alice in Wonderland (1932)
A Doll's House (1933)
Hedda Gabler (1933)
The Master Builder (1933)
Sailors of Cattaro (1934)
Black Pit (1935)
Golden Boy (1937)
The Cradle Will Rock (1937)
Casey Jones (1938)
Abe Lincoln in Illinois (1938)
Summer Night (1939)
Two on an Island (1940)
Oklahoma! (1943)
Burning Bright (1950)
The World of Sholom Aleichem (1953)
Mister Roberts (1954)
The Adding Machine (1956)
Diary of a Scoundrel (1956)
Volpone (1957, 1972)
Compulsion (1957)
Fiorello! (1959)
Romulus (1962)
In the Counting House (1962)
Dear Me, the Sky Is Falling (1963)
Hamlet (1964)
The Unknown Soldier and His Wife (1967)
1776 (1969)
The Caucasian Chalk Circle (1975)
The Most Dangerous Man in America (1976)

FILMS

Abe Lincoln in Illinois (1940)
I'm Still Alive (1940)
The Sea Wolf (1941)
Strange Alibi (1941)

Howard da Silva in Missles of October

Sergeant York (1941)
Bad Men of Missouri (1941)
Blues in the Night (1941)
Wild Bill Hickok Rides (1942)
Bullet Scars (1942)
Native Land (1942)
Juke Girl (1942)
The Big Shot (1942)
Reunion in France (1943)
Keeper of the Flame (1943)
Tonight We Raid Calais (1943)
Duffy's Tavern (1945)
The Lost Weekend (1945)
The Blue Dahlia (1946)
Two Years before the Mast (1946)
Blaze of Noon (1947)
Unconquered (1947)
They Live by Night (1948)
The Great Gatsby (1949)

Border Incident (1949)
The Underworld Story (1950)
Wyoming Mail (1950)
Tripoli (1950)
Fourteen Hours (1951)
Three Husbands (1951)
M (1951)
David and Lisa (1962)
It's a Mad, Mad, Mad, Mad World (1963)
The Outrage (1964)
Nevada Smith (1966)
1776 (1972)
The Great Gatsby (1974)
Smile, Jenny, You're Dead (TV, 1974)
Power (TV, 1980)
Mommie Dearest (1981)

TV

For the People (1965)

Sammy Davis, Jr.

Complete Entertainer

Singer, dancer, actor, comedian, impressionist—Sammy Davis, Jr., was one of the last great examples of the complete entertainer nurtured in vaudeville. Remarkably, he became a star in every field he pursued.

Sammy Davis, Jr., was born of a Baptist father and Roman Catholic mother in Harlem on December 8, 1925. His father was the lead dancer, and his mother a lead chorus girl, in Will Mastin's vaudeville troupe. The boy's paternal grandmother took care of him in Harlem while his parents traveled with the show.

When Davis was two years old, his parents separated and his father took him to join the Will Mastin players. At first, little Sammy was used only as a silent prop, making the audience laugh by mugging the actions of other performers. Later, he learned to sing and dance in the show.

At the age of seven, Davis won the title role in the two-reel movie *Rufus Jones for President* (1933), which starred Ethel Waters and was filmed in Brooklyn. Soon afterward he made another film, *Seasoned Greetings* (1933), with Charles Chaplin, Jr., and Chaplin's mother, Lita Grey, who wanted to adopt Sammy and take him to Hollywood to make him a movie star. But the Davis family decided to stay together.

In the mid-thirties, vaudeville began to die out, largely because of competition from sound movies. Will Mastin, a close friend of the Davis family, had to reduce his troupe down to just himself, Sammy Davis, Sr., and Sammy Davis, Jr. The child had already become the main attraction, and the new group was called Will Mastin's Gang, Featuring Little Sammy. After several other name changes, the group was eventually billed as the Will Mastin Trio, Featuring Sammy Davis, Jr. In the late 1930s and early 1940s, the trio worked across the United States and Canada many times. During that period Davis met the legendary tap dancer Bill ("Bojangles") Robinson and the young singer Frank Sinatra.

When Davis turned eighteen, he was drafted into the army. During basic training he encountered, blatant, brutal racial prejudice for the first time in his life. He was assigned to Special Services and performed in shows at camps across the country.

After Davis left the army, he rejoined the Will Mastin Trio. But vaudeville was dead, and the act went through some lean years, playing nightclubs in various cities. From 1947 to 1948, they toured in a show starring Mickey Rooney, from whom Davis learned much about live performing.

Young Davis constantly worked on developing new skills to freshen up the trio's act, which soon became a showcase for him, while the two older men tap-danced and soft-shoed in the background. Besides broadening his singing and dancing repertoire, he played various instruments and did impressions of singers, such as Dean Martin, and film stars, such as Humphrey Bogart, Marlon Brando, and James Cagney.

By the early 1950s, the trio, because of young Davis's growing talent and reputation, began to receive big-time engagements, notably on *The Eddie Cantor Show*, which was part of *The Colgate Comedy Hour* TV series. They also performed at

Sammy Davis, Jr.

Judaism seriously. He saw the affinity between the Jews and the blacks as oppressed peoples. Within months his conversion to Judaism was psychologically complete, the formal ceremony coming a few years later, in 1958.

Meanwhile, Davis made his show-business comeback. Wearing an eye patch (which was later replaced by a glass eye), he joined his father and Mastin for successful engagements at major American nightclubs. In fact, the publicity surrounding his accident actually increased the demand for the Will Mastin Trio.

In 1956 the trio performed in a Broadway musical written especially for Davis, *Mr. Wonderful*. The show was about a young black nightclub entertainer who becomes successful by virtue of his talent and will in the face of strong racial opposition. The production itself was widely criticized, but it lasted over a year because Davis gave such powerful performances.

Soon after *Mr. Wonderful* closed, the trio broke up, both Mastin and Sammy Davis, Sr., retiring. Sammy Davis, Jr. continued to perform in nightclubs and Broadway shows, appearing in the musical *Golden Boy* (1964) and the one-man show *Sammy* (1974). He also starred in *Stop the World—I Want to Get Off* (1978) at Lincoln Center's New York State Theater.

In the late 1950s Davis began to act in movies. He sang for the soundtrack of, but did not appear in, *Meet Me in Las Vegas* (1956). In *Anna Lucasta* (1959) he had a straight dramatic role as a jive-talking sailor. Perhaps his most memorable film role was that of Sportin' Life in the movie version of George Gershwin's opera *Porgy and Bess* (1959).

Davis went on to appear in many films, showing his versatility by successfully performing in

the famed Copacabana nightclub in New York City, which a few years earlier had refused, on racial grounds, to allow Sammy even to enter the building.

Then, in November 1954, while driving from Las Vegas to Los Angeles, Davis was in a horrible car accident, as a result of which he lost his left eye. One of his visitors during his hospital stay was Eddie Cantor, who earlier had given him a *mezuzah* as a gift and whose depth of understanding in this crisis favorably impressed the young man. Davis was also visited in the hospital by a rabbi, who was making routine rounds.

After Davis left the hospital, he began to study

dramas and comedies, musicals and nonmusicals. In *A Man Called Adam* (1966), he played a jazz musician who falls from greatness. In the musical *Sweet Charity* (1969), he played the hip revivalist Big Daddy. He also starred in *Convicts Four* (1962), a prison drama, and *Sergeants Three* (1962), a Western comedy.

Davis became a member of a famous group of friends called the Rat Pack, or the Clan. The group was led by Frank Sinatra and included Joey Bishop, Dean Martin, and Peter Lawford. Various members of the Rat Pack appeared with Davis in the movies *Ocean's Eleven* (1960), *Johnny Cool* (1963), *Robin and the Seven Hoods* (1964), and *One More Time* (1970). Davis's association with the Rat Pack led to fast living, heavy smoking, and hard drinking. Eventually, he developed liver and kidney ailments, and early in 1974 he was hospitalized with chest pains. After that, he moderated his habits.

Beginning in the late 1950s, Davis made numerous TV appearances. He hosted his own musical-variety specials and series, including the series *The Sammy Davis, Jr., Show* (1966) and *Sammy and Company* (1975–77). He also guest-hosted *The Tonight Show* and guest-starred in the anthology series *General Electric Theater*, the drama series *Mod Squad*, the comedy series *All in the Family*, and many other TV programs.

Davis was a major recording artist. The songs with which he was closely identified include "The Candy Man," "Mr. Bojangles," "That Old Black Magic," and "What Kind of Fool Am I?" He was also an author, publishing two autobiographical books, *Yes, I Can: The Story of Sammy Davis, Jr.* (with Jane and Bury Boyar, 1965) and *Hollywood in a Suitcase* (1980).

Davis was married three times. In the late 1950s, he wedded Loray White, a black dancer, but they divorced after only one year together. Shortly thereafter he married Swedish actress May Britt. They had a natural daughter (Tracey) and two adopted sons (Mark and Geoff). Because of their racially mixed marriage, Davis and Britt were subjected to many ugly remarks and incidents. In 1968 that marriage, too, ended in divorce. In 1970 he married Altovise Gore, another black dancer.

In the 1980s Davis appeared in the movie *The Cannonball Run* (1981), provided a voice for the soundtrack of the animated film *Heidi's Song* (1982), performed in the play *Two Friends* (1983), and played the Caterpillar in the movie *Alice in Wonderland* (TV, 1985). One of his last projects was a role in the heartwarming movie *The Kid Who Loved Christmas* (TV, 1990).

While still in the prime of his career, Davis died of cancer in Beverly Hills, California, on May 16, 1990.

SELECTED PERFORMANCES:

STAGE

Mr. Wonderful (1956)
Golden Boy (1964)
Sammy (1974)
Stop the World—I Want to Get Off (1978)
Two Friends (1983)

FILMS

Anna Lucasta (1959)
Porgy and Bess (1959)
Pepe (1960)
Ocean's Eleven (1960)
Sergeants Three (1962)
Convicts Four (1962)
Nightmare in the Sun (1964)
Robin and the Seven Hoods (1964)
A Man Called Adam (1966)
Salt and Pepper (1968)
Sweet Charity (1969)
The Pigeon (TV, 1969)
One More Time (1970)
The Trackers (TV, 1971)
Poor Devil (TV, 1973)
Sammy Stops the World (1978)
The Cannonball Run (1981)
Heidi's Song (animated, voice only, 1982)
Cracking Up (1983, originally released as
　Smorgasbord)
Cannonball Run II (1984)
Alice in Wonderland (TV, 1985)
Moon over Parador (1988)

Kirk Douglas

Rugged, Intelligent Actor

Kirk Douglas is one of the most highly accomplished actors of his generation. Throughout his career—as a villain, a hero, or a complex combination of the two—he has infused his best work with a unique mixture of ruggedness and intelligence.

Kirk Douglas was born of Russian immigrant parents in Amsterdam, New York, on December 9, 1916. His father's original surname was Danielovitch, but in America he changed it to Demsky. Kirk Douglas grew up as Issur Danielovitch Demsky.

Interested in acting from his earliest youth, Douglas performed in school productions. After graduating from high school, he attended Saint Lawrence University in Canton, New York, where he studied dramatics, served as president of the student body, and became an outstanding intercollegiate wrestler. He also wrestled in carnivals to earn extra money.

After graduating from college with a B.A. degree in 1938, Douglas moved to New York City, where he studied at the American Academy of Dramatic Arts from 1939 to 1941. During that period he made his Broadway debut performing a minor role in *Spring Again*. He also had bit parts in other productions.

When America entered World War II, Douglas joined the navy. He was injured fighting in the Pacific and was discharged in 1944. Returning to New York City, he resumed his work with minor stage roles.

Douglas got his big break when an old acting-school friend, Lauren Bacall, recommended him to the film producer Hal B. Wallis. Douglas was given a supporting role in *The Strange Love of Martha Ivers* (1947). He then played supporting roles in several other films. He finally reached stardom with his leading role in *Champion* (1949), that of a ruthless, egotistical boxer. Over the next several years, he proved his ability to handle a wide variety of roles. In *The Glass Menagerie* (1950), for example, he was the sensitive "gentleman caller" who raises the hopes of a vulnerable, handicapped girl.

During his early years as a star, Douglas was renowned primarily for his roles as neurotic villains. He created realistic characters who were obsessive to the point of self-destruction. In *Ace in the Hole* (1951), he played an amoral newspaper reporter. In *Detective Story* (1951) he was a New York City police detective destroyed through his hatred of lawbreakers. In *The Bad and the Beautiful* (1952), he portrayed a ruthless Hollywood producer.

Less villainous but equally obsessive were his characters in *The Juggler* (1953) and *Lust for Life* (1956). In the former film, Douglas played an ex-vaudevillian who is so affected by his experiences in Nazi concentration camps that he imagines he is still surrounded by brutes after World War II is over and he is safe in Israel. In the biopic *Lust for Life*, he portrayed the painter Vincent van Gogh, who drives himself mad through overwork.

Meanwhile, Douglas was turning increasingly toward heroic or high-principled roles. For example, he starred in Disney's adventure film

Twenty Thousand Leagues under the Sea (1954) as the harpooner Ned Land, who has some of the abrasive characteristics of Douglas's earlier roles but who also fulfills the heroic function of saving himself and his companions from Captain Nemo's submarine prison. Douglas also had the title role in the Italian adventure movie *Ulysses* (1955), a recounting of the ancient Greek's heroic struggles to return home after the Trojan War. In *Path of Glory* (1957), he played an outraged colonel trying to prevent the execution of three innocent World War I French soldiers, who are selected at random, charged with cowardice, and sentenced to die merely to save a general's vanity.

Douglas was a battler in real life as well. In the 1950s he fought the Hollywood blacklist, notably by insisting that Dalton Trumbo be credited for writing the screenplay for Douglas's *Spartacus* (1960), at a time when other banned writers had to work under assumed names. Douglas also fought the Hollywood studio system by becoming the first major actor to establish his own filmmaking company, called Bryna Productions, after his mother (whose original name was Bryna Sanglel).

Kirk Douglas

Douglas's later films represent a wide range of genres, and include the bitter modern-life drama *The Arrangement* (1969), the adventure *The Light at the Edge of the World* (1971), the space story *Saturn 3* (1980), and the light-hearted western *Draw!* (TV, 1984). In *Victory at Entebbe* (TV, 1976), he played an Israeli who pleads with his government to negotiate with terrorists who have hijacked a plane carrying his daughter.

Douglas has also served as a producer and director. For example, he produced and starred in the Broadway play *One Flew over the Cuckoo's Nest* (1963). He produced, directed, and starred in the movie *Posse* (1975).

Douglas has had two marriages. In 1943 he married Diana Dill, whom he had met when both were students at the American Academy of Dramatic Arts. They had two children, Michael and Joel. Michael became one of the finest actors of his generation.

In the early 1950s, Douglas's first marriage dissolved. In 1954 he wedded the movie publicist Anne Buydens, with whom he had his children Peter and Eric. She became deeply involved with Douglas's professional life, long serving as president of his corporation and producing his films. Peter became a movie producer, while Eric became an actor and appeared in films with his father, notably in *Remembrance of Love* (TV, 1982). In that movie the elder Douglas played a middle-aged widower and Holocaust survivor who unexpectedly meets a woman he loved, and separated from, when both were teenagers in a Polish ghetto during World War II; Eric played the same character as a youth.

Douglas was aging gracefully. Still athletic in appearance and movement in the 1980s, he was able to continue to infuse his roles with ruggedness and intelligence. In *Amos* (TV, 1985; produced by his son Peter), he played an elderly man who is injured in an auto accident and has to retire to a nursing home, where he fights, and literally gives his life, to restore dignity to the abused patients. In real life Douglas publicly spoke out for legislation to protect senior citizens from physical, financial, and emotional abuse.

In fact, Douglas has fought against injustice his entire life. In his autobiography, *The Ragman's Son* (1988), he describes his childhood struggles against anti-Semitism, poverty, and the stigma of his father's work as a rag-collector. His most memorable film roles form a kind of composite portrait of Douglas himself. He repeatedly, though perhaps unconsciously, chose to portray characters who struggle against overwhelming obstacles to attain goals, just as Douglas fought to rise above his beginnings. The boxer seeking the championship in *Champion* (1949), the movie producer clawing his way up the Hollywood ladder in *The Bad and the Beautiful* (1952), Doc Holliday rising from his deathbed for one more gun battle in *Gunfight at the O.K. Corral* (1957), the Roman slave fighting to free himself and his people in *Spartacus* (1960), the cowboy refusing to give up his way of life in *Lonely Are the Brave* (1962)—these and many similar roles all represent elements in Douglas's own strong character. He became famous in particular for his unparalleled ability to convey sheer rage.

Now in his senior years, Douglas has lost none of his intensity. Even after he received serious injuries in a helicopter crash in 1991, he went on working with as much energy as ever. In the 1990s he wrote several novels and continued to make films, including *The Secret* (TV, 1992), *Greedy* (1994), and *Take Me Home Again* (TV, 1994). In 1991 he received the American Film Institute's Lifetime Achievement Award, and in 1994 he was awarded the prestigious Kennedy Center Honor for his contribution to American cultural life.

In the spring of 1996, Douglas suffered a stroke that left him with a severe speech impediment. He fought back, and just two months later, he was able to speak for himself at the Academy Awards ceremonies, where he received an Oscar for lifetime achievement. In 1997 he published yet another autobiographical book, *Climbing the Mountain: My Search for Meaning*, in which he describes his struggle to recover from the stroke and his renewed interest in his Jewish heritage. In 1999 he received the Screen Actors Guild Lifetime Achievement Award. His victory over his physical disability gave hope to others similarly afflicted and exemplified once again the indomitable spirit that has made Kirk Douglas one of the great figures in film history.

SELECTED PERFORMANCES:

STAGE

Spring Again (1941)
The Three Sisters (1942)
Alice in Arms (1945)
The Wind Is Ninety (1945)
Woman Bites Dog (1946)
One Flew over the Cuckoo's Nest (1963)

FILMS

The Strange Love of Martha Ivers (1947)
Mourning Becomes Electra (1947)
Out of the Past (1947)
I Walk Alone (1948)
The Walls of Jericho (1948)
A Letter to Three Wives (1949)
My Dear Secretary (1949)
Champion (1949)
Young Man with a Horn (1950)
The Glass Menagerie (1950)
Along the Great Divide (1951)
Ace in the Hole (1951)
Detective Story (1951)
The Big Trees (1952)
The Vikings (1952)
The Big Sky (1952)
The Bad and the Beautiful (1952)
The Juggler (1953)
Act of Love (1954)
Twenty Thousand Leagues under the Sea (1954)
The Racers (1955)
Man without a Star (1955)

Kirk Douglas in Spartacus

Ulysses (1955)
The Indian Fighter (1955)
Lust for Life (1956)
Top Secret Affair (1957)
Gunfight at the O.K. Corral (1957)
Paths of Glory (1957)
Last Train from Gun Hill (1959)

The Devil's Disciple (1959)
Strangers When We Meet (1960)
Spartacus (1960)
The Last Sunset (1961)
Town without Pity (1961)
Lonely Are the Brave (1962)
Two Weeks in Another Town (1962)
For Love or Money (1963)
The Hook (1963)
The List of Adrian Messenger (1963)
Seven Days in May (1964)
In Harm's Way (1965)
Cast a Giant Shadow (1966)
The Heros of Telemark (1966)
Is Paris Burning? (1966)
The War Wagon (1967)
The Way West (1967)
The Brotherhood (1968)
A Lovely Way to Die (1968)
The Arrangement (1969)
There Was a Crooked Man. . . (1970)
The Light at the Edge of the World (1971)
Scalawag (1973)
Mousey (TV, 1974)
Posse (1975)
The Moneychangers (TV, 1976)
Victory at Entebbe (TV, 1976)
The Fury (1978)
The Chosen (1978)
The Villain (1979)
Saturn 3 (1980)
Home Movies (1980)
The Final Countdown (1980)
The Man from Snowy River (1982)
Remembrance of Love (TV, 1982)
Eddie Macon's Run (1983)
Draw! (TV, 1984)
Amos (TV, 1985)
Tough Guys (1986)
Queenie (TV, 1987)
Inherit the Wind (TV, 1988)
Oscar (1991)
The Secret (TV, 1992)
Greedy (1994)
Take Me Home Again (TV, 1994)

Richard Dreyfuss

Unconventional Star

Male film stars are traditionally tall, handsome, and macho. Richard Dreyfuss is, truth to tell, none of the above, yet he is one of the great stars of his era. With his title role as a poor young Jew pursuing success in *The Apprenticeship of Duddy Kravitz* (1974), Dreyfuss established his trademark character type: an aggressive but ordinary guy. In his numerous films since then, he has used his self-assertive style to transform his nondescript features into a new image of what a star can be. When he hit the big time, he believed that he was setting a trend for future stars, but the trend never came. He remains one of a kind.

⊰○⊱

Richard Stephan Dreyfuss was born in New York City, New York, on October 29, 1947. In 1956 he moved with his parents to Los Angeles. At the age of nine, he decided that he wanted to be an actor. He joined an acting group at a local Jewish community center, where he made his first stage appearances.

While attending Beverly Hills High School, Dreyfuss used to sneak into a local movie studio and absorb the atmosphere. During that time he also began to work on the professional stage at the Gallery Theater in Los Angeles.

After graduating from high school, Dreyfuss studied at San Fernando Valley State College. His schooling was interrupted when he was drafted. Refusing to serve on the grounds that he was a conscientious objector, he performed two years of alternative service as a file clerk at Los Angeles County General Hospital.

Meanwhile, Dreyfuss's acting career began to move forward. In the late 1960s and early 1970s he appeared in a few minor movies, such as *The Young Runaways* (1968); performed guest roles on TV series, such as *Mod Squad*; and acted in plays in Los Angeles and in New York City, making his Broadway debut in *But Seriously . . .* (1969). In 1972 he toured nationally in the play *The Time of Your Life*, starring Henry Fonda. His first important screen role was as the gangster Baby Face Nelson in *Dillinger* (1973).

The major turning point in Dreyfuss's career occurred when he was offered an important part in *American Graffiti* (1973), a nostalgic film about one summer night in the lives of teenagers in a California city in 1962. In his role as Curt Henderson, Dreyfuss portrayed a witty intellectual apprehensive about leaving his hometown to attend an Ivy League college.

Having shown promise in *American Graffiti*, Dreyfuss was then given the leading role in *The Apprenticeship of Duddy Kravitz* (1974). In that film he played a poor young Jew whose aggressive pursuit of success blinds him to the pain that he often inflicts on others. His next film was the thriller *Jaws* (1975), in which he portrayed a wisecracking scientist involved in a terrifying shark hunt. In 1976 he had an important role in the TV movie *Victory at Entebbe*, which was based on a true story. He played the Israeli colonel who was killed while leading the July 4, 1976, raid on the Entebbe Airport in Uganda to rescue Jewish hostages held by terrorists.

Richard Dreyfuss

In 1977 Dreyfuss starred in the Steven Spielberg classic, *Close Encounters of the Third Kind*. That year he also gave a critically acclaimed performance as an egocentric young actor in the comedy *The Goodbye Girl*. He then appeared in two Shakespearean dramas, playing Cassius in *Julius Caesar* (1978) and Iago in *Othello* (1979).

After starring in *The Competition* (1980), a film about a young pianist trying to establish himself, Dreyfuss skillfully played a very challenging role in the movie *Whose Life Is It Anyway?* (1981). Usually a very physical actor, he had to play a bedridden sculptor who has been paralyzed from the neck down following a car crash. Feeling that his life is useless now, the character challenges the doctors and nurses to let him die.

From the mid-eighties to the present, Dreyfuss has starred in a number of critically acclaimed and/or popular films. He costarred with Bette Midler in the film comedy *Down and Out in Beverly Hills* (1986) and with Danny DeVito in *Tin Men* (1987). He also appeared in *Stakeout* (1987), *Rosencrantz and Guildenstern Are Dead* (1991), *Silent Fall* (1994), *The American President* (1995), *Mr. Holland's Opus* (1996), and *The Call of the Wild* (TV, 1997). In *Oliver Twist* (TV, 1997) he played the wily old criminal Fagin, who feeds and shelters homeless London boys and teaches them how to pick pockets for his benefit.

Dreyfuss periodically returns to the stage. In 1998, for example, he performed in a Los Angeles production of *Curtains*.

In late 1985 Dreyfuss discussed his craft on the *Actors on Acting* TV series. He said that he is difficult to cast and that he looks forward to the day when audiences will become bored with perfect biceps and come to admire "short, slightly overweight Jewish neurotics."

Dreyfuss has a wide range of friends and interests which include liberal politics. He has expressed a desire to run for political office someday. His sociopolitical viewpoint is reflected in his definition of acting: "humanity expressing humanity."

In 1983 he married the actress-writer Jeramie Rain (also known as Susan Davis). They had three children, Emily, Benjamin, and Harry.

Richard Dreyfuss and Bette Midler

SELECTED PERFORMANCES:

STAGE

But Seriously ... (1969)
And Whose Little Boy Are You? (1971)
Line (1971)
The Time of Your Life (1972)
Major Barbara (1972)
Miss Julie (1976)
A Man of Destiny (1976)
The Tenth Man (1977)
Julius Caesar (1978)
Othello (1979)
Whose Life Is It Anyway? (1980)
A Day in the Life of Joe Egg (1981)
Total Abandon (1983)
The Hands of Its Enemy (1984)
Death and the Maiden (1992)
Curtains (1998)
House (1998)

Richard Dreyfuss in The Apprenticeship of Duddy Kravitz

FILMS

The Young Runaways (1968)
Hello Down There (1969)
Two for the Money (1972)
Dillinger (1973)
American Graffiti (1973)
The Apprenticeship of Duddy Kravitz (1974)
Jaws (1975)
Inserts (1976)
Victory at Entebbe (TV, 1976)
Close Encounters of the Third Kind (1977)
The Goodbye Girl (1977)
The Big Fix (1978)
The Competition (1980)
Whose Life Is It Anyway? (1981)
The Buddy System (1984)
Down and Out in Beverly Hills (1986)
Tin Men (1987)
Stakeout (1987)
Nuts (1987)
Moon over Parador (1988)

Always (1989)
Let It Ride (1989)
Postcards from the Edge (1990)
Once Around (1991)
Rosencrantz and Guildenstern Are Dead (1991)
Prisoner of Honor (TV, 1991)
What about Bob? (1991)
Another Stakeout (1993)
Lost in Yonkers (1993)
Silent Fall (1994)
The American President (1995)
Mr. Holland's Opus (1996)
Mad Dog Time (1996)
James and the Giant Peach (1996)
Oliver Twist (TV, 1997)
The Call of the Wild (TV, 1997)
Night Falls on Manhattan (1997)
Krippendorf's Tribe (1998)

TV

American Chronicles (1990)

Peter Falk

Columbo

As the seemingly bumbling but actually slyly brilliant homicide detective Lieutenant Columbo in the TV crime-drama series *Columbo* (1971–78, 1989–90) and in many made-for-TV movies, Peter Falk has become one of the most successful and beloved actors of his time. He has also repeatedly demonstrated his ability as a character actor in such diverse roles as a gangster, a comic stooge, and a 107-year-old man.

Peter Michael Falk was born in New York City, New York, on September 16, 1927. He was raised in Ossining, New York. At the age of three, he developed a malignant tumor in his right eye, which had to be removed. Since then he has used a glass eye. At first he was self-conscious about the artificial eye, but after he started playing games with neighborhood children, he and they simply joked about it.

At Ossining High School, Falk was an excellent student, a star athlete, and the president of his class. He also showed an interest in acting, performing in a number of school productions.

After graduating from high school in 1945, Falk spent one and a half years in the merchant marine. He then studied at Hamilton College in Clinton, New York, for two years before transferring to the New School for Social Research in New York City, where he earned a B.A. in political science (1951). Then, at Syracuse University, he obtained a master's degree in public administration (1953).

After applying unsuccessfully for a job with the CIA, Falk became a management analyst (or efficiency expert) with the Connecticut State Budget Bureau in Hartford. In his spare time, he performed with the Mark Twain Maskers in Hartford and studied acting under Eva Le Gallienne at the White Barn Theater in Westport (1955).

At the age of twenty-eight, Falk quit his job and moved to New York City, where he studied acting with various teachers, notably Sanford Meisner in 1957. He made his professional acting debut by appearing in an off-Broadway production of Molière's *Don Juan* (1956). For the next two years, he performed in numerous plays on the New York City stage, notably as the bartender in an acclaimed production of Eugene O'Neill's *The Iceman Cometh* (1956).

A theatrical agent advised Falk that his glass eye would prevent him from ever getting good parts in movies. Indeed, Harry Cohn, head of Columbia Pictures, after initially expressing an interest in Falk, rejected the young actor specifically because of the glass eye. Falk, however, never regarded his glass eye as a liability. He learned how to use it to his advantage—squinting with it to create effects of menace, humor, detachment, and so on, depending on the dramatic situation.

Other studio executives recognized Falk's talent and did not let the glass eye bother them. He made his film debut in 1958, playing a small part in *Wind across the Everglades*. Over the next few years, he came close to being permanently typecast as a gangster because of his solid performances as villains in several TV programs and movies, especially *Murder, Inc.* (1960), in which he portrayed a vicious assassin for a crime syndicate.

Peter Falk

Peter Falk as Columbo

A big breakthrough in Falk's career came with his performance in *Pocketful of Miracles* (1961), in which he again played a gangster, but this time with a touch of comedy. Many critics felt that Falk had outshone the film's stars, including Bette Davis and Glenn Ford.

Falk received more praise for his excellent performances in the late 1950s and early 1960s in TV anthology and drama series, such as *Omnibus*, *Studio One*, and *The Untouchables*. He gave a particularly fine performance as a drug addict in the episode "Cold Turkey" (1961) of *The Law and Mr. Jones*, and as a truck driver who picks up a pregnant hitchhiker in the episode "The Price of Tomatoes" (1962) of *The Dick Powell Show*. He also starred in the lighthearted TV series *The Trials of O'Brien* (1965–66), as an untidy, disorganized criminal attorney.

Meanwhile, Falk continued to appear in a variety of movie roles. He was a comic stooge to the villain in *The Great Race* (1965), a police lieutenant in the comedy *Penelope* (1966), and a Mafia leader in *Machine Gun McCain* (It., 1968; U. S., 1970).

From 1971 to 1978, Falk played the Los Angeles Police Department homicide detective Lieutenant Columbo, who became one of the most popular characters in TV history, in the crime-drama series *Columbo*. Disheveled in appearance, slurred in speech, and fumbling in manner, Columbo seems to be no match for the intelligent murderers whom he pursues. The villains at first underestimate him, then they gradually become aware of his truly sharp mind and forceful nature. In the end, his unrelenting pursuit pays off and he pounces on the criminals.

Falk continued to act in films while he worked on his TV series, and in the mid-sixties, he began to specialize in comic roles. In *Murder by Death* (1976), for example, he was Sam Diamond, a satirical imitation of the Sam Spade character played by Humphrey Bogart. In *The In-Laws* (1979), he played a bizarre CIA agent. In *All the Marbles* (1981), he gave a fine comic performance as the manager of women wrestlers.

During the 1989 to 1990 TV season, the *Columbo* series was revived, and Falk once again played the title role. After that season he appeared in the same role about once a year in special made-for-TV movies, including *Columbo Goes to College* (TV, 1990), *Columbo: No Time to Die* (TV, 1992), *Columbo: Butterfly in Shades of Grey* (TV, 1994), and *Columbo: Strange Bedfellows* (TV, 1995).

Though Falk is still best known as Columbo, he continues to skillfully play other kinds of roles. In the film *Roommates* (1995), he played Rocky Holeczek, a man who takes his orphaned grandson into his home to raise him and later becomes the boy's roommate in college. For this role, Falk, actually sixty-eight years old, had to age from seventy-five to 107. He costarred with Woody Allen in a made-for-TV version of Neil Simon's classic comedy *The Sunshine Boys* (produced 1995, aired 1997). In 1998 Falk returned to the New York City stage after an absence of over twenty-five years, playing the title role in Arthur Miller's *Mr. Peter's Connection*, a play about a former pilot trying to understand what happened to his life.

Falk has been married twice. In 1960 he wedded Alice (also reported as Alyce) Mayo, whom he had met when both were students at Syracuse University. They had two daughters, Jacqueline and Catherine (also reported as Katherine), before divorcing in 1976. The following year he married Shera Lynn Danese, an actress who costarred with Falk in *Columbo: A Trace of Murder* (TV, 1997).

SELECTED PERFORMANCES:

STAGE

Don Juan (1956)
The Iceman Cometh (1956)
Saint Joan (1956)
Diary of a Scoundrel (1956)
The Lady's Not for Burning (1957)
The Bonds of Interest (1958)
The Passion of Josef D. (1964)
The Prisoner of Second Avenue (1971)
Glengarry Glen Ross (1985)
Light Up the Sky (1987)
Mr. Peter's Connection (1998)

FILMS

Wind across the Everglades (1958)
The Bloody Brood (1959)
Murder, Inc. (1960)
Pocketful of Miracles (1961)
Pressure Point (1962)
The Balcony (1963)
It's a Mad, Mad, Mad, Mad World (1963)
Robin and the Seven Hoods (1964)
The Great Race (1965)
Penelope (1966)
Luv (1967)

Anzio (1968)
Machine Gun McCain (1968)
Prescription: Murder (as Columbo, TV, 1968)
Castle Keep (1969)
Husbands (1970)
A Step out of Line (TV, 1971)
Ransom for a Dead Man (as Columbo, TV, 1971)
A Woman under the Influence (1974)
Mikey and Nicky (1976)
Murder by Death (1976)
Griffin and Phoenix (TV, 1976)
The Cheap Detective (1978)
The Brink's Job (1978)
The In-Laws (1979)
. . . All the Marbles (1981)
Big Trouble (1986)
Der Himmel über Berlin (1987, Ger.; U.S., *Wings of Desire*, 1988)
Cookie (1989)
In the Spirit (1990)
Columbo Goes to College (TV, 1990)
Columbo and the Murder of a Rock Star (TV, 1991)
Columbo: No Time to Die (TV, 1992)
Columbo: A Bird in the Hand (TV, 1992)
The Player (1992)
Faraway, So Close (1993)
Columbo: It's All in the Game (TV, 1993)
Columbo: Butterfly in Shades of Grey (TV, 1994)
Columbo: Undercover (TV, 1994)
Columbo: Strange Bedfellows (TV, 1995)
Roommates (1995)
Columbo: A Trace of Murder (TV, 1997)
Pronto (1997)
The Sunshine Boys (TV, 1997, produced 1995)
Columbo: Ashes to Ashes (TV, 1998)

TV

The Trials of O'Brien (1965–66)
Columbo (1971–78, 1989–90)

Marty Feldman

Popeyed Comic

Marty Feldman was a rare comedian—one who could make audiences roar with laughter just by looking at them. With large bulging eyeballs as his central feature (the result of a thyroid condition brought on by a childhood accident), he developed subtle facial expressions—such as a sly smile or a blank look of pure innocence—that added layers of meaning to his work and set him apart from the more obvious, aggressive types of comics. Yet he was also a master of zany slapstick, performing most of his own pratfalls and movie stunts. He was short, with frizzy hair and a large, askew nose. "Physically," he admitted, "I am basically equipped to be a clown."

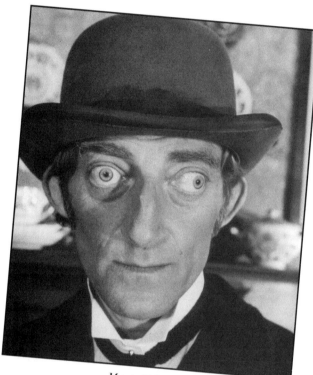

Marty Feldman

Marty Feldman was born in London, England, on July 8, 1934. He grew up in the rough East End section of the city, and at the age of fifteen, he quit school. His great dream at that time was to become a jazz trumpeter. In his late teens, he led his own jazz band.

Feldman was unable to make a living as a professional musician, so he began writing and selling jokes. Eventually, he graduated to writing comedy sketches for British radio and TV. Among those for whom he wrote was David Grost, who later asked Feldman to be one of the writer-performers, along with future Monty Python members Graham Chapman and John Cleese, on the TV series *At Last the 1948 Show* (1967). Feldman then had his own TV series, *Marty* (1968–69). He became one of the most popular entertainers in England, developing a cult following.

In 1969 Feldman appeared in his first film, the allegory *The Bed Sitting Room*, in which he had a small part as a male nurse. He then coscripted and starred in the comedy *Every Home Should Have One* (1970; American title, *Think Dirty*).

In the early 1970s, Feldman made appearances on American TV. He performed on the musical-variety series *The Golddiggers in London*, and he had his own series, *The Marty Feldman Comedy Machine*

Sid Caesar, Bernadette Peters, and Marty Feldman—three comic greats.

(1971–72), which was taped in London and then shown on American TV.

However, Feldman is best known to Americans for his roles in a handful of American films in which his unique comic gifts were featured. In Mel Brooks's *Young Frankenstein* (1974), Feldman played Igor (which he pronounced "eye-gore"), assistant to Dr. Frankenstein (played by Gene Wilder), a brain surgeon who follows in his ancestor's footsteps by creating a manlike creature. In Gene Wilder's *The Adventure of Sherlock Holmes' Smarter*

Brother (1975), Feldman took the role of Orville Sacker, a retired London detective who assists Sigerson Holmes (played by Wilder), just as Dr. Watson helped the more famous Holmes brother. In *Silent Movie* (1976), another Brooks film, Feldman played the assistant of a filmmaker (played by Brooks) who attempts to make a modern silent movie.

Later in life, Feldman tried his hand at directing. He cowrote, directed, and starred in *The Last Remake of Beau Geste* (1977), a spoof of old foreign-legion adventure yarns. He also cowrote, directed, and starred in the biting satire *In God We Tru$t* (1980), subtitled *Gimme That Prime Time Religion*. In that film Feldman played Brother Ambrose, a monk who, at the request of his superior, leaves his cloister to perform an errand in the big city, where he becomes involved with religious hucksters.

In his private life, Feldman was literate, sensitive, and reflective. "I see life as absurd," he said. "And there's dignity in the absurd."

On December 2, 1982, the world was deprived of one of its greatest comics when Feldman suddenly died of a massive heart attack in Mexico City, Mexico, where he had just finished his role in the film *Yellowbeard* (1983), a spoof of pirate movies. He also appeared in the posthumously released movie *Slapstick of Another Kind* (1984).

Feldman was survived by his wife of twenty-three years, Lauretta. She had served as associated producer of *In God We Tru$t*.

SELECTED PERFORMANCES:

FILMS

The Bed Sitting Room (1969)
Every Home Should Have One (1970, G.B.; U.S., *Think Dirty*)
Young Frankenstein (1974)
The Adventure of Sherlock Holmes' Smarter Brother (1975)
Silent Movie (1976)
The Last Remake of Beau Geste (1977)
In God We Tru$t (1980)
Yellowbeard (1983)
Slapstick of Another Kind (1984)

TV

At Last the 1948 Show (1967)
Marty (1968–69)
The Golddiggers in London (1970)
The Marty Feldman Comedy Machine (1971–72)

Harrison Ford

Most Popular Screen Hero

Harrison Ford is one of the most popular contemporary film actors. He is best known for his portrayals of heroic characters in action and adventure films, such as Han Solo in the *Star Wars* trilogy (1977–83) and Indiana Jones in *Raiders of the Lost Ark* (1981) and its sequels (1984–89). Ford's broad popular appeal is due, in large part, to the fact that the characters he plays are not one-dimensional swashbucklers. Rather, Ford's protagonists are vulnerable, contemplative men—they are heroes for the thinking person.

Harrison Ford was born in Chicago, Illinois, on July 13, 1942. His father comes from an Irish Catholic family, his mother from a Russian Jewish family.

As a child Ford had little interest in sports or schoolwork and virtually no interest in becoming an actor. For four years he majored in philosophy at Ripon College in Ripon, Wisconsin, without taking a degree. However, in his junior year, he took a drama class as an elective. Acting seemed to free him from his natural shyness and provided him, he later admitted, with his "first experience of working with a group of people on a clearly defined goal." After doing a season of summer stock in 1964 in Williams Bay, Wisconsin, he moved to Hollywood, California.

While appearing in *John Brown's Body* at a Laguna Beach playhouse in 1965, Ford was discovered by a talent scout for Columbia Pictures. Columbia signed Ford to a contract for an apprentice program at the studio, which aimed to groom him and other young actors and actresses for Hollywood stardom. He had bit parts in several movies, including *Luv* (1967), before he and the studio called it quits. Ford felt that "the attitude that they could manufacture a star from raw material was silly."

He soon signed a contract with Universal Pictures, which cast him in small roles in the film *Journey to Shiloh* (1968) and in episodes of some TV programs, such as *Gunsmoke* and *Ironside*. Universal lent him out for minor roles in the independent production *Zabriskie Point* (1970) (his part was eventually cut out) and for the Columbia picture *Getting Straight* (1970). At this point he decided not to accept another role until he was offered one that would clearly further his career. To earn a living, he turned to carpentry, at which he was self-taught.

Three years later he was finally given a good part, the supporting role of the hot-rodding Bob Falfa in the nostalgic coming-of-age film *American Graffiti* (1973). The movie was a tremendous success, yet, afterwards, Ford still wasn't being offered the kinds of roles he wanted. Over the next several years, he appeared in only a handful of productions, including *The Conversation* (1974) and *Dynasty* (TV, 1976). During that time carpentry remained his principal occupation.

Ford finally got his big break when he was offered the major role of Han Solo, the cocky pirate spaceship captain, in the space adventure *Star Wars* (1977). The film was an enormous hit, and Ford's career took off. He repeated his Han Solo role in two *Star Wars* sequels: *The Empire Strikes Back* (1980) and *Return of the Jedi* (1983).

Harrison Ford as Dr. Richard Kimble in The Fugitive

Meanwhile, Ford was selected to star in Steven Spielberg's *Indiana Jones* adventure trilogy. The series, which included the films *Raiders of the Lost Ark* (1981), *Indiana Jones and the Temple of Doom* (1984), and *Indiana Jones and the Last Crusade* (1989), was extremely successful and was responsible for making Ford a huge star.

During his Han Solo and Indiana Jones years, Ford consciously widened his acting range by taking different kinds of roles. He portrayed a psychologically broken Vietnam War veteran in *Heroes* (1977), an intellectual army colonel in *Apocalypse*

Now (1979), a bandit in the Old West comedy *The Frisco Kid* (1979), and a police detective in *Witness* (1985).

In the 1990s Ford continued to play roles that enabled him to demonstrate the depth and range of his skills as an actor. In *The Fugitive* (1993) he was Richard Kimble, a doctor who is falsely accused of murdering his wife and who flees the authorities while he searches for the real killer. In *Clear and Present Danger* (1994), he played a CIA deputy director who is assigned to investigate the murder of friends of the president. He portrayed a heroic United States president in the action thriller *Air Force One* (1997). In the comedy adventure *Six Days, Seven Nights* (1998), he was an experienced South Pacific airplane pilot.

With his first wife, Mary Louise Marquardt, whom he met at Ripon College and married in 1964, Ford had two children, Benjamin and Willard. The marriage ended in 1978. In 1983 he married Melissa Mathison, a screenwriter. They had a son, Malcolm, and a daughter, Georgia.

SELECTED PERFORMANCES:

STAGE

Take Her, She's Mine (1964)
Little Mary Sunshine (1964
Night of the Iguana (1964)
Dark of the Moon (1964)
Damn Yankees (1964)
Sunday in New York (1964)
John Brown's Body (1965)

FILMS

Dead Heat on a Merry-Go-Round (1966)
Luv (1967)
A Time for Killing (1967; G.B., *The Long Ride Home*)

Journey to Shiloh (1968)
Zabriskie Point (1970)
The Intruders (TV, 1970)
Getting Straight (1970)
American Graffiti (1973)
The Conversation (1974)
Judgment: The Court-Martial of Lt.
  William Calley (TV, 1975)
Dynasty (TV, 1976)
Star Wars (1977)
Heroes (1977)
The Possessed (TV, 1977)
Force 10 from Navarone (1978)
More American Graffiti (1979)
Apocalypse Now (1979)
Hanover Street (1979)
The Frisco Kid (1979)
The Empire Strikes Back (1980)
Raiders of the Lost Ark (1981)
Blade Runner (1982)
Return of the Jedi (1983)
Indiana Jones and the Temple of Doom
  (1984)
Witness (1985)
The Mosquito Coast (1986)
Frantic (1988)
Working Girl (1988)
Indiana Jones and the Last Crusade
  (1989)
Presumed Innocent (1990)
Regarding Henry (1991)
Patriot Games (1992)
The Fugitive (1993)
Jimmy Hollywood (1994)
Clear and Present Danger (1994)
Sabrina (1995)
The Devil's Own (1997)
Air Force One (1997)
Six Days, Seven Nights (1998)

Harrison Ford

John Garfield

New-Style Hero

In the mid-twentieth century, a new kind of leading man emerged in films. He was not always good at heart, strong in spirit, and victorious in the end. Instead, he was flawed, vulnerable, and sometimes defeated. Yearning for society to accept him and his aspirations, he must confront the harsh truths of modern urban life. Such characters were often played by Marlon Brando, Montgomery Clift, James Dean, Dustin Hoffman, Paul Newman, Steve McQueen, and Al Pacino. But the prototype was John Garfield.

John Garfield was born of Russian immigrant parents in New York City, on March 4, 1913. His father was a factory worker during weekdays, but on weekends and holidays he served as a cantor. The boy's original name was Jacob Garfinkle (with no middle name), but in his early childhood his parents informally added the name Julius in front of his given name and began to call him Julie.

Garfield spent part of his youth on the Lower East Side of Manhattan and in the Brownsville section of Brooklyn, where he became involved in the street life of the urban poor. His experiences there helped to form his social consciousness and his mannerisms as an actor.

At the time, however, he came close to becoming a real hoodlum. He averted that fate through the help of Angelo Patri, the principal of the Bronx junior high school that Garfield attended. Patri encouraged the boy to take up amateur boxing, at which he did fairly well. More important, Patri got Garfield interested in debate and dramatics.

After Garfield graduated from junior high school in 1928, Patri helped him get a scholarship to the drama workshop of the Heckscher Foundation. Garfield then began high school but dropped out in 1929. With Patri's financial help, Garfield next studied acting at the American Laboratory Theater. He also did odd jobs backstage for Theater Guild productions and made his Broadway debut with a one-night appearance in *The Camel through the Needle's Eye* (1929).

Garfield got his first big break when he was given a part in the Guild's production of *Red Rust* (1929). Soon afterward he joined the Civic Repertory Theater as an apprentice. There, he adopted the stage name Jules Garfield, which he continued to use until 1938.

In 1930 Garfield entered a Golden Gloves boxing tournament. The following year he hitchhiked to California, where he worked as a migrant farmworker. Returning to New York in 1932, he worked for a while as an assistant social director at a Jewish resort in the Catskills. He then acted in the play *Counsellor-at-Law* in New York City and on the road.

In 1933 Garfield had a tiny, uncredited part in the film musical *Footlight Parade*. That year he also had a minor part in the play *Peace on Earth*, which was produced by Theater Union, a left-wing theater company.

In 1934 Garfield became an apprentice with the Group Theater, another leftist theater company. He also married Roberta Seidman that year. They had three children: Katherine, who died in early childhood; David Patton, who became an actor in the early 1960s under the name John Garfield, Jr. (he later changed his name to John David Garfield); and Julie Roberta, who became an actress.

In 1935 Garfield was given an important role in *Awake and Sing!*, a play by Clifford Odets, the man who had helped Garfield get into the Group Theater. Early in 1937 he was offered the lead in *Having Wonderful Time*, a romantic comedy staged at Catskills resorts. That autumn he rejoined the Group Theater to appear in Odets's *Golden Boy*. The playwright had promised Garfield the lead role of Joe Bonaparte; however, Garfield was given the supporting role of the protagonist's brother-in-law.

Garfield then began his career as a film actor, signing with Warner Brothers in 1938. In his first movie, *Four Daughters* (1938), he played a cynical young loner. The character was appealing yet doomed—it was the kind of role that Garfield would play the rest of his career.

In Garfield's next film, *They Made Me a Criminal* (1939), he played a boxer who went into hiding after being framed for a killing. After making several more films, including *Dust Be My Destiny* (1939), he returned to Broadway in 1940 to appear in *Heavenly Express*.

John Garfield

A heart condition kept Garfield out of military service during World War II. But he frequently entertained troops overseas, and he made several war-related movies, including *Pride of the Marines* (1945), in which he portrayed a real-life blind American military hero. During that period, in 1942, he officially changed his legal name from Jacob Garfinkle to John Jules Garfield (he had changed his name from Jules Garfield to John Garfield when he signed with Warner Brothers).

Immediately after the war, Garfield made some of his most memorable films. In *The Postman Always Rings Twice* (1946), he was a drifter lured by love into adultery and murder. In *Humoresque* (1946) he played a violinist enmeshed in an affair with a wealthy married woman who helps his career. In *Body and Soul* (1947), he got an opportunity to show the real depth and range of his acting talent by playing an arrogant youthful boxer who ages into a disillusioned middle-aged champ. In *Gentleman's Agreement* (1947) he played the part of a young Jewish friend of the principal character, who pretends to be a Jew so that he can get material for a magazine article on anti-Semitism. It was unusual for a star of Garfield's stature to take such a small role, but it was something that he felt he "had to do." His performance was praised by the critics.

In 1947 Garfield was offered the part of Stanley Kowalski in the Broadway production of Tennessee Williams's *A Streetcar Named Desire*. He turned it down because he wanted more money than the producer offered. Ironically, this became the role that made young Marlon Brando a star.

Soon, however, Garfield returned to Broadway, as Joris Kuiper, a Dutch sea captain who attempts to rescue Jewish refugees, in *Skipper Next to God* (1948). That year he also appeared in the film *Force of Evil* (1948), in which he played a lawyer drawn into corruption.

Garfield continued to be active in film and in theater for the next few years. In his final appearance on the big screen, he played an outlaw dying in the gutter in *He Ran All the Way* (1951).

In 1951 Garfield was called before the House Committee on Un-American Activities to answer questions about his association with, and support of, various liberal causes and organizations. He succeeded in convincing the committee that he had never belonged to the Communist party but not that he was unacquainted with other party members. As bizarre and un-American as it now seems, the committee's attitude toward Garfield actually cast a shadow over him and dampened his career.

Early in 1952 Garfield appeared in the lead role in a Broadway revival of *Golden Boy*. It was to be his final role. He died in his sleep of heart failure (he had a long history of heart trouble, a condition that he neglected) in New York City on May 21, 1952, at the age of only thirty-nine.

SELECTED PERFORMANCES:

STAGE

Red Rust (1929)
Counsellor-at-Law (1932)
Lost Boy (1932)
Peace on Earth (1933)
Gold Eagle Eye (1934)
Waiting for Lefty (1935)
Awake and Sing! (1935)
Weep for the Virgins (1935)

The Case of Clyde Griffiths (1936)
Johnny Johnson (1936)
Having Wonderful Time (1937)
Golden Boy (1937, 1952)
Heavenly Express (1940)
Skipper Next to God (1948)
The Big Knife (1949)
Peer Gynt (1951)

FILMS

Four Daughters (1938)
They Made Me a Criminal (1939)
Blackwell's Island (1939)
Juarez (1939)
Daughters Courageous (1939)
Dust Be My Destiny (1939)
Castle on the Hudson (1940)
Saturday's Children (1940)
Flowing Gold (1940)
East of the River (1940)
The Sea Wolf (1941)
Out of the Fog (1941)
Dangerously They Live (1942)
Tortilla Flat (1942)
Air Force (1943)
The Fallen Sparrow (1943)
Thank Your Lucky Stars (1943)
Destination Tokyo (1944)
Between Two Worlds (1944)
Hollywood Canteen (1944)
Pride of the Marines (1945)
The Postman Always Rings Twice (1946)
Nobody Lives Forever (1946)
Humoresque (1946)
Body and Soul (1947)
Gentleman's Agreement (1947)
Force of Evil (1948)
We Were Strangers (1949)
Under My Skin (1950)
The Breaking Point (1950)
The Difficult Years (narrator, 1950)
He Ran All the Way (1951)

Jack Gilford

Wistful Comic Actor

Jack Gilford was one of the earliest stand-up comedians to abandon the traditional string-of-jokes routine and to perform acts with variety, originality, and distinct themes. He was a gifted mimic, able to imitate not only people, but also animals and even split-pea soup coming to a boil. He sang comic songs, including a rendition of "California, Here I Come" in Yiddish. In addition, he became an outstanding comic film and stage actor. A meek, sad-faced funnyman, he projected a uniquely wistful quality.

Jack Gilford was born in New York City, on July 25, 1907. His original name was Jacob Gellman.

Gilford began his career by performing as a comedian in amateur-night contests in 1934. Unable to break into professional show business, he became the manager of a cosmetics store. One day the entertainer Milton Berle entered the store and Gilford began to do comic imitations of famous personalities, including Laurel and Hardy. Berle later auditioned Gilford and gave him a job touring in vaudeville with the *Milton Berle Revue* (1935–38).

It was Berle who suggested that the young comedian change his surname. Gilford agreed, also changing his given name in the process.

During his association with Berle, Gilford also began to make solo vaudeville appearances. Soon he was touring the borscht circuit and performing in nightclubs, including New York City's Café Society Downtown and Café Society Uptown, where he performed off and on for many years.

In 1940 Gilford made his Broadway debut by appearing in *Meet the People*. Over the next few years he returned to the New York City stage in other shows, including *They Should Have Stood in Bed* (1942).

Gilford was turned down for military service during World War II because he was in psychotherapy. Instead, he toured the Pacific theater as an entertainer with the USO. He also acted in two films during the war, *Hey, Rookie* (1944) and *Reckless Age* (1944).

After the war Gilford continued to work as a comedian in vaudeville, in nightclubs, and on the borscht circuit. In the late 1940s and early 1950s he began to perform on television variety shows, including shows hosted by Garry Moore and Milton Berle. He also made one film, *Main Street to Broadway* (1953).

Then, Gilford's career as a TV and movie actor was interrupted by the McCarthy-era Communist witch-hunts. Although he was blacklisted in Hollywood, he was able to continue acting in theatrical productions. In 1950, for example, he had a nonsinging comic part, Frosch, in the operetta *Die Fledermaus* at the Metropolitan Opera. He played the same role in many subsequent productions. In *The World of Sholom Aleichem* (1953) he was the painfully shy Bontche Schweig, while in *The Diary of Anne Frank* (1955) he played the fussy, frightened Mr. Dussel. Gilford was the mute king Sextimus in *Once upon a Mattress* (1959), and in *A Funny Thing Happened on the Way to the Forum* (1962) he portrayed the timid slave Hysterium.

In the mid-1960s the blacklist lost its effective-

Jack Gilford

Jack Gilford

ness, and Gilford began to get TV and movie roles again. During the 1960s and 1970s he appeared as a guest star on many TV series, including *All in the Family, The Defenders, Get Smart,* and *Rhoda.* He was a regular on *The David Frost Revue* (1971) and *Apple Pie* (1978). Gilford's films during that period included *Mister Buddwing* (1966), *Enter Laughing* (1967), *Catch-22* (1970), *Save the Tiger* (1973), and *Seventh Avenue* (TV, 1977). And, he did not neglect the stage, performing in *The Sunshine Boys* (1973), *The Seven Year Itch* (1975), and other plays.

In the 1980s Gilford continued to act in plays and films and on TV. He played four roles in a revival of *The World of Sholom Aleichem* (1982), starred in the films *Wholly Moses!* (1980), *Happy* (TV, 1983), and *Hostage Flight* (TV, 1985), and appeared in TV commercials.

Gilford married the entertainer Madeline Lederman (stage name, Madeline Lee) in 1949. They had two children together, Joseph and Sam. She also had a daughter, Lisa, from a previous marriage.

Gilford died in New York City on June 4, 1990.

SELECTED PERFORMANCES:

STAGE

Meet the People (1940)
They Should Have Stood in Bed (1942)
It's All Yours (1942)
The New Meet the People (1943)
Alive and Kicking (1950)
The Live Wire (1950)
Die Fledermaus (1950 and many times thereafter)
The World of Sholom Aleichem (1953, 1982)
The Passion of Gross (1955)
Once Over Lightly (1955)
The Diary of Anne Frank (1955)
Romanoff and Juliet (1957)
Drink to Me Only (1958)
Look After Lulu (1959)
Once upon a Mattress (1959)
The Tenth Man (1959)
The Policeman (1961)
A Funny Thing Happened on the Way to the Forum (1962)
Cabaret (1966)
Three Men on a Horse (1969)
No, No Nanette (1971)
The Sunshine Boys (1973)
Anything Goes (1973)
The Seven Year Itch (1975)
Sly Fox (1976)
The Supporting Cast (1981)

FILMS

Hey, Rookie (1944)
Reckless Age (1944)
Main Street to Broadway (1953)
The Daydreamer (1966)
A Funny Thing Happened on the Way to the Forum (1966)
Mister Buddwing (1966)
Enter Laughing (1967)
The Incident (1967)
Who's Minding the Mint? (1967)
Catch-22 (1970)
They Might Be Giants (1971)
Save the Tiger (1973)
Harry and Walter Go to New York (1976)
Seventh Avenue (TV, 1977)
Wholly Moses! (1980)
Caveman (1981)
Cheaper to Keep Her (1981)
Goldie and the Boxer Go to Hollywood (TV, 1981)
Happy (TV, 1983)
Hostage Flight (TV, 1985)
Cocoon (1985)
Cocoon: The Return (1988)

TV

The David Frost Revue (1971)
Apple Pie (1978)

Hermione Gingold

Revue Comedienne and Character Actress

Hermione Gingold became famous by performing as a comedienne in British musical revues of the 1930s and 1940s. After moving to the United States in the fifties, she continued to perform in stage revues and musicals and became a beloved comic character actress in films.

H ermione Gingold was born in London, England, on December 9, 1897. She attended private school and studied acting at the Rosina Filippi School of the Theater in London.

Gingold made her first stage appearance in a kindergarten production of *Henry VIII*. She made her professional debut by playing a herald in *Pinkie and the Fairies* (1908). Over the next several years, she continued to gain professional stage experience. Soon she was performing Shakespeare at London's Old Vic theater and in the Bard's hometown of Stratford-on-Avon. Gingold also performed in other plays, such as *Little Lord Fauntleroy* (1931).

In the late 1930s Gingold began to appear in musical revues. By the 1940s she had become an expert comedienne and was performing in the most popular British revues of the day: *Sweet and Low* (1943), *Sweeter and Lower* (1944), and *Sweetest and Lowest* (1946).

Gingold made her American stage debut in a Cambridge, Massachusetts production of the revue *It's about Time* (1951). She then performed in a New York City revue *John Murray Anderson's Almanac* (1953). In an article about the show, an American critic called her "one of the funniest women in the world."

Over the next quarter of a century Gingold performed in numerous theatrical productions in both England and America. Her most memorable role was that of Madame Armfeldt, an elderly once-famous courtesan, in the Broadway production of Stephen Sondheim's musical *A Little Night Music* (1973).

Meanwhile, Gingold was performing on TV comedy-variety shows and was acting in films (she had made her film debut in the British movie *Someone at the Door* (1936)). She became a popular comic character actress and was particularly adept at playing haughty eccentrics. In the comedy *Bell, Book, and Candle* (1958), she played a modern-day witch. In *Gigi* (1958) she portrayed a woman who grooms her granddaughter to be a courtesan. For the animated film *Gay Purr-ee* (1962), she supplied the voice of the jaded Madame Rubens-Chatte. She was the wild wife of the mayor in *The Music Man* (1962). And she repeated her stage role in the filmed version of *A Little Night Music* (1977).

Gingold's talents extended beyond the stage and the screen. She made a number of recordings, including *La Gingold* (1956), a collection of speciality songs and revue material. And she authored many works, including articles, humorous essays, short stories, and the books *The World Is Square: My Own Unaided Work* (1945) and *Sirens Should Be Seen and Not Heard* (1963).

Gingold's first marriage was to the British publisher Michael Joseph. They had two sons: Stephen, who became director of London's Theater-in-the-Round, and Leslie, who became a

Hermione Gingold

Hermione Gingold

The Dippers (1922)
Little Lord Fauntleroy (1931)
From Morn to Midnight (1932)
The World of Ours (1935)
Spread It Abroad (1936)
Laura Garrett (1936)
The Gate Revue (1938)
Swinging the Gate (1940)
Rise above It (1941)
Sky High (1942)
Sweet and Low (1943)
Sweeter and Lower (1944)
Sweetest and Lowest (1946)
Slings and Arrows (1948)
Fumed Oak (1949)
Fallen Angels (1949)
It's about Time (1951)
John Murray Anderson's Almanac
  (1953)
The Sleeping Prince (1956)
First Impressions (1959)
From A to Z (1960)
Abracadabra (1961)
Milk and Honey (1961)
Oh, Dad, Poor Dad, Mamma's Hung
  You in the Closet and I'm Feelin'
  So Sad (1963)
Dumas and Son (1967)
Charley's Aunt (1968)
Highly Confidential (1969)
A Little Night Music (1973)
Side by Side by Sondheim (1978)

businessman. Gingold and Joseph divorced, and she later married Eric Maschwitz, an author and broadcasting program director. That marriage, too, ended in divorce.

In her later years Gingold made many appearances on American TV talk shows, including *The Merv Griffin Show* and *The Mike Douglas Show*. Her deep, expressive voice and her devastating wit made her an entertaining guest.

The incomparable Hermoine Gingold died in New York City on May 24, 1987, at the age of ninety.

SELECTED PERFORMANCES:

STAGE

Pinkie and the Fairies (1908)
The Merry Wives of Windsor (1909)
The Marriage Market (1913)
The Merchant of Venice (1914)
If (1921)

FILMS

Someone at the Door (1936)
Meet Mr. Penny (1938)
The Pickwick Papers (1952)
Around the World in Eighty Days (1956)
Gigi (1958)
Bell, Book, and Candle (1958)
The Naked Edge (1961)
Gay Purr-ee (animated, voice only, 1962)
The Music Man (1962)
I'd Rather Be Rich (1964)
Harvey Middleman, Fireman (1965)
Munster, Go Home! (1966)
Promise Her Anything (1966)
Jules Verne's Rocket to the Moon (1967, G.B.; U.S.,
  Those Fantastic Flying Fools)
Banyon (TV, 1971)
A Little Night Music (1977)

Elliott Gould

The Original Trapper John

A prolific performer, Elliott Gould has appeared in dozens of films and in numerous stage productions over the course of his long acting career. He is probably best known for his portrayal of Trapper John in the movie version of *M*A*S*H* (1970). Fame did not come easily for Gould, however. He struggled for many years with personal and professional problems before he finally settled into a comfortable career as a reliable dramatic leading man and supporting actor.

Elliott Gould was born in New York City, New York, on August 29, 1938. His original name was Elliott Goldstein. He grew up in Brooklyn, then moved to West Orange, New Jersey, with his parents when he was an adolescent.

Gould's mother encouraged him to enter show business, and when he was eight, she enrolled him in speech, singing, dance, and drama classes at Charles Lowe's Broadway school for youngsters in Manhattan. With other children from the school, little Elliott performed in vaudeville acts at temples, bar mitzvahs, weddings, and so on. They also performed on television. For his first TV appearance, his mother changed his stage name to Gould. At the age of eleven, he danced in an act with an adult professional vaudevillian at the famed Palace Theater.

Gould completed his formal education at the Professional Children's School in Manhattan. During his years there, he spent summer vacations performing on the borscht circuit and in summer stock. He graduated in 1955.

For the next several years, Gould struggled, getting occasional small parts in Broadway shows and on TV but often having to take odd jobs. In 1960 his prospects began to improve when he gave an impressive performance in the Broadway musical *Irma La Douce*. He began by playing an usher, a priest, and a warder, but he was later promoted to the role of Polyte-le-Mou.

Gould then won the lead in the Broadway musical comedy *I Can Get It for You Wholesale* (1962), but his work in that show was eclipsed by the explosive performance of the newcomer Barbra Streisand, who had a supporting role in the production. Gould and Streisand soon developed a romance, and they were married in 1963. They had one child, Jason, before separating in 1969 and divorcing in 1971. One reason for the tension in the marriage was that Gould's career floundered in the mid-sixties, while Streisand's flourished.

Gould found a new direction when he began to undergo psychoanalysis and to study with Lee Strasberg at the Actors Studio. Gould played an apathetic antihero in the short-lived Broadway play *Little Murders* (1967). In the movie *The Night They Raided Minsky's* (1968), he appeared as the harried manager of a 1920s burlesque house.

Gould finally got his big break when he was offered a role in the highly successful film *Bob and Carol and Ted and Alice* (1969). Playing Ted, an easy-going conventional man who has difficulty adjusting to the new sexual morality, Gould showed a surprising gift for light comedy.

Elliott Gould

Elliot Gould

and played a compulsive gambler in *California Split* (1974).

In the late 1970s and early 1980s, Gould again experienced a slump in his career, appearing in a succession of inconsequential films. Among them were *Harry and Walter Go to New York* (1976), *Capricorn One* (1978), and the Disney pictures *The Last Flight of Noah's Ark* (1980) and *The Devil and Max Devlin* (1981).

In the mid-1980s, Gould was able to revitalize his career by being more selective in his choice of roles. In *Over the Brooklyn Bridge* (1984) he played a Jewish restaurateur who is financially dependent on an uncle who disapproves of his Catholic girlfriend. In *Vanishing Act* (TV, 1986) Gould was an idiosyncratic police chief trying to solve a baffling mystery. His later films included *Lethal Obsession* (1988), *Bugsy* (1991), *Bloodlines: Murder in the Family* (TV, 1993), *Cover Me* (1995), *A Boy Called Hate* (1996), *Johns* (1997), and *Stephen King's "The Shining"* (TV, 1997).

Gould soon became one of the most popular actors of the early 1970s. In the hit movie *M*A*S*H** (1970) he was cast as Trapper John, a hip young surgeon who undermines army bureaucracy. It is probably the role by which he is best known, although it was later played by others in the TV series *M*A*S*H** and *Trapper John, M.D.*

In 1971, however, Gould suffered a nervous breakdown. For the next two years he was unable to work.

In 1973 Gould married Jennifer Bogart (they have two children, Molly and Sam) and made a comeback with his performance as the private detective Philip Marlowe in *The Long Goodbye*. He then had a role in the spy comedy *S*P*Y*S* (1974)

SELECTED PERFORMANCES:

STAGE

Rumple (1957)
Say, Darling (1958)
Irma La Douce (1960)
I Can Get It for You Wholesale (1962)
Drat! The Cat! (1965)
Little Murders (1967)
A Way of Life (1969)

FILMS

The Night They Raided Minsky's (1968)
Bob and Carol and Ted and Alice (1969)
Getting Straight (1970)
I Love My Wife (1970)
M*A*S*H (1970)
Move (1970)
Little Murders (1971)
The Touch (1971)
The Long Goodbye (1973)
S*P*Y*S (1974)
California Split (1974)
Busting (1974)
Whiffs (1976)
I Will, I Will... for Now (1976)
Harry and Walter Go to New York (1976)
A Bridge Too Far (1977)
Capricorn One (1978)
Matilda (1978)
Escape to Athena (1979)
The Muppet Movie (1979)
The Silent Partner (1979)
The Lady Vanishes (1979)
The Last Flight of Noah's Ark (1980)
Falling in Love Again (1980)
The Devil and Max Devlin (1981)
The Rules of Marriage (TV, 1982)
The Naked Face (1984)
Over the Brooklyn Bridge (1984)
Vanishing Act (TV, 1986)
Conspiracy: The Trial of the Chicago Eight (TV, 1987)
Lethal Obsession (1988)
Stolen: One Husband (TV, 1990)
Night Visitor (1990)
Bugsy (1991)
The Player (1992)
Beyond Justice (1992)
Wet and Wild Summer (1993)
Bloodlines: Murder in the Family (TV, 1993)
Cover Me (1995)
A Boy Called Hate (1996)
Four Tales of Two Cities (1996)
Camp Stories (1997)

City of Industry (1997)
Johns (1997)
Stephen King's "The Shining" (TV, 1997)

TV

E/R (1984–85)
Together We Stand (1986)
Sessions (1991)

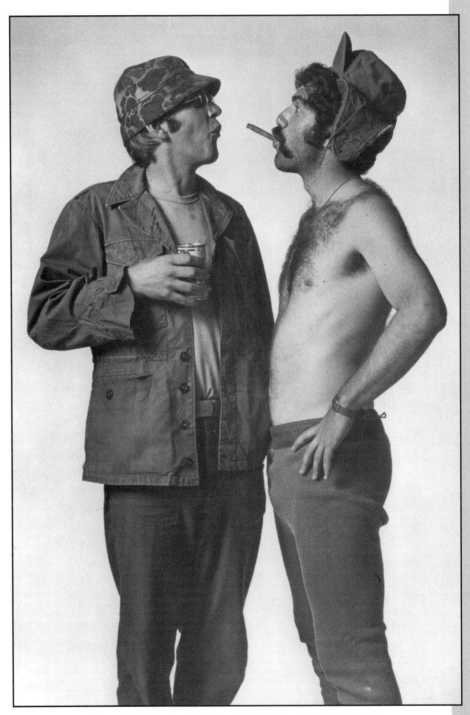

Donald Sutherland (left) and Elliot Gould in M*A*S*H

Lee Grant

Lee Grant's place in film history is twofold. First, she is a top-notch actress. Second, she was one of the most prominent victims and outspoken critics of the infamous blacklisting during the 1950s.

Lee Grant was born in New York City, New York, on October 31, 1931. (The date is so listed in *Who's Who in America.* Other sources give every year from 1926 through 1930.) Her original name was Lyova Haskell Rosenthal.

Grant was encouraged by her mother (a model and actress from Odessa, Russia) to enter the performing arts. In 1933 the child made her stage debut by appearing in a Metropolitan Opera production, and soon she was dancing in the Metropolitan Opera Ballet. Later she studied voice and violin at the Julliard School of Music.

After graduating from George Washington High School, Grant studied acting at the Neighborhood Playhouse School of the Theatre and then made her professional debut touring the nation as an understudy to Celeste Holm for the role of Ado Annie in *Oklahoma!* She appeared in a number of other productions, before making her Broadway debut in *Joy to the World* (1948).

In 1949 Grant became a member of the Actors Studio. That year she also gave an impressive performance in the Broadway drama *Detective Story,* stealing the show in a small role as a neurotic young shoplifter.

In 1950 Grant performed in *All You Need Is One Good Break* a play by Arnold Manoff, whom she married. They had one child, Dinah.

Grant next appeared in the filmed version of *Detective Story* (1951). Returning to Broadway, she was praised for her work in *Lo and Behold!* (1951).

In 1952 Grant became a victim of the Hollywood blacklisting inspired by the Communist witch-hunts of Senator Joseph McCarthy. She was placed on the blacklist simply because her husband allegedly had connections with Communists. For more than a decade Grant was offered very little television and film work. Her few screen appearances during that time included one season (1953-54) as Rose Peabody on the TV soap opera *Search for Tomorrow.*

During the 1950s, Grant spent most of her time as a homemaker for her husband, their daughter, and his children from a previous marriage. When family funds ran short, she worked in summer stock and occasionally acted in Broadway plays, such as *Wedding Breakfast* (1954) and *A Hole in the Head* (1957).

Finally, in the mid-1960s, after years of fighting the practice of blacklisting, Grant got her name cleared. One of her first roles after that experience was the role of Stella Chernak in the TV series *Peyton Place* (1965-66). The series was a hit, and it gave Grant the exposure she needed to re-establish herself as an actress.

In 1965 Grant's husband died. In 1967 she married the independent filmmaker Joseph Feury, with whom she had her daughter Belinda.

Since her return to major commercial films, Grant has been one of America's busiest and most successful actresses. She appeared in three popular movies almost immediately after she began working again: *Divorce American Style* (1967), *In the Heat of the Night* (1967), and *Valley of the Dolls* (1967). In *The Landlord* (1970) she was devastatingly funny as the hero's mother. In *Portnoy's Complaint* (1972) she played a caricatured Jewish mother. In *Shampoo* (1975) she gave a powerful performance as a devouring rich woman. In *Voyage of the Damned* (1976) she was one of a shipload of Jews sent by German Nazis to Cuba in 1939. Among her later films were *Damien: Omen II* (1978), *Visiting Hours* (1982), *Defending Your Life* (1991), and *The Substance of Fire* (1996).

Grant has also acted in many made-for-TV movies, beginning with *Night Slaves* (TV, 1970). In *Ransom for a Dead Man* (TV, 1971) the second of two pilots for the *Columbo* series, she costarred with Peter Falk, as a lawyer who executes an intricate plan to murder her husband. Grant also appeared in *What Are Best Friends For?* (TV, 1973), *The Spell* (TV, 1977), *Backstairs at the White House* (TV, 1979), and *Thou Shalt Not Kill* (TV, 1982). In the biopic *Will There Really Be a Morning?* (TV, 1983), she played the mother of the actress Frances Farmer. In *Mussolini: The Untold Story* (TV, 1985), she portrayed the dictator's wife. Grant's other TV movies included *Citizen Cohn* (TV, 1992) and *In My Daughter's Name* (TV, 1992).

Lee Grant

SELECTED PERFORMANCES:

STAGE

Joy to the World (1948)
Detective Story (1949)
All You Need Is One Good Break (1950)
Arms and the Man (1950)
Lo and Behold! (1951)
Wedding Breakfast (1954)
A Hole in the Head (1957)
The Captains and the Kings (1962)
The Maids (1963)
Electra (1964)
Love's Labour's Lost (1965)
Saint Joan (1966)
Plaza Suite (1968)
The Prisoner of Second Avenue (1971)
The Little Foxes (1975)

FILMS

Detective Story (1951)
Storm Fear (1955)
Middle of the Night (1959)
An Affair of the Skin (1963)
The Balcony (1963)
Terror in the City (1966)
Divorce American Style (1967)
In the Heat of the Night (1967)
Valley of the Dolls (1967)
The Big Bounce (1969)
Buona Sera, Mrs. Campbell (1969)
Marooned (1969)
The Landlord (1970)
There Was a Crooked Man . . . (1970)

Night Slaves (TV, 1970)
The Neon Ceiling (TV, 1971)
Ransom for a Dead Man (TV, 1971)
Plaza Suite (1971)
Portnoy's Complaint (1972)
Lieutenant Schuster's Wife (TV, 1972)
Partners in Crime (TV, 1973)
What Are Best Friends For? (TV, 1973)
Shampoo (1975)
Voyage of the Damned (1976)
Perilous Voyage (TV, 1976)
The Spell (TV, 1977)
Airport '77 (1977)
Damien: Omen II (1978)
When You Comin' Back, Red Ryder? (1979)
Backstairs at the White House (TV, 1979)
Little Miss Marker (1980)
Charlie Chan and the Curse of the Dragon Queen (1981)
The Million Dollar Face (TV, 1981)
For Ladies Only (TV, 1981)
Visiting Hours (1982)
Thou Shalt Not Kill (TV, 1982)
Bare Essence (TV, 1982)
Will There Really Be a Morning? (TV, 1983)
Mussolini: The Untold Story (TV, 1985)
The Big Town (1987)
Defending Your Life (1991)
Citizen Cohn (TV, 1992)
In My Daughter's Name (TV, 1992)
It's My Party (1996)
The Substance of Fire (1996)

Lee Grant

TV

Search for Tomorrow (1953-54)
Peyton Place (1965-66)
Fay (1975)

Lorne Greene

Ben Cartwright

Lorne Greene was best known for playing Ben Cartwright, the strong but compassionate father in the TV Western series *Bonanza* (1959-73). The series, among the longest-running in TV history, made him one of the most popular stars of his time.

Lorne Greene was born in Ottawa, Canada, on February 12, 1915. He developed a booming voice as an adolescent, and in high school he was cast in a play as one of two deaf people shouting at each other. While attending Queen's University in Kingston, he produced, directed, and acted in plays. He even changed his major from chemical engineering to languages (French and German) so that he would have more time for theater activities.

After receiving his B.A. (1937) from Queen's University, Greene spent two years in New York City, studying acting at the Neighborhood Playhouse School of the Theater and stage movement at Martha Graham's School of Contemporary Dance. Returning to Canada in 1939, he found acting jobs scarce, but because of his strong baritone voice, he was hired to read national news nightly over the Canadian Broadcasting Corporation radio network. (He soon came to be called the Voice of Canada). He also read parts in radio plays.

Greene married Rita Hands, of Toronto, in 1940. They had twins, Belinda and Charles, before divorcing in 1960. In 1961 he wedded Nancy Anne Deale, with whom he had one child.

After serving abroad in the Canadian army dur-

ing World War I, Greene returned to radio work in Toronto. There, he founded the Academy of Radio Arts to train broadcasting students. Still interested in stage work, he also helped to establish the Jupiter Theater in Toronto, a repertory group with which he directed or acted in dozens of plays. Additionally, he occasionally worked as an announcer for TV commercials and as a narrator for TV documentaries.

In the course of his radio broadcasting work, Greene experienced the problem of trying to determine how much time remained near the end of a program. To solve that problem, he developed a stopwatch that ran backward from 60 to 0. The device was produced and widely used.

In 1953 Green went to New York City to demonstrate his stopwatch for a TV executive. While there, he met Fletcher Markle, who had taught at Greene's Academy of Radio Arts. Markle induced Greene to appear on the American TV series *Studio One*, which Markle produced.

After appearing in two episodes of *Studio One*, Greene made his American stage debut by acting in the Broadway play *The Prescott Proposals* (1953). He then made several films, including *The Silver Chalice* (1954), *Peyton Place* (1957), and *The Buccaneer* (1958). He also began to appear in guest roles on other American TV shows, such as the anthology series *Alfred Hitchcock Presents*, *Omnibus*, and *Playhouse Ninety*.

In a 1959 episode of the TV western series *Wagon Train*, Greene played a particularly forceful character. His performance greatly impressed the NBC executives who were planning a new western series called *Bonanza*. They cast him—a

Lorne Greene

Lorne Greene

stern, Bible-reading, gun-toting patriarch. But Greene changed the character into, in his words, a "loving father who commands respect through the force of his own personality, a good man, a strong man, a decent man." Drawing on his own happy childhood, Greene modeled Ben Cartwright after his own father, Daniel Greene, a maker of orthopedic boots and shoes. The series ran from 1959 to 1973.

After Bonanza was cancelled, Greene starred in several other series, including *Battlestar Galactica* (1978-79) and *Code Red* (1981-82). Of special significance to Greene was the TV series *Last of the Wild* (or *Lorne Greene's Last of the Wild*, 1974-79). He was chairman of the National Wildlife Foundation, and he was a member of the board of directors of the American Horse Protection Association. He also served as the chairman of the American Freedom from Hunger Foundation.

In addition, Greene appeared in many films, mostly TV movies and miniseries. Among them were *Tidal Wave* (1975), *Roots* (TV, 1977), *The Bastard* (TV, 1978), and *A Time for Miracles* (TV, 1980). In the animated film *Heidi's Song* (1982) he supplied the grandfather's voice.

In 1986 he appeared in TV commercials for Alpo dog food, and he acted in the made-for-TV movie *The Alamo: Thirteen Days to Glory* (1987).

Greene died in Santa Monica, California, on September 11, 1987.

tall, heavily built man with a rugged, expressive face—in the role of the father, Ben Cartwright. NBC executives had two unusual reasons for creating the new show. First, they needed a hit show that could film in color in order to help RCA (NBC's parent company) sell more color TV sets. Second, they wanted a show that would feature an especially strong father-son relationship because of widespread concern about American soldiers' defections in Korea, which had been traced by a psychologist to momism.

Greene's charater was originally conceived as a

SELECTED PERFORMANCES:

STAGE

The Prescott Proposals (1953)
Julius Caesar (1955)
The Merchant of Venice (1955)
Speaking of Murder (1956)
Edwin Booth (1958)

FILMS

The Silver Chalice (1954)
Tight Spot (1955)

Autumn Leaves (1956)
Peyton Place (1957)
The Gift of Love (1958)
The Buccaneer (1958)
The Trap (1959)
The Errand Boy (1961)
Waco (1966)
Destiny of a Spy (TV, 1969)
The Harness (TV, 1971)
Tidal Wave (1975)
Nevada Smith (TV, 1975)
Man on the Outside (TV, 1975)
Roots (TV, 1977)
SST—Death Flight (TV, 1977)
The Trial of Lee Harvey Oswald (TV, 1977)
The Bastard (TV, 1978)
A Time for Miracles (TV, 1980)
Code Red (TV, 1981)
Heidi's Song (animated, voice only, 1982)
The Alamo: Thirteen Days to Glory (TV, 1987)

TV

Sailor of Fortune (1957)
Bonanza (1959–73)
Griff (1973–74)
Last of the Wild (or *Lorne Greene's Last of the Wild*, 1974–79)
Battlestar Galactica (1978-79)
Galactica 1980 (1980)
Code Red (1981–82)

Lorne Greene as Ben Cartright in an episode of Bonanza

Joel Grey

Master of Ceremonies

Joel Grey rose to stardom as the master of ceremonies in the Broadway and film versions of the offbeat musical *Cabaret*. Since then he has proven himself to be an exceptionally versatile actor, skillfully performing all types of dramamtic and comic roles.

Joel Grey was born in Cleveland, Ohio, on April 11, 1932. His original name was Joel Katz. His father was Mickey Katz, a popular comic musician in the American Yiddish musical theater. Mickey directed a vaudeville troupe in which his wife, Grace, performed and in which little Joel soon learned to sing and dance. The boy acted in his first play, *On Borrowed Time* (1941) at the Cleveland Playhouse.

The family later moved to Los Angeles, where Grey attended Alexander Hamilton High School and continued to work in his father's show. After graduating, the young man left his father's troupe, changed his stage name from Katz to Kaye and finally to Grey, and started performing a solo act in nightclubs.

In 1951, while working in Miami, Grey was spotted by Eddie Cantor and booked on Cantor's TV show. After that exposure, Grey got engagements at some of the best-known nightclubs in the country, including the Copacabana in New York City. His fast-paced act—singing, dancing, patter—was likened to the style of Danny Kaye's.

In spite of his new found success, Grey yearned to perform roles in theatrical productions. His parents and agents pressured him to remain a nightclub performer, and he became increasingly unhappy. By the age of nineteen, he had already developed a bleeding ulcer.

In the mid-1950s Grey finally abandoned his nightclub work and began to study acting at the Neighborhood Playhouse in New York City. He made his Broadway debut by appearing in *The Littlest Revue* (1956) and then played the title role in the TV special *Jack and the Beanstalk* (1956). Soon, he was making guest appearances on TV variety shows, including Ed Sullivan's

In 1958 Grey married Jo Wilder, an actress. They had two children, Jennifer and Jimmy. Jo was a stabilizing force in his life and career. "Before I was married, I was scattered," he admitted, "but afterwards I was able to zero in on my acting projects."

In the early 1960s Grey had a part in the movie *Come September* (1961), understudied several roles on Broadway, and acted in the off-Broadway black comedy *Harry, Noon, and Night* (1965). He began to build a reputation among theater people for his dynamism and versatility.

Grey got his big break when he was cast in the Broadway musical *Cabaret* (1966). As the heavily made-up, hollow-eyed master of ceremonies at Berlin's Kit Kat cabaret, he personified the decadence that set the stage for Hitler's takeover of Germany. *Cabaret* made Grey a star, and his part as the master of ceremonies is still the one by which he is best known.

In 1968 Grey appeared in the title role of *George M!*, a Broadway musical about the famous entertainer George M. Cohan. In 1972 Grey returned to nightclub work on an occasional basis. He then

Joel Grey

appeared in several shows that were not popular successes including the Broadway musical *Goodtime Charley* (1975); the off-Broadway play *Marco Polo Sings a Solo* (1977); and the Broadway show *The Grand Tour* (1979), a musical adaptation of a play about a Polish Jew, Jacobowsky (played by Danny Kaye in the 1958 movie version entitled *Me and Colonel*), who is escaping from the Nazis during World War II. *The Grand Tour* had a limited run, but Grey's role was personally meaningful to him. "I've never played a Jewish person before," he said. "I've played Nazis and Irishmen and WASPs—but never a Jew. It feels good."

Grey has, in fact, been involved in Jewish causes. In 1974 he served as West Coast chairman of the Committee to Free the Panovs. Valery Panov, a Jew, and his wife, Galina, were famed ballet dancers in the Soviet Union. The Panovs, who wanted to move to Israel, had been denied permission to leave Russia; they had also been forbidden to perform. Pressure from Western countries finally forced the Soviet government to let the Panovs leave. For his efforts, Grey received the Israel Cultural Award in 1974.

During the 1970s Grey began his film career in earnest. He was impressive in the filmed version of *Cabaret* (1972), and in the murder mystery *Man on a Swing* (1974) he played a straight dramatic role as a clairvoyant. In 1976 he appeared in two films: *Buffalo Bill and the Indians* and *The Seven-Per-Cent Solution*.

In 1980 Grey made his opera debut by performing in the New York City Opera production of the American premiere of Kurt Weill's *Silverlake*. He then appeared in a TV production of Gilbert and Sullivan's operetta *The Yeoman of the Guard* (TV, 1984). In 1987 he returned to the stage for a revival production of *Cabaret*.

In the 1990s Grey devoted much of his time to acting in films. He appeared in *Kafka* (1991), *The Music of Chance* (1993), and *Venus Rising* (1996). On the Broadway stage, he appeared as Amos Hart in the revival of the musical *Chicago* (1998).

SELECTED PERFORMANCES:

STAGE

On Borrowed Time (1941)
The Littlest Revue (1956)
Come Blow Your Horn (1961)

Joel Grey

Stop the World—I Want to Get Off (1963)
Half a Sixpence (1965)
Harry, Noon, and Night (1965)
Cabaret (1966, 1987)
George M! (1968)
1776 (1972)
Goodtime Charley (1975)
Marco Polo Sings a Solo (1977)
The Grand Tour (1979)
Silverlake (1980)
Chicago (1996)

FILMS

About Face (1952)
Come September (1961)
Cabaret (1972)
Man on a String (TV, 1972)
Man on a Swing (1974)
Buffalo Bill and the Indians; or, Sitting Bull's History Lesson (1976)
The Seven-Per-Cent Solution (1976)
The Yeoman of the Guard (TV, 1984)
Remo Williams: The Adventure Begins (1985)
Queenie (TV, 1987)
Marilyn and Me (TV, 1991)
Kafka (1991)
The Player (1992)
The Music of Chance (1993)
The Dangerous (1995)
Venus Rising (1996)

Buddy Hackett

Rubber Face

Buddy Hackett's humor is based on an endearing combination of helplessness and craftiness. His comic delivery is aided by his awkwardly pudgy body and by his puckish, elastic visage, which has been referred to as a "rubber face." He has appeared in films and on TV, but he is at his best on the stages of Las Vegas, where he has free reign to tell his raunchy anecdotes and to spontaneously interact with audience members.

Buddy Hackett was born in New York City, New York, on August 31, 1924. His original name was Leonard Hacker.

While growing up in Brooklyn, Hackett spent parts of his summer vacations on the borscht circuit as a waiter, bellhop, and toomler (that is, a creator of comic tumult). Soon after graduating from New Utrecht High School, he joined the army.

Returning to civilian life after World War I ended, he changed his name to Buddy Hackett and began to work in East Coast cafés and nightclubs as a comedian. He had little success, however, till he began performing in popular nightclubs in California in the early 1950s. Soon, he was getting engagements with major nightclubs and hotels throughout the country.

Almost overnight Hackett became a hot commodity. He appeared in the movies *Walking My Baby Back Home* (1953); *Fireman, Save My Child* (1954); the Broadway farce *Lunatics and Lovers* (1954); and the TV series *Stanley* (1956-57), in which he starred as the owner of a hotel-lobby newsstand.

In 1955 Hackett married the ex-dancer Sherry Cohen (stage name, Sherry Dubois). They had three children, Sandy, Ivy, and Lisa.

In 1958 Hackett gave a memorable and moving performance as a lovelorn rustic in the film *God's Little Acre* (1958). He next made a very successful appearance on David Susskind's TV talk show *Open End*. On that program Hackett showed the wit and the ad-libbing skills that had made him famous on the nightclub circuit. After his *Open End* performance he was in demand as a guest on TV talk shows and variety programs.

In the 1960s Hackett created delightful characters in a number of movies. In *The Music Man* (1962), for example, he was a stableboy who helps a con man to bilk a town.

From 1974 to 1976 Hackett was a regular panelist on the TV show *Celebrity Sweepstakes*. In 1978 he gave one of his most memorable performances, as the famed comedian Lou Costello in the TV biopic *Bud and Lou*.

In the 1980s and 1990s Hackett worked primarily in nightclubs, where he did not have to censor his humor. He also occasionally made guest appearances on TV, notably in episodes of the dramatic series *Quincy, M.E.* and *Murder, She Wrote*. Additionally, he performed in several films, including the Canadian film *Hey, Babe!* (1984) in which he played a washed-up entertainer who befriends a twelve-year-old orphan; the Disney animated picture *The Little Mermaid* (1989), in which he created the voice of the seagull Scuttle; and *Paulie* (1998).

Buddy Hackett doing what he does best.

SELECTED PERFORMANCES:

STAGE

Lunatics and Lovers (1954)
Viva Madison Avenue (1960)
I Had a Ball (1964)

FILMS

Walking My Baby Back Home (1953)
Fireman, Save My Child (1954)
God's Little Acre (1958)
All Hands on Deck (1961)
Everything's Ducky (1961)

The Wonderful World of the Brothers Grimm (1962)
The Music Man (1962)
It's a Mad, Mad, Mad, Mad World (1963)
Muscle Beach Party (1964)
The Good Guys and the Bad Guys (1969)
The Love Bug (1969)
Bud and Lou (TV, 1978)
Hey, Babe! (1984)
Scrooged (1988)
The Little Mermaid (animated, voice-only, 1989)
Paulie (1998)

TV

Stanley (1956-57)
Celebrity Sweepstakes (1974-76)

Laurence Harvey

Perfect Scoundrel

Laurence Harvey won international acclaim for his appearances in a series of films in which he played scoundrels. He gave unforgettable performances in such classic movies as *Room at the Top* (1959) and *The Manchurian Candidate* (1962).

Laurence Harvey was born in Yonishkis, Lithuania, on October 1, 1928. His original name was Larushka Mischa Skikne.

In 1934 Harvey moved with his parents to Johannesburg, South Africa, where he improved his English by attending movies. In 1943 he made his stage debut by appearing in *Cottage to Let* with the Johannesburg Repertory Company. In that same year, he ran away from home and joined the South African military service (he lied about his age). He fought in North Africa and Italy and was then assigned to an entertainment unit.

After being discharged, Harvey moved to England and briefly attended the Royal Academy of Dramatic Art in London. Soon he had offers from the American film studio Warner Brothers and from a classical-theater company in Manchester, England. Realizing that he needed to improve his acting skills and master the English language, he chose to remain in England. He stayed with the company from 1947 to 1951 (he became a British subject in 1947). During this period he changed his name to Laurence Harvey (his surname came from the fashinable Harvey Nichols department store in London).

Meanwhile, Harvey began to appear in British movies. His made his screen debut in *House of Darkness* (1948).

In 1951 Harvey made his London debut in the play *Hassan* (1951). He then joined the Royal Shakespeare Company in Stratford-upon-Avon, where he performed in many of the Bard's plays in 1952 and 1954. It was there that he first attracted serious critical attention, when he played Romeo in *Romeo and Juliet* (1954). He repeated his performance in a filmed version of the play (1954).

For several more years Harvey worked both on the stage and in films. He made his Broadway debut by playing Angelo, an eccentric stranger who becomes involved with three lonely women, in *The Island of Goats* (1955). In the late 1950s he began working almost exclusively in films, both in England in the United States.

Harvey became an international star with his performance as the ambitious, self-serving young schemer Joe Lampton in the British movie *Room at the Top* (1959). He then played similar roles in a series of films that became classics. In *Butterfield 8* (1960) he portrayed a philandering husband whose behavior toward his mistress drives her to suicide. He played a dissolute young doctor in *Summer and Smoke* (1961) and a brainwashed assassin in *The Manchurian Candidate* (1962). In *The Ceremony* (1963), which he also produced and directed, he was the leader of a holdup gang. In *Life at the Top* (1965), a sequel to *Room at the Top*, he re-created his Joe Lampton character.

Harvey's typical screen image was that of a bored, coldly impudent young man. But with his classical training and his native intelligence (though having little formal education, he could speak Dutch, English, French, German, and Italian), Harvey was able to give his villains depth.

Harvey sometimes played heros, too. For example, in *The Wonderful World of the Brothers Grimm* (1962) Harvey portrayed a likeable collector of fairy tales. He played Philip Carey, the clubfooted, tormented lover in *Of Human Bondage* (1964). And on the New York City stage, he had the role of King Arthur in the musical *Camelot* (1964).

In real life, Harvey's arrogant manner made him unpopular among many in his profession. He was also known for his strange antics. For example, during the gasoline rationing in London in 1956 he rode about the city on a chauffeur-driven motor scooter.

Harvey had three marriages. In 1957 he married the actress Margaret Leighton. They had met while they both were working at Stratford-upon-Avon. Later, they appeared together in the movie *The Good Die Young* (1955). They divorced in 1961.

In 1968 he wedded Joan Cohn, widow of Harry Cohn, head of Columbia Pictures. That marriage ended in divorce in 1972. He then married the young fashion model Paulene Stone. They had a daughter, Domino.

Harvey's third marriage was less than a year old when he died of cancer in London on November 25, 1973, at the age of only forty-five.

Laurence Harvey

SELECTED PERFORMANCES:

STAGE

Cottage to Let (1943)
The Man Who Ate the Popomack (1943)
Hassan (1951)
Coriolanus (1952)
As You Like It (1952)
Macbeth (1952)
Volpone (1952)
Romeo and Juliet (1954)
Troilus and Cressida (1954)
The Island of Goats (1955)
The Rivals (1956)
The Country Wife (1956)
Simply Heavenly (1958)
Henry V (1958)
Camelot (1964)

FILMS

House of Darkness (1948)

Man on the Run (1949)
The Black Rose (1950)
I Believe in You (1952)
Women of Twilight (1952, G.B.; U.S., *Twilight Women*)
King Richard and the Crusaders (1954)
Romeo and Juliet (1954)
Innocents in Paris (1955)
The Good Die Young (1955)
I Am a Camera (1955)
Storm over the Nile (1955)
Three Men in a Boat (1956)
The Truth about Women (1958)
The Silent Enemy (1958)
Room at the Top (1959)

Laurence Harvey

Expresso Bongo (1959)
Butterfield 8 (1960)
The Alamo (1960)
The Long and the Short and the Tall (1961, G.B.;
    U.S., *Jungle Fighters*)
Summer and Smoke (1961)
Two Loves (1961)
A Girl Named Tamiko (1962)
The Manchurian Candidate (1962)
Walk on the Wild Side (1962)
The Wonderful World of the Brothers Grimm (1962)
The Ceremony (1963)

The Running Man (1963)
Of Human Bondage (1964)
The Outrage (1964)
Darling (1965)
Life at the Top (1965)
The Spy with a Cold Nose (1966)
A Dandy in Aspic (1968)
The Magic Christian (1970)
Escape to the Sun (1972)
Night Watch (1973)
Welcome to Arrow Beach (1974, G.B.; U.S., *Tender
    Flesh* or *Cold Storage*)

Goldie Hawn

Kooky Comedienne

Goldie Hawn is widely regarded as the finest film comedienne since Carole Lombard. Combining slapstick with light romantic banter, and sexiness with innocence, Hawn typically portrays characters who are childlike but not stupid. Her success depends not on jokes but on comic timing, body language, and expressive openness.

Goldie Jeanne Hawn was born of a Jewish mother and Protestant father in Washington, D.C., on November 21, 1945. She was raised in Maryland.

At the age of three she began to study tap dancing and ballet, and at eleven she added modern dance lessons as well. Her father, who played violin, clarinet, and saxophone in society dance bands, gave her voice lessons.

As a teenager Hawn appeared in school and community dramatic productions. After graduating from Montgomery Blair High School in Silver Spring, Maryland, she studied drama for a year and a half at American University in Washington, D.C.

Hawn then worked as a professional dancer. She danced in summer-stock musicals, performed as a go-go dancer in a Manhattan discotheque, and appeared in a variety of other productions.

While dancing in the chorus on an Andy Griffith TV special in 1967, she was spotted by Art Simon, who became her agent. He helped her to get a small role as the wacky neighbor in the TV situation comedy *Good Morning, World* (1967–68).

Hawn then became a star with her regular appearances on the TV show *Laugh-in* (1968-70). Many of the characters that Hawn has played since have some of the same qualities.

In her first movie, *The One and Only, Genuine, Original Family Band* (1968), she played a small part as a giggly girl. Then, in *Cactus Flower* (1969), she had one of the leading roles and was praised

Goldie Hawn

137

Goldie Hawn and Kurt Russell

for her comic portrayal of the young mistress of a middle-aged dentist.

In *There's a Girl in My Soup* (1970) she again played a mistress. In *$* (1971) she was a call girl and an amateur bank robber. Her performance as the eccentric neighbor who falls in love with a young blind man in *Butterflies Are Free* (1972) firmly established her reputation as a fine comedienne. Among her other movies in the 1970s were *Shampoo* (1975) and *Foul Play* (1978).

In *Private Benjamin* (1980) she played the title role of a pampered young woman who has difficulty adjusting to life as a soldier. Hawn skillfully blended slapstick and romantic comedy in her performance. In *Swing Shift* (1984) she portrayed a lonely wife who finds work and romance in an aircraft plant during World War II. *In Protocol* (1984) she played a cocktail waitress who shakes up the State Department. In *Wildcats* (1986) she was a teacher who becomes the boys' football coach at a tough high school. She then played a spoiled heiress who develops amnesia in *Overboard* (1987).

In the early 1990s Hawn made several films, including *Bird on a Wire* (1990) and *Housesitter* (1992). Then she took a four-year break from acting. She returned in 1996 with two comedy films.

In *The First Wives Club* (1996) she was a fading movie star who joins forces with two other wronged wives in plotting revenge on their husbands. Hawn also participated in Woody Allen's homage to Hollywood musicals, *Everyone Says I Love You* (1996).

Hawn has been married and divorced twice. In 1969 she wedded the actor and film director Gus Trikonis. In the mid-1970s she divorced Trikonis and married the singer-comedian Bill Hudson, with whom she had two children, Oliver and Kate. In 1980 her second marriage ended in divorce. In recent years she has lived with the actor Kurt Russell, with whom she had her son Wyatt.

SELECTED PERFORMANCES:

FILMS

The One and Only, Genuine, Original Family Band (1968)
Cactus Flower (1969)
There's a Girl in My Soup (1970)
$ (1971)
Butterflies Are Free (1972)
The Girl from Petrovka (1974)
The Sugarland Express (1974)
Shampoo (1975)
The Duchess and the Dirtwater Fox (1976)
Foul Play (1978)
Private Benjamin (1980)
Seems like Old Times (1980)
Best Friends (1982)
Swing Shift (1984)
Protocol (1984)
Wildcats (1986)
Overboard (1987)
Bird on a Wire (1990)
Deceived (1991)
Crisscross (1992)
Death Becomes Her (1992)
Housesitter (1992)
The First Wives Club (1996)
Everyone Says I Love You (1996)
The Out-of-Towners (1999)

TV

Good Morning, W`orld (1967–68)
Laugh-in (1968-70)

Goldie Hawn and Steve Martin in a scene from Housesitter

Dustin Hoffman

Antihero

In the 1960s and 1970s Dustin Hoffman specialized in playing antiheros—defenseless characters caught in situations reflecting the complexity of the modern world. Later, he broadened the range of his roles and became one of the most versatile and highly regarded actors of his era.

Dustin Lee Hoffman was born in Los Angeles, California, on August 8, 1937. As a youth he was interested in becoming a classical pianist. After graduating from a Los Angeles high school in 1955, he enrolled at Santa Monica City College, where he majored in music (he also took an acting class). He then studied classical and jazz piano for a while at the Los Angeles Conservatory of Music.

However, early in 1957 he decided to become an actor. He began to study the fundamentals of his new profession at the Pasadena Playhouse. In 1958 he left for New York City, working in various community theaters along the way. After arriving at his destination, he auditioned and failed several times to enter Lee Strasberg's famous Actors Studio. Finally, he was accepted at the Studio, where his roommates were Robert Duvall and Gene Hackman.

At first, Hoffman earned his living in New York City by doing odd jobs. In 1959 he got a nonpaying role in a Sarah Lawrence College production of *Yes Is for a Very Young Man*. In 1961 he made his Broadway debut with a one-word line in *A Cook for Mr. General*.

Hoffman then made an important career move by joining the Theater Company of Boston as a character actor. He appeared in a number of plays with the company, giving a particularly fine performance in its production of Samuel Beckett's *Waiting for Godot* (1964).

Hoffman was then given his first significant Broadway job: assistant director of a revival of *A View from the Bridge* (1965). Over the next two years, however, he worked as an actor. His growing reputation culminated with his acclaimed performance in the off-Broadway comedy *Eh?* (1966).

Hoffman's first movie role was a bit part as a beatnik lover in *The Tiger Makes Out* (1967). He then had a leading role in the low-budget Italian-Spanish detective comedy *Madigan's Millions* (made in 1967, released in 1969). He finally got his big break when he was cast in the title role of *The Graduate* (1967). In that film he played Benjamin Braddock, an innocent, confused college graduate who is seduced by an older woman, played by Anne Bancroft. This legendary film, which was directed by Mike Nichols and which featured the famed Simon and Garfunkel soundtrack, made Hoffman an immediate sensation.

Hoffman's role in *The Graduate* was the start of a succession of great antiheroic characterizations he created during the 1960s and 1970s. He played the homosexual hustler Ratso Rizzo in *Midnight Cowboy* (1969); the irritable 122-year-old Jack Crabb, who claimed to be the sole survivor of Custer's last stand, in *Little Big Man* (1970); the weak, timid convict Louis Dega in *Papillon* (1973); the controversial real-life comedian Lenny Bruce in *Lenny* (1974); and the troubled and trapped student Babe Levy

Dustin Hoffman

critics and audiences with the depth and diversity of his performances in movies and on the stage. In the comic film *Tootsie* (1982), his brilliant performance as an unemployed actor who masquerades as a woman to win a role in a soap opera won him an Academy Award. In 1984 he starred as Willy Loman in a Broadway revival of Arthur Miller's *Death of a Salesman*. He reprised this role in a filmed version (TV, 1985). In the film comedy *Ishtar* (1987) he sang and danced as one of two (with Warren Beatty) no-talent songwriters on the road. One of the finest performances of his career was his portrayal of Raymond, an idiot savant, in the movie *Rain Man* (1988), also starring Tom Cruise. In 1989 he returned to the stage to play his first Shakespearean role, Shylock in the London and New York City productions of *The Merchant of Venice*.

Hoffman's film work in the 1990s continued to reflect his ever-widening range as an actor. In *Hook* (1991), an updated version of the Peter Pan story, he was the evil Captain Hook. In *Billy Bathgate* (1991) he played a ruthless racketeer. In *Outbreak* (1995) he played a conventional hero. He then portrayed a world-weary lowlife criminal in *American Buffalo* (1996).

Hoffman's most recent movies include the comedy *Wag the Dog* (1997) and the science-fiction film *Sphere* (1998).

in *Marathon Man* (1976). Hoffman also portrayed the real-life Watergate investigative reporter Carl Bernstein in *All the President's Men* (1976).

In 1969 Hoffman married Anne Byrne, a dancer. She had a daughter, Karina, from an earlier marriage. Hoffman and Byrne had another daughter, Jennifer. When Hoffman's marriage broke up in the late 1970s, he was particularly worried about the effect the divorce would have on his children. It was during this period that he was offered the role of the divorced parent Ted Kramer in *Kramer vs. Kramer*, opposite Meryl Streep, (1979). Hoffman was able to draw upon his personal experience while playing that role, creating one of his most sensitive performances to date.

In 1980 Hoffman married Lisa Gottsegen, a young law school graduate and photographer. They had four children, Jacob, Rebecca, Max, and Alexandra.

In more recent years Hoffman has impressed

SELECTED PERFORMANCES:

STAGE

A Cook for Mr. General (1961)
Endgame (1964)
Waiting for Godot (1964)
Three Men on a Horse (1964)
Harry, Noon, and Night (1965)
The Journey of the Fifth Horse (1966)
Eh? (1966)
The Old Jew (1966)
Jimmy Shine (1968)
Death of a Salesman (1984)
The Merchant of Venice (1989)

Dustin Hoffman in The Graduate

FILMS

The Tiger Makes Out (1967)
The Graduate (1967)
Midnight Cowboy (1969)
John and Mary (1969)
Madigan's Millions (1969)
Little Big Man (1970)
Straw Dogs (1971)
Who Is Harry Kellerman and Why Is He Saying Those Terrible Things about Me? (1971)
Papillon (1973)
Alfredo, Alfredo (1973)
Lenny (1974)
All the President's Men (1976)
Marathon Man (1976)
Straight Time (1978)

Agatha (1979)
Kramer vs. Kramer (1979)
Tootsie (1982)
Death of a Salesman (TV, 1985)
Ishtar (1987)
Rain Man (1988)
Family Business (1989)
Dick Tracy (1990)
Hook (1991)
Billy Bathgate (1991)
Hero (1992)
Outbreak (1995)
American Buffalo (1996)
Sleepers (1996)
Wag the Dog (1997)
Mad City (1997)
Sphere (1998)

Judy Holliday

Dumb-Blonde Genius

Judy Holliday had one of the most astonishing careers in show business. She performed in only a small number of plays and movies, most of them unremarkable except for her performances in them. She attained such a rapport with her audience and created such thoroughly endearing characterizations that her work continues to win the admiration of each new generation of movie buffs.

Holliday was generally typecast as a dumb blonde. In real life, however, she was a genius, with an IQ of 172. Her characterizations, then, were entirely artistic creations, enriched by her ability as a mimic, her vaudevillian talent, and her expressive vulnerability. She gave her dumb-blonde persona a high-pitched, piercing, childlike voice, but she could suddenly drop to a deep pitch to create a humorous effect. And with just a tiny inflection in her voice, she could quickly make a hilarious scene poignant.

J udy Holliday was born in New York City, New York, on June 21, 1921 (some sources report 1922). Her original name was Judith Tuvim.

Holliday's parents were of Russian descent, her maternal grandparents having fled their native land to avoid a czarist pogrom. From her father, Abraham, who was a professional fund-raiser for Jewish and socialist organizations, she derived her social consciousness. From her mother, Helen, who was a piano teacher, she acquired an interest in the arts.

When Holliday was six, her parents separated. She then lived with her mother and her grandmother.

In 1938 Holliday graduated from Manhattan's Julia Richman High School. Shortly thereafter she worked briefly as a switchboard operator for Orson Wells's Mercury Theater.

Then, with a few friends, including the future great songwriting team Betty Comden and Adolph Green, Holliday helped to form the Revuers, a topical cabaret act. They worked in nightclubs and had a thirty-two-week run on the radio. Holliday's gift for comedy became immediately apparent. During her stint with the Revuers, she changed her name from Judy Tuvim to Judy Holliday (*tuvim* is derived from the Hebrew word for holiday).

In 1943 the Revuers performed in Hollywood, California. While they were there, Holliday played bit parts in the movies *Winged Victory* (1944) and *Something for the Boys* (1944). Returning to New York City, the Revuers disbanded because Comden and Green had been asked to prepare the book and lyrics for Leonard Bernstein's musical *On the Town*. Holliday then won a small "moronic" part in the Broadway farce *Kiss Them for Me* (1945). She was the hit of the show.

Later that year Holliday was called in as a replacement for the female lead in the Broadway-bound play *Born Yesterday*. In just three days, she learned and rehearsed the role of Billie Dawn, a corrupt tycoon's dumb-blonde mistress whose latent sensitivities are awakened, who learns to think for herself, and who finally scores a moral and financial victory on behalf of all "little" people over the wealthy megalomaniac junkman. In early

Judy Holliday

1946 *Born Yesterday* hit Broadway and was a tremendous success. During the next few years Holliday played Billie Dawn well over a thousand times.

In 1948 Holliday married David Oppenheim, a clarinetist and later an executive with Columbia Records. They had one child, Jonathan, before divorcing in 1957.

In 1949 Holliday took a leave of absence from *Born Yesterday* to play a similar role in the film *Adam's Rib* (1949). The female star of that movie, Katharine Hepburn, credited Holliday with outshining both her and the film's male lead, Spencer Tracy.

Meanwhile, plans were being made for the movie of *Born Yesterday*, but Harry Cohn of Columbia Pictures hesitated to sign Holliday, who demanded a contract requiring that she make only one movie a year. She had requested this so that she could have more time to be with her husband. After a two-year search, however, it became evident to Cohn that no one else could match Holliday's brilliant stage portrayal of Billie Dawn. She was hired, and subsequently gave a memorable performance in this film.

In the early 1950s, Holliday frequently appeared on TV variety shows. But in 1952 she was called before a Senate subcommittee and questioned about her support of various causes alleged to be fronts for Communist activity. She purposely and skillfully adopted her scatterbrained Billie Dawn persona during her testimony, in which she exonerated herself and avoided naming others. Her ploy beautifully confounded the members of the subcommittee and exemplified the disdain with which level-headed Americans looked upon the extremists among the witch-hunters of the era. Garson Kanin, author of *Born Yesterday*, said, "Her behavior under pressure was a poem of grace."

Nevertheless, the subcommittee succeeded in casting a vague shadow over her. As a result, she was blacklisted from television for a number of years.

However, Holliday's movie career continued to blossom. She played her patented dumb-blonde characters in several films, including *It Should Happen to You* (1954), *Phffft* (1954), and *The Solid Gold Cadillac* (1956).

In 1956 Holliday returned to the Broadway stage to make her musical debut, playing Ella Peterson in *Bells Are Ringing*. Betty Comden and Adolph Green had tailored the role to most effectively utilize Holliday's unique talents.

While she was enjoying the peak of her success in *Bells Are Ringing*, she had a tempestuous love affair with Sydney Chaplin, son of Charlie Chaplin. But Sydney broke off the romance.

In late 1960 Holliday began work on the play that she felt would have the greatest impact on her artistic development: *Laurette*, which was based on the life of the actress Laurette Taylor, Holliday's idol. Just before its scheduled opening in Philadelphia, Holliday became ill and had to leave the show. The official reason given at the time was that she had a throat problem. Indeed, she did have such an affliction. But while the doctor was examining her, he also found a lump in

her left breast. The lump turned out to be malignant, and the breast had to be removed.

During her subsequent physical and psychological recovery, Holliday was greatly helped by the jazz saxophonist Gerry Mulligan, with whom she had a long-term romantic relationship. She recovered sufficiently to appear in the ill-fated stage musical *Hot Spot* (1963). It was her last professional appearance.

Holliday's life was marked by a series of painful reversals. As soon as she became a successful film actress, she was hauled into the Senate hearings. In the midst of her success with *Bells Are Ringing*, she was dropped by her lover. As soon as she found the great acting vehicle that she had long hoped for, *Laurette*, she became ill and had to leave the show.

Throughout her life Holliday went on periodic eating binges and struggled with the problem of being overweight. Insecure about her looks, she was always shocked when she turned heads in public. She may never have realized that she was actually one of the most appealing and lovable actresses of her time.

Unfortunately for everyone, her time was short. Holliday died of cancer in New York City on June 7, 1965, two weeks short of her forty-fourth birthday.

SELECTED PERFORMANCES:

STAGE

Kiss Them for Me (1945)
Born Yesterday (1946)
Dream Girl (1951)
Bells Are Ringing (1956)
Laurette (1960)
Hot Spot (1963)

FILMS

Winged Victory (1944)
Something for the Boys (1944)
Adam's Rib (1949)
Born Yesterday (1950)
The Marrying Kind (1952)
It Should Happen to You (1954)
Phffft (1954)
The Solid Gold Cadillac (1956)
Full of Life (1957)
Bells Are Ringing (1960)

Oscar Homolka

Green Screen Heavy

Oscar Homolka was one of filmdom's most memorable villains. He played a saboteur, a drunk, a spy, and numerous other unsavory characters.

O scar Homolka was born in Vienna, Austria, on August 12, 1898. He studied at the Royal Academy of Dramatic Arts in Vienna and then began his professional stage career in that city.

After spending two years in the Austrian army during World War I, Homolka returned to the stage. In 1918 he went to Berlin, where he became one of the director Max Reinhardt's leading men. Homolka mastered French and Polish and appeared in French and Polish plays as well. He also began to appear in German-language films in the 1920s.

In the early 1930s Homolka fled Germany to escape persecution, settling in Great Britain. He made his English-language stage debut with a performance as Dr. Mesmer in a Scottish production of *Mesmer* (1935). Later that year he began to work on the London stage. He then appeared in the British film *Rhodes of Africa* (1936) as President Kruger of the Dutch Transvaal, whose policies led to the Boer War.

In 1937 Homolka made his American film debut in *Ebb Tide* as a former ship captain who has become a drunken beachcomber. In 1940 he gave his first performance on the New York City stage, in *Grey Farm*. Homolka became a naturalized American citizen in 1943.

One of Homolka's most memorable roles was that of the bombastic but benevolent Uncle Chris in *I Remember Mama* (stage, 1944; film, 1948). But for Homolka, who played some of the most unforgettable heavies in film history, it was an uncharacteristic part. Because he had a rugged build, heavy facial features, bushy eyebrows, wickedly twinkling eyes, and a gravelly voice, he was usually cast as a villain. In Alfred Hitchcock's *Sabotage* (1936) Homolka was a saboteur who manufactures bombs in the back room of his theater in London. In *Comrade X* (1940) he portrayed a Russian commissar, while in *Anna Lucasta* (1949) he was an alcoholic father. In the comedy *The Seven Year Itch* (1955) he played an unsympathetic psychiatrist. In *Funeral in Berlin* (1966), *Billion Dollar Brain* (1967), and *The Tamarind Seed* (1974), he portrayed Russian spies.

Homolka was married five times. His fourth marriage was to Florence Meyer, daughter of Eugene Meyer, publisher of the *Washington Post*. Homolka's two surviving children, Lawrence and Vincent, were products of that marriage. His final and most successful marriage was to the actress Joan Tetzel. They had appeared together on Broadway in *I Remember Mama*.

In the mid-1960s Homolka moved to a rural setting in Sussex, England, after having lived about fifteen years in New York City. He died in Sussex on January 27, 1978. The cause of death was given as pneumonia, but friends said that he was weakened by grief over the loss of his wife, who had died just three months earlier.

SELECTED PERFORMANCES:

STAGE

Pygmalion (1932)
Mesmer (1935)
Close Quarters (1935)
Power and Glory (1938)
Grey Farm (1940)
The Innocent Voyage (1942)
I Remember Mama (1944)
The Last Dance (1948)
Bravo! (1948)
The Broken Jug (1950)
The Master Builder (1955)
Rashomon (1959)

FILMS

Der Kampf des Donald Westhof (1927, Ger.;
   U.S., *The Trial of Donald Westhof*)
Dreyfus (1930, Ger.; U.S., *The Dreyfus Case*)
Im Geheimdienst (1931, Ger.; U.S., *In the
   Employ of the Secret Service*)
Rhodes of Africa (1936, G.B.; U.S., *Rhodes*)
Sabotage (1936, G.B.; U.S., *The Woman
   Alone*)
Ebb Tide (1937)
Seven Sinners (1940)
Comrade X (1940)
The Invisible Woman (1941)
Rage in Heaven (1941)
Ball of Fire (1941)
Hostages (1943)
Mission to Moscow (1943)
The Shop at Sly Corner (1947, G.B.; U.S., *The Code
   of Scotland Yard*)
I Remember Mama (1948)
Anna Lucasta (1949)
The White Tower (1950)
Top Secret (1952, G.B.; U.S., *Mr. Potts Goes to
   Moscow*)
Prisoner of War (1954)
The Seven Year Itch (1955)
War and Peace (1956)
A Farewell to Arms (1957)
The Key (1958)

Mr. Sardonicus (1961)
Boys' Night Out (1962)
The Wonderful World of the Brothers Grimm (1962)
The Long Ships (1964)
Joy in the Morning (1965)
Funeral in Berlin (1966)
Billion Dollar Brain (1967)
The Happening (1967)
The Strange Case of Dr. Jekyll and Mr. Hyde (TV,
   1968)
Assignment to Kill (1969)
The Madwoman of Chaillot (1969)
The Executioner (1970)
Song of Norway (1970)
The Tamarind Seed (1974)
One of Our Own (TV, 1975)

Oscar Homolka

Harry Houdini

Legendary Escape Artist

Harry Houdini was the master showman of the early twentieth century. Through his unprecedented use of self-publicity, he became the most famous magician—and one of the most famous entertainers—of his time. No ordinary conjurer, Houdini virtually invented the art form of escape.

Harry Houdini was born in Budapest, Hungary, on March 24, 1874. His original name was Erik Weisz.

Shortly after his birth, his parents moved with him to the United States and settled in Wisconsin, first in Appleton and later in Milwaukee. The boy's name was Americanized to Erich Weiss. Houdini always claimed that he had been born in Appleton on April 6, 1874, probably because he strongly felt himself to be a native American and wanted the world to see him as such.

Houdini's father, Rabbi Mayer Weiss, had difficulty adjusting to life in America, and the family was very poor. The boy developed an interest in show business as a means of escaping poverty. His first public performance came at a neighborhood circus, probably in a trapeze act.

On his twelfth birthday Houdini ran away from home to look for work. By 1888 he had rejoined his family, which had moved to New York City. He worked at odd jobs, eventually becoming a cutter at a necktie factory.

Meanwhile, however, Houdini had been cultivating a growing interest in magic and feats of dexterity. He learned the rudiments of those skills by observing acts at sideshows and circuses and by reading books.

When he decided to seriously pursue a career in magic, he changed his nickname of Ehrie into Harry, and he derived his new surname of Houdini from the name of his idol, the magician Robert Houdini. Harry Houdini and his friend Jacob Hyman, a fellow worker at the necktie factory, put together a magic act and had small-time bookings as the Brothers Houdini. Later Hyman was replaced by one of Houdini's four real-life brothers, Theodore (later known as the independent magician Hardeen).

On April 3, 1891, Houdini left his factory job and went into show business full-time. He and his brothers played dime museums, beer halls, and small-time rural vaudeville theaters. At first they concentrated on magic, but Houdini soon began to add escape tricks to the act.

In 1894 Houdini married Wilhemina Beatrice Rahner, a Catholic girl, known as Bess or Bessie. Theodore left the act, which then became known as the Houdinis, starring Harry with Bess as his assistant.

In 1895 they played briefly at Tony Pastor's famous Music Hall in New York City. Over the next several years they struggled in poverty while appearing mostly in saloons, circuses, and dime museums.

At the turn of the century they traveled to Europe. During their five years there, Houdini developed the art of self-publicity, which he would use to tremendous advantage for the rest of his career. When he returned to the United States in 1905, he was a major celebrity.

In America, Houdini took advantage of a new forum, big-time urban vaudeville, to raise himself to an unprecedented level of popularity for a magician and escape artist. His great genius lay in his dramatic escape tricks. In "The Challenge Handcuff Act" he became the first escape artist to invite people from the audience to shackle him with real handcuffs, not the usual fake variety. In "The Chinese Water Torture Cell Escape" Houdini's ankles were padlocked and he was lowered head first into a glass container full of water. "Metamorphosis" was the rapid substitution of one person for another inside a locked and roped trunk. In "The Naked Test Prison Escape" he was stripped and locked in real prison or jail cells. In "The Overboard Box Escape" he was locked in a box, which was then tossed into a river. "The Straitjacket Escape" never ceased to amaze audiences as they watched him squirm out of the binding.

For those and other escapes, Houdini used his knowledge of mechanics, both human and nonhuman. When his escapes depended on sheer strength and physical dexterity, he performed in full view of his audience. But for more difficult tricks, he hid in a cabinet of one kind or another.

After World War I Houdini entered the filmmaking business. He starred in the serial *The Master Mystery* (1918–19) and then made several independent movies. The stories and the acting were not memorable, but the films did have some thrilling adventure featuring Houdini's physical dexterity.

He was also active as a writer. In *The Unmasking of Robert Houdini* (1908) he exposed the methods and claims of his former idol. *Miracle Mongers and Their Methods* (1921) was an exposé of fire-eaters, gravity-resisters, and other sideshow acts. Many of his essays were published posthumously in *Houdini on Magic* (1953).

Houdini long had an interest in death. That interest was intensified in 1913 when his beloved mother died and then in 1920 when he met Sir Arthur Conan Doyle, creator of the Sherlock Holmes fictional character and champion of spiritualism.

Harry Houdini

Houdini began to investigate spiritualism as a possible way of communicating with his mother. He soon discovered the tricks used by spiritualists, and by 1922 a strong denunciation of mediums had become a regular part of his own act. His book *A Magician among the Spirits* (1924) was a well-documented exposé of the phony mediums of the day.

On October 21, 1926, while in Montreal, Canada, for a performance, Houdini was approached by two youths from nearby McGill University. They asked if it was true that he had claimed he could take a punch in the midsection without being affected. He said yes; but before Houdini had time to brace himself, one of the youths threw a vicious blow to the older man's abdomen. Unknown to Houdini, the punch ruptured his appendix. Over the next few days he continued to work, though the pain increased steadily.

On October 24, just after a performance in Detroit, Michigan, he collapsed. An emergency operation was performed on his gangrenous appendix, but he died of advanced peritonitis in Detroit on October 31, 1926. At Houdini's own request he had a Jewish burial service at Mount Zion Temple in New York City.

After his death a furor arose when his widow said that he had promised to try to communicate with her from the "other world," conveying a secret message that he had whispered to her on his deathbed. During a series of seances in 1928 and 1929 the spiritualist Arthur Ford claimed to have received the message. At first Bess agreed with Ford; later she disagreed. Subsequent investigations showed that neither Ford nor Bess was a reliable witness.

SELECTED PERFORMANCES:

FILMS

The Master Mystery (1918–19)
The Grim Game (1919)
Terror Island (1920)
The Soul of Bronze (1921)
The Man from Beyond (1922)
Haldane of the Secret Service (1923)

Harry Houdini

Leslie Howard

Creator of "Natural" Acting

Leslie Howard created a new style of acting. In the 1920s on Broadway and then in the 1930s on film, he eschewed the excessive gestures and overwrought declamations traditional among actors. Instead, he used a "natural" approach, underplaying his parts with a relaxed manner that reflected his own personality. He was the principal forerunner of modern realistism in acting.

L eslie Howard was born in London, England, on April 3, 1893. His original name was Leslie Howard Steiner (his surname is so indicated on his birth records, though his daughter later spelled it Stainer).

Howard disliked school, but he enjoyed writing. In his early teens, he began to write stories, plays, and short musical comedies. He sold many thrillers to pulp magazines. To encourage him, his mother organized a neighborhood drama club, in whose plays both mother and son appeared.

Howard attended Dulwich College but, at his father's insistence, left at the age of nineteen to become a bank clerk. The outbreak of World War I gave him the opportunity to leave the bank, where he had never been happy. He enlisted in the military and was made a second lieutenant in the cavalry in 1915. In the spring of 1916, he was sent to France to fight. The next year he had to return to England because of shell shock. From his cavalry experience, he developed a great love of horses and eventually a passion for polo.

In 1916, before going to France, Howard had married Ruth Martin, daughter of a laundry manager. They had two children, Ronald (nicknamed Winkie) and Leslie Ruth (nicknamed Doodie). Howard was very close to his children and each child later wrote a book about Howard. Leslie Ruth's was called *A Quite Remarkable Father* (1959), Ronald's *In Search of My Father: A Portrait of Leslie Howard* (1981).

When Howard returned from France in 1917, he decided to become an actor (he dropped his original surname for his new career). He made his professional debut that year, touring the provinces in *Peg o' My Heart*. He made his London debut in early 1918 playing a small part in *The Freaks*.

Howard then became fascinated by movies and, in 1920, helped to form the small Minerva Films production company, with himself as managing director and leading actor. The company made three short comedies before going out of business.

Returning to the stage, Howard traveled to the United States, where he made his New York City debut in the fall of 1920 in *Just Suppose*. He spent the next several years in America, often appearing as the juvenile lead in light comedies. He then traveled back and forth between England and the United States, appearing in plays in both London and New York, including *Her Cardboard Lover* and *Escape*. The British often referred to him as "that American actor."

Howard never really enjoyed acting however. He performed mainly to earn enough money to have the freedom to pursue other activities. Still interested in writing, in the 1920s he sold several light essays (mostly about acting and the theater) to major American magazines, such as *Vanity Fair* and *The New Yorker*.

Leslie Howard

Leslie Howard

daring disguises, not with fists and swords. As Alan Squier in *The Petrified Forest* (1936) Howard portrayed a writer who sacrifices his life for a waitress. In *Pygmalion* (which he also codirected, 1938) he was Professor Henry Higgins, a linguist who turns an unwashed, uneducated girl into a lady. In the classic film *Gone with the Wind* (1939) he played Ashley Wilkes, a self-debating reluctant soldier.

Having no pretensions as an actor, Howard simply played himself: a dreamy, cultured, intelligent, honorable man often pitted against the brute forces in the world. He became the screen's foremost idealistic intellectual.

In 1939 England entered World War II. Howard, still a British citizen, returned from America to his homeland to aid the war effort. He helped (as producer, director, writer, and/or star) to make propaganda films showing the British viewpoint to American audiences. Outstanding among those films was the biopic *The First of the Few* (1942, released in the United States in 1943 as *Spitfire*), the story of R. J. Mitchell (played by Howard), designer of the Spitfire fighter plane. Howard also made weekly radio broadcasts to North America on the *Britain Speaks* program.

In the spring of 1943, at the request of the British Council, Howard went as a goodwill ambassador to the neutral nations of Spain and Portugal, where he gave a series of lectures. On the return flight his plane was shot down by German aircraft over the Bay of Biscay on June 1, 1943. His body was never recovered.

Howard also enjoyed directing and producing. In 1927 he directed and starred in the New York City production of *Murray Hill*, a farce that he had written. In 1928 he produced a London staging of *Her Cardboard Lover*, in which he again starred. Thereafter, he often served as producer or coproducer of the plays in which he appeared. Highlights of the rest of his stage career included his work in *Berkeley Square* (1929), *The Animal Kingdom* (1932), and *The Petrified Forest* (1935).

In 1930 Howard began to appear in major films. His first performance in the film *Outward Bound* (1930), as one of a group of ship passengers who slowly realize that they are dead, made a tremendous impression on audiences. He then appeared in a number of light comedies, but he is best remembered for his memorable characterizations in a series of outstanding films made between 1934 and 1939. In *Of Human Bondage* (1934) he played the lovesick Philip Carey. In *The Scarlet Pimpernel* (1935) he was Sir Percy Blakeney, a hero who fights the oppressive French with trickery and

SELECTED PERFORMANCES:

STAGE

Peg o' My Heart (1917)
Charley's Aunt (1917)
Under Cover (1917)
The Freaks (1918)
The Title (1918)
Our Mr. Hepplewhite (1919)
Mr. Pim Passes By (1920)
The Young Person in Pink (1920)
East Is West (1920)
Just Suppose (1920)
The Wren (1921)
Danger (1921)
The Truth about Blayds (1922)

A Serpent's Tooth (1922)
The Romantic Age (1922)
The Lady Cristilinda (1922)
Anything Might Happen (1923)
Aren't We All? (1923)
Outward Bound (1924)
The Werewolf (1924)
Isabel (1925)
Shall We Join the Ladies? (1925)
The Green Hat (1925)
The Way You Look at It (1926)
Murray Hill (1927)
Escape (1927)
Berkeley Square (1929)
Candlelight (1929)
The Animal Kingdom (1932)
This Side Idolatry (1933)
The Petrified Forest (1935)
Hamlet (1936)

FILMS

The Happy Warrior (1917)
The Lackey and the Lady (1919)
Bookworms (1920)
Five Pounds Reward (1920)
Outward Bound (1930)
Never the Twain Shall Meet (1931)
A Free Soul (1931)

Five and Ten (1931)
Devotion (1931)
Service for Ladies (1932, G.B.; U.S., *Reserved for Ladies*)
Smilin' Through (1932)
The Animal Kingdom (1932, U.S.; G.B., *A Woman in His House*)
Secrets (1933)
Captured (1933)
Berkeley Square (1933)
The Lady is Willing (1934)
Of Human Bondage (1934)
British Agent (1934)
The Scarlet Pimpernel (1935)
The Petrified Forest (1936)
Romeo and Juliet (1936)
It's Love I'm After (1937)
Stand-in (1937)
Pygmalion (1938)
Gone with the Wind (1939)
Intermezzo (1939, U.S.; G.B., *Escape to Happiness*)
From the Four Corners (1940)
Forty-ninth Parallel (1941, G.B.; U.S., *The Invaders*)
Pimpernel Smith (1941, G.B.; U.S., *Mister V*)
The First of the Few (1942, G.B.; U.S., *Spitfire*)

Sam Jaffe

Gunga Din and Dr. Zorba

Sam Jaffe left his unique imprint as a great character actor on a vast number of stage, film, and TV roles. He is probably best remembered for playing the title role in the film classic *Gunga Din* (1939) and starring as Dr. Zorba in the TV medical-drama series *Ben Casey* (1961-65).

Samuel Jaffe was born in New York City, on March 10, 1891. He grew up in the Lower East Side of Manhattan and attended Townsend Harris High School. As a child he occasionally appeared in shows with his mother, Ada Steinberg Jaffe, an actress in the Yiddish theater.

Jaffe studied engineering, earning his B.S. degree from City College of the City University of New York (1912). While he pursued his graduate studies at the Columbia University School of Engineering, he was a teacher, and then dean (1915–16), of mathematics at the Bronx Cultural Institute, a college-preparatory school. In 1918 he served as an army engineer.

Meanwhile, Jaffe was pursuing an interest in the theater. From 1915 to 1916 he appeared with the Washington Square Players, and in 1917 he worked with a Shakespearean repertory company. He made his Broadway debut in 1921 as Leibush in *The Idle Inn*.

Jaffe appeared in a number of Broadway plays over the next several years. Two of his most memorable roles were those of Yudelson in *The Jazz Singer* (1925) and Kringelein in *Grand Hotel* (1930).

Jaffe frequently played Jewish characters. Among them were Izzy Goldstein in *The Main Line* (1924), Eli Iskowvitch in *Izzy* (1924), Shylock in *The Merchant of Venice* (1938), and Jonah Goodman in *The Gentle People* (1939).

A special contribution of Jaffe's stage career was his cofounding (with George Freedley) of the famed Equity Library Theater in New York City (1943).

Beginning in the early 1930s much of Jaffe's time was spent acting in films. In his first movie, *The Scarlet Empress* (1934), he gave an impressive performance as the dissolute Grand Duke Peter of Russia. He soon became an extremely popular character actor. He was the venerable High Lama in *Lost Horizon* (1937) and the title character—the humble, ascetic, noble water-carrier for British soldiers—in *Gunga Din* (1939). In *Gentleman's Agreement* (1947), a film about anti-Semitism, he played a Jewish scientist, while in *The Asphalt Jungle* (1950) he portrayed a cool-headed criminal mastermind. In the science-fiction classic *The Day the Earth Stood Still* (1951) he was the space scientist Jacob Barnhardt, while in *Ben-Hur* (1959) he played a loyal steward in ancient Judea.

Starting in the 1950s Jaffe guest-starred on many TV series, such as *Bonanza, The Defenders, Night Gallery*, and *The Untouchables*. He became best known to TV audiences for his ongoing role as Dr. David Zorba, chief of neurosurgery, in the TV medical-drama series *Ben Casey* (1961–65).

Jaffe continued to work as an actor until he was in his nineties. A highlight of his later Broadway stage career was his memorable performance as Zero in *The Adding Machine* (1956). His last Broadway appearance was in the play *A Meeting by the River* (1979). His later movies included *Born Free* (1966), *The Old Man Who Cried Wolf!* (TV, 1970), and *Gideon's Trumpet* (TV, 1980). In October 1983, at the age of ninety-two, he performed his last film role, as a smuggler of illegal aliens in *On the Line*.

Jaffe was a man of wide-ranging talents and interests. He was an excellent pianist and composer of classical music, and he spoke at least six languages fluently. He supported many causes, including the security of Israel. A liberal, he had to endure a brief downswing in his career during the McCarthy era in the early 1950s.

Jaffe was married twice. In the mid-1920s he wedded the actress Lillian Taiz, who died in 1941. In 1956 he married the actress Bettye Ackerman, with whom he frequently acted (as in *Ben Casey*).

Jaffe died at the age of ninety-three in Beverly Hills, California, on March 24, 1984.

Sam Jaffe

SELECTED PERFORMANCES:

STAGE

The Clod (1915)
Youth (1918)
Mrs. Warren's Profession (1918)
Samson and Delilah (1920)
The Idle Inn (1921)
The God of Vengeance (1922)
The Main Line (1924)
Izzy (1924)
The Jazz Singer (1925)
Grand Hotel (1930)
Divine Drudge (1933)
The Bride of Torozko (1934)
The Eternal Road (1937)
A Doll's House (1937)
The Merchant of Venice (1938)
The Gentle People (1939)
King Lear (1940)
The King's Maid (1941)
Café Crown (1942)
Thank You, Svoboda (1944)
This Time Tomorrow (1947)
Mademoiselle Colombe (1954)
The Sea Gull (1954)

Saint Joan (1954)
The Adding Machine (1956)
Idiot's Delight (1970)
Storm in Summer (1973)
A Meeting by the River (1979)

FILMS

The Scarlet Empress (1934)
We Live Again (1934)
Lost Horizon (1937)
Gunga Din (1939)
Stage Door Canteen (1943)
13 Rue Madeleine (1947)
Gentleman's Agreement (1947)
The Accused (1949)
Rope of Sand (1949)
The Asphalt Jungle (1950)
Under the Gun (1951)
I Can Get It for You Wholesale (1951)
The Day the Earth Stood Still (1951)
The Barbarian and the Geisha (1958)
Ben-Hur (1959)

Sam Jaffe (right) as Gunga Din

Gunga Din (1939)
Damon and Pythias (1962)
Born Free (1966)
A Guide for the Married Man (1967)
Guns for San Sebastian (1968)
The Great Bank Robbery (1969)
Night Gallery (TV, 1969)
Quarantined (TV, 1970)
The Old Man Who Cried Wolf! (TV, 1970)
The Dunwich Horror (1970)

Bedknobs and Broomsticks (1971)
QB VII (TV, 1974)
Gideon's Trumpet (TV, 1980)
Battle beyond the Stars (1980)
Nothing Lasts Forever (1983)
On the Line (1983)

TV

Ben Casey (1961–65)

Al Jolson

Jazz Singer

Many people regarded Al Jolson as the greatest entertainer of his time. During his lifetime he was principally known for his performances in Broadway musical shows, but the work for which he is now best remembered is his role in *The Jazz Singer* (1927), the first important movie with sound.

Born sometime between 1880 and 1886 in Srednike, Lithuania—the exact date of his birth is not known—Al Jolson selected May 26, 1886, as the birth date that he preferred. His original name was Asa Yoelson.

In the early 1890s his father, Moses, moved to the United States. A few years later the elder Yoelson sent for his family, who joined him in Washington, D.C., where he had obtained a post as a cantor.

Moses strictly upheld Orthodox Jewish views and practices, while Asa and his older brother, Hirsch, were lax in such observances. Moreover, Moses taught both boys to sing, but he hated popular music, while it was precisely American popular culture that most interested his sons. The brothers sang in the streets to earn money from passersby and often ran away from home to try to break into show business. After Hirsch Americanized his given name to Harry, Asa followed suit by calling himself Al.

Al's first indoor show-business job was singing "Rosie, You Are My Posie" in a Bowery restaurant, where his payment was a meal. At the Bijou Theater in Washington, D.C., he sang from the audience as part of Eddie Leonard's act, later performing the same function there for the burlesque queen Jersey Lil. In 1899 he appeared on a stage for the first time as an extra in the New York City production of the London Jewish epic *Children of the Ghetto*.

Having Americanized their surname to Joelson (the change was initiated by Al), the brothers (known as the Joelson Brothers) began touring in vaudeville in a comedy act called *The Hebrew and the Cadet*. Because Al's voice was changing, Harry sang while Al whistled. During the show-business slump following the assassination of President McKinley in 1901, the boys were laid off.

After a couple of years in burlesque they returned to vaudeville in the comedy team Jolson, Palmer, and Jolson (a printer suggested the change in spelling because two "Joelsons" were too long for their business card). In their act, entitled *A Little of Everything*, Al used blackface for the first time, finding that with a mask on he could perform with greater abandon.

The team lasted about three years, after which Al developed a solo act. In San Francisco, one week after the great 1906 earthquake there, he made his first significant appearance in his solo vaudeville routine, again in blackface. His first great success, however, came when he performed as one of Lew Dockstader's Minstrels in New York City in 1909.

Jolson then began touring in vaudeville on his own again, still in blackface, and perfected his technique as he went along. Cultivating a style of singing derived from Afro-American music and blackface minstrelsy, he characteristically per-

Al Jolson

formed with an intoned declamation that emphasized the text rather than the melodic line. Yet he was also skilled at melodic invention, often improvising whistled choruses in the manner of jazz instrumentalists. In fact, much of his routine was improvised. Besides performing his rehearsed numbers, he sang songs on request, sometimes whistled or broke into a buck-and-wing, and kept up a lively extemporaneous monologue consisting of anecdotes, homilies, and confessions.

In 1911 Jolson began his meteoric rise to the position of Broadway's greatest attraction. He appeared that year in *La Belle Paree* and *Vera Violetta* and the next year at the famed Winter Garden Theater in the revue *The Whirl of Society*, in which he presented himself as the blackface character Gus, and performed on a special runway that had been erected for him in the orchestra pit. Jolson would use both the runway and the Gus character in many future shows.

In *The Honeymoon Express* (1913), Jolson employed for the first time two gestures that became his hallmark: falling to one knee and extending his arms in a pathetic appeal while singing. His original purpose, however, was not theatrical but practical: he was suffering from an ingrown toenail, and as he went down on one knee to take pressure off the painful digit, his arms flew out instinctively to compensate for the sudden immobility of his legs. But the favorable response of the audience induced him to keep the gestures as a regular feature in his performances.

Over the next several years, Jolson continued to score big successes in numerous Broadway productions, notably *Robinson Crusoe, Jr.* (1916), *Sinbad* (1918), and *Bombo* (1921). Most of the musicals had little plot interest. Jolson simply took over the last segment of each show to work his magic and bring the entertainment to a rousing climax. In his performances, he became closely identified with many songs, including "April Showers," "My Mammy," "Rock-a-bye Your Baby with a Dixie Melody" (his favorite song), "Swanee," and "Toot, Toot, Tootsie."

In the late 1920s, after the successful *Big Boy* (1925), Jolson's popularity began to fade with the changing fashions in theater. His last two shows, *The Wonder Bar* (1931) and *Hold On to Your Hats* (1940), performed without blackface, were not hits.

Jolson adapted to the changing times, and in the late 1920s he became a film actor. He debuted, in fact, in the first significant feature-length sound movie: *The Jazz Singer* (1927). Actually, this film is mostly a silent movie, with songs and just bits of dialogue audible. The first spoken words in the film occur when Jolson, after singing "Dirty Hands, Dirty Face," says, "Wait a minute! Wait a minute! You ain't heard nothin' yet," and then introduces his next song, "Toot, Toot, Tootsie."

The *Jazz Singer* was originally a Broadway play in which the main character, Jakie Rabinowitz, was modeled after Jolson himself. Jakie is a cantor's son who runs away from home to become the jazz singer Jack Robin. When his father dies, Jack gives up his big chance on Broadway and goes home to take over his father's cantorial duties at the synagogue. For the screen version, a final segment was added showing Jack singing in a Broadway musical entitled *The Jazz Singer*. George Jessel, the original Jakie Rabinowitz on Broadway, had been offered the screen role; but when he asked for too much money, he was replaced by Jolson.

Among Jolson's later films were *The Singing Fool* (1928); *Mammy* (1930); *Hallelujah, I'm a Bum* (1933); *Swanee River* (1939); and *Rhapsody in Blue* (1945).

Jolson also frequently performed on radio, both as the star of his own shows and as a guest on other programs. He hosted several variety series, including *Presenting Al Jolson* (1932–33), *The Kraft Music Hall* (1933–34, 1947–49), and *Shell Chateau* (1935–36). In 1936 he teamed up with two comics, Martha Raye and Parkyakarkus (real name, Harry Einstein), on *The Lifebuoy Program*, which was a hit show for several seasons.

Jolson's popularity waned again in the late 1930s and early 1940s. But the semibiographical movies *The Jolson Story* (1946) and *Jolson Sings Again* (1949) revived interest in him. He dubbed in the singing for Larry Parks (as Jolson) in the two films.

Jolson had four marriages. In 1906 he wedded Henrietta Keller, a chorus girl whom he had met in San Francisco; they divorced in 1919. He was then married to the Broadway dancer Alma Osborne, better known by the stage name Ethel Delmar, from 1922 to 1926.

In 1928 Jolson married the famed entertainer Ruby Keeler. They performed together a number of times. In 1929 Keeler starred on Broadway in *Show Girl*, in which she had a solo scene leading a women's chorus in the song "Liza." In one of Broadway's most famous incidents, Jolson appeared at the theater and sang "Liza" from the audience to calm his stage-frightened young wife. He returned for several more nights to perform the same function until Keeler felt secure on her own.

Jolson and Keeler adopted a son, whom they named Al Jolson, Jr. But this marriage, too, did not last; they parted in 1939 and divorced in 1940.

In 1945 Jolson married Erle Chenault Galbraith, an x-ray technician and fan from Little Rock, Arkansas. They adopted a son, Asa and, less formally, a daughter (Alicia).

Jolson was generous with his time for benefit performances, particularly during wartime. He helped to sell World War I Liberty Bonds, and he performed on the USO circuits during World War II and the Korean War.

Having just returned from a Korean tour, Jolson was stopping over in San Francisco when he died of a heart attack on October 23, 1950. His good friend George Jessel delivered the eulogy at Temple Israel in Los Angeles. The bulk of Jolson's estate, estimated at $4 million, was bequeathed to a number of institutions, including Jewish, Catholic, and Protestant charities.

SELECTED PERFORMANCES:

STAGE

La Belle Paree (1911)
Vera Violetta (1911)
The Whirl of Society (1912)

The Honeymoon Express (1913)
Dancing Around (1914)
Robinson Crusoe, Jr. (1916)
Sinbad (1918)
Bombo (1921)
Big Boy (1925)
Artists and Models (1926)
A Night in Spain (1927)
The Wonder Bar (1931)
Hold On to Your Hats (1940)

FILMS

The Jazz Singer (1927)
The Singing Fool (1928)
Say It with Songs (1929)
Mammy (1930)
Big Boy (1930)
Hallelujah, I'm a Bum (1933)
Wonder Bar (1934)
Go Into Your Dance (1935)
The Singing Kid (1936)
Rose of Washington Square (1939)
Swanee River (1939)
Rhapsody in Blue (1945)
The Jolson Story (voice only, 1946)
Jolson Sings Again (voice only, 1949)

RADIO

Presenting Al Jolson (1932–33)
The Kraft Music Hall (1933–34, 1947–49)
Shell Chateau (1935–36)
The Lifebuoy Program (1936–39)

Madeline Kahn

"Clown with the Face of an Angel"

Known to most people for her comic film roles, Madeline Kahn actually began her career in the performing arts as a classical opera singer. Later performing in musical comedy shows and then in motion pictures, Kahn eventually earned the reputation as one of the outstanding comic actresses in the industry. As a comedienne, Kahn has a unique ability to portray characters that exhibit seemingly contradictory traits: she can be physically sexy yet klutzy, vocally whining yet commanding, intellectually flighty yet conniving, and emotionally neurotic yet durable. Through all of these shifts and shades, she maintains a blank facial expression of neutrality and innocence. The film critic Rex Reed has dubbed Kahn "the clown with the face of an angel."

Madeline Kahn was born in Boston, Massachusetts, on September 29, 1942. Her original name was Madeline Gail Wolfson.

Kahn was raised in New York City. When she was very young, her parents separated. She lived with her mother, who supported the family by working as a secretary, an usher, a model, and a nightclub singer. When Madeline was about ten, her mother married a man named Kahn.

After Mrs. Kahn, bearing another child, abandoned her plans for a show-business career. However, she transferred her hopes to Madeline, who as a young girl was given lessons in piano, dance, and voice. She made her first professional appearance singing on the *Children's Hour*, a New York City radio program.

At Martin Van Buren High School in Queens, New York, young Kahn participated in several plays. At Hofstra University, she majored in drama for two years and then switched her major to music and later to speech, intending to become a speech therapist. Meanwhile, she continued her musical training and performances: she took private singing lessons, appeared as a classical singer in university productions, performed in an off-campus opera workshop, and worked as a singing waitress in a German restaurant.

Kahn graduated from Hofstra in 1964. She then taught for a while at a public school in Levittown, New York, but soon found that she did not care for this type of work.

Returning to show business, Kahn performed as a singing waitress in Bellmore, Long Island. She then went to New York City where she was cast in the chorus of the City Center's revival of Cole Porter's *Kiss Me, Kate* (1965). When its run was completed, Kahn joined the Green Mansions repertory group in upstate New York, where she sang opera and light opera during the next two years.

Kahn made her Broadway debut in the musical comedy *New Faces of 1968* (1968), in which she sang "Das Chicago Song," a parody of Bertolt Brecht and Kurt Weill musicals. In November 1968 she played the female lead in Leonard Bernstein's musical *Candide*, which was presented at New York's Lincoln Center honoring the composer's fiftieth birthday.

The late 1960s and early 1970s were produc-

Madeline Kahn

tive years for Kahn. She appeared in satirical revues at New York City's Upstairs at the Downstairs club, she performed in the Broadway musicals *Promenade* (1969) and *Two by Two* (1970), and she was a regular on the TV series *Comedy Tonight* (1970). In the Broadway drama *Boom Boom Room* (1973), she gave an impressive performance as Chrissy, a shallow, ambitious go-go dancer who is progressively degraded. In addition, she made numerous guest appearances on national TV talk shows hosted by Johnny Carson, Dick Cavett, Mike Douglas, David Frost, and Merv Griffin.

It was Kahn's film performances, however, that made her a star. She made her movie debut by playing Ryan O'Neal's shrewish, frustrated fiancee in *What's Up, Doc?* (1972). Kahn's comic performance nearly stole the show from the film's star, Barbra Streisand.

In her next movie, *Paper Moon* (1973), Kahn once again received accolades for her supporting role. She portrayed Trixie Delight, a Depression-era carnival dancer who teams up with a con man, played by Ryan O'Neal.

In Mel Brooks's western-movie spoof *Blazing*

Saddles (1974), Kahn gave one of her most hilarious performances. She played the saloon singer Lili von Shtupp, a devastating burlesque of Marlene Dietrich's style in the famous German film *The Blue Angel* (1930) and in the American Western *Destry Rides Again* (1939). Kahn's sexy Lili sneered, sulked, lisped, and pouted throughout this outrageously funny movie.

In Mel Brooks's horror-movie spoof *Young Frankenstein* (1974), Kahn played the role of Elizabeth, the primping, finicky fiancee of Dr. Frankenstein, played by Gene Wilder. Then in Gene Wilder's *The Adventure of Sherlock Holmes' Smarter Brother* (1975), a takeoff on nineteenth-century detective stories, she played Jenny Hill, a music-hall singer (and another sex tease) who constantly changes her identity. In Mel Brooks's *High Anxiety* (1977), a spoof of Alfred Hitchcock thrillers, Kahn portrayed Victoria Brisbane, a glamorous socialite. Kahn also starred in Brooks's *History of the World, Part I*.

In 1983 Kahn acted in the play *Blithe Spirit*; began her own TV situation-comedy series, *Oh, Madeline*; and made her Carnegie Hall debut by narrating a concert version of Offenbach's operetta *La Perichole*. She then appeared in the movies *Slapstick of Another Kind* (1984), *City Heat* (1984), and *Clue* (1985). During the 1987 to 1988 TV season, she appeared in the sitcom *Mr. President*. In 1989 she played Billie Dawn, a role made famous by Judy Holliday, in a Broadway revival of the classic comedy *Born Yesterday*.

In the 1990s Kahn continued to divide her time between TV, film, and stage roles. On the stage Kahn played Gorgeous Teitelbaum in the comedy-drama *The Sisters Rosensweig* (1992). Her film work included *Mixed Nuts* (1994) and *Nixon* (1995). Beginning in 1996 she played a recurring role on the TV sitcom *Cosby*.

Promenade (1969)
Two by Two (1970)
Boom Boom Room (1973)
Marco Polo Sings a Solo (1977)
She Loves Me (1977)
On the Twentieth Century (1978)
Blithe Spirit (1983)
La Perichole (1983)
Born Yesterday (1989)
The Sisters Rosensweig (1992–93)

FILMS

What's Up, Doc? (1972)
Paper Moon (1973)
From the Mixed-up Files of Mrs. Basil E. Frankweiler (1973)
Blazing Saddles (1974)
Young Frankenstein (1974)
At Long Last Love (1975)
The Adventure of Sherlock Holmes' Smarter Brother (1975)
High Anxiety (1977)
The Cheap Detective (1978)
The Muppet Movie (1979)
Simon (1980)
Happy Birthday, Gemini (1980)
Wholly Moses! (1980)
First Family (1980)
History of the World, Part I (1981)
Yellowbeard (1983)
Slapstick of Another Kind (1984)
City Heat (1984)
Clue (1985)
My Little Pony (1986)
Betsy's Wedding (1990)
For Richer, for Poorer (TV, 1992)
Mixed Nuts (1994)
Nixon (1995)
For Love Alone (TV, 1997)
Judy Berlin (1999)

SELECTED PERFORMANCES:

STAGE

Kiss Me, Kate (1965)
Upstairs at the Downstairs (1966)
New Faces of 1968 (1968)

TV

Comedy Tonight (1970)
Oh, Madeline (1983–84)
Mr. President (1987–88)
New York News (1995)
Cosby (1996–)

Danny Kaye

For the last thirty or more years of his life, Danny Kaye reigned as the world's undisputed prince of clowns. His work in behalf of UNICEF took him around the globe many times, and his humor—largely based on the universally understandable techniques of pantomime, mugging, and nonsense singing—won him the affection and admiration of people everywhere.

Danny Kaye was born of Russian immigrant parents in New York City, New York, on January 18, 1913. His original name was David Daniel Kaminski (sometimes spelled Kominski or Kominsky).

Kaye grew up in the Brownsville section of Brooklyn, one of the toughest districts in New York City. Even as a child he loved to make people laugh, and he often entertained his neighbors by singing and clowning around. During his school years he enjoyed and participated in many sports, which helped him to develop the strength, coordination, and sense of timing that he later applied to his physically demanding stage and film routines.

In his early teens Kaye got a job as a messenger boy in the office of a dentist, Dr. Samuel Fine. The doctor's teenage daughter, Sylvia, developed a crush on Kaye, but he was so busy that he never paid any attention to her. One day Dr. Fine caught his young employee making a kind of needlepoint design on a piece of wood with a dental drill. The doctor fired the boy on the spot.

Shortly after that incident, Kaye dropped out of high school and began trying to break into show business. His early efforts, such as performing at local parties, did not lead anywhere, and he had to take odd jobs for a while.

In 1929 Kaye went to work on the borscht circuit. There he combined the jobs of waiter, singer, actor, and comedian. His principal task was simply to keep the guests amused, which he often did by falling into the swimming pool—fully clothed, straw hat and all. In the language of the entertainment world, Danny was a toomler, that is, a creator of tumult.

Kaye continued to work as a toomler during the summers of 1930 to 1932. Finally, in the summer of 1933, he got a job as a full-fledged entertainer on the borscht circuit. That same year he was asked to join the dancing team of Dave Harvey and Kathleen Young. They formed a group called the Three Terpsichoreans. On the opening night of their show in Utica, New York, Kaye, an inexperienced dancer, accidentally fell during the performance. The audience began to laugh and applaud. Harvey whispered to him, "They love it. Don't get up." Kaye, in a false whisper that could be heard throughout the auditorium, replied, "I can't get up. I've split my pants!" Kaye's clowning became a regular part of the act, which played at vaudeville and burlesque theaters.

Late in 1933 the Three Terpsichoreans joined a revue troupe. The troupe worked its way westward across the United States and then sailed to Asia in February 1934. By then Kaye was singing and performing monologues in addition to dancing. To appeal to non-English-speaking audiences in Asian countries, Kaye learned to tell his stories in pantomime, to show emotions by making faces, and to entertain with scat singing, which consists of the expressive vocalizing of meaningless syllables with an occasional recognizable word for emphasis.

After the Asian tour ended, Kaye got a number of minor engagements in the United States. For a while he toured with the famous fan dancer Sally Rand, holding her fans to ensure that she was properly (that is, minimally) covered during her act. In 1938 he was hired for an important engagement at a London cabaret, but he failed to impress the British.

Kaye's career was at a standstill. He simply could not find the right material for his personality. Then, in 1939, he went to the Keystone Theater in New York City to audition for a job. Seated at the piano in the theater was an attractive brunette who looked vaguely familiar. She glanced up, smiled shyly, and said, "I know you, but I bet you don't remember me." It was Sylvia Fine, daughter of Dr. Samuel Fine. She was also the woman destined to change Danny Kaye's career and life.

They both got jobs that day, she as a pianist and songwriter and he as a performer, for *The Sunday Night Revue*. The show folded after only one night, but it was just the beginning for Kaye and Fine. That summer they worked together again, putting on *The Straw Hat Revue* at Camp Tamiment, a Jewish resort camp in the Poconos in Pennsylvania. In the autumn the show made it to Broadway, where Kaye finally began to develop a reputation and a following.

The new boost to his career can be traced directly to Sylvia Fine's sparkling melodies and absurd lyrics, perfectly tailored to showcase Kaye's personality and talent for dialect singing and for patter (humorous, rapid-fire) songs. There was, for instance, "Anatole of Paris," in which Kaye sang as a schizophrenic modiste with blue hair.

In early 1940 Kaye and Fine were married. They had one child, Dena, who became a successful writer.

Later in 1940 Kaye was hired at the elite New

Danny Kaye

York City nightclub La Martinique. After a shaky start, he was calmed down and technically advised by Sylvia. Soon he settled into a tremendously successful, now legendary, engagement. His biggest single song success at that time was Sylvia's "Stanislavsky," in which Kaye, in Russian dialect, poked fun at the Soviet artists of the Moscow Art Theater, where students were taught to "become" inanimate objects.

Thereafter, Sylvia continued to be the most important force in his career, not only writing much of his material but also serving as his personal coach and critic.

Kaye's performances at La Martinique led to a part in the major Broadway musical *Lady in the Dark* in early 1941. Later that year he appeared in another stage show, *Let's Face It*.

When the United States entered World War II Kaye tried to enlist for military service, but he

Danny Kaye sings to an attentive group of schoolchildren in Hans Christian Andersen.

was rejected because he had a sacroiliac problem. He then aided the war effort by appearing at benefits and rallies to help sell war bonds and by performing at military camps and hospitals. He also appeared in the USO tours in Europe.

During the war Kaye began to make movies through which his talent became known worldwide. His first film was *Up in Arms* (1944). There followed a series of movies designed as vehicles for Kaye's unique comedic and musical versatility. Through the 1940s there were *Wonder Man* (1945), *The Kid from Brooklyn* (1946), *The Secret Life of Walter Mitty* (1947), *A Song Is Born* (1948), and *The Inspector General* (1949).

One of his most endearing performances came in his portrayal of the title character in the musical film *Hans Christian Anderson* (1952). He also sang in the movies *On the Riviera* (1951), *Knock on Wood* (1954), *White Christmas* (1958), *The Five Pennies* (1959), *On the Double* (1961), *Pinocchio* (TV, 1976), and *Peter Pan* (TV, 1976).

Kaye proved himself as a straight actor as well, notably in the films *Me and the Colonel* (1958), in which he played a Jewish refugee fleeing 1940 France in the company of an anti-Semitic Polish colonel; *The Man from the Diner's Club* (1963); *The Madwoman of Chaillot* (1969); and *Skokie* (TV, 1981), in which he played a Holocaust survivor confronting resurgent Nazism in contemporary America.

Kaye also performed on radio and TV. He hosted *The Danny Kaye Show* on radio (1945-46) and the very successful TV variety series of the same name (1963-67).

Also notable was his return, after a nearly thirty year absence, to the Broadway stage in the musical *Two by Two* (1970), based on the biblical story of Noah. But he always preferred the freedom of concert appearances, where he could exercise his ability to improvise. Kaye, though he could not read music, frequently appeared on the podium with major orchestras, such as the Israel Philharmonic, conducting them with inspired hilarity.

He maintained his love of sports. In 1976 he became a founder and part owner of the Seattle Mariners professional baseball team. In 1981 he sold most, and in 1983 the remainder, of his interest in the club.

The dominant factor in Kaye's life for many years was his work in behalf of the United Nations International Children's Emergency Fund (UNICEF). From 1953 on he was UNICEF's official ambassador-at-large to the world's children. He went into remote areas of Europe, Asia, Africa, and Latin America to visit children who were undernourished, diseased, or orphaned by war. Exuding an obviously genuine affection for them, he entertained the children while teams of UNICEF workers administered medical and other aid.

In 1957 he hosted the TV program *The Secret Life of Danny Kaye*, in which he presented children of various countries to demonstrate the work of UNICEF. In 1983, while Kaye was recuperating from a successful heart bypass operation, UNICEF saluted him for his thirty years of service by naming him as an honorary delegate to the UNICEF Executive Board.

Kaye did not slow down much after his surgery. On January 1, 1984, he acted as the grand marshal of the Rose Parade. He also continued to make UNICEF tours and to appear as a conductor. In September 1985, for example, he comically conducted the Los Angeles Philharmonic Orchestra at the Hollywood Bowl in a benefit for a musician's fund.

Complications stemming from his operation finally took their toll, and Kaye died in Los Angeles on March 3, 1987.

Because his humor was never unkind, was always solidly based in humility, was universal in appeal, and was channeled into helping the world's children, Kaye was internationally recognized as one of humanity's greatest treasures and as an independent ambassador of goodwill to people everywhere.

SELECTED PERFORMANCES

STAGE

The Sunday Night Revue (1939)
The Straw Hat Revue (1939)
Lady in the Dark (1941)
Let's Face It (1941)
Two by Two (1970)

FILMS

Up in Arms (1944)
Wonder Man (1945)
The Kid From Brooklyn (1946)
The Secret Life of Walter Mitty (1947)
A Song Is Born (1948)
The Inspector General (1949)
On the Riviera (1951)
Hans Christian Andersen (1952)
Knock on Wood (1954)
White Christmas (1954)
Assignment Children (UNICEF short, 1955)
The Court Jester (1956)
Me and the Colonel (1958)
Merry Andrew (1958)
The Five Pennies (1959)
On the Double (1961)
The Man from the Diner's Club (1963)
The Madwoman of Chaillot (1969)
Pinocchio (TV, 1976)
Peter Pan (TV, 1976)
Skokie (TV, 1981)

RADIO

The Danny Kaye Show (1945-56)

TV

The Danny Kaye Show (1963-67)

Jack Klugman

Oscar Madison and Dr. Quincy

For many years Jack Klugman was a dependable, but relatively unknown, character actor on TV, in film, and in the theater. Then, in the early seventies, Klugman hit it big by starring as Oscar Madison in the popular TV sitcom *The Odd Couple* (1970–75). He later played the title role in the dramatic TV series *Quincy, M.E.* (1977–83).

Jack Klugman was born in Philadelphia, Pennsylvania, on April 27, 1922. He studied drama at the Carnegie Institute of Technology in Pittsburgh and at the American Theater Wing in New York City. He appeared in several plays when he was in his late twenties, which included a touring company of *Mister Roberts* (1950-51), and he made his Broadway debut in a revival of *Golden Boy* (1952) when he was thirty. Two years later he was offered a regular role in the short-lived TV soap opera *The Greatest Gift*.

Klugman made his film debut in *Timetable* (1956). The following year he gave a memorable performance as one of the jurors in the movie *Twelve Angry Men* (1957).

During the late 1950s and early 1960s Klugman received steady work as a character actor. Noteable performances at this time included a successful run, opposite Ethel Merman, in the famed Broadway musical *Gypsy*; the film *Cry Terror* (1958); and the film *Days of Wine and Roses* (1962). He also made guest appearances on TV series such as *Ben Casey*, *Playhouse Ninety*, *Studio One*, *Twilight Zone*, and *The Untouchables*. In 1964 he had a regular role in the TV comedy series *Harris against the World*.

A turning point in Klugman's career occurred in 1965, when he succeeded Walter Matthau in the role of Oscar Madison in Neil Simon's sensational Broadway comedy *The Odd Couple*. When the play was made into a TV series five years later, Klugman was again offered the role of Oscar Madison, which he played to perfection opposite Tony Randall's equally brilliant Felix Unger, Madison's roommate. The two men, Unger obsessively neat and Madison easygoing and sloppy, made their match as New York's beloved odd couple. The hit series ran until 1975, and made Jack Klugman (and Oscar Madison) a household name.

Many episodes of *The Odd Couple* featured the actress Brett Somers as Oscar's ex-spouse, Blanche. In real life Klugman and Somers had married in 1956. They had two children, David and Adam, before divorcing in 1978.

After *The Odd Couple* ended its TV run Klugman appeared in the films *Two Minute Warning* (1976) and *One of My Wives Is Missing* (TV, 1976). Then, much to the surprise of those who thought Klugman would be handicapped as an actor because TV viewers so closely identified him with the Oscar Madison character, he created a colorful, well-rounded new character in the TV crime-drama series *Quincy, M.E.* (pilot, 1976; series, 1977–83). As a medical examiner in the Los Angeles coroner's office, Dr. Quincy (Klugman) solved crimes and espoused humanitarian causes, many of them directly related to current real-life issues, such as pollution, mental health, and "orphan drugs" (medicines for diseases that are too rare to be economically profitable for drug companies to produce). Klugman reached a new peak in his career with his passionate portrayal of the emotionally involved and professionally committed Dr. Quincy.

After *Quincy, M.E.* ended, Klugman worked on a number of projects. In 1984 he starred as Lyndon Johnson in a California stage production of the one-man show *Lyndon.* He played a father in conflict with his son in the TV comedy series *You Again?* during the 1986 to 1987 season. In 1989 he appeared in the made-for-TV movie *Around the World in Eighty Days.*

However, he was then stricken with a major illness. A heavy smoker for many years, Klugman was diagnosed with throat cancer in 1973. By 1989 his condition was so bad that one of his vocal cords had to be surgically removed. He lost control of his voice and thought his career was over, but his old friend and costar Tony Randall boosted Klugman's morale and encouraged him to work again. With the help of therapy, Klugman bounced back, and in 1991 he and Randall appeared together in a one-night Broadway revival of the original *The Odd Couple.* They later made a movie sequel to their TV series, *The Odd Couple: Together Again* (TV, 1993), and appeared in a four-month revival of the original play in London (1996). Klugman and Randall also performed together on Broadway in *Three Men on a Horse* (1993) and in Neil Simon's comedy *The Sunshine Boys* (1997–98).

Since his illness Klugman has tried to spend more time with his companion, Barbara Neugass, and on his horse farm in Temecula, California. His horse Jaklin Klugman took third place in the 1980 Kentucky Derby.

Jack Klugman

The Odd Couple (1965, 1991, 1996)
*The Sudden and Accidental Re-education of Horse
    Johnson* (1968)
Lyndon (1984)
I'm Not Rappaport (1987)
Three Men on a Horse (1993)
The Sunshine Boys (1997–98)

SELECTED PERFORMANCES:

STAGE

Stevedore (1949)
Saint Joan (1949)
Bury the Dead (1950)
Mister Roberts (1950)
Golden Boy (1952)
Coriolanus (1954)
A Very Special Baby (1956)
Gypsy (1959)

FILMS

Timetable (1956)
Twelve Angry Men (1957)
Cry Terror (1958)
Days of Wine and Roses (1962)
Act One (1963)
I Could Go On Singing (1963)
The Yellow Canary (1963)
Fame Is the Name of the Game (TV, 1966)
The Detective (1968)
The Split (1968)

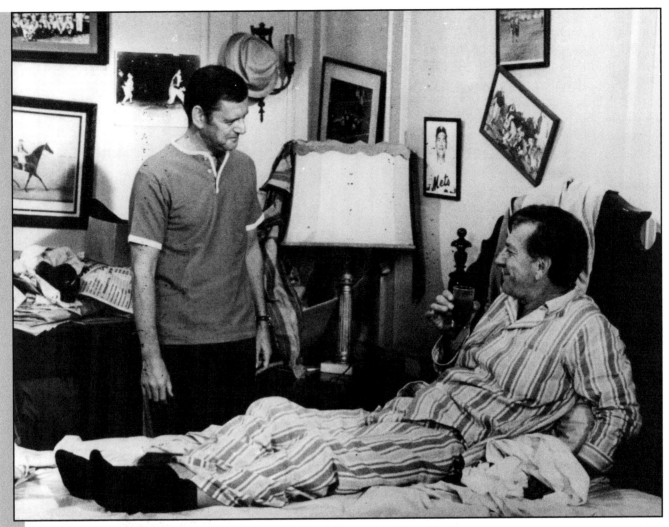

Tony Randall (left) and Jack Klugman in The Odd Couple

Goodbye, Columbus (1969)
Who Says I Can't Ride a Rainbow! (1971)
Poor Devil (TV, 1973)
The Underground Man (TV, 1974)
One of My Wives Is Missing (TV, 1976)
Two Minute Warning (1976)
Around the World in Eighty Days (TV, 1989)
The Odd Couple: Together Again (TV, 1993)
Parallel Lives (TV, 1994)

Dead God (1996)
The Twilight of the Golds (TV, 1997)

TV

The Greatest Gift (1954–55)
Harris against the World (1964–65)
The Odd Couple (1970–75)
Quincy, M.E. (1977–83)
You Again? (1986–87)

Harvey Korman

Master of Sketch Comedy

Harvey Korman has long been an effective comedy character actor in theatrical and made-for-TV movies. He's best known, however, for his performances in comedy sketches on the variety series *The Danny Kaye Show* (1963–67) and *The Carol Burnett Show* (1967–77).

Harvey Herschel Korman was born in Chicago, Illinois, on February 15, 1927. His parents separated when he was four, and he was raised by his mother. "My childhood stunk," he later admitted. "We were poor, and there's the no-father bit."

When Korman was in seventh grade, he joined an after-school theater workshop. Through the workshop he got some juvenile roles in industrial films. Later, he appeared in plays at Senn High School.

After attending Wright College of the City Colleges of Chicago and serving in the United States Naval Reserve (1945–46), Korman studied acting for four years (1946–50) at the Goodman School of Drama in Chicago. In 1950 he moved to New York City, where he shared an apartment with another aspiring young actor, Tom Bosley. By November of that year Korman had a walk-on role in *The Tower beyond Tragedy*, and the following month he played a small part as an Arab in *Captain Brassbound's Conversion*. But he soon realized that further advancement within the theater does not come easily.

For the next ten years Korman worked odd jobs while struggling to make it as an actor. He went back to the Midwest and performed in stock productions in Chicago and Milwaukee. He then returned to New York City, where he became so despondent over his lack of success that he contemplated suicide. Psychotherapy saved him, however, and he returned to Chicago where he began to work again.

In 1960 Korman married Donna Ehlert, a fashion model and charm-school teacher whom he had met on a blind date in Milwaukee. They had two children—a daughter, Maria, and a son, Christopher—before divorcing in 1977. In 1982 he married Deborah Fritz, with whom he had two more daughters, Katherine and Laura.

In the early 1960s Korman's career finally took off. Seymour Berns, who had directed him in a Chicago production of *Mr. and Mrs.*, invited Korman to California to appear on the TV variety series *The Red Skelton Show*, which Berns directed. Korman performed on that program several times and also made guest appearances on other TV shows, such as *Dennis the Menace*, *The Donna Reed Show*, and *Dr. Kildare*.

In 1963 Korman got his big break. Through Berns, he got a job as a regular member of the supporting cast in the new TV variety series *The Danny Kaye Show*. Korman soon proved to be a master of sketch comedy on TV. A brilliant straight man for Danny Kaye, he played a Nazi prison-camp commandant, a Gypsy fiddler, and many other roles.

In 1967 that series ended and Korman joined the cast of *The Carol Burnett Show*. He stayed with the show for ten years, becoming during that time

Harvey Korman

Harvey Korman

one of TV's preeminent comedy-sketch performers. He often appeared as Carol Burnett's husband. Many of the sketches poked fun at specific Hollywood movies or TV soap operas.

While at the peak of his TV fame, Korman described himself as not a comedian but "an actor doing comedy." "I don't look for gags," he said. "I look for characters."

In 1977 Korman left *The Carol Burnett Show* and made a pilot for *The Harvey Korman Show*. In 1978 the weekly series began, but it lasted only five months. During the 1980 to 1981 TV season he

costarred in the TV comedy series *The Tim Conway Show*. In both his own series and Conway's, Korman continued to show his expertise in sketch comedy.

Korman began to appear in movies in the early 1960s. He gave particularly fine performances in the satire *Lord Love a Duck* (1966), in the romantic comedy *The April Fools* (1969), and as the phony king in the musical *Huckleberry Finn* (1974).

In the seventies Korman joined the goup of actors and actresses who were regularly cast in Mel Brooks's comedies. In *Blazing Saddles* (1974) Korman was Hedley Lamarr, an unctuous, land-grabbing lawyer. In *High Anxiety* (1977) he again played a villain, the sadomasochistic psychiatrist Dr. Charles Montague. He also appeared in Brooks's *History of the World, Part I* (1981).

Korman showed great dramatic depth in the biopic *Bud and Lou* (TV, 1978), a film about the unhappy private lives of the comedy team of Bud Abbott and Lou Costello. Korman poignantly portrayed the epileptic, heavy-drinking straight man Abbott.

From the mid-1970s to the mid-1980s Korman starred in a number of films, many made-for-TV, including *The Love Boat* (TV, 1976), *Herbie Goes Bananas* (1980), *Trail of the Pink Panther* (1982), *Carpool* (TV, 1983), and *Alice in Wonderland* (TV, 1985). In 1986 he was cast in the comedy series *Leo and Liz in Beverly Hills*. Here he played an upstart trying to fit in among the rich and famous. Korman also starred in the funny but short-lived sitcom *The Nutt House* (1989).

In the 1990s Korman was especially active in movies. These included *Betrayal of the Dove* (1993); *Radioland Murders* (1994); *The Flintstones* (1994), as the voice of the Dictabird; and *Jingle All the Way* (1996).

SELECTED PERFORMANCES:

FILMS

Living Venus (1961)
Gypsy (1962)
The Last of the Secret Agents? (1966)
Lord Love a Duck (1966)
The Man Called Flintstone (1966)
Three Bites of the Apple (1967)
Don't Just Stand There (1968)
The April Fools (1969)
Three's a Crowd (TV, 1969)
Suddenly Single (TV, 1971)
Blazing Saddles (1974)
Huckleberry Finn (1974)
The Love Boat (TV, 1976)
High Anxiety (1977)
Bud and Lou (TV, 1978)
Americathon (1979)
Herbie Goes Bananas (1980)
First Family (1980)
History of the World, Part I (1981)
Trail of the Pink Panther (1982)
The Invisible Woman (TV, 1983)
Carpool (TV, 1983)
Alice in Wonderland (TV, 1985)
The Longshot (1986)
Munchies (1987)
Crash Course (TV, 1988))
Based on an Untrue Story (TV, 1993)
Betrayal of the Dove (1993)
Radioland Murders (1994)
The Flintstones (voice-only, 1994)
Dracula: Dead and Loving It (1995)
Jingle All the Way (1996)

TV

The Danny Kaye Show (1963–67)
The Carol Burnett Show (1967–77)
The Harvey Korman Show (1978)
The Tim Conway Show (1980–81)
Leo and Liz in Beverly Hills (1986)
The Nutt House (1989)

Bert Lahr

Cowardly Lion

Bert Lahr is best known for his comic, heart-warming portrayal of the Cowardly Lion in the 1939 film classic *The Wizard of Oz*, but he was far more than a one-role performer. The last great American comedian to be nurtured in classic burlesque, Lahr eventually became one of the few performers to triumph not only in low comedy and high comedy but also in literary drama.

Bert Lahr was born in New York City, New York, on August 13, 1895. His original name was Irving Lahrheim. His father was German-born and his mother was of German descent. For the first six years of his life Lahr spoke only German.

As a youngster, Lahr enjoyed making his friends laugh by clowning around, and he often earned money by street singing in his neighborhood, the Bronx. He first discovered the thrill of performing on stage when he performed in his eighth-grade class show.

Lahr disliked the regimentation of school, and he paid little attention to his studies, though he loved to read on his own. When he was ordered to repeat the eighth grade, he simply dropped out of school at the age of fourteen. For six months he did odd jobs. Then, in 1910, he began to find work in various professional kid acts (shows in which kids satirized classroom life). Irving Lahrheim became Bert Lahr.

In 1917 Lahr entered burlesque. Soon thereafter he established a common-law marriage with Mercedes Delpino, a chorus girl whom he had met in 1916. They had one child, Herbert.

In burlesque Lahr began to carve his individual identity as a "Dutch" (that is, German-dialect) comic out of the block of low-comedy stock humor. He experimented with funny gestures and faces, and he learned how to build humorous situations as opposed to merely telling unrelated jokes. Much of his humor was based on exaggerated dialect and on malapropisms, as in this passage from a song: "Ouououououououooch—how dot voman could cook!—Her oyshters and fishes were simply—[in sensuous delight] malicious!"

By the early 1920s burlesque was in trouble because of competition from theater revues and silent films. So, in 1922 Lahr graduated from burlesque to vaudeville.

In vaudeville he teamed up with his wife Mercedes for the comedy sketch *What's the Idea?* Mercedes played a sensual woman, while Lahr was a drunken, ill-dressed, wild-spirited policeman. The line "What's the idea?" played a prominent part in the sketch. And when he took his bows, he yelled at the audience, "What's the idea? That's the ideeeea?"

In 1927 Lahr made the step up to Broadway by appearing in the revue *Harry Delmar's Revels*, followed by the musical comedy *Hold Everything* (1928). In 1929 he made his first movie, *Faint Heart*.

Even as his career was skyrocketing, his relationship with Mercedes was disintegrating. She began to suffer from mental illness, and in 1930 she was committed to an institution.

Jack Haley, Ray Bolger, Judy Garland, and the inimitable Cowardly Lion of Bert Lahr.

Lahr's stock soon rose so high that the grand Broadway impresario Florenz Ziegfeld picked him to star in the last Ziegfeld extravaganza, *Hot-Cha!* (1932). After Ziegfeld's death in 1932 his competitor George White developed close association with the young comedian. In *George White's Music Hall Varieties* (1932) Lahr ventured for the first time into satire, spoofing the English matinee idol Clifton Webb. Other 1930s stage shows featuring Lahr included *Life Begins at 8:40* (1934), *George White's Scandals of 1936* (1935), and *Du Barry Was a Lady* (1939).

Hollywood also beckoned. In 1931 he made a filmed version of *Flying High*, in which he had appeared onstage the previous year.

In the later 1930s he made several movies, notably *The Wizard of Oz* (1939), in which he played the Cowardly Lion. The film's lyricist, E.Y. Harburg, had promoted Lahr for the part because "everybody's heart goes out to him. He must be somebody who embodies all this pathos and sweetness, yet puts on this comic bravura. Bert had that quality to such a wonderful degree."

Lahr, as the Cowardly Lion, incongruously and hilariously used New York City colloquial pronunciations (such as *noive* for *nerve*) even though the character was set in the imaginary land of Oz. Absolute gems of comic-song interpretation were Lahr's renditions of "If I Only Had the Nerve" and "If I Were King of the Forest." He gave both humor and humanity to his Cowardly Lion. It was the role by which he remained best known for the rest of his life.

In 1940 Lahr married Mildred Schroeder, whom he had met in 1931 when she was a chorus girl. They had two children, John and Jane. John became a drama critic and wrote the definitive biography of his father, *Notes on a Cowardly Lion* (1969).

In the early 1940s Lahr continued to make films, such as *Ship Ahoy* (1942) and *Meet the People* (1944). The later years of that decade were spent mostly on the stage, as in *Burlesque* (1946) and *Make Mine Manhattan* (1948). In the early 1950s he had roles in the play *Two on the Aisle* (1951) and the movies *Mr. Universe* (1951) and *Rose Marie* (1954).

In the late 1950s Lahr also began to appear on TV. He frequently performed his old revue routines on Ed Sullivan's variety show.

In 1956 Lahr played Estragon in Samuel Beckett's complex modernistic play *Waiting for Godot*. Lahr's approach was instinctive and theatrical, not intellectual. He saw the play as "two men trying to amuse themselves on earth by playing jokes and little games." His performance was universally praised.

Waiting for Godot opened a whole new chapter in Lahr's career. He began to appear in other great literary plays, such as televised productions of Shaw's *Androcles and the Lion* (1956) and Molière's *The School for Wives* (1956). In 1957 he starred in Feydeau's classic French farce *Hotel Paradiso*. In 1960 he played Bottom in Shakespeare's *A Midsummer Night's Dream* and, without any knowledge of the Bard's writings or tradition, won the Best Shakepeare Actor of the Year Award. In 1964 he starred in *Foxy*, a musical adaptation of Jonson's *Volpone*. His final work in the classics was as Pisthetairos in Aristophanes' *The Birds* (1966).

Lahr's last performance was in *The Night They Raides Minsky's* (1968), fittingly a story about burlesque. He died of cancer (not pneumonia as reported at the time) in New York City on December 4, 1967.

SELECTED PERFORMANCES:

STAGE

Harry Delmar's Revels (1927)
Hold Everything (1928)
Flying High (1930)
Hot-Cha! (1932)
George White's Music Hall Varieties (1932)
Life Begins at 8:40 (1934)
George White's Scandals of 1936 (1935)
The Show Is On (1936)
Du Barry Was a Lady (1939)
Seven Lively Arts (1944)
Harvey (1945)
Burlesque (1946)
Make Mine Manhattan (1948)
Two on the Aisle (1951)
Waiting for Godot (1956)
Hotel Paradiso (1957)
Visit to a Small Planet (1957)
The Girls against the Boys (1959)
Romanoff and Juliett (1959)
A Midsummer Night's Dream (1960)
The Beauty Part (1962)
Foxy (1966)
The Birds (1966)

FILMS

Faint Heart (1929)
Flying High (1931)
Happy Landing (1934)
Merry-Go-Round of 1938 (1937)
Love and Hisses (1938)
Just around the Corner (1938)
Josette (1938)
Zaza (1939)
The Wizard of Oz (1939)
Sing Your Worries Away (1942)
Ship Ahoy (1942)
Meet the People (1944)
Always Leave Them Laughing (1949)
Mr. Universe (1951)
Rose Marie (1954)
The Second Greatest Sex (1956)
Androcles and the Lion (TV, 1956)
The School for Wives (TV, 1956)
The Night They Raided Minsky's (1968)

Martin Landau

Distinctive Character Actor

Gaunt and swarthy, Martin Landau has often been cast in sinister roles. But his character acting skills are considerable, and he can play a wide range of parts. For example, he portrayed the kindhearted woodcarver Geppetto in *The Adventures of Pinocchio* (1996).

Martin Landau was born in New York City, New York, on June 20, probably 1930 (some sources give 1928, 1933, or 1934). He studied at the Art Students League and worked for a time as a staff artist and cartoonist with the *New York Daily News*, but his interest in theater took him to the Actors Studio in New York City, where he studied dramatics.

In 1951 Landau made his stage debut by appearing in *Detective Story* at a theater in Maine. That year he also gave his first performance in New York City, in the play *First Love* (1951). During the next few years, he acted in a number of plays, including *Goat Song* (1953) and *Middle of the Night* (1957).

In the late 1950s Landau began appearing in movies. He developed a reputation as a skilled character actor, performing in such films as *Pork Chop Hill* (1959), *North by Northwest* (1959), *Cleopatra* (1963), and *Nevada Smith* (1966).

Landau is best known to many for his work on the TV espionage-adventure series *Mission: Impossible* (1966-69). He played Rollin Hand, a master of disguise.

Also in *Mission: Impossible* was the actress Barbara Bain, whom Landau had married in 1957. They had two children—Susan, now a writer and producer, and Juliet, an actress—before divorcing.

After the *Mission Impossible*, series ended, Landau continued to be in demand in films and on television. He appeared in the popular film *They Call Me Mister Tibbs* (1970). In *Welcome Home, Johnny Bristol* (TV, 1972) he starred as a Vietnam veteran returning to an imaginary home in the United States. In the science-fiction TV series *Space: 1999* (1975–77) he starred as Commander John Koenig. Landau's wife, Barbara Bain, was also featured in the show.

Over the next two decades Landau had important roles in many films. In *The Fall of the House of Usher* (TV, 1982), Edgar Allan Poe's gothic horror story, he starred as Roderick Usher. He gave outstanding performances in *Without Warning* (1980), *Tucker: The Man and His Dream* (1988), and *Crimes and Misdemeanors* (1989).

The highlight of Landau's work in the 1990s was his portrayal of the famed horror-movie actor Bela Lugosi in the comedy-drama biopic *Ed Wood* (1994). He won that year's Oscar for Best Supporting Actor for his performance. Landau also impressed audiences in *By Dawn's Early Light* (TV, 1990), *Joseph* (TV, 1995), *The Adventures of Pinocchio* (1996), and *B.A.P.S.* (1997). In *Rounders* (1998) he played the mentor of a poker player.

Landau currently teaches acting at the Actors Studio West. His former students include Jack Nicholson and Oliver Stone. With two other partners, Landau has also formed a film production company, Firestorm Pictures.

STAGE

Detective Story (1951)
First Love (1951)
The Penguin (1952)
Stalag 17 (1952)
Goat Song (1953)
Middle of the Night (1957)

FILMS

Pork Chop Hill (1959)
North by Northwest (1959)
The Gazebo (1960)
Stagecoach to Dancers' Rock (1962)
Cleopatra (1963)
The Greatest Story Ever Told (1965)
The Hallelujah Trail (1965)
Nevada Smith (1966)
They Call Me Mister Tibbs (1970)
A Town Called Hell (1971)
Black Gunn (1972)
Welcome Home, Johnny Bristol (TV, 1972)
Savage (TV, 1973)
Strange Shadows in an Empty Room (1977)

Meteor (1979)
The Last Word (1979)
The Death of Ocean View Park (TV, 1979)
Without Warning (1980)
Alien's Return (1980)
The Harlem Globetrotters on Gilligan's   Island (TV, 1981)
Alone in the Dark (1982)
The Fall of the House of Usher (TV, 1982)
The Being (1983)
*The Return of the Six-Million-Dollar Man and the
    Bionic Woman* (TV, 1987)
Tucker: The Man and His Dream (1988)
Crimes and Misdemeanors (1989)
The Neon Empire (TV, 1989)
Real Bullets (1990)
Max and Helen (TV, 1990)
By Dawn's Early Light (TV, 1990)
Paint It Black (1990)
Firehead (1991)
Mistress (1992)
Legacy of Lies (TV, 1992)
12:01 (TV, 1993)
Eye of the Stranger (1993)
No Place to Hide (1993)

Sliver (1993)
Intersection (1994)
Ed Wood (1994)
Joseph (TV, 1995)
*The Adventures of
    Pinocchio* (1996)
City Hall (1996)
The Long Way Home
    (1997)
B.A.P.S. (1997)
Rounders (1998)
*Bonanno: A Godfather's
    Story* (TV, 1999)

TV

Mission: Impossible
    (1966–69)
Space: 1999 (1975–77)

Woody Allen instructs Martin Landau in Ed Wood.

Louise Lasser

Mary Hartman

Louise Lasser is probably best known as the star of the groundbreaking TV series *Mary Hartman, Mary Hartman* (1976-77). She has also played a wide range of roles in films and theatrical productions and is specifically associated with certain movies of Woody Allen, to whom she was married.

L ouise Lasser was born in New York City, New York, on April 11, 1939. She majored in political science for three years at Brandeis University near Boston, where she also appeared in student musicals. She did not graduate from Brandeis, but instead returned to New York City and studied acting with Sanford Meisner of the Neighborhood Playhouse School of the Theater. She also studied philosophy and literature at the New School for Social Research.

In 1962 Lasser made her Broadway debut, as Barbra Streisand's replacement in the musical comedy *I Can Get It for You Wholesale*. The following year Lasser began a promising career as a nightclub singer in New York City. But she was unable to continue her club work for very long because it made her excessively nervous.

In 1964 Lasser appeared in the off-Broadway improvisational revue *The Third Ear*. She then made her film debut, playing a small part in *What's New, Pussycat?* (1965). The movie was written by Woody Allen, who was in the film as well.

Lasser and Allen had met in 1961. In 1966 they married, and in 1970 they divorced. She appeared in several of Allen's film comedies, even after their breakup, including *Take the Money and Run* (1969), *Bananas* (1971), and *Everything You Always Wanted to Know about Sex* (*but Were Afraid to Ask)* (1972).

Lasser became nationally famous for playing the title role in the satirical TV soap opera *Mary Hartman, Mary Hartman* (1976-77). It was the first TV series to deal with such previously taboo subjects as adultery, anti-Semitism, venereal disease, and masturbation. As Mary Hartman, Lasser played a pigtailed, thirtyish, often bewildered housewife trying to face the modern world.

When *Mary Hartman, Mary Hartman* completed its run, Lasser returned to film. In Marty Feldman's brilliant religious satire *In God We Tru$t* (1980), Lasser had the role of a kindhearted prostitute who helps a monk (played by Feldman) adapt to life in the modern secular city. In *Crimewave* (1985) she portrayed a woman being pursued by killers. Lasser's later films include *Nightmare at Shadow Woods* (1987), *Modern Love* (1990), and *Sudden Manhattan* (1997). She has also appeared in a number of TV movies. Among them were *Just Me and You* (TV, 1978) and *For Ladies Only* (TV, 1981).

SELECTED PERFORMANCES:

STAGE

I Can Get It for You Wholesale (1962)
The Third Ear (1964)
Henry, Sweet Henry (1967)
Lime Green (1969)
The Chinese (1970)
Marie and Bruce (1980)

Louise Lasser

What's New, Pussycat? (1965)
Take the Money and Run (1969)
Bananas (1971)
Such Good Friends (1971)
Everything You Always Wanted to Know about Sex
    *(*but Were Afraid to Ask)* (1972)
Slither (1973)
Coffee, Tea, or Me? (TV, 1973)
Isn't It Shocking? (TV, 1973)
Just Me and You (TV, 1978)
Stardust Memories (1980)
In God We Tru$t (1980)
For Ladies Only (TV, 1981)
Crimewave (1985)
Nightmare at Shadow Woods (1987)
Surrender (1987)
Frankenhooker (1990)
Modern Love (1990)
The Night We Never Met (1993)
Sudden Manhattan (1997)
Happiness (1998)

TV

Mary Hartman, Mary Hartman (1976–77)
It's a Living (1981–82)

Sam Levene

Sour-Faced Character Actor

For over fifty years, Sam Levene was one of the most dependable, respected, and beloved character actors in America. His bushy eyebrows, prominent mustache, sour face, and pronounced New York City accent (despite his diction lessons) became familiar to millions of people through his stage and film appearances.

Sam Levene was born in Russia on August 28, 1905. His original name was Samuel Levine; early in his show-business career, he changed the *i* in his surname to an *e* so that he would not be confused with another actor of the time named Sam Levine.

Brought to the United States when he was two years old, Levene grew up in New York City. After graduating from Stuyvesant High School in 1923, he went to work in his older brother's dressmaking business.

In 1925, to further his career as a salesman, Levene attempted to rid himself of his Yiddish accent by enrolling in diction classes at the American Academy of Dramatic Arts. He soon became a full-time student at the academy, from which he graduated in 1927.

That year Levene made his Broadway debut, in *Wall Street*. For the next eight years he worked steadily on the stage, but he remained a relatively unknown actor until he played the role of Patsy, a racing addict, in *Three Men on a Horse* (1935). He made his movie debut in a filmed version (1936) of the same story.

Over the next forty-five years Levene regularly appeared on the New York City stage. Among his most successful roles were those of Gordon Miller, a producer desperately trying to keep his troupe together on a shoestring budget, in *Room Service* (1937); Officer Finkelstein, a Jewish policeman who must find the murderer of a Nazi diplomat, in *Margin for Error* (1939); and Sidney Black, an aggressive producer, in *Light Up the Sky* (1948). The role by which he became best known was that of the cocky Nathan Detroit in the famed Damon Runyon musical *Guys and Dolls* (1950). *In Fair Game* (1957), *Make a Million* (1960), and *Paris is Out!* (1970), Levene carried the shows, creating endearing comic characters out of even the most stereotyped Jewish role. He gave a magnificent performance as Al Lewis, an ex-vaudevillian, in the original Broadway production of Neil Simon's comedy *The Sunshine Boys* (1972). He also had important roles in *Heartbreak House* (1959) and *The Royal Family* (1975).

Levene was also in demand as a film actor. Among his early films were *After the Thin Man* (1936), *The Shopworn Angel* (1938), and *Golden Boy* (1939). During World War II, he appeared in *Action in the North Atlantic* (1943) and *The Purple Heart* (1944). In *The Killers* (1946) he played a detective, in *Boomerang* (1947) a reporter, and in *Brute Force* (1947) a prison inmate. He gave one of his most affecting performances as the gentle Jewish murder victim in *Crossfire* (1947), which was one of the earliest movies to take a stand against racial intolerance. Levene also starred in *The Babe Ruth Story* (1948), *Sweet Smell of Success* (1957), *Act One* (1963), and *And Justice for All* (1979).

Sam Levene

Sam Levene and Esther Rolle

Levene married Constance Hoffmann in 1953. They had one son, Joseph, before divorcing.

In 1980 Levene played his final role, as Samuel Horowitz in *Horowitz and Mrs. Washington*. He performed the part on Broadway and then again in Toronto. In December of that year he returned home to New York City. The last time he was seen alive was on Christmas Day. He died sometime between then and December 28, when his body was discovered by his son.

SELECTED PERFORMANCES:

STAGE

Wall Street (1927)
Jarnegan (1928)
Tin Pan Alley (1928)
Solitaire (1929)
Street Scene (1929)
Headquarters (1929)

This Man's Town (1930)
The Up and Up (1930)
Three Times the Hour (1931)
Wonder Boy (1931)
Dinner at Eight (1932)
Yellow Jack (1934)
The Milky Way (1934)
Spring Song (1934)
Three Men on a Horse (1935)
Room Service (1937)
Margin for Error (1939)
A Sound of Hunting (1945)
Light Up the Sky (1948,1970,1971,1975)
Guys and Dolls (1950)
The Matchmaker (1954)
The Hot Corner (1956)
Fair Game (1957)
Middle of the Night (1958)
Heartbreak House (1959)
The Good Soup (1960)
Make a Million (1960)
Devil's Advocate (1961)
Let It Ride (1961)
Seidman and Son (1962)
Café Crown (1964)
The Last Analysis (1964)
Fidelio (1965)
The Impossible Years (1966)
Don't Drink the Water (1968)
Three Men on a Horse (1969)
Paris Is Out! (1970,1971)
A Dream out of Time (1970)
The Sunshine Boys (1972)
Dreyfus in Rehearsal (1974)
Sabrina Fair (1975)
The Royal Family (1975)
The Prince of Grand Street (1978)
Goodnight Grandpa (1978)
Horowitz and Mrs. Washington (1980)

Three Men on a Horse (1936)
After the Thin Man (1936)
Yellow Jack (1938)
The Shopworn Angel (1938)
The Mad Miss Manton (1938)
Golden Boy (1939)
Married Bachelor (1941)
Shadow of the Thin Man (1941)
Sunday Punch (1942)
Sing Your Worries Away (1942)
Grand Central Murder (1942)
The Big Street (1942)
Destination Unknown (1942)
Action in the North Atlantic (1943)
I Dood It (1943)
Gung Ho! (1944)
The Purple Heart (1944)
Whistling in Brooklyn (1944)
The Killers (1946)
Boomerang (1947)
Brute Force (1947)
Crossfire (1947)
Killer McCoy (1948)
The Babe Ruth Story (1948)
Guilty Bystander (1950)
With These Hands (1950)
Dial 1119 (1950)
Three Sailors and a Girl (1953)
The Opposite Sex (1956)
Designing Woman (1957)
Sweet Smell of Success (1957)
Slaughter on Tenth Avenue (1957)
Kathy O' (1958)
Act One (1963)
A Dream of Kings (1969)
Last Embrace (1979)
. . . and Justice for All (1979)

Jerry Lewis

Great Clown

Jerry Lewis is America's last great clown. As a stand-up comic and a film actor, he has repeatedly proven himself to be the preeminent master of the clown's special forte—the blending of physical comedy and poignancy.

Lewis began his career as a stand-up comedian with goofy physical routines. Later his act became more sophisticated, though he by no means eschewed slapstick and mugging. Now his principal asset is sheer charisma.

As a film comedian Lewis uses mugging and wild bodily movements for much of his humor. He is also adept at disguises and multiple characterizations. At the heart of his comedy is the notion that one can reduce the pain of shyness and failure through cathartic laughter.

As a filmmaker (writer-director-star) Lewis tends to create episodic pictures. Individual episodes frequently turn into glorious moments of comic timing and visual inventiveness.

Jerry Lewis was born in Newark, New Jersey, on March 16, 1926. His original name was Joseph Levitch. He came from a show-business family: his father, Daniel Levitch (stage name, Danny Lewis) was one of the last vaudevillians, while his mother, Rachel Levitch (née Brodsky), was a pianist.

Young Lewis began experimenting with musical-comedy routines at an early age. When he was fifteen, he was expelled from Irvington (New Jersey) High School for punching the principal, who had made an anti-Semitic remark. He was transferred to Irvington Vocational High School, but on his sixteenth birthday, he quit school forever.

Lewis then became a professional performer. He used his father's professional surname as his stage name and adopted the first name Jerry because he wanted to avoid confusion with the comedian Joe. E. Lewis and the boxer Joe Louis. Soon, Lewis had a successful solo act at theaters in Baltimore, Philadelphia, Boston, and elsewhere.

In 1944 Lewis married Patti Palmer (real name, Esther Calonico), a singer whom he had met while both were working at a theater in Detroit. They had six sons—Gary, Ronnie, Scott, Chris, Anthony, and Joseph. Gary became a popular vocalist, led his own band, and appeared a number of times with his father in movies and on TV.

During the period of time after the collapse of his marriage, his career went through two years at low ebb. He performed on the borscht circuit, in theaters, and in nightclubs, but the work was not steady.

Then, in 1946 in New York City, Lewis was introduced to the singer Dean Martin by their mutual friend Sonny King, also a singer. Martin and Lewis soon formed a nightclub act. Martin's real name was Paul Dino Crocetti, and privately, Lewis always called him Paul, while Martin referred to Lewis as pallie, Jew, or pardner.

The crooning Dean Martin and clowning Jerry Lewis played off each other perfectly. Their act was a mix of prepared gags and ad-libs. While Martin tried to sing, Lewis would make faces, pop up with prop buckteeth, perform eccentric dances, and generally destroy the straight man, demolish the orchestra, and attack the audience (spilling food, putting cigars into drinks, and so on). The

Jerry Lewis

team quickly became the hottest act in show business, and in 1948 they hit the big time with their appearance at the Copacabana nightclub in New York City.

That year they also made their first TV appearances, performing on the first show of Ed Sullivan's *Toast of the Town* and on Milton Berle's *The Texaco Star Theater*. From 1949 to 1952 they hosted their own radio show, and from 1950 to 1955 they had their own TV series (rotating with other hosts on *The Colgate Comedy Hour*).

Meanwhile, the duo was making films, debuting in *My Friend Irma* (1949). They starred in a string of popular movies in the 1950s, including *At War with the Army* (1951), *Sailor Beware* (1952), *The Caddy* (1953), *Three Ring Circus* (1954), *You're Never Too Young* (1955), and their final movie together, *Hollywood or Bust* (1956).

In 1956 after at least two years of increasing tension between Martin and Lewis, and to the horror of their fans, the incomparable team of Dean Martin and Jerry Lewis split up. The most serious problems between them began when Martin exploded at being relegated to a clearly secondary role in *Three Ring Circus*. Even before then, Martin's contribution to the team's success was largely overlooked by filmmakers, critics, and fans (though not by Lewis). Martin finally rebelled, stating that he was tired of playing the stooge, and began to psychologically isolate himself from Lewis. And Lewis, emotionally drained by his efforts to renew the original chemistry between Martin and himself, initiated the legal dissolution of their partnership. Their last performance together was at the Copacabana on July 25, 1956.

Lewis's first film on his own was *The Delicate Delinquent* (1957). Playing the title role, he created one of his most memorable screen moments when, pretending to be a hoodlum, he feigned a knife attack on a woman social worker and warned her, "Stay away, baby. I'm flippin'."

During the 1960s Lewis made some of his most popular films. In *The Bellboy* (1960) he gave one of his finest performances, his brilliant slapstick skill equaling that of the masters of silent-film comedy. In *The Nutty Professor* (1963), Lewis played the title role without his usual idiot-kid image. *The Family Jewels* (1965) provided Lewis with a vehicle for a tour de force performance. He played seven roles: Willard, the chauffeur; Uncle

Jerry Lewis

James, the old ferryboat captain; Uncle Everett, the circus clown; Uncle Eddie, the airline pilot; Uncle Julius, the fashion photographer; Uncle Skylock, the private investigator; and Uncle Bugs, the gangster. Julius was a spinoff of the nutty professor, while the gap-toothed, cheerful, and optimistic—but wholly incompetent—Eddie ranks as one of Lewis's most inspired creations.

In his post-Martin films, Lewis has often served as producer, director, or writer, in addition to star. Examples include *The Delicate Delinquent* (producer), *The Bellboy* (producer, director, writer), *The Ladies' Man* (misspelled without the apostrophe in the film, 1961; producer, director, writer), *The Errand Boy* (1961; director, writer), *The Family Jewels* (producer, director), *The Big Mouth* (1967; producer, director, writer), and *Which Way to the Front?* (1970; producer, director).

In the early 1970s Lewis made *The Day the Clown Cried*, a film set in Germany during the Nazi era.

Jerry Lewis, the master of physical comedy.

He played the part of Helmut, once a great clown but now wasted by drinking that was brought on by his abhorrence of the Nazi regime. Helmut is arrested by the Gestapo, interned in a concentration camp, and forced into clowning to help control Jewish children being marched to the ovens. The film remains unreleased, locked up in Stockholm where it was made, because of ongoing litigation about lack of payments from the producer, Nathan Wachsberger.

After making *The Day the Clown Cried*, Lewis did not make any more films during the 1970s. In his autobiography, *Jerry Lewis in Person* (with Herb Gluck, 1982), he explained his action. Filmgoers were "crying out for happy entertainment," he wrote, but filmmakers were providing works "tainted by the grime of 'realism' and magnified on celluloid." The industry "was eroding under a heavy flood of X-rated films." Fed up, Lewis

stayed away from filmmaking for a number of years.

Lewis busied himself with other projects, however, notably his volunteer work as national chairman of the Muscular Dystrophy Association (MDA). He had become formally involved with battling the disease in 1950, when he banded together with others to help raise funds to create a muscular dystrophy facility that opened at Columbia University in 1959. In 1966 he gave his first annual *Jerry Lewis Labor Day Telethon* in behalf of MDA. The first two telethons were broadcast in the New York City area only, but since 1968 the show has been networked to many other parts of the country.

Lewis returned to films when he wrote, directed, and starred in *Hardly Working* (1981). In that film he played a circus clown who loses his job and tries various other lines of work, bungling them all. He also cowrote, directed and starred in *Cracking Up* (1983, originally released as *Smorgasbord*), a film about a misfit recalling his failures. In *The King of Comedy* (1983) Lewis played his first straight dramatic role, as a TV talk-show host kidnapped by a deranged would-be comedian played by Robert DeNiro.

In 1982 Lewis divorced his wife, Patti. In December of that year, just after he completed his part in *The King of Comedy*, he suffered a serious heart attack—so serious, in fact, that he was clinically dead for several seconds. Emergency double-bypass surgery was performed, and he recovered well. In 1983 he married the dancer Sandra, or SanDee (Sam) Pitnick, whom he had met when he hired her for a part in *Hardly Working*. Soon afterwards they moved from Los Angeles to Las Vegas, and in 1992 they adopted a daughter, Danielle.

From the mid-1980s to the mid-1990s, Lewis performed his comedy act in Las Vegas and other cities, and of course continued hosting his annual telethons. He also made more movies. He gave a powerful performance in the fact-based dramatic movie *Fight for Life* (TV, 1987), in which he portrayed Dr. Bernard Abrams, an optometrist who fights to get permission to use a special drug for his daughter's myoclonic epilepsy and then fights again to make the drug available to other children as well. Lewis's other films during the 1980s and 1990s included *Slapstick of Another Kind* (1984), *Mr. Saturday Night* (1992), and the Disney comedy *Funny Bones* (1995).

In 1995 Lewis was offered his first role in a Broadway show. He had always wanted to appear on Broadway, so he eagerly accepted. The role was that of Mr. Applegate, the devil, in a revival of the musical comedy classic *Damn Yankees*. "He's a mischievous kid, just an older one," Lewis said. Lewis played Mr. Applegate for 185 performances on Broadway, then toured the United States for two years with the show. In 1997 he began an extended international tour. Having been brought into the show in the middle of its original run Lewis made the role of Mr. Applegate entirely his own, adding his own quips to the original dialogue.

Lewis, more than any other comedian of his time, has generated a wide range of opinions about his abilities. Many American critics consider his "mugging" to be merely a species of low comedy, whereas many European critics rank his clowning antics as comparable to those of the great Charles Chaplin. Some commentators deplore his sentimentality, yet others see his efforts as reflections of a genuine social awareness and concern for the little guy. Perhaps, as is usual in such cases, the truth about the totality of his work lies between the extreme views of his unyielding disparagers and his fanatic followers. Yet, for his gift of countless hours of laughter to millions of ordinary viewers around the globe, he deserves to be ranked as one of the funniest men of his time. And for his courage to clown with compassion, Jerry Lewis, after the death of Red Skelton in 1997, can certainly now be regarded as America's reigning great clown.

SELECTED PERFORMANCES:

STAGE

Damn Yankees (1995–98)

FILMS

My Friend Irma (1949)
At War with the Army (1951)

A toothless Jerry in one of his priceless comic poses.

That's My Boy (1951)
Sailor Beware (1952)
Jumping Jacks (1952)
The Stooge (1953)
Scared Stiff (1953)
The Caddy (1953)
Money from Home (1954)
Living It Up (1954)
Three Ring Circus (1954)
You're Never Too Young (1955)
Artists and Models (1955)
Pardners (1956)
Hollywood or Bust (1956)
The Delicate Delinquent (1957)
The Sad Sack (1957)
Rock-a-bye Baby (1958)
The Geisha Boy (1958)
Don't Give Up the Ship (1959)
Visit to a Small Planet (1960)
The Bellboy (1960)
Cinderfella (1960)
The Ladies' Man (1961)
The Errand Boy (1961)
It's Only Money (1962)
The Nutty Professor (1963)
It's a Mad, Mad, Mad, Mad World (1963)
Who's Minding the Store? (1963)
The Patsy (1964)

Dean Martin and Jerry Lewis in Sailor Beware.

The Disorderly Orderly (1964)
The Family Jewels (1965)
Boeing Boeing (1965)
Three on a Couch (1966)
Way . . . Way Out (1966)
The Big Mouth (1967)
Don't Raise the Bridge, Lower the River (1968)
Hook, Line, and Sinker (1969)
Which Way to the Front? (1970)
Hardly Working (1981)
Cracking Up (1983, originally released as *Smorgasbord*)
The King of Comedy (1983)
Slapstick of Another Kind (1984)
Retenez-moi ou je fais un malheur (1984, Fr.; U.S., *To Catch a Cop*)

Fight for Life (TV, 1987)
Cookie (1989)
Mr. Saturday Night (1992)
Funny Bones (1995)
Arizona Dream (1995)

RADIO

The Martin and Lewis Show (1949–52)

TV

The Dean Martin, Jerry Lewis Show (1950–55, part of *The Colgate Comedy Hour*)
The Jerry Lewis Show (1963, 1967-69)
Will the Real Jerry Lewis Please Sit Down (animated, voice-only, 1970–72)
Wiseguy (1988–89)

Hal Linden

Barney Miller

Hal Linden first achieved star recognition as a performer in Broadway musicals. He later proved himself to be a serious actor in theatrical and made-for-TV movies. Today he is best known for his portrayal of a New York City police detective in the popular TV series *Barney Miller* (1975–82).

Hal Linden was born in New York City, New York, on March 20, 1931. His original name was Harold Lipshitz.

Linden graduated from the High School of Music and Art in New York City (1948) attended Queens College of the City University of New York (1948–50), and graduated with a B.B.A. degree from City College of the City University of New York (1952). After his college graduation, he spent two years in the army (1952–54). There he performed in revues for the special-services division.

Early in his show business career Linden was a saxophonist and singer. He performed in the bands of Sammy Kaye, Bobby Sherwood, and Boyd Raeburn.

Linden studied voice in New York City with Lou McCollogh from 1953 to 1956 and with John Mace from 1958 to 1964. From 1954 to 1955 Linden studied acting as well in New York City at the American Theater Wing. He also studied acting with Paul Mann and Lloyd Richards.

Linden made his stage debut as a member of the chorus in a stock-company production of the musical *Wonderful Town* in Hyannis, Massachusetts,

in 1955. He then worked in New York City as an understudy to Sydney Chaplin (son of Charles Chaplin) as Jeff Moses in the Broadway musical *Bells Are Ringing*. Linden succeeded Chaplin in the lead role in 1958. In the filmed version of *Bells Are Ringing* (1960) Linden had a minor role as the nightclub singer performing "The Midas Touch."

During the next dozen years, Linden worked regularly in theatrical productions, particularly musicals, throughout the United States. Among the shows were *Wish You Were Here* (Massachusetts, 1961) about life at a Jewish summer camp, *The Pajama Game* (New Jersey, 1963), and *The Education of H*Y*M*A*N K*A*P*L*A*N* (New York City, 1968), about the efforts of Jewish immigrants to make themselves at home in America. He received rave reviews for his fine performance as Meyer Rothschild in the original Broadway production of the musical *The Rothschilds* (1970).

In the early 1970s, Linden began his film acting career. In *Mr. Inside/Mr. Outside* (TV, 1973) he played a police detective. He also acted in the farce *How to Break Up a Happy Divorce* (TV, 1976); the disaster movie *Starflight: The Plane That Couldn't Land* (TV, 1983); and the biopic *My Wicked, Wicked Ways: The Legend of Errol Flynn* (TV, 1985), in which he played the film magnate J. L. Warner.

Meanwhile, Linden was becoming more and more familiar to TV viewers through his title role in the TV comedy series *Barney Miller* (1975-82). As Captain Miller, chief of detectives at a New York City police precinct, Linden created a strong but compassionate and humanitarian character.

Linden also starred in the TV series *Blacke's Magic* (1986). He played a retired magician who

Hal Linden

Wonderful Town (1955)
Strip for Action (1956)
Bells Are Ringing (1958)
Angel in the Pawnshop (1960)
Wildcat (1960)
Wish You Were Here (1961)
Anything Goes (1962)
The Pajama Game (1963)
The Sign in Sidney Brustein's Window (1964)
Something More! (1964)
Remains to Be Seen (1966)
The Boys from Syracuse (1966)
The Apple Tree (1966)
Ilya, Darling (1967)
*The Education of H*Y*M*A*N
   K*A*P*L*A*N* (1968)
The Love Match (1968)
Three Men on a Horse (1969)
The Rothschilds (1970)
Room Service (1983)
I'm Not Rappaport (1986)
Man of La Mancha (1989)
Unfinished Stories (1991)
Gypsy of the Year (1993)
The Sisters Rosensweig (1993)

FILMS

Bells Are Ringing (1960)
Mr. Inside/Mr. Outside (TV, 1973)
The Love Boat (TV, 1976)
How to Break Up a Happy Divorce (TV, 1976)
When You Comin' Back, Red Ryder? (1979)
Father Figure (TV, 1980)
Starflight: The Plane That Couldn't Land (TV, 1983)
The Other Woman (TV, 1983)
My Wicked, Wicked Ways: The Legend of Errol Flynn
   (TV, 1985)
A New Life (1988)
Dream Breakers (TV, 1989)
The Colony (TV, 1995)
Just Friends (1996)
Out to Sea (1997)

TV

Barney Miller (1975–82)
Blacke's Magic (1986)
Jack's Place (1992–93)
The Boys Are Back (1994–95)

uses his knowledge of magic to solve baffling crimes. Later in the 1980s Linden's work included the film *A New Life* (1988) and an American tour as Don Quixote in the great musical *Man of La Mancha*.

In the 1990s Linden often gave concerts as a vocalist of popular songs. Sometimes, he also played the clarinet performing, for example, Mozart's *Clarinet Concerto*. Meanwhile, Linden remained exceptionally active as an actor. Among his many projects were the play *Unfinished Stories* (Los Angeles, 1991); the TV drama series *Jack's Place* (1992–93), in which he played a restaurant owner; the play *Gypsy of the Year* (New York City, 1993); the TV sitcom *The Boys Are Back* (1994–95), in which he played a recent retiree whose peace is disturbed by family members; and the films *The Colony* (TV, 1995) and *Out to Sea* (1997).

Linden married the actress Frances Martin in 1958. They had four children—Amelia, Jennifer, Nora, and Ian.

Herbert Lom

Chief Inspector Dreyfus

During his long career as a character actor, Herbert Lom has played such diverse roles as Adolf Hitler, Napoleon, the phantom of the opera, a kindhearted psychiatrist, and the king of Siam. But the role for which he is best known is that of Chief Inspector Dreyfus, the comic foil in the Pink Panther series of films.

◄◦►

Herbert Lom was born in Prague, Bohemia, in 1917 (the precise date of birth is unknown). His original name was Herbert Charles Angelo Kuchacevich ze Schluderpachern.

Lom began his stage career in Prague. Moving to England in 1939, he studied acting at the Vic-Wells School. From 1940 to 1946, he worked on radio for the European Service of the British Broadcasting Corporation (BBC). He also acted in touring and repertory companies.

Lom made his film debut by portraying Adolf Hitler in *Mein Kampf* (1940). For many years thereafter, he was frequently cast as a heavy. His characterizations of villains were enhanced by use of a Charles Boyer-like Continental accent and manner. Lom played Napoleon in *The Young Mr. Pitt* (1942) and in *War and Peace* (1956). He also played a Balkan crook in *State Secret* (1950), an impulsive gangster in *The Ladykillers* (1956), and the title role in *The Phantom of the Opera* (1962).

However, Lom was always capable of playing a wide range of roles. In *The Seventh Veil* (1945), for example, he played a psychiatrist sympathetically treating a woman concert pianist. He later

Herbert Lom

played a similar role in the TV series *The Human Jungle* (1964). He appeared on the London stage as the King in the musical *The King and I* (1953).

In the 1960s Lom effectively pulled away from being typecast in sinister parts. The single most important step in that direction was his role in the "Pink Panther" series of comedy films as the neurotic French policeman Chief Inspector Charles Dreyfus, who is plagued by his subordinate Inspector Jacques Clouseau (played by Peter Sellers). Lom played the part in *A Shot in the Dark* (1964), *The Return of the Pink Panther* (1975), *The Pink Panther Strikes Again* (1976), *Revenge of the Pink Panther* (1978), *Trail of the Pink Panther* (1982), *Curse of the Pink Panther* (1983), and *Son of the Pink Panther* (1993).

Though he is now best known as Chief Inspector Dreyfus, Lom has continued to play a variety of other roles. His later films included *And Then There Were None* (1975), *King Solomon's Mines* (1985), *Ten Little Indians* (1990), and *The Masque of the Red Death* (1991).

Lom was formerly married to Dina Scheu. They had two sons and a daughter before divorcing.

SELECTED PERFORMANCES:

STAGE

The Seventh Veil (1951)
The Trap (1952)
The King and I (1953)
Betzi (1975)

FILMS

Mein Kampf (1940)
The Young Mr. Pitt (1942)
The Dark Tower (1943)
The Seventh Veil (1945)
Appointment with Crime (1946)
Night Boat to Dublin (1946)
Dual Alibi (1947)
Good Time Girl (1948)
Night and the City (1950)
The Black Rose (1950)
State Secret (1950)
The Ladykillers (1956)
War and Peace (1956)

I Accuse! (1958)
Chase a Crooked Shadow (1958)
The Roots of Heaven (1958)
I Aim at the Stars (1960)
El Cid (1961)
Mysterious Island (1961)
The Frightened City (1962)
I Like Money (1962)
The Phantom of the Opera (1962)
Tiara Tahiti (1963)
No Tree in the City (1964)
A Shot in the Dark (1964)
Return from the Ashes (1965)
Treasure of Silver Lake (1965)
Bang! Bang! You're Dead! (1966)
Gambit (1966)
Eve (1968)
Villa Rides (1968)
Ninety-nine Women (1969)
Uncle Tom's Cabin (1969)
Assignment to Kill (1969)
Journey to the Far Side of the Sun (1969)
Mister Jerico (TV, 1970)
Asylum (1972)
And Now the Screaming Starts (1973)
And Then There Were None (1975)
The Return of the Pink Panther (1975)
The Pink Panther Strikes Again (1976)
Revenge of the Pink Panther (1978)
The Lady Vanishes (1979)
Peter and Paul (TV, 1981)
Trail of the Pink Panther (1982)
Curse of the Pink Panther (1982)
The Dead Zone (1983)
Memed My Hawk (1984)
Lace (TV, 1984)
King Solomon's Mines (1985)
Ten Little Indians (1990)
River of Death (1990)
The Masque of the Red Death (1991)
The Devil's Daughter (1992)
Son of the Pink Panther (1993)

TV

The Human Jungle (1964)

Peter Lorre

Neurotic Villain

Peter Lorre was a unique talent in the history of films. He was capable of depicting the most evil of villains, yet he also had a genuine flair for comedy. He was just as adept at being slithery and sinister as he was at being cute and lovable. His distinct mannerisms and voice made him one of the most widely copied actors by comic impressionists.

Peter Lorre was born in Rozsahegy (in German, Rosenberg), Hungary, on June 26, 1904. His original name was Ladislav Loewenstein (sometimes given as Laszlo Lowenstein).

After moving several times, his family settled in Vienna, Austria. There, in his teens, he changed his name to Peter Lorre and began to appear in plays. In 1924 he worked in Breslau in Zurich before returning to Vienna in 1925. For the next three years he labored in obscurity but learned his craft well.

Lorre finally began to receive some recognition when he gave a number of outstanding performances in Berlin, beginning with his role as the village idiot in *Pioniere in Ingolstadt* ("Engineers in Ingolstadt," 1929). In *Dantons Tod* ("Danton's Death," 1929) he portrayed a sadistic "philosopher of terror." In *Frühlings Erwachen* ("Spring's Awakening," 1929,) he played a fourteen-year-old boy who, confused by moral conflicts arising from the difficulty of puberty, commits suicide.

Soon after his Berlin debut, Lorre began to live with the well-known German actress Cacilie Lvovsky (who later simplified her name to Celia Lovsky). She introduced him to the great film director Fritz Lang, who cast him in the lead of the movie *M* (1931), a story about a child murderer. Lorre brilliantly conveyed the weakness, desperation, and self-loathing of the compulsive killer. His sudden shifts from whining and groveling to indignation were to characterize many of his later parts as well.

M brought Lorre worldwide renown, but he initially refused offers from Hollywood. He was afraid that the commercially oriented American filmmakers would typecast him forever as a middle-aged villain. Lorre struggled, at least in his younger years, to force producers to give him a variety of challenging roles. "Acting," he once said, "if money is its only object, is childish and undignified work. There must be some higher motive."

After the release of *M* Lorre continued to act in German-language films until 1933. That year the Nazis rose to power in Germany and Lorre fled first to Austria, then to France, and then, in 1934, to England.

Though his English was as yet poor, he soon acted in the British film *The Man Who Knew Too Much* (1934) directed by Alfred Hitchcock. Lorre played one of a band of spies who kidnap a young girl and attempt a political assassination. He gave his character a sad, desperate quality that made his performance stand out from the usual way of playing such roles. While in England he married Celia Lovsky.

In July 1934 Lorre moved to the United States to work for Columbia Pictures (the studio executives had promised him some artistic freedom).

Peter Lorre

Peter Lorre

played characters of different nationalities and ethnicities, including Arab, French, German, Hungarian, Mexican, and Russian.

In 1941 Lorre portrayed a strange gentleman crook in *The Maltese Falcon*. A similar part was played by Sidney Greenstreet. Audiences enjoyed the contrast and interplay between the two villains—Lorre was small and quiet, Greenstreet was large and loud—and they appeared together again in *Casablanca* (1943), *Passage to Marseille* (1944), *The Mask of Dimitrios* (1944), *Three Strangers* (1946), and *The Verdict* (1946).

Lorre was also cast in horror films. He appeared with Boris Karloff and Bela Lugosi in *You'll Find Out* (1940) and starred in *The Face behind the Mask* (1941), in which he again displayed his gift for pathos. He also starred in *The Beast with Five Fingers* (1946). Meanwhile, he also displayed is gift for comedy, notably in *Arsenic and Old Lace* (1944).

In 1945 Lorre divorced his first wife and married Karen Verne, a former actress. They separated only a few years later. In 1950 he met Annemarie Brenning (or Stoldt) when both were staying at a sanatorium. She soon became his secretary, and in 1953 they married. They had one child, Catherine.

Unhappy with his career in Hollywood, Lorre went to Germany, where he wrote, directed, and starred in the film *Der Verlorene* ("The Lost One," 1951). Ironically, though he had grown weary of being typecast as a neurotic killer, he decided to portray the homicidal Nazi scientist in this unsuccessful movie.

Around this time Lorre began to suffer from high blood pressure and obesity. His facial expression seemed to convey a perpetual comical melancholy.

In 1952 Lorre returned to America. His career was now quickly fading. He played minor roles in *Twenty Thousand Leagues under the Sea* (1954), *Silk Stockings* (1957), and *Voyage to the Bottom of the Sea* (1961). He played a caricature of his earlier serious roles in the comic-horror movies *Tales of Terror* (1962), *The Raven* (1963), and *The Comedy of Terrors* (1964).

After several months, however, no suitable material had appeared, and Lorre was lent to Metro-Goldwyn-Mayer (MGM) for *Mad Love* (1935). He played a brilliant but sexually unfulfilled plastic surgeon who derives pleasure from watching the torture of an actress in a Grand Guignol production. Lorre, who had shaved his head for the part, made the character extremely repulsive yet, gave him some humanity and pathos.

Lorre had accepted the lead in *Mad Love* with the condition that Columbia would give him the role of Raskolnikov, another brilliant but disturbed person, in a filmed version of Dostoevski's novel *Crime and Punishment*. Lorre was happy to have the chance to appear in such a serious work, but the film, released in 1935, was only moderately successful.

In 1936 Lorre returned briefly to England to appear in Hitchcock's *Secret Agent*. He then came back to America and from 1937 to 1939 star as the Japanese detective Mr. Moto in the "Mr. Moto" series of detective movies. In his career Lorre

In the early 1960s Lorre separated from his third wife. He died in Los Angeles, California, on March 23, 1964.

SELECTED PERFORMANCES:

STAGE

Pioniere in Ingolstadt (1929)
Happy End (1929)
Dantons Tod (1929)
Frühlings Erwachen (1929)
Die Quadratur des Kreises ("Squaring the Circle," 1930)
Mann Ist Mann ("Man Is Man," 1931)
Geschichten aus dem Wiener Wald ("Tales from the Vienna Woods," 1931)

FILMS

M (1931)
Bomben auf Monte Carlo ("The Bombardment of Monte Carlo," 1931)
Die Koffer des Herrn O. F. ("The Trunks of Mr. O. F.," 1931)
Fünf von der Jazzband ("The Jazzband Five," 1932)
Schuss im Morgengrauen ("A Shot at Dawn," (1932)
F.P. 1 Antwortet Nicht ("F.P. 1 Doesn't Answer," 1932)
Der Weisse Dämon ("The White Demon," 1932)
Was Frauen Träumen ("What Women Dream," 1933)
Unsichtbare Gegner ("Invisible Opponent," 1933)
Der Haut en Bas ("From Top to Bottom," 1933)
The Man Who Knew Too Much (1934)
Mad Love (1935)
Crime and Punishment (1935)
Secret Agent (1936)
Mr. Moto Takes a Vacation (1939)
Strange Cargo (1940)
I Was an Adventuress (1940)
Island of Doomed Men (1940)
Stranger on the Third Floor (1940)
You'll Find Out (1940)
The Face behind the Mask (1941)
Mr. District Attorney (1941)
They Met in Bombay (1941)
The Maltese Falcon (1941)

All through the Night (1942)
Invisible Agent (1942)
The Boogie Man Will Get You (1942)
Casablanca (1943)
Background to Danger (1943)
The Constant Nymph (1943)
The Cross of Lorraine (1943)
Passage to Marseille (1944)
The Mask of Dimitrios (1944)
Arsenic and Old Lace (1944)
The Conspirators (1944)
Hollywood Canteen (1944)
Hotel Berlin (1945)
Confidential Agent (1945)
Three Strangers (1946)
Black Angel (1946)
The Chase (1946)
The Verdict (1946)
The Beast with Five Fingers (1946)
My Favorite Brunette (1947)
Casbah (1948)
Rope of Sand (1949)
Quicksand (1950)
Double Confession (1950)
Der Verlorene ("The Lost One," 1951)
Beat the Devil (1954)
Twenty Thousand Leagues under the Sea (1954)
Meet Me in Las Vegas (1956)
Congo Crossing (1956)
Around the World in Eighty Days (1956)
The Buster Keaton Story (1957)
Silk Stockings (1957)
The Story of Mankind (1957)
Hell Ship Mutiny (1957)
The Sad Sack (1957)
The Big Circus (1959)
Scent of Mystery (1960)
Voyage to the Bottom of the Sea (1961)
Tales of Terror (1962)
Five Weeks in a Balloon (1962)
The Raven (1963)
The Comedy of Terrors (1964)
Muscle Beach Party (1964)
The Patsy (1964)

RADIO

Mystery in the Air (1947)
Nightmare (1953)

Paul Lukas

Suave Hungarian Leading Man

—◀○▶—

Paul Lukas played lovers, villains, and intellectuals in many Hollywood films from the 1920s to the 1960s. Perhaps his greatest role was that of the Nazi fighter Kurt Muller in *Watch on the Rhine* (1943).

—◀○▶—

Paul Lukas was born on a railway train as it was pulling into Budapest, Hungary, on May 26, 1895. His original name was Pal Lukacs (He later anglicized it when he moved to become a film actor.). After attending the Hungarian equivalent of high school, he served during World War I in the Austro-Hungarian army. He was wounded in action against the Russians in 1915.

Released from the army, Lukas studied briefly at the Royal Academy of Acting in Budapest (1915). He then began his professional career by working for two years at the opera house in the little Hungarian town of Kassa. There, he sang in opera and operetta choruses and performed in plays, working his way up from small roles to such parts as Shylock in *The Merchant of Venice* and Othello in *Othello*. He then spent nine years at Budapest's Comedy Theater, where he played more than sixty different roles in plays by a variety of playwrights.

In 1927 the American film producers Jesse Lasky and Adolph Zukor saw Lukas on the Budapest stage and signed him to make movies. He had already appeared in numerous European silent movies; and when he moved to the United States, it was with the intention of making more silent movies. However, soon after Lukas's arrival in Hollywood, silent movies were replaced by sound movies. Lukas, of course, spoke with an accent, but he quickly mastered English well enough to act in American films.

In his early years in American movies Lukas, because of his suave, dominating manner, was often cast as a Continental seducer, as in *The Shopworn Angel* (1929) and *Dodsworth* (1936), or as a sophisticated foreign villain, as in *The Lady Vanishes* (1938) and *Confessions of a Nazi Spy* (1939). But he was actually a fine, versatile actor. In his Broadway debut he played the tired consumptive Dr. Rank in Ibsen's *A Doll's House* (1937).

Lukas became famous for his starring performance in *Watch on the Rhine* as the worn-out Kurt Muller, a gentle German engineer whose work in the anti-Fascist German underground forces him into exile in America but who finally returns to Germany to continue his fight against Nazism. Lukas imbued the part with sorrow, humility, and human compassion, yet also with a fiery, invincible spirit.

Lukas's roles as lovers, villains, and exhausted intellectuals were actually quite far removed from his true nature. Always athletic and energetic, he was a skilled wrestler and an avid weightlifter in his youth. Later he took up tennis, fencing, and horseback riding. He was also a licensed airplane pilot.

In his later films Lukas frequently played kindly old men, as in *Lord Jim* (1965). Particularly memorable was his role in Walt Disney's production of Jules Verne's *Twenty Thousand Leagues under the Sea* (1954). Lukas portrayed Professor Pierre Arronax, a specialist in sea creatures, who

Paul Lukas

is captured by the misanthropic genius Captain Nemo and confined aboard his submarine, the *Nautilus*. The gentle Arronax convinces Nemo to make peace with the world and to share his fantastic scientific knowledge with humankind. But Nemo is ambushed by warships, and he orders the *Nautilus*, with its scientific secrets, to make a final trip to the ocean floor. Lukas's Professor Arronax epitomized the idealistic conception of the humanitarian scientist altruistically pursuing knowledge.

Lukas was married twice. He wedded Gizella (nicknamed Daisy) Benes in 1927. She died in 1962, and in 1963 he married Anna Dreisens.

Lukas died in Tangier, Morocco, on August 15, 1971.

Paul Lukas

SELECTED PERFORMANCES:

STAGE

A Doll's House (1937)
Watch on the Rhine (1941)
Call Me Madam (1950)
Flight into Egypt (1952)
The Wayward Saint (1955)

FILMS

Two Lovers (1928)
Three Sinners (1928)
Loves of an Actress (1928)
The Night Watch (1928)
The Woman from Moscow (1928)
Manhattan Cocktail (1928)
The Shopworn Angel (1929)
The Wolf of Wall Street (1929)
Half Way to Heaven (1929)
Behind the Makeup (1930)
Slightly Scarlet (1930)
Young Eagles (1930)
The Benson Murder Case (1930)
The Devil's Holiday (1930)
Grumpy (1930)
Anybody's Woman (1930)
Unfaithful (1931)
City Streets (1931)
The Vice Squad (1931)
Women Love Once (1931)
The Beloved Bachelor (1931)
Strictly Dishonorable (1931)
No One Man (1932)

Tomorrow and Tomorrow (1932)
Thunder Below (1932)
A Passport to Hell (1932)
Downstairs (1932)
Rockabye (1932)
Grand Slam (1933)
Kiss before the Mirror (1933)
Sing, Sinner, Sing (1933)
Captured (1933)
The Secret of the Blue Room (1933)
Little Women (1933)
The Countess of Monte Cristo (1934)
Glamour (1934)
Affairs of a Gentleman (1934)
I Give My Love (1934)
The Fountain (1934)
The Casino Murder Case (1935)
Age of Indiscretion (1935)
The Three Musketeers (1935)

I Found Stella Parish (1935)
Dodsworth (1936)
Ladies in Love (1936)
Espionage (1937)
Dinner at the Ritz (1937)
The Lady Vanishes (1938)
Confession of a Nazi Spy (1939)
Captain Fury (1939)
Strange Cargo (1940)
The Ghost Breakers (1940)
The Monster and the Girl (1941)
Chinese Den (1941)
They Dare Not Love (1941)
Lady in Distress (1942)
Watch on the Rhine (1943)
Hostages (1943)
Uncertain Glory (1944)

Address Unknown (1944)
Experiment Perilous (1944)
Deadline at Dawn (1946)
Temptation (1946)
Whispering City (1947)
Berlin Express (1948)
Kim (1950)
Twenty Thousand Leagues under the Sea (1954)
The Roots of Heaven (1958)
Scent of Mystery (1960)
The Four Horsemen of the Apocalypse (1962)
Tender Is the Night (1962)
Fifty-five Days at Peking (1963)
Lord Jim (1965)
Sol Madrid (1968)
The Challenge (TV, 1970)

Marx Brothers

Madcap Comedy Team

The Marx Brothers remain unmatched in the range of their comedic accomplishments. No other team or individual has so well combined nonsense, slapstick, satire, pantomime, black humor, and witty dialogue. At the heart of their comedy was their refusal to be molded by the pompous powers of convention. The boys thumbed their noses at the establishment (often personified on stage and screen by the stately Margaret Dumont, their favorite comic foil). They never played overtly Jewish roles, but they exuded the Jewish urban experience through their streetwise Lower East Side language, their ingenious (albeit eccentric) debates reminiscent of the Talmud, and especially their sense of alienation from the mainstream of society. A Marx Brothers performance was a wild conglomeration of pure madcap energy and anarchy.

All of the brothers were born in New York City, but only Groucho's and Zeppo's births were officially recorded with the city government, and for many years Groucho fibbed about his true age. (About 85 percent of the births and deaths in New York City were unrecorded by the government before 1898, by which time more stringent reporting requirements had been established.) Consequently, many different birth dates for the brothers have been published. The following birth dates are based on the best recent evidence: Chico (originally Leonard), August 21, 1887; Harpo (originally Adolph, later Arthur), November 23,

1888; Groucho (originally Julius), October 2, 1890; and Zeppo (originally Herbert), February 25, 1901. Another brother, Gummo (originally Milton; born October 23, 1892), left the team in the early years.

Their father, Sam (Frenchy) Marx (originally Simon Marrix), was an unsuccessful tailor who had immigrated to the United States from Alsace-Lorraine. Their mother, Minnie Marx (originally Minna Schoenberg), had come to America from Germany, where her parents had operated a traveling theatrical troupe. Her father was a magician, her mother a harpist. One of Minnie's brothers changed his name to Al Shean and became a famous American vaudeville comedian in the team Gallagher and Shean (beginning in 1910).

The older boys left school early to pursue separate careers in show business. Chico, for example, played the piano in nickelodeons, brothels, and vaudeville theaters. Harpo, whose principal musical instrument was the harp, played the piano (though he knew only two tunes) in a nickelodeon, a job he had inherited from Chico. And Groucho sang with various groups, including Gus Edwards's famous vaudeville kid act.

Then Minnie decided to form a group of singers. She recruited three of her sons—Harpo, Groucho, Gummo—and a friend, Lou Levy—and called them the Four Nightingales. "Minnie's Boys" toured from 1907 to 1910, and during that time they moved to Chicago, the center of the small-time vaudeville circuits in which the group performed.

The Four Nightingales were strictly a singing group until one memorable day in Nacogdoches, Texas. While they were performing in an outdoor theater, a mule caused a disturbance nearby. Most of the audience went out to watch the mule. When some of the people straggled back, the boys—furious at being topped by a mule—hurled insults at the audience (for example, Groucho's "Nacogdoches is full of roaches"). The audience loved the "jokes" and laughed hysterically. Thus, the boys entered a new phase of their show business careers.

Soon they developed a comedy schoolroom show called *Fun in Hi Skule*, which they used from 1910 to 1913. At first they were billed as the Three Marx Brothers, and the cast consisted of Harpo, Groucho, Gummo, and several others. Then Chico joined the act, which became the Four Marx Brothers and Company. In 1913 the show evolved into *Mr. Green's Reception*, and in 1914 it became *Home Again*, which was written by Al Shean.

Before 1914 the brothers were still known by their original given names (though Adolph had earlier changed his name to Arthur). It was during a 1914 poker game in Galesburg, Illinois, that they were dubbed with the names by which they would become famous. They and their poker partner, a monologist named Art Fisher, were noting how the popular comic-strip character Sherlock the Monk had spawned such vaudeville names as Nervo, Henpecko, and Tightwado. Fisher applied the same naming system to the Marxs. He called Leonard, known for his success in chasing pretty girls, or chicks, Chicko (the *k* was later accidentally dropped by a typesetter, and the name became Chico, though it was still pronounced to rhyme with "chick" not "cheek"). Arthur, the harpist, became Harpo. Julius, the moody one, became Groucho. Milton, who wore gumshoes to help ward off colds, was henceforth Gummo.

During World War I, Gummo was drafted into the army. He never returned to the act, choosing instead to become a businessman. His place was taken by the youngest brother, Herbert, who was named Zeppo when he joined the act.

In 1919 the Marx Brothers got an engagement at the prestigious Palace Theater in New York City. Soon they were the biggest attraction in all of vaudeville. That year they also performed in their first musical comedy, *The Cinderella Girl*, which was staged in Battle Creek, Michigan and ran for only three days. In 1920 or 1921 they made a silent movie, *Humor Risk*, which was so bad that they destroyed it. But the musical revue *I'll Say She Is!* was a tremendous success. It opened in Philadel-

phia in the summer of 1923. After touring with the show for a year, they took it to Broadway, where it was also a hit. Next, they starred in two extremely successful Broadway musical comedies: *The Cocoanuts* (1925) and *Animal Crackers* (1928).

The Marx Brothers gained their greatest fame through movies, beginning with filmed the versions of *The Cocoanuts* (1929) and *Animal Crackers* (1930). In the former film, the boys are involved in the Florida land boom. In *Animal Crackers* they are guests at a party where thieves covet a valuable oil painting. Groucho portrayed one of his most memorable roles in that film—Captain Jeffrey Spaulding, a bumbling African explorer.

The brother's first two movies were shot on the East Coast. The boys made the rest of their movies in Hollywood. In *Monkey Business* (1931) they stow away on a ship, crash a party, and reluctantly catch some crooks. *Horse Feathers* (1932) is a spoof of college life, especially football. Groucho, as Professor Quincy Adams Wagstaff, played the newly appointed president of the school. In *Duck Soup* (1933) Groucho was Rufus T. Firefly, president of the mythical land of Freedonia, which wages war on its scheming neighbor Sylvania. A highlight of *Duck Soup* is the mirror scene, in which Harpo, who is being chased by Groucho, accidentally smashes a large mirror and then pretends to be Groucho's mirror image in a series of intricate and hilarious moves.

In the team's first five movies, plots were barely begun when the Marx Brothers started to destroy them by shifting attention to a series of tangential comedy routines showcasing the boys in various combinations. Each of the brothers had a clearly developed character that he portrayed in every film.

The principal figure on the screen was Groucho, who wore an ill-fitting frock coat, a carry-over from his days as the schoolmaster in *Fun in Hi Skule* and a parody of the uniform of the society that he mocked. He also had a painted-on mustache, constantly smoked and flicked a cigar, insinuatingly twitched his eyebrows, and uttered savage wisecracks at virtually everyone and everything. Groucho would alternatingly romance and insult his favorite target, the pompous character played by Margaret Dumont, who symbolized all of conventional society. "You've got beauty, charm, money," he told her in *Animal Crackers*. "You have got money, haven't you? Because if you haven't, we can quit right now." In *Duck Soup* Dumont said

Groucho, Chico, and Harpo harass a bellhop in The Cocoanuts.

to Groucho, "As chairwoman of the reception committee, I welcome you with open arms." To which Groucho replied, "Is that so? How late do you stay open?" "Remember," he said to his brothers in the same film, "you're fighting for this woman's honor, which is probably more than she ever did."

Groucho was a master of verbal-humor delivery. He could get laughs even with material that would fall flat coming from other comedians. For example, in his courtroom defense of Chico in *Duck Soup*, Groucho said, "Chicolini here may talk like an idiot and look like an idiot, but don't let that fool you. He really *is* an idiot."

Groucho sang comic songs with a unique nasal twang and outrageous, lovable mockery. He expressed the essence of the Marx Brothers spirit when he sang "Whatever It Is, I'm against It" in

Horse Feathers. In *Animal Crackers* he performed the nonsense song "Hello, I Must Be Going" and the self-descriptive "Hooray for Captain Spaulding," which became his theme song for the rest of his career.

Chico's humor was largely based on his use of a mock Italian accent and his misuse of the English language. In *The Cocoanuts*, for example, he confused "viaduct" with "why a duck." In *Duck Soup* Groucho asked, "Have you got a license [to sell peanuts]?" To which Chico replied, "No, but my dog—he's got millions of 'em." In the same movie he confused "elephant" and "irrelevant," "tanks" and "thanks," and so on. Chico supplied a constant stream of puns and fractured-language humor in all of their films.

He was also the "real" world's link with the

silent Harpo, whom only Chico could understand. When Harpo honked his horn, pulled faces, or threw wild fits, Chico translated the meanings of these gestures.

A fine instinctive pianist, Chico provided the Marx Brothers films with many lighthearted melodious moments at the piano. He applied comedy even to his pianoism, especially in his technique of "shooting the keys," that is, pointing his index finger like a pistol, using his thumb as a trigger, and striking a key.

Harpo portrayed a totally uninhibited, childlike mute. His stage character became mute when Al Shean accidentally included only a few lines for Harpo in his script for *Home Again*. Shean compensated for his oversight by asking Harpo to use pantomime. He was so good at it that he became one of the world's most beloved pantomimists.

In Harpo's character he gave himself over completely to his instincts, from simple exuberance (as in his wildly stamping and scattering documents at a passport inspection) to lechery (as in his literally chasing women while honking his horn). His brothers frequently played straight men to his zaniness, as when Groucho, in *The Cocoanuts*, fed Harpo flowers and a telephone, and when Chico, in several films, deciphered messages that Harpo conveyed through charades.

Harpo's most characteristic prop was a fright wig. In vaudeville he had used a red wig, but the red showed up too dark on the screen in *The Cocoanuts*. Consequently, from *Animal Crackers* on, he used a blonde wig.

He also carried a rubber horn to "communicate" with others and wore an overcoat with enormous interior pockets, where he stored all sorts of bizarre objects, including a blowtorch, an ice-cream cone, a cup of coffee, and a ton of silverware—obviously pilfered—which dropped to the floor, piece by piece, to his embarrassment and the audience's delight.

In every Marx Brothers show, Harpo pulled a face called a "Gookie," in which he puffed out his cheeks and crossed his widened eyes. The look was named after a New York City cigar roller named Gookie, who unintentionally made the face as he worked in a cigar store, where Harpo, as a youngster, spotted and copied the expression.

Harpo created many beautiful moments on the screen with his harp playing. He had no formal lessons, and he tuned the instrument eccentrically,

yet he became a highly admired harpist, being especially adept at improvising on popular tunes.

Zeppo played the straight man to Groucho and generally supplied the romantic relief: he got the girl but not the gags. He also sang the romantic ballads.

After *Duck Soup* Zeppo left the team and opened what came to be one of the largest talent agencies in show business. At the same time, Gummo gave up his dress-manufacturing business to become Zeppo's partner, specifically as manager of the three remaining Marx Brothers.

The first five Marx Brothers films, made for Paramount Pictures, were dominated by the team's comic anarchy at the expense of plot and of production values (such as direction and camera work). Their methods bordered on the surreal and appealed to a rather narrow urban audience. Then they signed with MGM. Through the influence of MGM executive Irving Thalberg, their next two films had more structured plots, stronger production values, and a broader audience appeal.

In *A Night at the Opera* (1935) the brothers pave the way for the happiness of two young opera singers by deflating an unfair opera director and an egotistical tenor. A highlight of the film is the stateroom scene: the three Marx Brothers and a dozen other people are gradually squeezed into a tiny room; when Margaret Dumont opens the door to visit Groucho (as Otis B. Driftwood), the bodies pour out at her feet.

In *A Day at the Races* (1937) the Marx Brothers help a young woman to raise money for her sanatorium by assisting her boyfriend's horse in winning a big race. Groucho played Dr. Hugo Z. Hackenbush, a veterinarian who tries to pass himself off as a people doctor. In one scene, Chico pretends to be a tutti-frutti (in his lingo, "tutsifrutsi") ice-cream salesman at a racetrack, while actually selling Groucho phony betting aids. In another scene, Harpo pounds a piano until it falls apart, leaving only the inside "harp" which he proceeds to play.

Irving Thalberg died in 1936. His efforts had helped the Marx Brothers to reach the zenith of their career, but with Thalberg gone, their later movies never rose to the same plateau.

In *Room Service* (1938) they are penniless theatrical producers trying to find ways to stay in a hotel until they can find a backer. In *At the Circus*

(1939) they save a circus from bankruptcy. Groucho played the shyster lawyer J. Cheever Loophole and sang the delightfully risqué "Lydia, the Tattooed Lady."

In *Go West* (1940) the brothers tackle a western villain. The rousing finale is a train chase in which they literally tear their train apart to fuel the wood-burning engine. In *The Big Store* (1941) they save a department store from crooks.

After *The Big Store* the team split up for several years, but then they got together again, chiefly because Chico needed the money. In *A Night in Casablanca* (1946) they rout Nazi refugees in a North African hotel. Their last film as a team was *Love Happy* (1950), in which they search for a stolen diamond necklace. The story was concieved by Harpo, who for the first time had the limelight.

All three brothers were in the movie *The Story of Mankind* (1957) but not as a team; each appeared in scenes that did not include the othe two brothers. The last time that all three appeared together on a screen was in the TV play "The Incredible Jewel Robbery" (1959) on *General Electric Theater*.

In their late years however, they did remain active in separate careers. In the 1950s Chico and Harpo had a dual act in nightclubs and at country fairs. Chico's solo work included guest-starring in the TV play "Papa Romani" (1950) on *The Bigelow Theater*, hosting the TV variety series *The College Bowl* (1950-51), and playing the piano in numerous engagements. Harpo's solo work included guest-starring in a 1955 episode of the TV comedy series *I Love Lucy*, in which he and Lucy recreated the famous mirror scene from *Duck Soup*; appearing in the dramas "The Red Mill" (1958) and "Silent Panic" (1960) on TV's *The Du Pont Show*; and playing the harp in numerous engagements. He also published his autobiography, *Harpo Speaks!* (with Rowland Barber, 1961).

Groucho's fame continued to grow after the team broke up. He served as the wisecracking host of the quiz show *You Bet Your Life* on both radio (1947–51) and TV (1950-61), for which he grew a real mustache to replace the painted-on one that he had used on the stage and in movies). He also acted in several films, including *Copacabana* (1947), *A Girl in Every Port* (1952), and *Skidoo* (1968). Besides working on his own TV show, he made many guest appearances on the small screen. A longstanding fan of Gilbert and Sullivan's oper-

ettas, Groucho particularly enjoyed playing Ko-Ko, the Lord High Executioner, in *The Mikado* on TV in 1960. In 1972 he performed a one-man show at Carnegie Hall in New York City.

Groucho read voraciously and became a skilled writer. He coauthored (with Norman Krasna) the play *Time for Elizabeth* (1948) and wrote the humorous books *Beds* (1930), a history of sleeping accommodations, and *Many Happy Returns!* (1942), and indictment of the Internal Revenue Service. He also wrote the autobiographical books *Groucho and Me* (1959), *Memoirs of a Mangy Lover* (1963), *The Groucho Letters* (1967), *The Secret Word Is Groucho* (with Hector Arce, 1976), and *The Groucho Phile* (1976)

In real life Chico was the charmer of the brothers. An inveterate womanizer and gambler, he was very successful as the former, less so as the latter. In 1924 he married Betty Karp, a dancer. They had a daughter, Maxine, who wrote the book *Growing Up with Chico* (1980). That marriage ended in divorce, and in 1958 he wedded the actress Mary De Vithas (also known as Mary Dee). In 1961 Chico entered the Cedars of Lebanon Hospital in Los Angeles. He was released, but soon died in his Beverly Hills home of a heart ailment on October 11, 1961

The real-life Harpo was much like his fictional character—sweet, gentle, and puckish. In 1936 he married the actress Susan Fleming, a former *Ziegfeld Follies* showgirl. They adopted four children, William, Alexander, Minnie, and James. Harpo finally broke his professional silence in January 1963 when he annouced his retirement just after giving a stage performance. The following year he underwent heart surgery at Mount Sinai Hospital in Los angeles, where he died on September 28, 1964.

The real life Groucho was shy, thoughful, and kindhearted, much in contrast with his smart-alecky fictional character. But his fame as a caustic wit in films was so great the he felt obligated to live up to his reputation in real life as well. The conflict between his natural shyness and his desire to please others by insulting them often led him to great inner turmoil.

In his private life, Groucho had a wide range of interests. A literate, articulate man, he corresponded with such notables as T. S. Eliot, James Thurber, and E. B. White. He was also a liberal activist.

Groucho was married three times. In 1920 he married Ruth Johnson, who had been hired for the Marx Brothers vaudeville act as Zeppo's dancing partner. Groucho and Ruth had two children, Arthur and Miriam. Arthur became a prominent writer of movie and TV scripts and of biographical-autobiographical books, including *Son of Groucho* (1972).

After divorcing Ruth Johnson in 1942, Groucho married the aspiring singer-dancer Catherine (or Kay) Gorcey in 1945. She had previously been married to the actor Leo Gorcey, one of the Dead End Kids. Groucho and Kay had a daughter, Melinda, who, as a youth, performed as a singer-dancer-actress, sometimes appearing with her father, as in *The Mikado* and on *You Bet Your Life*. His second marriage ended in divorce in 1951.

Groucho wedded the former model Eden Hartford (originally Eden Higgins) in 1954. She had a bit part with him in *The Story of Mankind*. They divorced in 1969.

Shortly after that divorce he began to receive secretarial help from the aspiring actress Erin Fleming. She later became his companion and business manager.

In his final years Groucho was considerably slowed down by a major heart attack and by several small strokes. His last few months of life were marred by a bitter legal battle between Erin Fleming and his son, Arthur, for the conservatorship of Groucho's considerable estate. Andy Marks, Arthur son, was eventually named conservator. Groucho died of pneumonitis at Cedars-Sinai Medical Center in Los Angeles on August 19, 1977.

Gummo, who had acted as Groucho's agent in the 1950s, died in Palm Springs, California, on April 21, 1977.

Zeppo, in real life, was a witty person and a shrewd businessman. He was married twice. In 1927 he wedded the actress Marion Benda (originally Marion Bimberg), with whom he had a son, Timothy, before divorcing in 1937. His second wife, Barbara, divorced Zeppo in 1973 and later married Frank Sinatra. Zeppo made his last public appearance in 1977, when he testified in favor of Groucho's companion, Erin Fleming, in the conservatorship hearing. Zeppo died of lung cancer in Palm Springs on November 30, 1979.

SELECTED PERFORMANCES:

STAGE

Chico, Harpo, Groucho, Zeppo:
I'll Say She Is! (1924)
The Cocoanuts (1925)
Animal Crackers (1928)

FILMS

Chico, Harpo, Groucho, Zeppo:
The Cocoanuts (1929)
Animal Crackers (1930)
Monkey Business (1931)
Horse Feathers (1932)
Duck Soup (1933)

Chico, Harpo, Groucho:
A Night at the Opera (1935)
A Day at the Races (1937)
Room Service (1938)
At the Circus (1939)
Go West (1940)
The Big Store (1941)
A Night in Casablanca (1946)
Love Happy (1950)
The Story of Mankind (1957)

Groucho:
Copacabana (1947)
Mr. Music (1950)
Double Dynamite (1951)
A Girl in Every Port (1952)
Skidoo (1968)

RADIO

Groucho:
You Bet Your Life (1957-51)

TV

Chico:
The College Bowl (1950-51)

Groucho:
You Bet Your Life (1950-61)

Jackie Mason

Rabbi Turned Comedian

Jackie Mason is one of the most successful comedians in America today, but his climb to the top was unusually long and hard. For years he could not get movie and TV roles because many Jewish studio and TV executives felt that he sounded "too Jewish" to win a broad-based following. According to Mason, "What they really mean is that I remind them of where they come from, and they don't like that." Many other Jews were sensitive about the Jewish image he presented through his impudent manner and through such jokes as this: "Money is not the most important thing in the world. Love is. Fortunately, I love money." Mason, however, has steadfastly refused to give up the ethnic ambience of his monologues. "To give up your identity plays into the hands of anti-Semitism," he maintains. Furthermore, the differences between Jews and Gentiles are legitimate fodder for humor: "If there wasn't a difference," he quips, "I wouldn't have an act."

Mason does not just tell jokes; he creates in-telligent, humorous oral essays. His social commentary covers such subjects as sex, dating, hookers, money, politics, Israel, psychiatry, TV weathermen, and current events. He also mimics James Cagney, Ted Kennedy, Henry Kissinger, pop singers, and other personalities. His specialty is stories that center on the stereotyped differences between ethnic groups—including Jews, WASPs, Poles, Chinese, Japanese, Mexicans, Italians, and Puerto Ricans. Put-downs, aimed at himself as well as others, are a staple in his act.

Mason performs with a deadpan, bewildered expression on his face. As he speaks he emphasizes points by jabbing the air with his right index finger or by using chopping movements with his hands. His delivery is marked by rapid talking, staccato articulation, and a singsong cadence. He frequently stresses the final word of a phrase or clause. He speaks with an overtly Jewish inflection, and he often uses Yiddish words.

Jackie Mason was born in Sheboygan, Wisconsin, on June 9, 1930 (according to the most reliable sources, though in his autobiography the date is given as the "fourth year of . . . the 1930s"). His original name was Yacov Moshe Maza.

Mason grew up on the Lower East Side of Manhattan. He came from a long paternal line of rabbis; his three older brothers followed that tradition. At eighteen Mason became a cantor, and after taking a B.A. degree in psychology at the City College of New York and completing the seminary course at Yeshiva University, he was ordained a rabbi.

As a rabbi in Weldon, North Carolina, and in Pittston, Pennsylvania, Mason was uncomfortable, but he continued out of deference to his father's wishes. He spiced up his services with humor, and after a couple of years, he began taking jobs as a comedian in Jewish resorts in the Catskill Mountains, pretending to his father that this work was only a "hiatus."

After his father died in 1957, Yacov Maza became Jackie Mason, full-time comedian. He worked during the summers on the borscht circuit and the rest of the year at New York City nightclubs and strip joints, where his clean material and Jewish accent prevented him from being a rousing success.

Feeling guilty about his career change, Mason sought help in psychoanalysis, an experience that inspired "neurotic" jokes before Woody Allen became famous for them. "When I went to a football game," Mason would say, "every time the players went into a huddle I thought they were talking about me."

Mason also began to experiment with routines that took listeners through a stream-of-consciousness maze, notably his classic bit on psychiatry: "My analyst said, 'We have to try to find the real you.' I said to myself, 'Why do I need him?' I could call my friends. They know where I've been. And what if I find the real me and he's even worse than I am? I don't make enough money for myself—I need a partner? Besides, if this is not the real me, why should I pay the fifty dollars? Collect it from the real me.'"

In 1960 Mason got his big break when he was invited to appear on Steve Allen's national TV show. Soon Mason was working at top nightclubs, such as Manhattan's Copacabana and Blue Angel, and on other TV programs, including those hosted by Perry Como, Garry Moore, and Jack Paar.

One of Mason's most popular routines in the early 1960s was his impersonation of Ed Sullivan, host of the TV show widely regarded as the pinnacle of prime-time exposure. Sullivan invited Mason to appear on *The Ed Sullivan Show* many times. On October 18, 1964, Mason was performing on the show when Sullivan, out of camera range, digitally signaled the amount of time Mason had left. This gesture distracted the attention of the studio audience away from the comedian, who tried to recapture it by jokingly imitating Sullivan, holding up various fingers to the audience and saying, "I've got a finger for you and a finger for you and a finger for you." Sullivan, mistakenly believing that Mason had flipped the forbidden middle finger, became furious backstage and told the comedian, "I'll destroy you in show business." Sullivan canceled Mason's contract and refused to pay him his fee for the night's performance. Later a New York state supreme court

judge viewed a kinescope of the show and cleared Mason. Sullivan and Mason reconciled and the comic returned to Sullivan's show in 1966.

Nevertheless, serious long-term damage had already been done to Mason's career. He was widely seen as a troublemaker, a censored comedian, and a bad representative of the Jewish community.

In 1966 and 1967 a series of events endangered his physical safety. His Las Vegas act included some jokes about Frank Sinatra's relationships with women. After receiving some anonymous threatening telephone calls, he was shot at in his hotel room on November 6, 1966. On February 13, 1967, he was attacked with punches as he sat in his parked car in Miami, Florida.

Soon afterwards Mason experienced other crucial career reversals. He formed his own production company, JaMa Productions, Inc., and starred in the Broadway play *A Teaspoon Every Four Hours* (1969) and the motion picture *The Stoolie* (1972). Both flopped.

Mason then returned to square one and retraced his original route to popularity. From the mid-1970s to the early 1980s he appeared as a guest on TV shows, worked hotels and nightclubs, and even performed at trade shows. He appeared as the gas-station owner in the comedy *The Jerk* (1979) and as the first Jew in Mel Brooks's *History of the World, Part I* (1981).

The springboard to Mason's current great success was his one-man show *The World According to Me!* After running for six months in southern California theaters (first in Hollywood, then in Beverly Hills), the show opened on Broadway in December 1986.

"I should have been a doctor," Mason said in his act. "In what other profession can a man tell a woman to take off her clothes and send the bill to her husband?" One of his favorite targets was Richard Nixon. "People say I shouldn't pick on Nixon. He's got phlebitis. I say it's syphilis. You can't screw 200 million people and wind up with phlebitis." He brought the house down with an eight-minute impression of President Ronald Reagan trying to explain his lack of complicity in the Iran-Contra covert-operations scam then under congressional investigation: "They say it was going on in my own basement. Why should I go to the basement? I'm the president." Mason's act was loaded with jokes based on ethnic stereotypes.

"My best friend is half-Italian, half-Jewish. If he can't buy it wholesale, he steals it." "I love the Puerto Ricans. I go to Puerto Rico all the time. I like to visit my hubcaps." "Every Jew loves food. What do you think Jews talk about for breakfast? Where to eat lunch. At lunch, where should we have dinner? Dinner, where should we have coffee?... The only people who never had a cockroach are white Protestant American Gentiles. There's no food in the house. After all, how much can a cockroach drink?...You never see a Jew in a bar, except if he gets lost looking for a piece of cake." "If a Gentile has a boat, he's out on excursions. There's no bigger schnook in the world than a Jew with a boat. All he wants is to show it to you. I know five thousand Jews with boats. I never saw one move yet."

The success of Mason's one-man Broadway show brought him many other lucrative projects. He came out with book, record-album, and cable-TV versions of the show. In 1987 he appeared in a popular Honda TV commercial, and in 1988 he starred in the comedy film *Caddyshack II*. In the summer of 1988 he returned to his Broadway show for another run before closing later that year. That fall he published an autobiographical book, *Jackie Oy! Jackie Mason from Birth to Rebirth* (with Ken Gross).

From September to November 1989 he starred in the TV sitcom *Chicken Soup*, which did well in the ratings but was reportedly dropped because of its strong ethnic slant.

In the 1990s Mason repeatedly returned to Broadway in different one-man shows. He prepared fresh material for *Brand New* (1990-91), *Politically Incorrect* (1994-95), and *Love Thy Neighbor* (1996-97).

"All my comedy is social and psychological commentary," Mason says. He wants to help people see through "the restriction of conventionality." His mission is rooted in the Talmud. "The Talmud is the study of logic," he explains. "Every time I see a contradiction or hypocrisy in somebody's behavior, I think of the Talmud and build the joke from there."

Jackie Mason

SELECTED PERFORMANCES:

STAGE

Enter Solly Gold (1965)
A Teaspoon Every Four Hours (1969)
The World According to Me! (1986-88)
Brand New (1990-91)
Politically Incorrect (1994-95)
Love Thy Neighbor (1996-97)

FILMS

Operation Delilah (1966)
The Stoolie (1972)
The Jerk (1979)
History of the World, Part I (1981)
The Perils of P.K. (1986)
Caddyshack II (1988)

TV

Chicken Soup (1989)

Walter Matthau

Sardonic Actor

Walter Matthau spent many years working as a character actor, frequently playing villains. But since his mid-forties, he has been a major star known especially for the unique quality of comical derisiveness that he brings to his comedy roles.

Walter Matthau was born in New York City, New York, on October 1, 1920. His original name was Walter Matuschanskayasky.

His father, Melas Matuschanskayasky, had been an Eastern Rite Catholic priest in czarist Russia. After leaving the priesthood, Melas met and married Rose Berolsky, a Jew, in Lithuania and then immigrated to the United States, where the family name became Matthow. Later Walter changed the spelling to Matthau.

Melas (now Milton) left his family when his son was three. The boy was raised by his mother in the Jewish milieu of New York City's Lower East Side. As a youngster he worked in the refreshment concessions at various theaters. At the age of eleven he was given a small role in a Yiddish-language play. He later performed in school plays at Seward Park High School, from which he graduated in 1939.

After working odd jobs for several years he enlisted in the air force in 1942. Returning to civilian life at the end of World War II, he studied acting under Erwin Piscator at the Dramatic Workshop of the New School for Social Research in New York. During that time Matthau performed in Dramatic Workshop productions, in summer stock, and on TV.

In 1948 Matthau reached Broadway as an understudy for seven characters in *Ann of a Thousand Days,* playing various roles on separate occasions. Over the next few years he worked his way up until, in 1951, he was offered a leading role in *Twilight Walk.* He continued to work on both Broadway and TV for several years, earning the respect of colleagues but remaining unkown to the public.

In 1955 Matthau finally landed a major role in a successful play: *Will Success Spoil Rock Hunter?* He also got parts in two movies that year, *The Kentuckian* and *The Indian Fighter.* In both films he played a supporting role as a villain.

Matthau then played a variety of supporting roles in such films as *Bigger Than Life* (1956), *A Face in the Crowd* (1957), *Onionhead* (1958), *Lonely Are the Brave* (1962), *Ensign Pulver* (1964), and *Goodbye Charlie* (1964). Real success, however, still eluded him. He gained wide recognition for his comic portrayal of a haughty French aristocrat in the Broadway play *A Shot in the Dark* (1961).

Matthau finally reached genuine stardom with his role as Oscar Madison in Neil Simon's Broadway comedy *The Odd Couple* (1965). Simon had written the work with Matthau in mind, and the character of Oscar turned out to be the major role in a top script that had always eluded the actor. Matthau readily identified with Oscar's easygoing lifestyle (though not with the character's sloppiness) and sardonic humor, a quality that has characterized much of the actor's work.

Matthau then gave another outstanding performance, as the conniving shyster lawyer in the film comedy *The Fortune Cookie* (1966). While making that movie, Matthau had a major heart attack. He thereupon decided to limit himself principally to filmacting, which he felt was less exhausting than stage work. (In 1976 he had heart bypass surgery to help prevent further problems.)

Matthau reprised his Oscar Madison role in the filmed version of *The Odd Couple* (1968). He solidified his star status with outstanding comic performances in *Hello Dolly!* (1969), as a grouchy merchant who eventually mellows; *Plaza Suite* (1971), as three different characters; *Kotch* (1971), as a septuagenarian; *The Sunshine Boys* (1975), as an old vaudevillian; *The Bad News Bears* (1976), as a down-at-heel children's baseball coach; *Buddy, Buddy* (1981), as a hit man; *The Survivors* (1983), as a gas-station owner battling a right-wing military unit; and *Movers and Shakers* (1985), as a Hollywood executive trying to produce a box-office hit from a best-selling sex book.

The highlights of his work in the 1990s were the films made with his old friend Jack Lemmon, with whom he had starred in earlier pictures, including *The Odd Couple*. They hit the jackpot with the films *Grumpy Old Men* (1993) and *Grumpier Old Men* (1995), in which they both played retirees, neighbors, and friends who constantly battle each other in a small midwestern town. In *Out to Sea* (1997) they play losers who get jobs as dance instructors so that they can court and swindle wealthy widows. In *The Odd Couple II* (1998), Matthau and Lemmon reprised their roles as Oscar Madison and Felix Unger, reunited in a rented car on the roads of California.

Matthau is married to the former Carol Marcus. They met in 1955 when they both were working in *Will Success Spoil Rock Hunter?* In 1959 they got married, and in that year they also appeared together in the movie *Gangster Story*. They had one child, Charles (who has become an important director). It was Matthau's second marriage, since he had earlier been married for a time to Grace Johnson, with whom he had his children, David and Jennifer. Matthau has used David and Charles, as well as Lucy Saroyan (his stepdaughter by way of Johnson's earlier marriage, to the author William Saroyan), in some of his movies.

Walter Matthau

SELECTED PERFORMANCES:

STAGE

The Aristocrats (1946)
Ann of a Thousand Days (1948)
The Liar (1950)
Twilight Walk (1951)
Fancy Meeting You Again (1952)
One Bright Day (1952)
The Glass Menagerie (1952)
In Any Language (1952)
The Grey-Eyed People (1952)
The Ladies of the Corridor (1953)
Guys and Dolls (1955)

Will Success Spoil Rock Hunter? (1955)
The Wisteria Trees (1955)
Once More with Feeling (1958)
A Shot in the Dark (1961)
Once There Was a Russian (1961)
The Odd Couple (1965)
Juno and the Paycock (1974)

FILMS

The Kentuckian (1955)
The Indian Fighter (1955)
Bigger Than Life (1956)
Slaughter on Tenth Avenue (1957)
Voice in the Mirror (1958)
Onionhead (1958)
King Creole (1958)
Ride a Crooked Trail (1958)
Gangster Story (1959)
Strangers When We Meet (1960)
Lonely Are the Brave (1962)
Who's Got the Action? (1962)
Charade (1963)
Island of Love (1963)
Ensign Pulver (1964)
Goodbye Charlie (1964)
Fail Safe (1964)
Mirage (1965)
The Fortune Cookie (1966)
A Guide for the Married Man (1967)
The Odd Couple (1968)
The Secret Life of an American Wife (1968)
Candy (1968)
Hello, Dolly! (1969)
Cactus Flower (1969)
A New Leaf (1971)
Plaza Suite (1971)
Kotch (1971)

Pete 'n' Tillie (1972)
Charley Varrick (1973)
The Laughing Policeman (1973)
The Taking of Pelham One Two Three (1974)
Earthquake (credited as Walter Matuschanskayasky, 1974)
The Front Page (1974)
The Sunshine Boys (1975)
The Bad News Bears (1976)
Casey's Shadow (1978)
House Calls (1978)
California Suite (1978)
Little Miss Marker (1980)
Hopscotch (1980)
First Monday in October (1981)
I Ought to Be in Pictures (1982)
The Survivors (1983)
Movers and Shakers (1985)
The Couch Trip (1988)
JFK (1991)
Mrs. Lambert Remembers Love (TV, 1991)
Against Her Will: An Incident in Baltimore (TV, 1992)
Dennis the Menace (1993)
Grumpy Old Men (1993)
Incident in a Small Town (TV, 1994)
I.Q. (1994)
Grumpier Old Men (1995)
I'm Not Rappaport (1996)
The Grass Harp (1996)
Out to Sea (1997)
The Odd Couple II (1998)
The Marriage Fool (TV, 1998)

TV

Tallahassee 7000 (filmed 1959, syndicated 1961)

Bette Midler

Queen of Camp

Bette Midler, the self-styled Divine Miss M, rose to fame in the 1970s through her lively, sometimes bizarre, song-and-comedy stage shows. She performed not only contemporary rock songs but also material from as far back as the 1930s, often imitating the styles of the artists most closely identified with the tunes. To evoke the aura of those earlier years, she wore gold lamé gowns, garter belts, toreador pants, and platform shoes. She used vulgar language profusely, appeared as a giant hot dog and as a female King Kong, and used such props as wheelchairs and mermaid tails. Breasts were one of her favorite topics; once, she said that she had weighed her own breasts on a mail scale: "I won't tell you how much they weigh, but it cost $87.50 to send them to Brazil." She frequently boasted at being "the last of the truly tacky women" who do "trash with flash and sleaze with ease." Observers soon dubbed her the Queen of Camp.

Yet this "truly tacky woman" later proved herself to be capable of handling fully developed comedy roles. Her performances in such motion pictures as *Down and Out in Beverly Hills* (1986), *Ruthless People* (1986), *Outrageous Fortune* (1987), and *Beaches* (1988) firmly established her as an outstanding film comedienne.

Bette Midler was born in Honolulu, Hawaii, on December 1, 1945, not long after her parents had arrived from New Jersey. Her mother named her after the actress Bette Davis; but Mrs. Midler, like many other fans, mistakenly thought that Davis pronounced her first name "Bet" (instead of the correct "Bet-ty"). Thus, Bette Midler's given name has always been pronounced "Bet."

In Hawaii the Midlers were the only white people in a predominantly Oriental community. Bette pretended to be Portuguese because, as she later explained, "Portuguese people were accepted. Jews were not. I was an alien, a foreigner—even though I was born there."

She was also sensitive about the fact that she was an overweight, plain-looking child. As she has put it, "I was an ugly, fat little Jewish girl with problems." But she soon found an excellent way to build her self-esteem—performing. In first grade she won a prize for singing "Silent Night, Holy Night." After that she was featured in many school and amateur productions. All during her youth she dreamed of becoming a professional actress. When she attended the University of Hawaii for one year, she studied drama.

In 1965 Midler got a bit part (as the seasick wife of a missionary) in the movie *Hawaii* (1966), which was being filmed on location. When the movie company traveled to Los Angeles to finish filming, she went with it.

After the movie was completed she moved to New York City to begin a stage career. After struggling for a few months, she landed a job in the chorus of the hit Broadway musical *Fiddler on the Roof* (1966). The next year she was promoted to the role of Tzeitel, one of the show's major parts. She remained with *Fiddler on the Roof* for three years.

Bette Midler

Bette Midler

wrote two books: *A View from a Broad* (1980), which covers her adventures when she took her act on a world tour and *The Saga of Baby Divine* (1983), a poetic fairy tale, ostensibly for children, about living life to the fullest.

Midler never abandoned her original ambition to be an actress. Her first important movie role was in *The Rose* (1979). In that film she played a hard-living, ill-fated rock singer.

Comedy, however, was her true calling and a natural outgrowth of her humorous stage acts. She appeared in the 1982 film comedy *Jinxed*, but friction with others involved in the production soured her on an immediate return to movies.

In August 1983, while touring with her act *De Tour*, she fainted from overwork. When she recovered, she stated that she was ready to switch to a full-time comedy career, which she felt would be less exhausting than her music shows had been.

Soon she issued her first all-comedy album, *Mud WILL Be Flung Tonight!* (recorded live at a Los Angeles club in 1985). In her performance she hurled insults at celebrities, such as Madonna and Bruce Springsteen. She also defended her breast obsession: "Do they dump on the pope 'cause all he ever talks about is God?"

Midler returned to films in a series of comedies, beginning with *Down and Out in Beverly Hills* (1986). In that film she played a shallow, trendy nouveau-riche woman who takes in a transient in an effort to learn the meaning of life. In *Ruthless People* (1986) Midler played a screechy Bel Air heiress who is so overbearing that her kidnappers keep marking down the ransom money demanded from her husband, who does not want her back at any price. In *Outrageous Fortune* (1987) she played a brassy, vulgar, street-smart con artist. Midler gave a hilarious performance as a set of identical twins in the switched-body plot of *Big Business* (1988). In Disney's animated feature *Oliver and Company*

Midler then decided to concentrate on a singing career. She got her big break in 1970, when she was hired as a singer at the Continental Baths, a New York City Turkish bath for male homosexuals. Her work there led to requests for her to appear on David Frost's and Johnny Carson's TV shows. Soon she was in demand at leading nightclubs and theaters across the country.

In 1971 Midler appeared in the rock opera *Tommy* with the Seattle Opera Company, and in 1973 she performed at the famed Palace Theater in New York City. Her New York City revue *Clams on the Half Shell* (1975) was very successful. In 1979 she starred in the bawdy one-woman Broadway show *Divine Madness*. The show was made into a film in 1980.

In 1972 Midler released her first album, *The Divine Miss M* (1972). Her later albums included *Live at Last* (1977) and *No Frills* (1983). She also

(1988), she supplied the voice of the "world's most conceited pooch." In *Beaches* (1988) Midler expanded her range by playing a Bronx-bred Jew who realizes that she will never attain true personal happiness even as she boasts of her successful show-business career.

Midler married Martin von Haselberg (alias Harry Kipper), a performing artist and commodities trader, in 1984. They had a daughter, Sophie.

Midler continued to be active in films during the 1990s. She starred with Woody Allen in *Scenes from a Mall* (1991) and played one of three wronged wives who join forces to plot revenge against their husbands in *The First Wives Club* (1996). Her other films included *Gypsy* (TV, 1993) and *That Old Feeling* (1997).

Bette Midler

SELECTED PERFORMANCES:

STAGE

Fiddler on the Roof (1966)
Salvation (1970)
Tommy (1971)
Clams on the Half Shell (1975)
Divine Madness (1979)
De Tour (1983)

FILMS

Hawaii (1966)
The Divine Mr. J. (1974)
The Rose (1979)
Divine Madness (1980)
Jinxed (1982)
Down and Out in Beverly Hills (1986)
Ruthless People (1986)

Outrageous Fortune (1987)
Big Business (1988)
Oliver and Company (animated, voice-only, 1988)
Beaches (1988)
Stella (1990)
For the Boys (1991)
Scenes from a Mall (1991)
Hocus Pocus (1993)
Gypsy (TV, 1993)
The First Wives Club (1996)
That Old Feeling (1997)

Marilyn Monroe

Sex Symbol

—◦—

Marilyn Monroe, a convert to Judaism, rose to fame as a dumb-blonde sex symbol. But many of her performances, as in *Bus Stop* (1956), reveal the psychological subtleties of a gifted actress.

—◦—

Marilyn Monroe was born of non-Jewish parents in Los Angeles, California, on June 1, 1926. Her original name was Norma Jean Mortensen. Her mother, originally named Gladys Monroe, had been married first to a man named Baker and then to a man named Mortensen, who soon deserted her. It is believed, however, that Marilyn Monroe's natural father was C. Stanley Gifford, a fellow employee at the studio where Gladys worked as a film technician.

Gladys came from a family with a history of mental illness, and she was frequently institutionalized. Her daughter, who went by the name Norma Jean Baker in her childhood, spent her early years in a succession of foster homes and in an orphanage.

In 1942 Monroe dropped out of high school to marry James Dougherty, an aircraft production worker. After he entered the merchant marine for World War II service, she supported herself by working in a defense plant and by part-time modeling.

In 1946 Monroe divorced Dougherty and decided to try to break into show business. She bleached her previously dark hair, got an agent, and changed her name (Marilyn after the actress Marilyn Miller, Monroe after her mother's maiden name).

Monroe managed to get a screen test, which led to a movie contract. She made her first film appearance in *Scudda-Hoo! Scudda-Hay!* (1948), but her brief close-ups were cut and she remained in the picture only as an extra in the distance. In *Dangerous Years* (1948) her bit part made the final cut. Finally, in the minor musical *Ladies of the Chorus*, (1949) she had one of the leading roles. During the production of *Ladies of the Chorus*, she began her first serious dramatic study, under Natasha Lytess.

There followed a year during which Monroe could get no film work. She earned her living by modeling.

Returning to movies, she made a brief, sexy appearance in the Marx Brothers film *Love Happy* (1950) and acted in several minor pictures. She also had small parts in the important movies *The Asphalt Jungle* (1950) and *All about Eve* (1950). In both films she played inexperienced young women protégées of worldly older men. She was beginning to attract attention through her sensuous presence, her wiggly walk, and her little-girl voice.

While she was filming *Clash by Night* (1952), it became nationally known that Monroe had posed for a full-length nude photograph being used on a widely distributed calendar. She and her press agents turned the discovery to their own advantage and used the publicity to increase her market value.

In 1953 Monroe became a movie star almost overnight when she played a gold-digging chorus girl in the hit comedy *Gentlemen Prefer Blondes*. In *How to Marry a Millionaire* (1953) she costarred with Betty Grable and Lauren Bacall as three models who share a penthouse and scheme to marry wealthy men.

In January 1954, after a well-publicized courtship, Monroe married the retired baseball player Joe DiMaggio, the great "Yankee Clipper." It was a brief and stormy marriage, ending in divorce in October of that year. The culminating factor in the breakup was Monroe's willingness to perform a particular scene for the movie *The Seven Year Itch* (1955): she stood over a sidewalk grating while an updraft billowed her skirt and exposed more of her than DiMaggio thought proper. A still of that scene was enlarged to a height of sixty feet and used to advertise the motion picture.

Meanwhile, Monroe continued to make serious efforts to improve her acting. She was eventually recognized by film critics as a fine comedienne. Her style often involved a touch of self-satire as she played the coquette.

From 1954 on, Monroe periodically studied with Lee and Paula Strasberg at the famed Actors Studio in New York City. The Strasbergs encouraged her to attempt serious dramatic parts and to use the Method technique of internalizing her roles. One of her best efforts along those lines was in *Bus Stop* (1956), in which she imbued her dumb-blonde character with a poignancy and emotional depth not apparent in her earlier work.

In June 1956 Monroe married the Jewish playwright Arthur Miller (author of *Death of a Salesman*). It was at this time that she converted to Judaism.

Monroe then appeared in the popular movies *The Prince and the Showgirl* (1957), *Some Like It Hot* (1959), and *Let's Make Love* (1960). Her performance in *Some Like It Hot* was an overt parody of her usual dumb-blonde screen character.

Marilyn Monroe

By this point Monroe was already having marital problems again. It seemed that she needed a man who could be a father figure by day and a lover by night. Above all, he had to devote himself entirely to her. Miller, busy with his own successful career, could not satisfy her.

Consequently, while filming *Let's Make Love*, she became the aggressor in a love affair with her costar, the French actor Yves Montand. He was already married to the actress Simone Signoret, and he eventually broke off his relationship with Monroe.

For several years Monroe had been showing signs of increasing mental and emotional deterioration: insomnia, addiction to sleeping pills, erratic behavior, frequent outbursts of temper, and reliance on psychiatric help. Her instability may have been rooted in her childhood loneliness and aggravated by pressures from studios and the press, by exploitation at the hands of close associates, by her own ambition, and by the loss of two pregnancies during her marriage to Miller.

In 1960, while working on *The Misfits* (1961), a film for which Miller wrote the screenplay, Monroe was often late or psychologically unable to function. Her role, tailored for her by her husband, was the deepest and most complex of her career. Though once again a dumb-blonde, the character showed a touching vulnerability, compassion, and capacity to love. In January 1961, shortly after completing the movie, Monroe and Miller divorced.

Later that year she spent some time in a New York City mental hospital. Then she began work on the film *Something's Got to Give*. However, she was dismissed because she showed up for work only twelve days during the first month of shooting. Shortly thereafter she was rehired, but before filming could resume, she was found dead at her home in the Brentwood section of Los Angeles on August 5, 1962.

An autopsy revealed a lethal amount of barbiturates in her system, and her death was declared a probable suicide. In recent years speculation has risen about possible complexities in Monroe's death. Some even claim that she was murdered. But in 1985 Los Angeles officials looked into the matter and decided that the case did not require reopening.

Joe DiMaggio arranged Monroe's funeral. Lee Strasberg, in his eulogy for her, captured her essence when he spoke of her "childlike naiveté which was at once so shy and yet so vibrant."

SELECTED PERFORMANCES:

FILMS

Scudda-Hoo! Scudda-Hay! (1948)
Dangerous Years (1948)
Ladies of the Chorus (1949)
Love Happy (1950)
A Ticket to Tomahawk (1950)
The Fireball (1950)
Right Cross (1950)
The Asphalt Jungle (1950)
All about Eve (1950)
Let's Make It Legal (1951)
Home Town Story (1951)
As Young As You Feel (1951)
Love Nest (1951)
We're Not Married (1952)
O. Henry's Full House (1952)
Clash by Night (1952)
Don't Bother to Knock (1952)
Monkey Business (1952)
Niagara (1953)
Gentleman Prefer Blondes (1953)
How to Marry a Millionaire (1953)
River of No Return (1954)
There's No Business like Show Business (1954)
The Seven Year Itch (1955)
Bus Stop (1956)
The Prince and the Showgirl (1957)
Some Like It Hot (1959)
Let's Make Love (1960)
The Misfits (1961)

Zero Mostel

Unpredictable Comic Actor

Zero Mostel possessed an unusually wide range of comedic talents. He was a huge man, yet he moved with balletic grace and Chaplinesque physical control. As a stand-up comedian, he mixed low comedy with subtle observations about human behavior. In his stage and screen roles, he proved himself to be a master of pure slapstick, yet he could also act with insightful sensitivity.

Zero Mostel was born in New York City, New York, on February 28, 1915. His original name was Samuel Joel Mostel, an anglicization of his Hebrew name, Simcha Yoel Mostel.

Mostel graduated from Seward Park High School in 1931 and from City College of the City University of New York in 1935. His B.A. degree was in art, but after finishing college, he had a series of menial jobs in factories and on docks. During that time he developed a strong interest in social causes.

Later, he was hired by the Work Projects Administration (WPA) to teach art at various museums. Mostel, however, was a natural-born zany, and his lectures soon turned into hilarious routines. When word spread about his lectures, he began to get calls to entertain at various local functions, where he would pick up a few extra dollars.

Mostel's first formal engagement as a professional comedian was at a nightclub called Café Society Downtown, where he debuted early in 1942. He was an immediate hit. It was the club's press agent who gave Mostel the name Zero, hoping to make people say, "Here's a man who's made

something of nothing." Later, Mostel playfully told interviewers a number of lies about the origin of the name, such as that it was a reflection of his standing in school or of the state of his bank account.

Among Mostel's stand-up comedy routines was an impression of Charles Boyer: "Let me run through your hair, Hedy—barefoot." In another he gave a lecture as a nutty professor of ornithology; the punch line, delivered with a mad leer, was "Birds mate, you know!" Mostel also adopted the persona of a shy schoolteacher who had to give a sex lecture. Satirizing a senator making a speech on the Japanese bombing of Pearl Harbor, Mostel gave this brilliant concluding line to his blustering politician: "What the hell was Hawaii doing in the Pacific?"

Within the next few months Mostel performed on the radio series *The Chamber Music Society of Lower Basin Street*; made his Broadway debut, in *Keep 'Em Laughing*; and went to Hollywood to make his first movie, *Du Barry Was a Lady* (1943), but his work in the movie consisted only of a few of his nightclub routines, and he soon returned to New York City.

Mostel was then drafted into the army. After six months he developed an ulcer and was discharged.

In 1944 he married Kathryn (or Kate) Harkin, a dancer with the famous Rockettes at the Radio City Music Hall. They had two children, Joshua and Tobias. Joshua became an actor and appeared in the films *Going Home* (1971), *Harry and Tonto* (1974), and *Seventh Avenue* (TV, 1977). Kate Mostel and Madeline Gilford, with some help from their husbands, Zero Mostel and Jack Gilford, wrote

Zero and Maria Karnilova sing "Do You Love Me?" in a scene from Fiddler.

170 Years of Show Business (1978), a book about all four of their lives.

Through the rest of the 1940s and the early 1950s Mostel's career advanced slowly. He was blacklisted during much of that time for his earlier involvement with progressive social causes. His stage work during those years included roles in the comedy *Beggar's Holiday* (1946) and the drama *A Stone for Danny Fisher* (1954). He often appeared as a villain, as in the movies *Panic in the Streets* (1950) and *The Enforcer* (1951).

In 1958 Mostel began to come out from under the shadow of blacklisting when he was cast as Leopold Bloom in the off-Broadway show *Ulysses in Nighttown*. Finally, in 1961, Mostel reached stardom when he played John, a clerk who turns into a wild animal, in the play *Rhinoceros*. His performance in that play was described by one critic as "sidesplitting and terrifying." That was followed by his memorable performance as the conniving ancient Roman slave Pseudolus in the musical comedy *A Funny Thing Happened on the Way to the Forum* (1962).

Mostel reached the peak of his career when he starred as Tevye, a poor Jewish milkman, in the original Broadway production of the musical *Fiddler on the Roof* (1964). He repeated the role in several revivals in later years.

Mostel then began to devote more time to acting in movies. He appeared in filmed versions of *A Funny Thing Happened on the Way to the Forum* (1966) and *Rhinoceros* (1974). In *The Producers* (1967) he played Max Bialystock, a seedy Broadway producer who devises an elaborate scheme to cheat his backers out of their money. In *The Angel Levine* (1970), he was Morris Mishkin, a Jewish tailor beset by problems. He gave a fine performance in *The Front* (1976), a film about the witch-hunting McCarthy era, during which Mostel, in real life, had been blacklisted. For the animated film *Watership Down* (1978), he supplied the voice of Kehaar.

Mostel was a brilliant and unpredictable comic actor, both on and off the stage. He performed virtually anywhere he happened to be. For example, he once shaved his good friend Sam Jaffe (the great actor) in Sardi's restaurant, using as shaving cream the whipped cream of Jaffe's strawberry shortcake.

Mostel published two books about himself. *Zero by Mostel* (1965) consists mostly of photographs of him. *Book of Villains* (with Israel Shenker, 1976) has many photographs of him in various villainous poses.

Mostel spent the first half of 1977 touring major American cities in *Fiddler on the Roof*. In September of that year he was in Philadelphia to try out for the new play *The Merchant*. He deeply believed in the play because it addressed some important aspects of anti-Semitism. While he was in Philadelphia he suddenly died of a burst aorta on September 8, 1977.

SELECTED PERFORMANCES:

STAGE

Keep 'Em Laughing (1942)
Top-Notches (1942)
Beggar's Holiday (1946)
Flight into Egypt (1952)
A Stone for Danny Fisher (1954)
Once Over Lightly (1955)
Good As Gold (1957)
Ulysses in Nighttown (1958, 1974)
Rhinoceros (1961)
A Funny Thing Happened on the Way to the Forum (1962)
Fiddler on the Roof (1964, 1971, 1977)
The Latent Heterosexual (1968)

FILMS

Du Barry Was a Lady (1943)
Panic in the Streets (1950)
The Enforcer (1951)
Sirocco (1951)
Mr. Belvedere Rings the Bell (1951)
The Guy Who Came Back (1951)
The Model and the Marriage Broker (1952)
A Funny Thing Happened on the Way to the Forum (1966)
The Producers (1967)
Great Catherine (1968)
The Great Bank Robbery (1969)
The Angel Levine (1970)
The Hot Rock (1972)
Rhinoceros (1974)
The Front (1976)
Watership Down (animated, voice-only, 1978)

RADIO

The Chamber Music Society of Lower Basin Street (1942)

TV

Off the Record (1949)

Paul Muni

Man of Many Faces

The great character actor Paul Muni sought roles that were, he said, "vital and lifelike." For his exceptional versatility, he was dubbed the Man of Many Faces.

Paul Muni was born in Lemberg, Austria, on September 22, 1895. His original name was Mehilem Meyer ben Nachum Favel Weisenfreund. His parents called him by the Austrian nickname "Muni" or its diminutive "Munya".

Muni's parents were itinerant performers who sang, danced, and acted in European ghettos until they moved to the United States in 1901. Muni began to perform in Yiddish theaters in 1908. Soon, he developed a wide range of theatrical skills, including performing in burlesque and acting in Yiddish versions of plays by Ibsen and Strindberg.

From 1918 to 1926, Muni toured with the Yiddish Art Theater troupe and became one of the most highly regarded Yiddish actors in the country. He gave a particularly fine performance in *Hard to Be a Jew* (1920), as Ivanov, an aristocratic young Russian Christian who trades places with a Jewish student to prove that it is not difficult to be a Jew, that discrimination does not really exist.

In 1921 Muni married the actress Bella Finkel. In 1923 he became a naturalized American citizen.

The young Yiddish star made his English-speaking stage debut in 1926 by playing the role of Morris Levine, the aged Orthodox Jewish father in *We Americans on Broadway*. He was Benny Horowitz, a tough just out of prison, in *Four Walls* (1927), in which his wife also acted. (She retired from the stage soon afterward.)

Muni went to Hollywood to make *The Valiant* (1929) and *Seven Faces* (1929), two of the earliest talkies. Urged by studio executives to adopt an Americanized stage name, he chose the name Paul Muni, which he used for all his stage and film work from 1929 on.

Returning to Broadway, Muni played the gangster Saul Holland in *This One Man* (1930). He then became famous in the English-language theater by playing George Simon, a dynamic Jewish lawyer, in the heartwarming play *Counsellor-at-Law* (1931).

Over the next several years Muni conquered the film world as well. He had long been renowned in the Yiddish theater for his use of theatrical makeup and his acting skills in portraying characters of widely assorted ages and physical types. Using those skills in his film roles, he became a character actor par excellence. For example, in *Scarface* (1932) he played a scarred thug who turns coward when the law captures him. In *I Am a Fugitive from a Chain Gang* (1932) he was an innocent man who, after being duped into participating in a robbery and sentenced to inhuman treatment on a Southern chain gang, escapes only to find that he must resort to a life of crime to survive. In *The Good Earth* (1937) he played a Chinese farmer.

Muni remains perhaps best known for his screen portrayals of real-life people in three reverent biopics. He played the title character in *The Story of Louis Pasteur* (1936), the scientist fighting for sterilization of medical instruments; *The Life of Émile Zola* (1937), as the French writer crusading against the unjust imprisonment of the military officer (and Jew) Alfred Dreyfus; and *Juarez* (1939), as the famed Mexican statesman.

Muni's wife regularly helped him on the set while he was making films. At the end of each scene he would look at her for her signs of approval or disapproval.

In 1939 Muni returned to the stage to perform in *Key Largo* as King McCloud, a wartime deserter who attempts to atone for his faithlessness. From that point on Muni alternated roughly equally between stage and film work.

In 1943 Muni participated in *We Will Never Die*, a pageant decrying the Nazi horrors in Europe. It consisted of three parts: "The Roll Call," a recitation of the names of great Jews in the arts and sciences from ancient times to the modern era; "Jews in the War," a dramatization of the contributions of American Jewish war heroes; and "Remember Us," a presentation of reports about the slaughters in Nazi Europe.

Muni portrayed Joseph Elsner, Chopin's teacher, in the fictionalized biopic *A Song to Remember* (1945). In 1946 Muni played Tevya in the drama-pageant *A Flag Is Born*, which was designed to aid and explain the cause of Zionism. In 1949 he replaced Lee J. Cobb as Willy Loman in the Broadway play *Death of a Salesman*.

In 1955 Muni performed in the explosive play *Inherit the Wind*, based on the famous Scopes Monkey Trial of 1925. Eventually he played both leading parts: the agnostic Henry Drummond (in real life, Clarence Darrow), who defends a young teacher's right to teach the Darwinian theory of evolution in a high-school classroom, and the religious fanatic Matthew Harrison Brady (in real life, William Jennings Bryan), who prosecutes the young man.

In the movie *The Last Angry Man* (1959) Muni gave a memorable performance as a rugged old doctor who has dedicated his life to helping the poverty-stricken residents of his New York City neighborhood.

Paul Muni

Muni spent his last years living in Montecito, California. He died at his home there on August 25, 1967.

SELECTED PERFORMANCES:

STAGE

Two Corpses at Breakfast (1908)
The Gold Chain (1920)
Hard to Be a Jew (1920)
Anathema (1923)
Wolves (1924)
Sabbethai Zvi (1924)
We Americans (1926)
Four Walls (1927)

Paul Muni (right) in Fugitive of a Chain Gang

This One Man (1930)
Rock Me, Julie (1931)
Counsellor-at-Law (1931)
Key Largo (1939)
Yesterday's Magic (1942)
We Will Never Die (1943)
A Flag Is Born (1946)
They Knew What They Wanted (1949)
Death of a Salesman (1949)
Inherit the Wind (1955)
At the Grand (1958)

FILMS

The Valiant (1929)
Seven Faces (1929)
Scarface (1932)
I Am a Fugitive from a Chain Gang (1932)
The World Changes (1933)

Hi, Nellie! (1934)
Bordertown (1935)
Black Fury (1935)
Dr. Socrates (1935)
The Story of Louis Pasteur (1936)
The Good Earth (1937)
The Woman I Love (1937)
The Life of Emile Zola (1937)
Juarez (1939)
We Are Not Alone (1939)
Hudson's Bay (1941)
Commandos Strike at Dawn (1943)
Stage Door Canteen (1943)
A Song to Remember (1945)
Counter-Attack (1945)
Angel on My Shoulder (1946)
Stranger on the Prowl (1953)
The Last Angry Man (1959)

Leonard Nimoy

Mr. Spock

Leonard Nimoy has long been a versatile character actor. He is best known however, for his role as Mr. Spock in the TV science-fiction series *Star Trek* (1966-69) and in many Star Trek movies.

Leonard Nimoy was born of Russian immigrant parents in Boston, Massachusetts, on March 26, 1931. He played juvenile roles at the Elizabeth Peabody Playhouse in Boston. There, at the age of seventeen, he had the role of the teenager Ralphie in *Awake and Sing!*, a play about a matriarchal Jewish family during the Great Depression. "This role," Nimoy later explained, "the young man surrounded by a hostile and repressive environment, so touched a responsive chord that I decided to make a career of acting."

Nimoy went to Boston College on a drama scholarship but dropped out after a few months. Moving to California, he took classes at the Pasadena Playhouse and had minor roles on TV and in the films *Queen for a Day* (1951) and *Rhubarb* (1951). He was given the title role in the movie *Kid Monk Baroni* (1952), about a facially disfigured boxer from the streets of New York City. Nimoy, who had been raised in a primarily Italian neighborhood in Boston, closely identified with his part as the socially outcast prizefighter.

For the next two years Nimoy was cast in supporting roles. In *Old Overland Trail* (1953) he played an Indian, and in *Them!* (1954), a science-fiction classic, he had a bit part as a military pa-per-pusher. In real life, he went on to serve in the army from 1954 to 1956.

When Nimoy returned to civilian life, he worked at odd jobs and resumed his acting career. In 1956 he got his first important TV role, in an episode of the *West Point* series. He then played an alien in the science-fiction movie *Satan's Satellites* (1958).

From 1958 to 1960 Nimoy studied acting in Hollywood with Jeff Corey. From 1960 to 1962 he assisted Corey as a dramatic instructor. In 1962 he opened his own acting studio, which he ran for three years. His teaching methods were greatly influenced by Stanislavski.

During his years as a student and a teacher Nimoy continued to get work as an actor. He made guest appearances on TV series, such as *Dr. Kildare*, and he starred in a Hollywood stage production of *Deathwatch* (1960) and in the filmed version of the play (1966).

Nimoy got his big break in 1966 when he was cast as Mr. Spock, the pointy-eared half human-half alien, in the famous TV science-fiction series *Star Trek* (1966-69). Spock was the first officer of the starship *Enterprise*, which engaged in various adventures as it traveled through space. The series developed a cult of fanatic fans called "Trekkies." Nimoy himself became a popular hero as Spock.

Nimoy had a regular role in the popular TV international-intrigue adventure series *Mission: Impossible* (1969-71). Then, in the summer of 1971, he toured as Tevye in the musical *Fiddler on the Roof*. Late in 1971 he performed in a San Diego, California, production of *The Man in a Glass*

Leonard Nimoy

Leonard Nimoy

Nimoy also became involved with other activities, such as composing and recording songs. A committed liberal, he participated in the Vietnam antiwar movement, served as a delegate to the Democratic Central Committee in 1971 and 1972, campaigned for Eugene McCarthy for president in 1972, became a member of the American Civil Liberties Union, supported the United Farm Workers, and taught at Synanon (the controversial self-help program for former drug addicts).

Meanwhile, Nimoy was also broadening his acting range. He starred as a psychiatrist in the Broadway play *Equus* (1977) and played a similar role in a remake of the classic science-fiction movie *Invasion of the Body Snatchers* (1978). From 1978 to 1980 he performed in the one-man stage show *Vincent* (which he also wrote and directed), portraying Theo van Gogh, brother of the famed painter Vincent van Gogh. He played Golda Meir's husband, Morris Myerson, in the movie *A Woman Called Golda* (TV, 1982).

But Nimoy's popularity is still largely the result of his performances as Mr. Spock. He has played the role in a series of full-length movies: *Star Trek: The Motion Picture* (1979); *Star Trek II: The Wrath of Khan* (1982); *Star Trek III: The Search for Spock* (1984); *Star Trek IV: The Voyage Home* (1986); *Star Trek V: The Final Frontier* (1989); and *Star Trek VI: The Undiscovered Country* (1991).

In the 1990s Nimoy acted in a number of films that allowed him to show his versatility. Among them were *Bonanza: Under Attack* (TV, 1995), *David* (TV, 1997); and *Brave New World* (TV, 1998). He also narrated the documentary film *A Life Apart: Hasidism in America* (1997).

Nimoy met Sandra (Sandi) Zober when both were acting at the Pasadena Playhouse. They married in 1954 and had two children, Julie and Adam, before divorcing. In 1988 he married Susan Bay (also reported as Bey).

Booth. In 1973 he starred as an escapee from a Nazi concentration camp in a New York City production of *Full Circle*.

From 1973 to 1975 Nimoy provided the voice of Spock for an animated *Star Trek* TV series. In 1976 he became host and narrator for the syndicated TV documentary series *The Coral Jungle*, about the undersea world, and *In Search of . . .*, which attempted to explain such mysteries as ghosts, monsters, and strange phenomena.

In the mid-1970s, Nimoy became active as a writer. In 1975 he published his autobiography, *I Am Not Spock*. His other books focus on his poetry and photography. They included *You and I* (1973), *We Are All Children Searching for Love* (1977), and *Come Be with Me* (1979).

SELECTED PERFORMANCES:

STAGE

Awake and Sing! (1948)
Stalag 17 (1951)
A Streetcar Named Desire (1955)
Cat on a Hot Tin Roof (1959)
Deathwatch (1960)
Monserrat (1963)
Irma La Douce (1965)
Fiddler on the Roof (1971)
The Man in the Glass Booth (1971)
Oliver! (1972)
Full Circle (1973)
Camelot (1973)
One Flew over the Cuckoo's Nest (1974)
The King and I (1974)
Caligula (1975)
The Fourposter (1975)
Twelfth Night (1975)
My Fair Lady (1976)
Sherlock Holmes (1976)
Equus (1977)
Vincent (1978-80)

FILMS

Queen for a Day (1951)
Rhubarb (1951)
Kid Monk Baroni (1952)
Old Overland Trail (1953)
Them! (1954)

Satan's Satellites (1958)
The Balcony (1963)
Deathwatch (1966)
Valley of Mystery (1967)
Catlow (1971)
Assault on the Wayne (TV, 1971)
Baffled! (TV, 1973)
The Alpha Caper (TV, 1973)
The Missing Are Deadly (TV, 1975)
Invasion of the Body Snatchers (1978)
Star Trek: The Motion Picture (1979)
Seizure: The Story of Kathy Morris (TV, 1980)
A Woman Called Golda (TV, 1982)
Marco Polo (TV, 1982)
Star Trek II: The Wrath of Khan (1982)
Star Trek III: The Search for Spock (1984)
Star Trek IV: The Voyage Home (1986)
Star Trek V: The Final Frontier (1989)
Star Trek VI: The Undiscovered Country (1991)
Never Forget (TV, 1991)
The Pagemaster (1994)
Bonanza: Under Attack (TV, 1995)
David (TV, 1997)
A Life Apart: Hasidism in America (narrator, 1997)
Brave New World (TV, 1998)

TV

Star Trek (1966-69)
Mission: Impossible (1969-71)
Star Trek (animated, voice only, 1973-75)
The Coral Jungle (1976)
In Search of . . . (1976-82)

Lilli Palmer

Multitalented Artist

The German-born actress Lilli Palmer contributed intelligent and sophisticated performances to many English-language films from the 1930s to the 1980s. In her later years, she also became a successful painter and writer.

Lilli Palmer was born in Posen, Germany, on May 24, 1914. Her original name was Maria Lilli Peiser.

Palmer was raised in Berlin. Her mother had been an actress, and Palmer herself began to perform in amateur plays at the age of ten. In April 1932 she graduated from high school and also from drama school.

Later that year Palmer left Berlin and joined the players at the Darmstadt State Theater, where she soon made her professional debut. In 1933, however, Hitler took over Germany and her career was halted by the government. Moving to Paris, she literally sang for her supper at cabarets and strip joints.

Palmer then went to England, where she got roles in English-language movies, such as *Crime Unlimited* (1934), *Secret Agent* (1936), and *Thunder Rock* (1942). She also appeared on the stage in *Tree of Eden* (1938), *Little Ladyship* (1939), and other plays.

In 1943 Palmer married famed British actor Rex Harrison. They had one child, Rex Carey Alfred Harrison, whom they always called Carey (Harrison's original surname).

In 1945 Palmer and Harrison made their first movie together: *The Rake's Progress* (released as *Notorious Gentleman* in the United States). She played an Austrian Jew who marries, and is then swindled by, the rake. Late that year Palmer and Harrison moved to the United States.

Palmer soon was appearing in Hollywood movies. She gave impressive performances in *Cloak and Dagger* (1946) and *Body and Soul* (1947). In the latter film she played a sophisticated French painter who profoundly affects the life of an American boxer (portrayed by John Garfield).

Palmer and Harrison continued to appear together in plays and films. They acted in the Broadway productions of *Bell, Book, and Candle* (1950), *Venus Observed* (1952), and *The Love of Four Colonels* (1953). They also starred in the films *The Long Dark Hall* (1951) and *The Fourposter* (1952).

Their marriage was slowly dissolving, however. In 1957 they were divorced, and later that year Palmer married the Argentine film star Carlos Thompson.

In the mid-1950s Palmer began to make French and German films in addition to British and American pictures, but only a few roles were worthy of her talents. In *The Counterfeit Traitor* (1962), set in the Hitler era, she played a German resistance fighter who is executed by a Nazi firing squad. In *The Boys from Brazil* (1978) she was the sister and helper of a Nazi-hunter (played by Laurence Olivier).

In later years Palmer increasingly occupied herself with other artistic endeavors. She became a respected painter, and her canvases were hung in major galleries. She also showed remarkable ability as a writer. Her books included *Change Lobsters—and Dance: An Autobiography* (German, 1974;

English, 1975), *The Red Raven* (German, 1977; English, 1978), and *Night Music* (German, 1981; English, 1982).

Palmer continued to act up until the last year of her life. Her last role was that of Natalya in the miniseries *Peter the Great* (TV, 1986).

Palmer died in Los Angeles, California, on January 27, 1986.

Lilli Palmer

SELECTED PERFORMANCES:

STAGE

Road to Gandahar (1938)
The Tree of Eden (1938)
Little Ladyship (1939)
You, of All People (1939)
Ladies into Action (1940)
No Time for Comedy (1941)
My Name is Aquilon (1949)
Caesar and Cleopatra (1949)
ANTA Album (1950)
Bell, Book, and Candle (1950)
Venus Observed (1952)
The Love of Four Colonels (1953)
A Song at Twilight (1966)
Suite in Three Keys (1966)

FILMS

Crime Unlimited (1934)
Secret Agent (1936)
Command Performance (1937)
A Girl Must Live (1938)
The Door with Seven Locks (1940)
Thunder Rock (1942)
The Gentle Sex (1943)
The Rake's Progress (1945, G.B.; U.S., *Notorious Gentleman*)
Cloak and Dagger (1946)
Body and Soul (1947)
My Girl Tisa (1948)
No Minor Vices (1949)
The Long Dark Hall (1951)
The Fourposter (1952)
Main Street to Broadway (1953)
But Not for Me (1959)

Modigliani of Montparnasse (1961)
The Pleasure of His Company (1961)
The Counterfeit Traitor (1962)
Miracle of the White Stallions (1963)
Adorable Julia (1964)
Torpedo Bay (1964)
The Amorous Adventures of Molly Flanders (1965)
And So to Bed (1965)
Operation Crossbow (1965)
Jack of Diamonds (1967)
Devil in Silk (1968)
The High Commissioner (1968)
Oedipus the King (1968)
Sebastian (1968)
De Sade (1969)
Hard Contract (1969)
Hauser's Memory (TV, 1970)
The House That Screamed (1971)
Murders in the Rue Morgue (1972)
The Boys from Brazil (1978)
The Holcroft Covenant (1985)
Peter the Great (TV, 1986)

TV

The Lilli Palmer Show (1951)
Lilli Palmer Theater (1956)
The Zoo Gang (1975)

Nehemiah Persoff

Powerful Supporting Actor

Nehemiah Persoff has earned his reputation as an actor primarily by playing supporting roles. Even so, his forceful, well-rounded characterizations are often more memorable than those of leading men.

Nehemiah Persoff was born in Jerusalem, Palestine, on August 14, 1920. He immigrated to the United States in 1929.

Persoff studied at the Hebrew Technical Institute in New York City (1934–37), worked as an electric-motor repairman in the signal department of the New York City subway system (1939–41), and served in the U.S. army (1942–45).

Returning to civilian life in New York City, Persoff decided to become an actor. He studied under Stella Adler, Elia Kazan, Lee Strasberg, and others. Since 1948 he has been a member of the Actors Studio.

Persoff made his stage debut in a Naverhill, Massachusetts, summer production of *Of Mice and Men* (1947). Later that year he made his New York City debut by appearing in *Galileo*. Over the next several years, he continued to perform regularly as a character actor on the New York City stage, as in *Richard III* (1949), *Peter Pan* (1950), and *Peer Gynt* (1951).

In 1952 Persoff returned to Israel. He played Tom in a Tel Aviv production of *The Glass Menagerie*. He also appeared there in *Volpone*.

In 1953 Persoff returned to New York City to act in the play *Camino Real*. Over the next couple of years he performed in *Golden Boy* (1954) and several other stage works.

Persoff's career took off in the mid-1950s when he began appearing on TV. He had a supporting role in the original TV version of the play "Marty" (1953) on the *Philco Television Playhouse*, portrayed Pablo in "For Whom the Bell Tolls" (1958) on *Playhouse Ninety*, and appeared in many other plays on anthology series during TV's golden age.

For many years Persoff has been one of the busiest guest performers on American TV drama and comedy series. He has had roles on *Alfred Hitchcock Presents*, *Barney Miller*, *Gilligan's Island*, *Hawaii Five-O*, *Marcus Welby*, *Rawhide* and many other shows. In 1986 he appeared in an episode of the fantasy series *Highway to Heaven*.

Persoff has also appeared as a supporting actor in numerous films. In his early movies, he frequently portrayed heavies, as in his gangster roles in *The Harder They Fall* (1956), *Al Capone* (1959), and *Some Like It Hot* (1959). In *Fate Is the Hunter* (1964), he played an airline executive scheming for a promotion. His other films included *Mafia* (1969); *Red Sky at Morning* (1971); *Psychic Killer* (1976); *Ziegfeld: The Man and His Women* (TV, 1978); and *Condominium* (TV, 1980). In *Sadat* (TV, 1983) he played Leonid Brezhnev, head of the Soviet Union. In *Yentl* (1983), Barbra Streisand's homage to Jewish life and especially to her father, Persoff was the father of the title character (played by Streisand). In the animated films *An American Tail* (1986) and *An American Tail: Feivel Goes West* (1991), he provided the voice for the Jewish mouse Papa Mousekewitz.

Persoff occasionally returns to the stage. He gave a powerful performance in the one-man show *Aleichem Sholem—Sholem Aleichem* (1971). He played Rabbi Arielke in *The Dybbuk* (1975).

Persoff married Thia Persov in 1951. They had four children: Jeffrey, Dan, Perry, and Dahlia.

Persoff has explained the source of his energy and determination as follows: "I suspect that one of the most powerful forces shaping my life when I was growing up in the U.S.A. was that German with the small mustache who questioned the right of my people (and therefore me) to live. He put the burden of proof on me, personally. I was then determined to develop whatever talent I had to prove worthy of the gift of life. The habit of work remained with me in later years."

Nehemia Persoff

SELECTED PERFORMANCES:

STAGE

Of Mice and Men (1947)
The Male Animal (1947)
The Devil's Disciple (1947)
Hay Fever (1947)
Galileo (1947)
Sundown Beach (1948)
Richard III (1949)
Montserrat (1949)
Peter Pan (1950)
King Lear (1950)
Peer Gynt (1951)
The Glass Menagerie (1952)
Volpone (1952)
Camino Real (1953)
Detective Story (1953)
The Road to Rome (1953)
Mademoiselle Colombe (1954)
Golden Boy (1954)
Reclining Figure (1954)
Tiger at the Gates (1955)
Only in America (1959)
Rosebloom (1970)
Aleichem Sholem—Sholem Aleichem (1971)
The Dybbuk (1975)
Handy Dandy (1985)
Two (1991)

FILMS

A Double Life (1947)
The Naked City (1948)
On the Waterfront (1954)
The Harder They Fall (1956)
The Wild Party (1956)
The Wrong Man (1956)

Men in War (1957)
This Angry Age (1958)
The Badlanders (1958)
Never Steal Anything Small (1959)
Green Mansions (1959)
Al Capone (1959)
Some Like It Hot (1959)
The Big Show (1961)
The Comancheros (1961)
The Hook (1963)
Fate Is the Hunter (1964)
A Global Affair (1964)
The Greatest Story Ever Told (1965)
The Money Jungle (1968)
The Dangerous Days of Kiowa Jones (TV, 1966)
Escape to Mindanao (TV, 1968)
Panic in the City (1968)
The Power (1968)
The Girl Who Knew Too Much (1969)
Mafia (1969)
The People Next Door (1970)
Cutter's Trail (TV, 1970)
Red Sky at Morning (1971)

Lieutenant Schuster's Wife (TV, 1972)
The Sex Symbol (TV, 1974)
The Stranger Within (TV, 1974)
Eric (TV, 1975)
Francis Gary Powers: The True Story of the U-2 Spy Incident (TV, 1976)
Psychic Killer (1976)
Voyage of the Damned (1976)
Killing Stone (TV, 1978)
Ziegfeld: The Man and His Women (TV, 1978)
The Word (TV, 1978)
The Rebels (TV, 1979)
The French Atlantic Affair (TV, 1979)
F.D.R.: The Last Year (TV, 1980)
The Henderson Monster (TV, 1980)
Turnover Smith (TV, 1980)
Condominium (TV, 1980)
Sadat (TV, 1983)
Yentl (1983)
An American Tail (animated, voice-only, 1986)
The Last Temptation of Christ (1988)
Twins (1988)
An American Tail: Feivel Goes West (animated, voice-only, 1991)

Nehemiah Persoff

Molly Picon

Yiddish Variety Star

Molly Picon was the preeminent performer to emerge from the Yiddish variety theater. Her large eyes resembled Eddie Cantor's, her miming abilities compared with Harpo Marx's, and her comic manner recalled Fanny Brice's. But Picon was Picon. The diminutive (five-foot-tall) star had a special versatility and dramatic-comedic depth (she has been called the Yiddish Helen Hayes). She acted in humorous sketches; wrote and sang songs, such as "A Day in the Life of a New York Woiking Goil;" and constantly surprised her audiences with new stunts and acrobatics, such as tap dancing, roller skating, entering the stage on a horse, playing musical instruments, and performing dangerous feats while swinging from a rope. One of her trademark stunts was somersaulting, which she continued to do on the stage until she was in her sixties. She not only headlined in the Yiddish theater but she was also a successful performer in vaudeville, on Broadway, in nightclubs, and in film.

M olly Picon was born in New York City, New York, in 1898. When she was about three years old, she moved with her parents to Philadelphia.

At the age of five, billed as Baby Margaret, she began to win money for her singing and dancing at amateur contests. She also performed in early movie theaters, known as nickelodeons.

In 1904 Picon joined Michael Thomashefsky's Yiddish repertory company in Philadelphia, where she played juvenile roles for the next three years. She then appeared in plays at Philadelphia's Arch Street Theater (1908–1912) and performed in cabaret shows (1912–15). She left William Penn High School after her second year so that she would have time to earn more money on the stage.

From 1918 to 1919 Picon toured in a vaudeville act called *The Four Seasons*. That work took her to Boston, where she was hired in 1919 by Jacob Kalich, head of a Yiddish repertory company. At that time Picon was largely ignorant of Jewish culture. Kalich, a highly literate man, educated her.

Later in 1919 Picon married Kalich, whom she nicknamed Yonkel. In 1920 she delivered a stillborn baby girl. A pelvic problem prevented her from having other children, but later the couple took youngsters into their home as part of the Foster Parents' Plan for War Children.

Picon rapidly became a major Yiddish star, especially in comedy. She performed with her husband's troupe at the Boston Grand Opera House (1919–20) and then toured with the company in Europe (1920–22). Returning to the United States, she settled in New York City and appeared in such shows as *Yankele* (1923), *Shmendrik* (1924), *Rabbi's Melody* (1926), and *Hello, Molly!* (1928). With her husband she toured Europe, the Near East, South Africa, and Argentina in the early 1930s. She then returned to work in New York City.

With the decline of the Yiddish theater, Picon began working on Broadway, debuting there as Becky Felderman in *Morning Star* (1940). Then came World War II, during which she toured

Molly Picon

Molly Picon

musical-comedy movies made in Poland: *Yiddle mit'n Fiddle* (1936, released in America in early 1937 with English subtitles as *Yiddle with His Fiddle*) and *Mamale* (1938, released in America in 1938 with English subtitles as *Little Mother*). She did not begin to make English-language movies until many years later, beginning in 1963 with the comedy *Come Blow Your Horn* (1963), in which she played the mother of two fast-living sons. In the filmed version of the musical *Fiddler on the Roof* (1971), she played Yente the Matchmaker; her husband also had a role in that film. In *For Pete's Sake* (1974), she was a motherly madam. She also appeared in *Murder on Flight 502* (TV, 1975) and *Cannonball Run II* (1984).

Picon wrote her family biography in the book *So Laugh a Little* (1962). She also wrote an autobiography, *Molly!* (with Jean Bergantini Grillo, 1980).

In March 1985, for her contributions to the Jewish performing arts, Picon received one of the first ten Goldie Awards (named after Abraham Goldfaden, father of the Yiddish theater). She died in Lancaster, Pennsylvania, on April 6, 1992.

American military camps. In 1946 she and her husband entertained Holocaust survivors in European displaced-persons camps.

After the war Picon continued to work in both Yiddish and English plays. Perhaps the highlight of her stage career was her performance as Clara Weiss, an American widow looking for a husband in Israel, in the musical *Milk and Honey*. She starred in the show on Broadway from 1961 to 1962 and in the national touring company from 1963 to 1964.

Picon also played a Jewish widow, Mrs. Jacoby, in *A Majority of One* (1960, 1965, 1966). She appeared in the revue *How to Be a Jewish Mother* (1967); played Dolly Levi in *Hello, Dolly!* (1971); and gave a one-woman show in Yiddish, *Hello, Molly!* (1979).

Picon frequently appeared on TV. In 1949 she hosted the variety show *The Molly Picon Show*.

Picon's film career began with two Yiddish

SELECTED PERFORMANCES:

STAGE

Gabriel; The Silver King; Sappho; Uncle Tom's Cabin; Shulamite (1904–1907)
Girl of the Golden West; God of Revenge; Medea; King Lear; The Kreutzer Sonata (1908–1912)
Broadway Jones (1915)
Bunty Pulls the Strings (1915)
The Four Seasons (1918)
Yankele (1923)
Zipke (1924)
Shmendrik (1924)
Gypsy Girl (1925)
Molly Dolly (1926)
Rabbi's Melody (1926)
Little Devil (1926)
Kid Mother (1927)
Little Czar (1927)
Raizelle (1927)
Mazel Brocke (1928)
Hello, Molly! (1928)
Girl of Yesterday (1931)

Norma Crane as Golde and Molly Picon (right) as Yente in a scene from Fiddler on the Roof

Love Thief (1931)
Kale Loift (1936)
Morning Star (1940)
Oy Is Dus a Leben (1942)
For Heaven's Sake (1948)
Sadie Is a Lady (1949)
Abi Gezunt (1950)
Mazel tov Molly (1950)
Take It Easy (1950)
Make Momma Happy (1953)
Farblonjet Honeymoon (1956)
The Kosher Woman (1959)
A Majority of One (1960)
Milk and Honey (1961)
Dear Me, the Sky Is Falling (1965)
Madame Mousse (1965)
The Rubaiyat of Howard Klein (1967)
How to Be a Jewish Mother (1967)
Paris Is Out! (1970)

The Front Page (1970)
Hello, Dolly! (1971)
How Do You Live with Love? (1975)
Something Old, Something New (1977; also in
    retitled version, *Second Time Around*, 1978).
Hello, Molly! (1979)

FILMS

Yiddle mit'n Fiddle (1936, Pol. in Yid.; U.S.,
    Yiddle with His Fiddle)
Mamale (1938, Pol. in Yid.; U.S., *Little Mother*)
Come Blow Your Horn (1963)
Fiddler on the Roof (1971)
For Pete's Sake (1974)
Murder on Flight 502 (TV, 1975)
Cannonball Run II (1984)

TV

The Molly Picon Show (1949)

Luise Rainer

Poignantly Winsome Actress

With only a handful of film roles to her credit, Luise Rainer made a lasting impression with her petite size, wide soulful eyes, and poignant winsomeness. She is especially remembered for her work in *The Great Ziegfeld* (1936) and *The Good Earth* (1937).

Luise Rainer was born in Vienna, Austria, on January 12, 1910 (some sources give 1909 or 1912). At the age of sixteen she began to appear on the Viennese stage under the direction of the famed producer-director Max Reinhardt.

In the early 1930s Rainer made a few films in Austria and Germany. A talent scout for the American film company MGM discovered her in Vienna and signed her to a Hollywood movie contract.

Rainer got her big break when Myrna Loy walked out on the filming of *Escapade*. Rainer replaced Loy in the movie, which was released in 1935.

Rainer became a major star as a result of her outstanding performance in her next movie, *The Great Ziegfeld* (1936). Playing the actress Anna Held, the unhappy first wife of the impresario Florenz Ziegfeld, Rainer made a lasting impression on audiences across the country. Perhaps the most memorable moment in the film occurs when Anna calls her ex-husband on the telephone to congratulate him on his forthcoming marriage (to the actress Billie Burke, played by Myrna Loy) and emotionally begins, "Hello, Flor?—Yes, this is Anna."

Rainer's next performance, as a passive but strong Chinese peasant wife in *The Good Earth* (1937), was also well received. But her next five films were unsuccessful. The best of the lot was *The Great Waltz* (1938), in which she played Poldi Vogelhuber in an apocryphal story of the Viennese waltz composer Johann Strauss II. However, Rainer's strong Vienese accent made her difficult to cast, and she was criticized for being overly emotional.

After performing in the film *Dramatic School* (1938), she left the industry for several years. During that time she appeared on the New York City stage in a few plays, notably *Saint Joan* (1940).

In 1937 Rainer married the playwright Clifford Odets, but they soon developed marital problems, and divorced a few years later.

Rainer returned to movies one last time, in *Hostages* (1943), after which she permanently retired from films. She had had one of the most notable, but also one of the briefest, careers of any major movie actress.

In the mid-1940s Rainer married the American publisher Robert Knittel, moved with him to London, and had a daughter, Franceska. She later made only rare appearances on TV and in stage plays, as in the New York City production of *The Lady from the Sea* (1950). Her principal activity more recently has been painting, for which she has shown a great talent. An exhibition of her paintings was held at the Patrick Seale Gallery in London in 1978.

Rainer has also taken up recitation. She recited Tennyson's narrative poem Enoch Arden, with background music by Richard Strauss, during tours of the United States in the early 1980s.

SELECTED PERFORMANCES:

STAGE

Behold the Bride (1939)
Saint Joan (1940)
A Kiss for Cinderella (1942)
The Lady from the Sea (1950)

FILMS

Escapade (1935)
The Great Ziegfeld (1936)
The Good Earth (1937)
The Emperor's Candlesticks (1937)
Big City (1937)
The Toy Wife (1938)
The Great Waltz (1938)
Dramatic School (1938)
Hostages (1943)
The Gambler (1997 in Europe,
     1999 in U.S.)

Luise Rainer

Tony Randall

Supreme Light-Comedy Actor

Frequently playing an intelligent but lonely, frustrated bumbler, Tony Randall is regarded by many critics as the supreme light-comedy actor of his time. He is probably best known to most Americans for playing the role of Felix Unger in the TV sitcom *The Odd Couple* (1970-75).

Tony Randall was born in Tulsa, Oklahoma, on February 26, 1920. His original name was Leonard Rosenberg.

As a high school student, Randall tried out for, but failed to get roles in, school plays. Undaunted by his failure, he studied speech and drama for one year at Northwestern University, then went to the Neighborhood Playhouse School of the Theater in New York City, where he was taght acting by Sanford Meisner and movement by Martha Graham.

In the summer of 1939, as Anthony Randall, he made his first stage appearances by acting in productions at the Upper Ferndale Country Club. He made his New York City debut in 1941, when he played a Chinese character in *The Circle of Chalk* at the Dramatic Workshop of the New School for Social Research. He then acted in other plays, such as *The Corn Is Green* (1942). During this period Randall married Florence Mitchell (also reported as Gibbs), whom he had met when both were students at Northwestern. He then spent four years (1942-46) in the U. S. army.

Returning to civilian life, Randall began to develop a reputation as a skilled character actor

through his appearances on radio soap operas, such as *Life's True Story*. He was a regular on the radio adventure series *I Love a Mystery* (1949-52). He also resumed his stage career. He toured in *The Barretts of Wimpole Street* (1947) playing the stuttering brother. In 1947 he made his Broadway debut by appearing as Scarus in Shakespeare's *Antony and Cleopatra*. In *To Tell You the Truth* (1948), a sex comedy about the Garden of Eden, he played Adam. In 1949 he had the role of Major Domo in *Caesar and Cleopatra*.

During the 1950s Randall played in a wide range of roles on Broadway. Shortening his stage name to Tony Randall, he portrayed an alcholic movie star in *Oh, Men! Oh, Women!* (1954), a satire on psychoanalysis. In *Inherit the Wind* (1955) he was the sarcastic newsman E. K. Hornbeck. And in the musical comedy *Oh, Captain!* (1958), he displayed his singing and dancing talents.

Randall also worked on television in the 1950s. From 1950 to 1952 he appeared in the soap opera *One Man's Family*. In the popular sitcom *Mister Peepers* (1952–55) he played the supporting role of Harvey Westkit, a swaggering but ineffectual high-school English teacher.

Randall made his movie debut in the filmed version of *Oh, Men! Oh, Women!* (1957) as a patient in love with his analyst's fiancée. Then, in *Will Success Spoil Rock Hunter?* (1957), he had the title role as a sheepish advertising executive. Randall next gave impeccable performances in a series of film comedies, including *Pillow Talk* (1959) and *Send Me No Flowers* (1964).

Randall is best known for playing Felix Unger

in the TV comedy series based on Neil Simon's play *The Odd Couple*. Unger is an obsessively neat perfectionist who constantly irritates his sloppy, generally easygoing roommate, Oscar Madison (played by Jack Klugman). Though Randall was not in the original Broadway cast or in the movie of *The Odd Couple*, he was in the touring company before it was made into a TV series.

Randall later starred in two other TV comedy series. In *The Tony Randall Show* (1976–78) he played the widower and father Judge Walter Franklin. In *Love, Sidney* (1981-83) he had the title role as a lonely middle-aged bachelor who shares his Manhattan apartment on a platonic basis with a young woman and her daughter.

Randall also continued to make films, including *Kate Bliss and the Ticker Tape Kid* (TV, 1978), *Foolin' Around* (1980), and *Sidney Shorr: A Girl's Best Friend* (TV, 1981; which led to the TV series *Love, Sidney*). In *Off Sides* (TV, made 1980, telecast 1984) he portrayed a bearded guru who coaches a hippie football team. He also appeared in the films *Hitler's SS: Portrait in Evil* (TV, 1985), *My Little Pony* (1986), and Agatha Christie's *The Man in the Brown Suit* (TV, 1989).

Randall is also busy outside the sphere of acting. He is a classical-music—especially opera—buff and frequently appears at concerts and operas as a commentator or supporter. For example, he has often participated in the "Opera Quiz" segments aired during intermissions of live Metropolitan Opera broadcasts. And on December 31, 1984, he served champagne to the members of the New York Philharmonic during a *Live from Lincoln Center* telecast.

In 1984 Randall participated in a New York City radio program commemorating the anniversary of the atomic bombing of Hiroshima. He was especially active in the movement to free Soviet Jews, and he lent his name to many public rallies in their behalf.

In the 1990s Randall acted in several theatrical and made-for-TV films, including *Fatal Instinct* (1993) and *The Odd Couple: Together Again* (TV,

Tony Randall

1993). But Randall's principal interest became theater. He is founder and artistic director of the American classical repertory group, National Actors Theater in New York City. Here, he performed in *The Government Inspector* (1994) and *The School for Scandal* (1995). The group has also presented productions of *Saint Joan* (1993), *Timon of Athens* (1993), and the musical *Gentlemen Prefer Blondes* (1995) With his old costar Jack Klugman, Randall also costarred in revivals of the play *The Odd Couple* (1991 and 1996), *Three Men on a Horse* (1993), and *The Sunshine Boys* (1997-98).

In 1995 Randall married his second wife, the

actress Heather Harlan. They have had two children to date, Julia, born in 1997, and Jefferson, born in 1998, when Randall was seventy-eight years old.

SELECTED PERFORMANCES:

STAGE

The Circle of Chalk (1941)
Candida (1941)
The Corn Is Green (1942)
The Barretts of Wimpole Street (1947)
Antony and Cleopatra (1947)
To Tell You the Truth (1948)
Caesar and Cleopatra (1949)
Oh, Men! Oh, Women! (1954)
Inherit the Wind (1955)
Oh, Captain! (1958)
Arms and the Man (1960)
Goodbye Again (1961)
UTBU (1966)
The Odd Couple (1970, 1976, 1991, 1996)
The Music Man (1978)
A Little Hotel on the Side (1992)
Saint Joan (1993)
Three Men on a Horse (1993)
Timon of Athens (1993)
The Government Inspector (1994)
The School for Scandal (1995)
The Sunshine Boys (1997-98)

FILMS

Oh, Men! Oh, Women! (1957)

Will Success Spoil Rock Hunter? (1957)
No Down Payment (1957)
The Mating Game (1959)
Pillow Talk (1959)
The Adventures of Huckleberry Finn (1960)
Let's Make Love (1960)
Lover Come Back (1961)
Boys' Night Out (1962)
Island of Love (1963)
The Brass Bottle (1964)
Robin and the Seven Hoods (1964)
Send Me No Flowers (1964)
Seven Faces of Dr. Lao (1964)
Fluffy (1965)
The Alphabet Murders (1966)
Bang! Bang! You're Dead! (1966)
Hello Down There (1969)
Kate Bliss and the Ticker Tape Kid (TV, 1978)
Scavenger Hunt (1979)
Foolin' Around (1980)
Sidney Shorr: A Girl's Best Friend (TV, 1981)
Off Sides (TV, 1984)
Hitler's SS: Portrait in Evil (TV, 1985)
My Little Pony (1986)
Sunday Drive (TV, 1986)
Agatha Christie's "The Man in the Brown Suit" (TV, 1989)
Gremlins 2: The New Batch (1990)
Fatal Instinct (1993)
The Odd Couple: Together Again (TV, 1993)

RADIO

I Love a Mystery (1949–52)

TV

One Man's Family (1950–52)
Mister Peepers (1952–55)
The Odd Couple (1970–75)
The Tony Randall Show (1976–78)
Love, Sidney (1981–83)

Paul Reiser

Star of "Mad About You"

Paul Reiser became famous as a stand-up comedian. He is best known today, however, as a major TV star by virtue of his roles in the hit sitcoms *My Two Dads* (1987-90) and *Mad about You* (1992-99).

Paul Reiser was born in New York City, New York, on March 30, 1956. As a child he was the class cutup. While in high school, he often went to Greenwich Village comedy clubs to observe the comedians. He attended the State University of New York at Binghamton, where he majored in music and participated in theatrical productions.

After graduating from college in 1977, Reiser worked in his father's wholesale health-food business by day and performed in Manhattan comedy clubs at night. After a year of doing this, he decided to devote himself full-time to comedy. His career made steady progress over the next few years, and he began to perform in comedy clubs across the country.

Reiser's casual style of stand-up comedy appeared to be improvised but was actually carefully crafted. He pushed back the sleeves of his sweater and talked to his audience about everyday things that he observed or experienced. One of his favorite devices was the what-bothers-me line, as when he confessed his irritation at people who gave directions like "the road curves, but you stay straight." On the subject of pets, he said that "dog is man's best friend because they think alike."

Reiser got his big break when he was offered a role in the movie *Diner* (1982). He played Modell, who enters a diner but never orders anything, preferring to pester and mooch food from others.

Reiser's outstanding performance in *Diner* led to invitations to perform on the late-night variety shows hosted by Johnny Carson and David Letterman. He then got supporting roles in the films *Beverly Hills Cop* (1984) and *Aliens* (1986). In the film comedy *Odd Jobs* (1986) he starred as a confused but likable guy who bungles his way through life until he stumbles into heroism by capturing some car thieves; the role was an extension of his comedy-club persona. In 1987 he received high praise from fans and critics for his HBO special *Out on a Whim*.

Poised for stardom, Reiser was asked to play the lead in the TV comedy series *My Two Dads* (1987–90), a show about two men awarded joint custody of a preteen girl because either of them could have been her father. Reiser played Michael Taylor, a straitlaced business executive who contrasted with the other dad, an avant-garde artist. The show was a hit and it made Reiser a star.

During the run of *My Two Dads*, in 1988, Reiser married. He had met his wife, Paula, in 1982, when she was a student and comedy-club waitress. Later, she became a psychotherapist. They had a son, Ezra. In 1992 Reiser and the writer Danny Jacobson created a sitcom about a Manhattan-based newlywed couple, Paul and Jamie Buchman, with Reiser playing the husband. Like Reiser, Jacobson had recently married, and both men wanted the new series, *Mad about You*, to be a realistic portrayal of everyday husband-and-wife relationships. To that end, Reiser often drew story ideas from events in his own home. After a slow start on the ratings chart,

Paul Reiser

Helen Hunt and Paul Reiser

the series collected a large following. When it ended in 1999, it was still one of the most popular shows on TV.

While working on *Mad about You*, Reiser continued to work on other projects. He appeared in several movies, including *The Tower* (TV, 1993), *Mr. Write* (1994), and *Bye Bye, Love* (1995). Having studied married life for *Mad about You*, he reported his findings in the books *Couplehood* (1994) and *Babyhood* (1997).

Don Rickles

Insult Comedian

Don Rickles has long been one of America's leading stand-up comedians. The basis of his humor is insult, and he has been labeled the Merchant of Venom and, ironically, Mr. Warmth.

Donald Jay Rickles was born in New York City, New York, on May 8, 1926. He was raised in a strict Orthodox household, and he has remained a committed Jew all his life.

After serving in the U. S. navy during World War II, Rickles studied acting at the American Academy of Dramatic Arts in New York City. His goal was to become a dramatic actor, but he could not get enough acting work to earn a living (he had parts on the TV anthology series *Stage Seven* and in the film dramas *Run Silent, Run Deep* (1958) and *The Rat Race* (1960). To earn money he did stand-up comedy on the side, especially at strip joints. The patrons at such places, anxious to see the girls, heckled Rickles, who soon learned that he could get laughs by firing right back. He developed an act based on insulting his audience members, often by ridiculing their ethnicity or appearance. His favorite epithets were "dummy" and "hockey puck." Rickles has described his style as a kind of catharsis, "a satire of attitudes and prejudices." He claims never to have had a serious confrontation with an insulted fan.

In 1956 Rickles gave an important performance at the Slate Brothers Club in Los Angeles, where he insulted a special member of the audience—Frank Sinatra. Rickles's hilarious performance won him the respect of show-business insiders, but major public success with general audiences eluded him for some years to come.

By the mid-1960s Rickles's shift from dramatic acting to comedy was fulfilled. His abrasive style seemed to suit the social turbulence of the decade, and he became a popular comedian during that period.

Rickles's style, involving interplay with audience members, was especially effective in live performances. Since the 1960s he has worked at the most prestigious nightclubs, hotels, and casinos in New York City, Los Angeles, Las Vegas, Miami, and elsewhere.

Television, too, has been an important vehicle for Rickles. Besides appearing as a guest comedian on most of the major talk and variety shows, he has starred in his own series. *The Don Rickles Show* (1968-69) was a part-game, part-variety program that he hosted. In 1972 he starred as an advertising executive in the sitcom also titled *The Don Rickles Show*. More successful was *C.P.O. Sharkey* (1976–78), a sitcom in which he starred as Chief Petty Officer Otto Sharkey, a navy drill instructor. In a 1982 episode of the sitcom *Archie Bunker's Place*, he gave a fine seriocomic performance as an obnoxious—but lonely and pitiful—roomer who dies. In 1989 Rickles guest-starred as an insulting talk-show host on the sitcom *Newhart*. He also cohosted the comedy series *Foul-ups, Bleeps, and Blunders* (1984-85) and appeared in the short-lived sitcom *Daddy Dearest* (1993).

Rickles continues to take on occasional film roles. He appeared in three of the beach comedies of the 1960s: *Bikini Beach* (1964), *Muscle Beach Party*

Don Rickles

(1964), and *Beach Blanket Bingo* (1965). He was also featured in the farce *Enter Laughing* (1967), the war comedy *Kelly's Heroes* (1970), the horror comedy *Innocent Blood* (1992), and the crime drama *Casino* (1995). In the computer-animated hit *Toy Story* (1995), he provided the voice of Mr. Potato Head.

Rickles married Barbara Sklar, a secretary, in 1965. They had two children, Mindy and Lawrence.

SELECTED PERFORMANCES:

STAGE

The Odd Couple (1967)

FILMS

Run Silent, Run Deep (1958)
The Rat Race (1960)
X: The Man with X-Ray Eyes (1963)
Bikini Beach (1964)
Muscle Beach Party (1964)
Beach Blanket Bingo (1965)
Enter Laughing (1967)
The Money Jungle (1968)
Where It's At (1969)
Kelly's Heroes (1970)
For the Love of It (TV, 1980)
Innocent Blood (1992)
Casino (1995)
Toy Story (animated, voice-only, 1995)
Dennis the Menace Strikes Again (1998)
Quest for Camelot (1998)
Dirty Work (1998)

TV

The Don Rickles Show (1968–69, 1972)
C.P.O. Sharkey (1976–78)
Foul-ups, Bleeps, and Blunders (1984–85)
Daddy Dearest (1993)

Joan Rivers

The "Can We Talk?" Comedienne

Joan Rivers is the most successful woman in the history of stand-up comedy. Among the first and few comediennes to use insult humor (traditionally a male province), she ridicules flaws and neuroses in herself, in celebrities, and in Americans at large. Her favorite topics are physical appearance, lifestyle, and sexuality. Rivers sets a tone of informality, as if gossiping with close friends, through her signature phrase, "Can we talk?"

Joan Rivers was born in Brooklyn in New York, on June 8, 1933. Her original name was Joan Alexandra Molinsky.

While attending the Adelphi Academy preparatory school in Brooklyn, she participated in the drama program and placed second in a *Photoplay* acting contest. Shortly after graduation, she landed a small role in the movie *Mr. Universe* (1951).

Under pressure from her mother, Rivers put aside her acting ambitions and studied English and anthropology at Barnard College in New York City. After graduating in 1954, she entered the business world, eventually becoming fashion coordinator for the entire chain of Bond clothing stores. She also married Jimmy Langer, son of the merchandiser for the Bond stores, but her desire to return to performing led to the annulment of the marriage in 1958.

In 1960, after she had struggled for a couple of years as an actress, she started performing a comedy act. Her initial goal was to earn money to support her acting career. She worked in strip joints, Catskill resorts, and seedy nightclubs.

From 1961 to 1962 Rivers was a member of the Chicago-based improvisational acting troupe Second City. The group's stream-of-consciousness comedy technique taught her to trust her own comedic impulses.

In 1962 she returned to New York City, where she discovered discovered Lenny Bruce and admired the way he generated comedic material from personal pain and insight. Rivers, too, began to speak, as she later reported, "directly and personally to the audience," telling jokes about herself as a nervous, unattractive loser whom her mother could not marry off. "She is so desperate to get me married," Rivers told her audience, "that if a murderer called, she'd say, 'So, he has a temper.'"

From 1963 to 1964 Rivers toured with Jim Connell and Jake Holmes in a song-and-comedy team named Jim, Jake, and Joan. The group was moderately successful, but she soon decided to go solo.

Rivers got her first big break in February 1965, when she appeared on *The Tonight Show*. She and host Johnny Carson developed an instant rapport, and he pronounced her a future star.

Soon Rivers was being booked at the best comedy clubs in the country. She also began to record comedy albums, appeared in the Broadway comedy *Fun City* (1972), and became a familiar face on TV. From 1969 to 1971 she hosted *That Show*, her own talk program. Throughout the 1970s she frequently guest-hosted *The Tonight Show*.

By the early 1980s Rivers was applying her acid wit to celebrities. On Elizabeth Taylor's weight problem: "This woman has more chins than a Chinese phone book!" On the wardrobe of Queen

Joan Rivers

Rivers Show (1989–93), the gossip show *Joan Rivers' Gossip, Gossip, Gossip* (1992–93), and the shopping program *Can We Shop?* (1994).

Rivers has also succeeded as an actress. She gave outstanding performances on Broadway as Kate Jerome in Neil Simon's play *Broadway Bound* (1988) and as the title character, Lenny Bruce's mother, in *Sally Marr . . . and Her Escorts* (1994). Her other acting credits include roles in the theatrical films *Rabbit Test* (1978), *Les Patterson Saves the World* (1987), and *Spaceballs* (1987) as the voice of Dot Matrix. She also appeared in the made-for-TV movies *How to Murder a Millionaire* (TV, 1990) and *Tears and Laughter: The Joan and Melissa Rivers Story* (TV, 1994), in which she portrayed herself.

Multitalented, Rivers has proven herself to be a gifted writer in many genres. She cowrote the play *Fun City* (1972), the TV movie *The Girl Most Likely to . . .* (TV, 1973), and the theatrical film *Rabbit Test*, which she also directed. From 1973 to 1976 she wrote a nationally syndicated column for the *Chicago Tribune*. Her book *The Life and Hard Times of Heidi Abromowitz* (1984) was a fictional biography of "the most renowned tramp since Charlie Chaplin." *Enter Talking* (with Richard Meryman, 1986) was the first in a series of autobiographical books, the most recent being *Bouncing Back: I've Survived Everything . . . and I Mean Everything . . . and You Can Too!* (1997).

Rivers's second husband was Edgar Rosenberg, a producer whom she married in 1965. They had a daughter, Melissa. In 1987, depressed over his failing health, Rosenberg committed suicide. Griefstricken, Rivers buried herself in her work.

Rivers served as national chairperson of the Cystic Fibrosis Society, and she was the first major entertainer to headline fund-raising for AIDS. As of 1998 she was dating Orin Lehman, great-grandson of the founder of Lehman Brothers, the Wall Street investment firm.

Elizabeth of England: "Gowns by Helen Keller." On Nancy Reagan's "bulletproof" hair: "If they ever combed it, they'd find Jimmy Hoffa." Some critics accused Rivers of cruelty, but her jokes were all in fun. She did not spare herself either: "I'm Jewish. If God had wanted me to exercise, He would've put diamonds on the floor!"

From 1983 to 1986 Rivers was the first permanent guest host of *The Tonight Show*. In 1986 she hosted six one-hour specials, called *Joan Rivers: Can We Talk?*, for British TV. From October 1986 to May 1987 she directly competed against her old friend Johnny Carson by hosting her own late-night variety program, *The Late Show Starring Joan Rivers*. Later, she hosted the talk program *The Joan*

(Left to right) Miss Piggy, Frank Oz, and Joan Rivers

SELECTED PERFORMANCES:

STAGE

Fun City (1972)
Broadway Bound (1988)
Sally Marr . . . and Her Escorts (1994)

FILMS

Mr. Universe (1951)
The Swimmers (1968)
Rabbit Test (1978)
Uncle Scam (1981)
The Muppets Take Manhattan (1984)
Les Patterson Saves the World (1987)

Spaceballs (voice-only, 1987)
How to Murder a Millionaire (TV, 1990)
Lady Boss (TV, 1992)
Serial Mom (1994)
*Tears and Laughter: The Joan and Melissa Rivers
    Story* (TV, 1994)

TV

That Show (1969-71)
Joan Rivers: Can We Talk? (1986)
The Late Show Starring Joan Rivers (1986-87)
The Joan Rivers Show (1989-93)
Joan Rivers' Gossip, Gossip, Gossip (1992-93)
Can We Shop? (1994)

Edward G. Robinson

Filmdom's Preeminent Tough Guy

During his sixty-year career, Edward G. Robinson firmly established himself as one of America's greatest actors. He was especially noted for his powerful portrayals of gangsters and other tough-guy roles.

Edward G. Robinson was born in Bucharest, Romania, on December 12, 1893. His original name was Emanuel Goldenberg.

Because the Romanian government was engaged in the systematic persecution of Jews, the Goldenbergs left Romania and moved to the United States in 1902. Young Robinson attended New York City's Townsend Harris High School and City College of the City University of New York. He dropped out of college after his sophomore year so that he could study acting at the American Academy of Dramatic Arts.

While he was at the American Academy, he was urged to change his name because it was too long, too foreign, and (he suspected) too Jewish. He selected Edward (after the current king of England) Robinson (after a character in an English comedy). His middle initial stood for his original surname. "Deep down in my deepest heart," he later wrote in his autobiography, *All My Yesterdays* (with Leonard Spigelgass, 1973), "I am, and have always been, Emanuel Goldenberg."

In 1913, soon after leaving the American Academy, Robinson joined an Albany, New York, stock company with which he made his professional acting debut in *Paid in Full*. Returning to New York City, he began to make a name for himself by performing three separate roles in the play *Under Fire* (1915). For the next decade he served as a reliable supporting actor in numerous stage productions.

In 1926 Robinson married actress Gladys Lloyd, with whom he had appeared in *Henry Behave* (1926). They had one child, Edward G. Robinson, Jr. (always referred to as Manny).

Robinson got his big break in 1927 when he won the role of gangster Nick Scarsi in *The Racket*.

Robinson was not interested in making movies, but economic pressures finally induced him to give in to the lure of a Hollywood movie contract. He appeared in several minor films, then starred as the title character, a ruthless mobster, in *Caesar* (1931). His performance in *Caesar* was brilliant, and the film made Robinson a star. He played a number of other racketeer or tough-guy types in films throughout the 1930s, including *The Little Giant* (1933), *Barbary Coast* (1935), and *The Last Gangster* (1937). He soon became filmdom's preeminent performer of such roles.

In the early 1930s Robinson began to experience marital troubles when his wife decided to go back to work as an actress. Robinson helped her to get roles in his movies *Smart Money* (1931), *Five Star Final* (1931), *The Hatchet Man* (1932), and *Two Seconds* (1932). The tensions between them eased, at least temporarily.

Meanwhile Robinson was gradually receiving opportunities to show the wide range of his acting abilities. He displayed his flair for comedy in *The Whole Town's Talking* (1935) and *A Slight Case of Murder* (1938). He gave deeply moving performances in *Dr. Ehrlich's Magic Bullet* (1940), a film

Edward G. Robinson

about a scientist trying to find a cure for venereal disease, and *A Dispatch from Reuters* (1940), a movie about the founder of the news service. *In Brother Orchid* (1940) he convincingly portrayed a gangster-turned-monk.

Robinson's versatility reflected his general intelligence and personal cultivation. He read voraciously, spoke numerous languages (and read Hebrew), built a remarkable art collection, painted some fine pictures himself, and loved great music (his favorite composer was Beethoven).

In the 1940s Robinson continued to give memorable film performances. In *The Sea Wolf* (1941) he portrayed the maniacal captain of a ship. In *The Stranger* (1946) he hunted Nazi war criminals. Guilt haunted his characters in several movies: in *Scarlet Street* (1946) he was a milquetoast who is driven to murder and who lets another man be executed for the crime; in *The Red House* (1947) he was a man who loses his mind because of the horrible secret that he keeps about the red house, where he committed double murder; and in *All My Sons* (1948) he was a manufacturer who sold defective airplane parts to the government during World War II and who finally kills himself when he learns that his treachery indirectly caused the death of his own son. In *Key Largo* (1948) he played another gangster role.

In 1943 Robinson was one of the stars featured in Ben Hecht's pageant *We Will Never Die*, which was designed to make people aware of the Nazi horrors in Europe. The program was comprised of three parts: "The Roll Call," a recitation of the names of great Jews in the arts and sciences from ancient times to the modern era; "Jews in the War," a dramatization of the contributions of American Jewish war heroes; and "Remember Us," a presentation of reports about the slaughters in Nazi Europe.

Edward G. Robinson

Through the years Robinson had closely identified himself with many social and political causes promoting peace, democracy, and the betterment of the lives of minorities. By the late 1940s the Communist witch-hunt in America was in full swing, and Robinson, because of his fame, was one of the principal targets. At his own request he testified before the House Committee on Un-American Activities in 1947, 1950, and 1952. Nevertheless, he was blacklisted as a Communist sympathizer by major producers from the late 1940s through the mid-1950s.

Robinson fought back, taking whatever acting roles he could get and going back to the stage in *Darkness at Noon* (1951) and *Middle of the Night* (1956). Finally, the famed producer-director Cecil B. DeMille helped Robinson return to Hollywood films by giving him a major role in the biblical epic *The Ten Commandments* (1956).

During this same period Robinson's marriage finally fell apart. His wife had threatened divorce times and had been in and out of mental hospitals for many years. In 1956 Robinson divorced her, and as part of the property settlement, he had to give up his valuable art collection.

In 1958 Robinson married Jane Bodenheimer Adler, director of a firm through which the first Mrs. Robinson had purchased clothes for many years. With Jane he finally found the love and peace that had always been missing from his life. She was highly knowledgeable about painting, and she helped him to build another art collection.

At an age when most actors retire, Robinson kept working and showed no loss of energy or skill. From 1954 to 1971 he guest-starred in numerous TV series, including *For the Defense* (1954), *Playhouse Ninety* (1958), *General Electric Theater* (1961), and *Night Gallery* (1971). Among his later movies were *A Hole in the Head* (1959), *The Prize* (1964), *The Cincinnati Kid* (1965), *Mackenna's Gold* (1969), and *Song of Norway* (1970).

Robinson's portrayals of elderly men were dignified and richly evocative as in his role of the witness to a crime that no one believes really happened in *The Old Man Who Cried Wolf!* (TV, 1970). In *Soylent Green* (1973) he played his final movie role, that of Sol Roth, a serene philosopher who, in a horribly deprived New York City of 2022, gives up his life to prove that a new kind of food (soylent green) is made of human flesh.

In his last years Robinson suffered from serious health problems. He had a heart attack in Africa while filming *A Boy Ten Feet Tall* (1965). In 1966 he was in a near-fatal auto accident. In 1970 it was discovered that he had cancer of the bladder. After many sessions of cobalt treatment, he appeared to have made a remarkable recovery, but cancer finally took his life in Los Angeles, California, on January 26, 1973.

SELECTED PERFORMANCES:

STAGE

Paid in Full (1913)
Under Fire (1915)
Under Sentence (1916)
The Pawn (1917)
The Little Teacher (1918)
First Is Last (1919)
Night Lodging (1919)
Poldekin (1920)
Samson and Delilah (1920)
The Idle Inn (1921)
The Deluge (1922)
Banco (1922)
Peer Gynt (1923)
The Adding Machine (1923)
Launzi (1923)
A Royal Fandango (1923)
The Firebrand (1924)
Androcles and the Lion (1925)
The Man of Destiny (1925)
The Goat Song (1926)
The Chief Thing (1926)
Henry Behave (1926)
Juarez and Maximilian (1926)
Ned McCobb's Daughter (1926)
The Brothers Karamazov (1927)
Right You Are If You Think You Are (1927)
The Racket (1927)
A Man with Red Hair (1928)
Kibitzer (1929)
Mr. Samuel (1930)
Darkness at Noon (1951)
Middle of the Night (1956)

FILMS

The Bright Shawl (1923)
The Hole in the Wall (1929)
Night Ride (1929)
A Lady to Love (1930)
Outside the Law (1930)
East Is West (1930)
The Widow from Chicago (1930)
Little Caesar (1931)
Smart Money (1931)
Five Star Final (1931)
The Hatchet Man (1932)
Two Seconds (1932)
Tiger Shark (1932)
Silver Dollar (1932)

The Little Giant (1933)
I Loved a Woman (1933)
Dark Hazard (1934)
The Man with Two Faces (1934)
The Whole Town's Talking (1935)
Barbary Coast (1935)
Bullets or Ballots (1936)
Thunder in the City (1937)
Kid Galahad (1937)
The Last Gangster (1937)
A Slight Case of Murder (1938)
The Amazing Dr. Clitterhouse (1938)
I Am the Law (1938)
Confessions of a Nazi Spy (1939)
Blackmail (1939)
Dr. Ehrlich's Magic Bullet (1940)
Brother Orchid (1940)
A Dispatch from Reuters (1940)
The Sea Wolf (1941)
Manpower (1941)
Unholy Partners (1941)
Larceny, Inc. (1942)
Tales of Manhattan (1942)
Destroyer (1943)
Flesh and Fantasy (1943)
Tampico (1944)
Mr. Winkle Goes to War (1944)
Double Indemnity (1944)
The Woman in the Window (1945)
Our Vines Have Tender Grapes (1945)
Scarlet Street (1946)
Journey Together (1946)
The Stranger (1946)
The Red House (1947)
All My Sons (1948)

Key Largo (1948)
Night Has a Thousand Eyes (1948)
House of Strangers (1949)
It's a Great Feeling (1949)
My Daughter Joy (1950)
Actors and Sin (1952)
Vice Squad (1953)
Big Leaguer (1953)
The Glass Web (1953)
Black Tuesday (1954)
The Violent Men (1955)
Tight Spot (1955)
A Bullet for Joey (1955)
Illegal (1955)
Hell on Frisco Bay (1956)
Nightmare (1956)
The Ten Commandments (1956)
A Hole in the Head (1959)
Pepe (1960)
My Geisha (1961)
Two Weeks in Another Town (1962)
The Prize (1964)
Good Neighbor Sam (1964)
Robin and the Seven Hoods (1964)
The Outrage (1964)
Cheyenne Autumn (1964)
A Boy Ten Feet Tall (1965)
The Cincinnati Kid (1965)
The Biggest Bundle of Them All (1968)
Operation St. Peter's (1968)
Never a Dull Moment (1968)
Mackenna's Gold (1969)
Song of Norway (1970)
The Old Man Who Cried Wolf! (TV, 1970)
Soylent Green (1973)

Jill St. John

Beautiful Leading Lady

For many years Jill St. John was cast in roles that focused attention on her great physical beauty. Later, when given the opportunity to broaden her range, she proved to be a fine actress.

Jill St. John was born in Los Angeles, California, on August 19, 1940. Her original name was Jill Oppenheim. She began to act professionally when she was only six years old. She worked in radio on several episodes of the series *One Man's Family*, and she made her TV debut in a 1948 production of *A Christmas Carol*. By the time she was sixteen, she had performed on radio over a thousand times and on TV at least fifty times.

In 1957 St. John married the millionaire Neil Durbin. They divorced in 1959, and the following year she married another wealthy man, Lance Reventlow. The marriage dissolved in 1963. In 1967 she wedded entertainer Jack Jones, whom she divorced in 1969.

Meanwhile, St. John had begun her film career, debuting in *Summer Love* (1958). She also appeared in *The Roman Spring of Mrs. Stone* (1961), *Tender Is the Night* (1962), *Come Blow Your Horn* (1963), *The Oscar* (1966), and other movies.

St. John had been educated at UCLA, and the American diplomat Henry Kissinger once referred to her as "one of the brightest women I have ever met." Yet her physical beauty was so striking that for years she was consistently cast in roles that merely exploited her sexuality. She was even cast as a "Bond girl" in the James Bond spy movie *Diamonds Are Forever* (1971).

Eventually, however, St. John was able to break away from these sexist stereotypes. For example, she played the tough warden of a women's prison in *The Concrete Jungle* (1982). In the 1983 to 1984 TV season she appeared in *Emerald Point, N.A.S.*, and later she had a role in the made-for-TV movie *Out There* (TV, 1995).

St. John now spends much of her time at her Aspen, Colorado, home, where she runs a clothing (sweater) business. She is married to the actor Robert Wagner.

SELECTED PERFORMANCES:

STAGE

Love Letters (1998)

FILMS

Summer Love (1958)
The Remarkable Mr. Pennypacker (1959)
Holiday for Lovers (1959)
The Lost World (1960)
The Roman Spring of Mrs. Stone (1961)
Tender Is the Night (1962)
Come Blow Your Horn (1963)
Who's Been Sleeping in My Bed? (1963)
Who's Minding the Store? (1963)
Honeymoon Hotel (1964)
The Liquidator (1966)
The Oscar (1966)
Fame Is the Name of the Game (TV, 1966)
How I Spent My Summer Vacation (TV, 1967)
Banning (1967)
Eight on the Lam (1967)
The King's Pirate (1967)

Jill St. John

Tony Rome (1967)
The Spy Killer (TV, 1969)
Foreign Exchange (TV, 1970)
Diamonds Are Forever (1971)
Sitting Target (1972)
Brenda Starr (TV, 1976)
Telethon (TV, 1977)

Hart to Hart (TV, 1979)
Rooster (TV, 1982)
The Concrete Jungle (1982)
Out There (TV, 1995)

TV

Emerald Point, N.A.S. (1983–84)

Joseph Schildkraut

First Actor to Play Otto Frank

◄O►

Joseph Schildkraut was one of the most respected actors of his time, capable of playing any kind of leading or supporting role. He
achieved his greatest fame for his portrayal
of Otto Frank in both the stage (1955) and
film (1959) versions of *The Diary of Anne
Frank*.

◄O►

Joseph Schildkraut was born in Vienna, Austria,
on March 22, 1896. From an early age, Joseph
traveled extensively with his father, Rudolf
Schildkraut, an internationally famous actor.

Joseph's first love was music. He studied violin and piano at the Imperial Academy of Music
in Berlin, from which he graduated with honors in
1911, at the youthful age of fifteen.

Later that year he moved to the United States
because his father had been engaged to act in German (and later Yiddish) plays in New York City.
Joseph, against his father's wishes, then decided
to become an actor. He studied at the American
Academy of Dramatic Arts, where his classmates
included Paul Muni, William Powell, and Edward
G. Robinson. Shortly after graduating in 1913, he
made his professional acting debut, touring as the
juvenile lead in *The Romantics*.

Later that year he returned with his parents to
Europe and settled in Berlin. There he was cast
with his father in *The Prodigal Son*. Soon he began
to study with Albert Bassermann, the single greatest influence on Schildkraut as an actor.

Still an Austrian citizen (he became a naturalized American citizen in 1938), Schildkraut was inducted into the Austrian army for World War I
service (1914-16). In 1918 he hit his full stride as
an actor by appearing in three consecutive hits in
Vienna: *Jeremiah*, *The Coral*, and *Shadow Dance*.

In 1920 Schildkraut returned to New York City,
where he was soon chosen to play the title role, a
carnival barker, in *Liliom* (1921). The play was a
tremendous success, and it shot the young actor
to stardom. With his new status he was asked to
play his first important part in a movie (having
earlier made a few minor film appearances), the
D.W. Griffith production *Orphans of the Storm*
(1921).

Meanwhile, he continued to appear in *Liliom*.
In 1922 during its long run, he married the young
actress Elise Bartlee. They divorced in 1931.

Soon after finishing *Liliom*, Schildkraut starred
in two other important stage roles: the title role in
Peer Gynt (1923) and the roguish artist-lover
Benvenuto Cellini in *Firebrand* (1924). In the later
1920s he made movies in Hollywood, including
The King of Kings (1927), in which he acted with
his father, *Tenth Avenue* (1928), and *Show Boat*
(1929).

In the early 1930s Schildkraut went to England
to do film work. While in London he met Marie
McKay, whom he married in Vienna in 1932.

In Vienna, Schildkraut intended to accept a
stage engagement. However, the anti-Semitism in
the city had become so great that he decided to
return to New York City.

In the early 1930s he appeared on the American stage in *Camille* (1932), *Alice in Wonderland*
(1932), *Between two Worlds* (1934), and other plays.
He also returned to Hollywood to make numer-

ous films, including *Viva Villa!* (1934), *The Crusades* (1939), and *The Shop around the Corner* (1940). For his portrayal of Captain Dreyfus in *The Life of Émile Zola* (1937), Schildkraut won international acclaim.

Returning to the stage, he played *Clash by Night* (1941), *Uncle Harry* (1942), and *The Cherry Orchard* (1944). In the late 1940s, while under contract with Republic Pictures, he was cast in a number of undistinguished films.

In 1951 he appeared on Broadway in *The Green Bay Tree*, and in 1953 he played in the New York City Center's production of Shakespeare's *Love's Labour's Lost*. Unable to find significant film roles, Schildkraut began to work heavily in a new medium—television. From 1949 to 1955 he appeared in over eighty-five live TV shows, some of them for *Joseph Schildkraut Presents* (1953–54), an anthology series of dramas that he hosted.

In October 1955 he returned to the stage and created a memorable characterization as Otto Frank in *The Diary of Anne Frank*, the true story of the young girl who, with family and friends, fled Hitler's Nazi Germany and hid in an Amersterdam attic until she was arrested and later killed in a concentration camp. Schildkraut himself regarded his work in that play as the high point of his career and life. In his autobiography, *My Father and I* (as told to Leo Lanis, 1959), he explained that he had never before "felt such an intimate relationship with a play, never such an identification with a part."

Anne Frank's diary wrote the epitaph to the one-hundred-year history of the "emancipated" Germanized Jew. Rudolf Schildkraut had been a symbol of that era; the Jew who proudly thought of himself as a German, who assimilated German culture, and who in turn enriched the arts for all German people. Joseph Schildkraut, through his simple, humble, dignified portrayal of Otto Frank, paid homage not only to the Franks but also to his own father, who after arriving in America, finally came to realize that, in Joseph's words, "his soul and heartbeat were Jewish, not German."

Schildkraut re-created the role in the filmed version of *The Diary of Anne Frank* (1959). In 1962 his wife, Marie, died, and in 1963 he married the young actress Leonora Rogers. His last performance came as Nicodemus in the movie *The Greatest Story Ever Told* (1965). He died in New York City on January 21, 1964.

Joseph Schildkraut

Shildkraut had appeared in several dozen plays, over sixty films, and nearly one hundred TV productions. His acting range was extremely wide, from a romantic lead to virtually any kind of a supporting-character role. His hallmark was economy of gesture.

Schildkraut's heart was in the theater, which, like his father, he viewed as a "moral institution." Art he said, should "plant in the hearts and minds of the bewildered and frustrated the seeds of understanding, hope, goodness, and humanity."

SELECTED PERFORMANCES:

STAGE

The Romantics (1913)
The Prodigal Son (1913)
Jeremiah (1918)
The Coral (1918)

Shadow Dance (1918)
Pagans (1921)
Liliom (1921)
Peer Gynt (1923)
The Fireband (1924)
An American Tragedy (1932)
Camille (1932)
Dear Jane (1932)
Alice in Wonderland (1932)
Between Two Worlds (1934)
Tomorrow's a Holiday! (1935)
Clash by Night (1941)
Uncle Harry (1942)
The Cherry Orchard (1944)
The Green Bay Tree (1951)
Love's Labour's Lost (1953)
The Diary of Anne Frank (1955)

FILMS

Orphans of the Storm (1921)
Dust of Desire (1923)
The Song of Love (1924)
The Road to Yesterday (1925)
Young April (1926)
The King of Kings (1927)
The Heart Thief (1927)
His Dog (1927)
The Forbidden Woman (1927)
Tenth Avenue (1928)
The Blue Danube (1928)
Show Boat (1929)
The Mississippi Gambler (1929)
Cock o' the Walk (1930)
Carnival (1931)
Blue Danube (new version, 1932)

Viva Villa! (1934)
Sisters under the Skin (1934)
Cleopatra (1934)
The Crusades (1935)
The Garden of Allah (1936)
Slave Ship (1937)
Souls at Sea (1937)
The Life of Emile Zola (1937)
Lancer Spy (1937)
The Baroness and the Butler (1938)
Marie Antoinette (1938)
Suez (1938)
Idiot's Delight (1939)
The Three Musketeers (1939)
Mr. Moto Takes a Vacation (1939)
The Man in the Iron Mask (1939)
Lady of the Tropics (1939)
The Rains Came (1939)
Pack Up Your Troubles (1939)
The Shop around the Corner (1940)
Phantom Raiders (1940)
Rangers of Fortune (1940)
Meet the Wildcat (1940)
The Parson of Panamint (1941)
The Cheaters (1945)
Monsieur Beaucaire (1946)
The Plainsman and the Lady (1946)
Northwest Outpost (1947)
Old Los Angeles (1948)
The Diary of Anne Frank (1959)
King of the Roaring Twenties (1961)
The Greatest Story Ever Told (1965)

TV

Joseph Schildkraut Presents (1953–54)

George Segal

Thoughtful Leading Man

———◄○►———

Regardless of the type of role George Segal plays—serious or comic—he approaches it with wit and intelligence. A versatile actor, he is equally skilled at playing thoughtful, complex characters and light, comic-romantic roles.

◄○►

George Segal was born in New York City on February 13, 1934. While growing up in Great Neck, New York, he regularly entertained children with magic tricks at parties. After attending George School, a privately run Quaker institution in Pennsylvania, he enrolled at Haverford College and then transferred to Columbia University, where he received a B.A. degree in 1955.

After working as an usher and at other theater-related jobs, Segal began to get bit parts. He had, for example, a small role in a Broadway revival of Eugene O'Neill's *The Iceman Cometh* in 1956.

That year he also married Marion Sobol, a former TV story editor. They had two children, Elizabeth and Polly.

Following a brief stint in the army, Segal returned to the stage and continued to perform without any spectacular results. He appeared in *Antony and Cleopatra* (1959), *Gideon* (1961), and a variety of other plays. Then, after playing a couple of minor roles in movies, including *The Young Doctors* (1961), he finally began to receive serious attention as an actor when he played the brother in the Broadway show *Rattle of a Simple Man* (1963).

Segal became a major star with his performance in the movie *King Rat* (1965). In that film he played

a conniving American corporal who breeds rats and sells their flesh as game meat to his deceived fellow inmates at a prisoner-of-war camp during World War II. He also gave an impressive performance in *Ship of Fools* (1965), a film that explores relationships among a shipload of Jews and non-Jews on a German passenger vessel in 1933.

Over the next several years, Segal gave strong performances in a number of films and plays. He was highly praised for his portrayal of Biff, Willy Loman's son, in the 1966 TV production of *Death of a Salesman*. In the movie *Who's Afraid of Virginia Woolf?* (1966) he played a young teacher caught up in a vicious battle between an older colleague and the latter's wife. In *Bye Bye Braverman* (1968), a comic film about New York City Jewish intellectuals, he had the lead. *In No Way to Treat a Lady* (1968) Segal combined serious and humorous elements in his characterization of a police detective hunting a serial killer.

Indeed, through the years Segal has shown that he can play intensely serious roles and light, comic-romantic leads with equal skill. In the detective story *Trackdown: Finding the Goodbar Killer* (TV, 1983) and the psychological thriller *The Cold Room* (TV, 1984), he was cast in serious roles. In *The Owl and the Pussycat* (1970), on the other hand, he had an opportunity to demonstrate his skills as a comic actor. His light, sophisticated performance in *A Touch of Class* (1973) has been favorably compared with the work of Cary Grant. He was also effective in the title role of the decidedly unsubtle film *The Zany Adventures of Robin Hood* (TV, 1984), a broad spoof of the old Sherwood Forest legend. In the wild satirical comedy *Many Happy Returns*

George Segal

appeared in a great many movies, including *Look Who's Talking* (1989), *For the Boys* (1991), *Seasons of the Heart* (TV, 1994), *The Mirror Has Two Faces* (1996), and *The November Conspiracy* (1997). In March 1997 he began a recurring role as Jack Gallo, a women's magazine publisher, in the popular sitcom *Just Shoot Me!*

SELECTED PERFORMANCES:

STAGE

The Iceman Cometh (1956)
Don Juan (1956)
Antony and Cleopatra (1959)
Our Town (1959)
Leave It to Jane (1959)
Gideon (1961)
Rattle of a Simple Man (1963)
The Knack (1964)
Requiem for a Heavyweight (1985)

FILMS

The Young Doctors (1961)
Act One (1963)
Invitation to a Gunfighter (1964)
The New Interns (1964)
King Rat (1965)
Ship of Fools (1965)
Lost Command (1966)
The Quiller Memorandum (1966)
Who's Afraid of Virginia Woolf? (1966)
The St. Valentine Day Massacre (1967)
Bye Bye Braverman (1968)
No Way to Treat a Lady (1968)
The Bridge at Remagen (1969)
The Girl Who Couldn't Say No (1969)
The Southern Star (1969)
The Owl and the Pussycat (1970)
Where's Poppa? (1970)
Loving (TV, 1970)
Born to Win (1971)
The Hot Rock (1972)
Blume in Love (1973)
A Touch of Class (1973)
The Terminal Man (1974)
California Split (1974)
The Black Bird (1975)

George Segal

(TV, 1986), he played a man who is victimized by, and then wages war on, the Internal Revenue Service.

Though Segal has worked fairly steadily throughout his career, he spent many years in a drug-induced mental fog. He began to use drugs in the 1960s, but his work was most seriously affected from the mid-1970s to the early 1980s, particularly by cocaine. Finally, he kicked the habit cold turkey by spending two weeks in a Palm Springs, California, motel room, where he was aided by Linda Rogoff, whom he married in 1982. She died in 1996, and that year he married Sonia Schultz Greenbaum.

From the late 1980s to the mid-1990s, Segal

George Segal in one of his early movies

Russian Roulette (1975)
The Dutchess and the Dirtwater Fox (1976)
Fun with Dick and Jane (1977)
Rollercoaster (1977)
Who Is Killing the Great Chefs of Europe? (1978)
Lost and Found (1979)
The Last Married Couple in America (1980)
Carbon Copy (1981)
The Deadly Game (TV, 1982)
Trackdown: Finding the Goodbar Killer (TV, 1983)
The Cold Room (TV, 1984)
The Zany Adventures of Robin Hood (TV, 1984)
Not My Kid (TV, 1985)
Stick (1985)
Many Happy Returns (TV, 1986)
Look Who's Talking (1989)
For the Boys (1991)
Look Who's Talking Now (1993)
Taking the Heat (TV, 1993)

Seasons of the Heart (TV, 1994)
Following Her Heart (TV, 1994)
Direct Hit (1994)
Army of One (1994)
The Babysitter (1995)
The Good Doctor: The Paul Fleiss Story (TV, 1996)
The Cable Guy (1996)
Flirting with Disaster (1996)
It's My Party (1996)
The Mirror Has Two Faces (1996)
The November Conspiracy (1997)
Houdini (TV, 1998)

TV

Take Five (1987)
Murphy's Law (1988–89)
The Naked Truth (1997–98)
Just Shoot Me! (1997–)

Jerry Seinfeld

Comedian of His Generation

Jerry Seinfeld began his career in show business as a stand-up comedian in small comedy clubs. He eventually worked his way up to performing in large concert halls and amphitheaters. After making many guest appearances on TV, he hit the jackpot with his own sitcom, *Seinfeld* (1990-98), which became one of the most popular series in the history of television.

J erry Seinfeld was born in Brooklyn, New York, on April 29, 1954. He grew up in Massapequa, New York. His father, who painted and sold business signs, had a gift for making people laugh. Seinfeld later recalled, "I watched the effect he would have on people, and I thought that was for me."

In 1976, shortly after graduating from Queens College of the City University of New York with a major in theater and communications, Seinfeld began performing at small comedy clubs in New York City. "They weren't even clubs," he later admitted. "They were restaurants with a table missing."

In 1980 he moved to Los Angeles where he struggled through some lean months. He then landed a recurring, though short-lived, role as Frankie on the TV sitcom *Benson* (1980–81).

Seinfeld got his big break in 1981 when he made his first of many appearances on *The Tonight Show*. Later, he also became a favorite guest performer on *Late Night with David Letterman* and on HBO specials. By the late 1980s he was one of the busiest comedians in the country, making about three hundred appearances per year.

Part visual comedian and part lighthearted social commentator, Seinfeld characteristically explores humorous topics from all angles, as in this bit about a strand of hair in a bathroom:

"I don't like other people's showers. There's a problem with temperature adjustment. And there's always that little hair stuck on the wall. You want to get rid of it, but you don't want to touch it. You wonder how it got that high in the first place. Maybe it's got a life of its own. I don't want to get involved. So you have to aim the shower head at the hair, but then it always seems to just miss the hair. So you have to get a little water in your hands, go over there—[he throws imaginary water at the imaginary hair and watches it slither down the tile wall]."

Seinfeld's humor is not only very insightful, it's also clean. "My jokes are about clean subjects, and they're very thought-out," he explains. "Most comedians who use a lot of profanity—they're using it for fast punchlines . . . I can put a joke together well enough that I don't need dirty words."

Seinfeld, who writes all of his own material, is an observational humorist. When, for example, he watched the Winter Olympics, he was baffled by the biathlon, which consists of cross-country skiing and rifle shooting: "How many Alpine snipers are into this? It's like combining swimming and strangling a guy. I don't get the sport."

Among Seinfeld's other sidesplitters are these:

"Dogs are broke all their lives. You know why they have no money? No pockets. They see

258

change on the street—there's nothing they can do about it.

"You go to the store and buy Grape Nuts. No grapes, no nuts. What's the story there?"

"If he's the best man, why is the bride marrying the groom??

Having proved his popularity and durability as a comedian, Seinfeld was offered a chance for his own TV sitcom. The pilot, aired in 1989, was called *The Seinfeld Chronicles*. In 1990 the series began, called, simply, *Seinfeld*. Often referred to as a "show about nothing," the series revolved around four young, obviously flawed friends dealing with the daily problems of living in a modern urban environment (set in New York City). Seinfeld starred as himself, a comedian. His friends were Elaine, his ex-girlfriend; George, a bumbling worrywart; and the offbeat Kramer, an eccentric entrepreneur. The show was at or near the top of the TV ratings throughout most of the 1990s, even during its final 1997 to 1998 season. Seinfeld decided to end the series because he wanted to leave while it was still popular and because he felt ready to step aside from comedy and try other things. He had already branched out into writing, producing a book of humor, *SeinLanguage* (1993). The final episode of his series aired in May 1998 to one of the largest viewing audiences in the history of television..

He immediately returned to stand-up comedy. In August 1998 he appeared in an HBO comedy special, *Jerry Seinfeld: I'm Telling You for the Last Time*, which was broadcast live from a Broadway theater.

SELECTED PERFORMANCES:

FILMS

The Ratings Game (TV, 1984)

TV

Benson (1980-81)
Seinfeld (1990-98)

Peter Sellers

Comic Genius

Peter Sellers was a comedy chameleon. Not intrinsically a funny man, he nevertheless revealed a comic genius through a series of brilliant and hilarious screen characterizations of incredible variety. He frequently portrayed multiple roles in a single film. His best-known character, whom he played in the "Pink Panther" series of motion pictures, was the inept French police detective Inspector Jacques Clouseau.

Peter Sellers was born of a Protestant father and Jewish mother in the Southsea district of Portsmouth, England, on September 8, 1925. His father, Bill Sellers, was a pianist, while his mother, Peg Sellers (née Marks), was part of a family theatrical touring company created by her mother. Bill met Peg when he was asked to join the troupe.

Peter Sellers began his own attempt at a show-business career in 1941 when he teamed up with a friend, Derek Altman, to form a song-and-joke act. Soon, he took up the drums and played with various groups, including his father's touring band, which entertained wartime troops and munition workers. Sellers himself served in the Royal Air Force from 1943 to 1946.

Returning to civilian life, Sellers had a liaison with a woman whom he later called Sky Blue. The union produced a daughter, who was immediately put up for adoption. He never saw the child.

Meanwhile, his attempts to revive his career as a drummer met with little success. He worked up a variety act—jokes, comic impersonations, and a little drumming and ukele playing—and began to appear in music halls.

In 1948 Sellers telephoned a producer and impersonated the voices of two radio stars (Kenneth Horne and Richard Murdoch). Impressed, the producer hired him for some radio appearances. Sellers was an immediate hit, and he soon found himself inundated with offers for radio and concert engagements.

In 1949 he and a few friends, calling themselves the Goons, made a recording of a comedy act and sent it to some radio producers. Two years later the Goons were given their own radio series, called *Crazy People*. In 1952 the program became known as *The Goon Show*. One of England's most popular radio programs, the zany, anarchic, surrealistic *Goon Show* lasted till January 1960 and made Sellers famous.

Meanwhile, Sellers also made his first movies. He began with a spinoff of the Goon characters in *Penny Points to Paradise* (1951), appeared as one of the eccentric robbers in the classic *The Ladykillers* (1956), and gave an impressive performance as the comical elderly movie projectionist in *The Smallest Show on Earth* (1957). In the film *The Naked Truth* (1958), Sellers was given his first opportunity to demonstrate his abilities as a comic chameleon. Playing a devious British actor who disguises himself in several other roles, Sellers portrayed a Scottish quizmaster, an aging bureaucrat, an Irish terrorist, and a hunter who knows nothing about guns.

In 1958 he starred in the stage satire *Brouhaha* as the sultan of a small Persian Gulf state. But

Peter Sellers

Duchess Gljoriana, and the shy, lovesick commander-in-chief of the army. *In I'm All Right, Jack* (1959), a brilliant satire of British management and labor practices, he played Fred Kite, the pompous, pathetically ignorant union leader.

At about that time Sellers began to develop a personal characteristic that lasted for the rest of his life: while he was making a film, he would be overtaken in real life by the character that he was playing. For example, in a rare noncomedic role, he played a vicious stolen-car dealer in *Never Let Go* (1960); for many hours after work each day, he continued to act boorishly and to shout at people in the thug's rasping voice.

Sellers's first American movie was *Lolita* (1962). After that, he regularly appeared in both American and British films. Often, the films contained international stars and were shot at international locations. One such movie was *The Pink Panther* (1964), which was filmed in Rome with French (Capucine), Italian (Claudia Cardinale), American (Robert Wagner), and British (Sellers and David Niven) stars. In *The Pink Panther* Sellers created one of the most universally popular characters of the modern cinema: the bumbling French detective Inspector Jacques Clouseau. This part was originally given to Peter Ustinov, who reportedly withdrew from the film out of disappointment that Ava Gardner was not cast opposite him.

Sellers got his basic idea for Inspector Clouseau from a box of Captain Webb matches. The label on the box pictured Captain Webb, the first man to swim across the English Channel to France. He

Sellers's temperament was unsuited for the legitimate theater. Unable to sustain his interest in a single part for a long period of time, he kept changing his character and causing problems for the other performers. He left the show in February 1959 and never took another stage role.

His comic genius found its natural medium in films. In *The Mouse That Roared* (1959), a film set in a mythical European duchy, Sellers played three parts: the wily prime minister, the aged Grand

had a big mustache and a facial expression that Sellers associated with the ostentatious virility affected by some Frenchmen. At that moment, that actor decided to give the foolish Clouseau a big mustache and a great dignity, feeling that "a forgivable vanity would humanize him and make him kind of touching." Sellers also invented Clouseau's strange French accent, while the film's director, Blake Edwards, suggested the character's physical clumsiness, which would make his dignity even funnier.

Sellers played Clouseau again in *A Shot in the Dark* (1964), *The Return of the Pink Panther* (1975), *The Pink Panther Strikes Again* (1967), and *Revenge of the Pink Panther* (1978)

One of Seller's most memorable achievements came in *Dr. Strangelove; or, How I Learned to Stop Worrying and Love the Bomb* (1964). He played three roles; the liberal-humanist president of the United States, the captive English RAF captain, and the mad German nuclear scientist Dr. Stranglove, whose right arm uncontrollably reasserts its inbred violence (attempting to strangle himself) and Fascism (giving the Nazi salute).

On a lighter note were his roles in the comedies *The World of Henry Orient* (1964), as a lecherous and lousy concert pianist; *What's New, Pussycat?* (1965), as a nutty psychiatrist; *The Wrong Box (*1966), as the disreputable Dr. Pratt; *I love You, Alice B. Toklas* (1968) a s a Jewish lawyer who becomes a hippie; *There's a Girl in My Soup* (1971) as an aging playboy; *Murder by Death* (1976) as the Chinese sleuth Sidney Wang; and the Prisoner of Zenda (1979), as both the cockney hansom cabdriver and the monarch of a mythical kingdom.

Seller's greatest role was as Chauncy Gardiner (or Chance the gardener) in *Being There* (1979), an allegory of American society's worship of the appearance of things rather than their substance. Chance has spent his entire life inside the home and walled garden of the millionaire whose plants he tends. All he knows of life comes from what he has seen of it on TV. When the millionaire dies, Chance is turned out into the world. Through other people's illusions about him, he comes to be seriously thought of as a candidate for the presidency of the United States.

Seller's work in *Being There* shows his artistry at its peak. The role of Chance required a naive character who had been tranquilized against the harsh realities of the world and benumbed into a permanent passivity by his overexposure to the slick packaging of TV. In creating the part, Sellers felt that the key was the voice, which he eventually derived as an offshoot of the childlike, innocent voice of Seller's favorite comedian—Stan Laurel. Then came the leisurely walk and the rest of the passionless character.

In real life Sellers was an ardent romantic, falling in love easily and frequently. In 1951 he married the aspiring actress Anne Hayes. They had two children, Michael and Sarah. In 1963 he divorced Anne, and in 1964 he wedded the actress Britt Ekland, with whom he had his daughter Victoria. Sellers and Ekland appeared together in *After the Fox* (1966) and *The Bobo* (1967) before divorcing in 1968. Michael, with Sarah and Victoria, wrote the book *P.S. I Love You: An intimate Portrait of Peter Sellers* (1981).

From 1970 to 1974 Sellers was married to the socialite Miranda Quarry. Through the years, however, he had had romances with many others, including Sophia Loren, who appeared with him in *The Millionairess* (1960), and Liza Minnelli, who costarred with him in *Soft Beds and Hard Battles* (1974).

His final and greatest love was for actress Lynne Frederick, whom he married in 1977. She helped him through the illness of his last years and served (at his pleading) as a buffer in his dealings with other people. She appeared with him in *The Prisoner of Zenda*.

Seller's last role was in *The Fiendish Plot of Dr. Fu Manchu* (1980). He was preparing to do another Inspector Clouseau movie, *The Romance of the Pink Panther*, when he died of a long-standing heart ailment (he had had attacks in 1964, 1977, and 1979) in London, England, on July 24, 1980.

In 1982 the movie *Trail of the Pink Panther* was created from outtakes and previously unused sequences originally filmed for earlier comedies in the "Pink Panther" series.

SELECTED PERFORMANCES

STAGE

Brouhaha (1958)

FILMS

Penny Points to Paradise (1951)
Down among the Z-Men (1952)

Orders Are Orders (1954)
John and Julie (1955)
The Ladykillers (1956)
The Smallest Show on Earth (1957)
The Naked Truth (1958, G.B.; U.S., *Your Past Is Showing*)
Up the Creek (1958)
Tom Thumb (1958)
Carlton-Browne of the F.O. (1959, G.B.; U.S., *Man in a Cocked Hat*)
The Mouse That Roared (1959)
I'm All Right, Jack (1959)
Two-Way Stretch (1960)
The Battle of the Sexes (1960)
Never Let Go (1960)
The Millionairess (1960)
Mr. Topaze (1961)
Only Two Can Play (1962)
The Waltz of the Toreadors (1962)
Lolita (1962)
The Dock Brief (1962)
The Wrong Arm of the Law (1963)
Heavens Above (1963)
The Pink Panther (1964)
Dr. Strangelove; or, How I Learned to Stop Worrying and Love the Bomb (1964)
The World of Henry Orient (1964)
A Shot in the Dark (1964)
What's New, Pussycat? (1965)

The Wrong Box (1966)
After the Fox (1966)
Casino Royale (1967)
Woman Times Seven (1967)
The Bobo (1967)
The Party (1968)
I Love You, Alice B. Toklas (1968)
The Magic Christian (1970)
Hoffman (1970)
There's a Girl in My Soup (1971)
Alice's Adventures in Wonderland (1972)
Where Does It Hurt? (1972)
Soft Beds and Hard Battles (1974, G.B.; U.S., *Undercovers Hero*)
The Optimists of Nine Elms (1974)
The Great McGonagall (1975)
The Return of the Pink Panther (1975)
Murder by Death (1976)
The Pink Panther Strikes Again (1976)
Revenge of the Pink Panther (1978)
The Prisoner of Zenda (1979)
Being There (1979)
The Fiendish Plot of Dr. Fu Manchu (1980)
Trail of the Pink Panther (1982)

RADIO

The Goon Show (as *Crazy People*, 1951-52; as *The Goon Show*, 1952-60

William Shatner

Captain Kirk

—◄○►—

One of the major stars of his generation, William Shatner has earned plaudits for his work on the stage, on the screen, and on TV. The role by which he is best known is that of Captain Kirk on the TV series *Star Trek* (1966-69) and in a number of *Star Trek* films.

—◄○►—

William Shatner was born in Montreal, Canada, on March 22, 1931. He developed an interest in acting when, as a small child in a summer-camp play, he had a profoundly moving experience while portraying a Jewish boy in Europe during the Nazi era.

After graduating from McGill University (1952), Shatner performed in plays at a Montreal theater during the summers of 1952 and 1953. In the winters of 1952 to 1953 and 1953 to 1954, he played juvenile roles with the Canadian Repertory Theater in Ottawa. He then performed at the Stratford Shakespeare Festival in Ontario (1954-56), again frequently in juvenile roles.

Moving to New York City, Shatner made his Broadway debut in *Temburlaine the Great* (1956) and played Robert Lomax in the very successful play *The World of Suzie Wong* (1958). He also began to appear in films. In *The Brothers Karamazov* (1958) he played the youngest brother. In *The Explosive Generation* (1961) he starred as a teacher trying to implement sex education in a high school. In *The Intruder* (1962) he starred as a violent bigot. In *Judgment at Nuremberg* (1961), as a military officer, and *The Outrage* (1964), as a preacher, he gave strong performances in supporting roles.

From his earliest days in the United States, Shatner appeared on TV. His work in anthology series during the medium's golden age included performances in "All Summer Long" (1956) on *Goodyear Playhouse*, "Oedipus Rex" (1957) on *Omnibus*, and "Walk with a Stranger" (1958) on *The U.S. Steel Hour*. He also made guest appearances on *Alfred Hitchcock Presents* (1957, 1960), *Twilight Zone* (1960, 1963), and *Dr. Kildare* (1961, 1966). In the short-lived series *For the People* (1965) he had a regular role as an assistant district attorney.

Shatner finally became a major star when he was cast as Captain Kirk in the TV adventure series *Star Trek*. Kirk commanded the starship *Enterprise*, which was commissioned by the United Federation of Planets to seek out new life and new civilizations. The show ran for only three seasons (1966-69), but it has remained extremely popular in syndication ever since. Its fanatic followers are known as "Trekkies."

After *Star Trek* was canceled, Shatner continued to make guest appearances on TV shows, including *Mission: Impossible* (1971), *Hawaii Five-O* (1972), and other series. From 1973 to 1975 he supplied Kirk's voice for an animated version of *Star Trek* on TV. From 1982 to 1986 he starred in the title role of the TV police-drama series *T.J. Hooker*, and from 1989 to 1996, he hosted the popular true-life series *Rescue 911*. In 1999 he guest-starred as the Giant Head, an extraterrestrial leader, on the sitcom *Third Rock from the Sun*.

Shatner's Captain Kirk persona continues to be a major factor in his career. He played the character again in the theatrical movies *Star Trek: The Motion Picture* (1979); *Star Trek II: The Wrath of*

Khan (1982); *Star Trek III: The Search for Spock* (1984); *Star Trek IV: The Voyage Home* (1986); *Star Trek V: The Final Frontier* (1989); *Star Trek VI: The Undiscovered Country* (1991); and *Star Trek: Generations* (1994).

Through all those years of making TV series and *Star Trek* films, Shatner remained exceptionally busy acting in other movies. Among them were *Owen Marshall, Counselor at Law* (TV, 1971), *The Bastard* (TV, 1978), *The Kidnapping of the President* (1980), *Blood Sport* (as T. J. Hooker, TV, 1986), *Columbo: Butterfly in Shades of Grey* (TV, 1994), and *Double Play* (Canada, 1996; U.S., *The Prisoner of Zenda*, TV, 1997).

Incredibly, Shatner found time to write many books, including the science-fiction novel *TekWar* (1989) and several spinoffs, such as *TekKill* (1996) and *TekNet* (1997). *TekWar* became a movie (TV, 1994) and a TV series (1995), in both of which Shatner served as an actor and a director.

In the 1990s Shatner developed an extreme case of tinnitus (a sensation of noise due to a malfunction in the ear), caused by his earlier refusal to wear earplugs when filming near explosions. He said he came near to suicide before finally receiving proper care in the form of a special ear device.

Shatner has been married three times. He was wedded to actress Gloria Rand from 1956 to 1969, and to Marcy Lafferty from 1973 to 1994. In 1997 he married Nerine Kidd, who died tragically in a drowning accident in 1999. Shatner has four children, Melanie, Leslie, Lisabeth, and Daniel.

William Shatner

SELECTED PERFORMANCES:

STAGE

Tom Sawyer (1952)
Measure for Measure (1954)
The Taming of the Shrew (1954)
Oedipus Rex (1954)
Julius Caesar (1955)

The Merchant of Venice (1955)
Kind Oedipus (1955)
The Merry Wives of Windsor (1956)
Henry V (1956)
Temburlaine the Great (1956)
The World of Suzie Wong (1958)
A Shot in the Dark (1961)
The Tender Trap (1970)
Remote Asylum (1971)
Tricks of the Trade (1977)
Otherwise Engaged (1978)

FILMS

The Brothers Karamazov (1958)
The Explosive Generation (1961)
Judgment at Nuremberg (1961)
The Intruder (1962)
The Outrage (1964)
Sole Survivor (TV, 1970)
Vanished (TV, 1971)
Owen Marshall, Counselor at Law (TV, 1971)
The People (TV, 1972)
The Hound of the Baskervilles (TV, 1972)
Incident on a Dark Street (TV, 1973)
Go Ask Alice (TV, 1973)
The Horror at 37,000 Feet (TV, 1973)
Pioneer Woman (TV, 1973)
Indict and Convict (TV, 1974)
Pray for the Wildcats (TV, 1974)
The Barbary Coast (TV, 1975)
The Devil's Rain (1975)
Perilous Voyage (TV, 1976)
Testimony of Two Men (TV, 1977)
The Bastard (TV, 1978)
Little Women (TV, 1978)

Crash (TV, 1978)
Disaster on the Coastline (TV, 1979)
Star Trek: The Motion Picture (1979)
The Kidnapping of the President (1980)
The Babysitter (TV, 1980)
Airplane II: The Sequel (1982)
Visiting Hours (1982)
Star Trek II: The Wrath of Khan (1982)
Star Trek III: The Search for Spock (1984)
Secrets of a Married Man (TV, 1984)
North Beall and Rawhide (TV, 1985)
Blood Sport (TV, 1986)
Star Trek IV: The Voyage Home (1986)
Broken Angel (TV, 1988)
Star Trek V: The Final Frontier (1989)
Star Trek VI: The Undiscovered Country (1991)
Bill and Ted's Bogus Journey (1991)
A Family of Strangers (TV, 1993)
National Lampoon's Loaded Weapon I (1993)
Columbo: Butterfly in Shades of Grey (TV, 1994)
Star Trek: Generations (1994)
TekWar (TV, 1994)
Double Play (Canada, 1996; U.S., *The Prisoner of Zenda*, TV, 1997)

TV

For the People (1965)
Star Trek (1966-69)
Star Trek (animated, voice only, 1973-75)
Inner Space (1974)
The Barbary Coast (1975-76)
T. J. Hooker (1982-86)
Rescue 911 (1989-1996)
TekWar (1995)

Norma Shearer

Early Product of the Star System

In the early 1920s, Norma Shearer became one of the first great Hollywood stars. She was also one of the very few stars to be equally successful in both silent and sound movies. Shearer's great asset was not acting skill but personality—her star quality. She had charm, poise, elegance, and—when given free rein—wit and spirit.

Norma Shearer was born of non-Jewish parents in Westmount, a suburb of Montreal, Canada, on August 15, 1902. (The date is so recorded on her birth certificate, though during her lifetime the day was usually given as August 10, with the year listed as early as 1900 and as late as 1904.)

In 1920 she moved with her mother and sister, Athole, to New York City. There, the girls began to get jobs as extras in silent movies. Athole soon dropped out of the business (though she later married the film director Howard Hawks). Norma continued her extra work and did some modeling.

Her first significant acting role was that of a wholesome daughter of a minister in *The Stealers* (1920). She had her first leading role in *The Man Who Paid* (1922), a melodrama set in the Canadian Northwest.

After making several more movies in the East, she was signed by the producer Irving Thalberg to work for the Mayer Company in Hollywood (though in her early years in California she was also occasionally lent to other studios). Shearer began in minor films. Having never formally studied act-

ing, she learned her craft simply by doing it. In 1924 Mayer became part of Metro-Goldwyn-Mayer (MGM), Shearer's professional home for the rest of her career.

Shearer began to blossom as an actress from her role in *The Snob* (1924), in which she played a young woman who marries a snobbish professor. In *He Who Gets Slapped* (1924) she was a bareback rider in a circus.

At that point Irving Thalberg, who was one of the creators of the Hollywood "star" system (his other stars included Lon Chaney, Sr. and Greta Garbo), expanded Shearer's appeal by casting her in comedy roles. Her first such role was in *Excuse Me* (1925) as a young woman who, with her fiancé, encounters many trials and tribulations while trying to locate a minister to perform a marriage ceremony. The romantic comedy-drama *A Slave of Fashion* (1925) was the first movie to show her in a glamorous wardrobe, for which she later became famous both offscreen and on.

The year 1927 was a major turning point in Shearer's career and life. Her performance in *The Demi-Bride* (1927), a French farce, helped to make her one of the most popular comediennes of her time.

Meanwhile, her professional association with Thalberg had developed into a close personal relationship as well, and in September 1927 they were married. Thalberg came from an Orthodox Jewish family, and when Shearer visited his parents, as she later reported, she "found peace and contentment in their religion. I wanted peace and contentment in our marriage. I decided I had no particular religious convictions—that I could find

Norma Shearer

Norma Shearer became one of the few silent-screen stars to successfully make the transition to sound pictures. Her first speaking role was as the title character in *The Trial of Mary Dugan* (1929). In an emotional yet restrained performance that surprised many observers in its effectiveness, she played an ex-showgirl accused of murdering her lover. In *The Divorcée* (1930) she played a free-spirited woman involved with her ex-husband's best friend. It was one of Shearer's few roles in which she strayed from conventional virtue—she was best known for playing genteel women, as in the romantic tearjerker *Smilin' Through* (1932).

In 1932 Shearer became a naturalized American citizen and appeared in the filmed version of Eugene O'Neills celebrated play, *Strange Interlude*. She then starred in two more prestige films. In *The Barretts of Wimpole Street* (1934), she played the poet Elizabeth Barrett, an invalid whose life is dominated by her father until she meets, and falls in love with, the poet Robert Browning. Shearer next played Juliet in *Romeo and Juliet* (1937).

it in the Jewish faith. I loved Irving so much that I wanted our children brought up in the same way he had been." Thus, she converted to Judaism. They had two children, Irving and Katherine.

Thalberg again began to expand Shearer's range and to change her image by placing her in prestige movies. She was cast, for example, in the silent-movie version of the famed operetta *The Student Prince* (1927), in which she displayed a quality of appealing tender fragility.

At about that time, sound entered filmmaking. Douglas Shearer, Norma's brother, became the head sound engineer at MGM, a post that he held for thirty-nine years.

Thalberg died in 1936 at the age of only thirty-seven. Shearer considered retiring, but after a period of rest, she returned to play the lead in *Marie Antoinette* (1938). In *The Women* (1939) she again played a genteel role, as a woman whose marriage is failing because of the interference of a hussy.

Shearer was offered the part of the selfish, unscrupulous Scarlett O'Hara in *Gone with the Wind* (1939). In fact, she accepted the role until she began to receive letters from her fans, urging her not to take the part. The role was eventually given to Vivien Leigh.

Shearer's last movie was *Her Cardboard Lover*.

In the same year that the film was released, 1942, she married the skier Martin Arrouge (in a Christian ceremony), who was fourteen years her junior. She then retired.

After retiring, Shearer continued to stay involved in the movie industry. In the mid-1940s she discovered Janet Leigh. In 1956 she met Robert J. Evans, a young New York clothing manufacturer; noticing his resemblance to her first husband, she was instrumental in getting Evans the role of Thalberg in the Lon Chaney biopic *Man of a Thousand Faces* (1957).

In 1980 Shearer, ill and for the previous several years a virtual recluse, entered the Motion Picture and Television Country House and Hospital in Woodland Hills, California. She died there on June 12, 1983.

SELECTED PERFORMANCES:

FILMS

The Stealers (1920)
The Man Who Paid (1922)
The Bootleggers (1922)
Channing of the Northwest (1922)
A Clouded Name (1923)
Man and Wife (1923)
The Devil's Partner (1923)
Pleasure Mad (1923)
The Wanters (1923)
Lucretia Lombard (1923)
The Trail of the Law (1924)
The Wolf Man (1924)
Broadway after Dark (1924)
Broken Barriers (1924)
Married Flirts (1924)
Empty Hands (1924)

The Snob (1924)
He Who Gets Slapped (1924)
Excuse Me (1925)
Lady of the Night (1925)
Waking Up the Town (1925)
A Slave of Fashion (1925)
Pretty Ladies (1925)
The Tower of Lies (1925)
His Secretary (1925)
The Devil's Circus (1926)
The Waning Sex (1926)
Upstage (1926)
The Demi-Bride (1927)
After Midnight (1927)
The Student Prince (1927)
The Latest from Paris (1928)
The Actress (1928)
A Lady of Chance (1928)
The Trial of Mary Dugan (1929)
The Last of Mrs. Cheyney (1929)
The Hollywood Revue (1929)
Their Own Desire (1929)
The Divorcée (1930)
Let Us Be Gay (1930)
Strangers May Kiss (1931)
A Free Soul (1931)
Private Lives (1931)
Strange Interlude (1932)
Smilin' Through (1932)
Riptide (1934)
The Barretts of Wimpole Street (1934)
Romeo and Juliet (1937)
Marie Antoinette (1938)
Idiot's Delight (1939)
The Women (1939)
Escape (1940)
We Were Dancing (1942)
Her Cardboard Lover (1942)

Dinah Shore

Popular TV Personality

Dinah Shore was one of America's most popular singers in the 1940s. From the 1950s to the 1980s, she became a beloved national institution through her TV variety and talk shows.

D inah Shore was born in Winchester, Tennessee, on March 1, 1917. Her original name was Frances Rose Shore.

When she was eighteen months old, she was stricken with poliomyelitis, which caused a paralysis in her right leg and foot. She went through six years of rigid physical therapy, and her mother encouraged her to participate in ballet and in vigorous outdoor exercise. The illness made her shy yet ambitious to prove her worth despite this infirmity. Besides excelling in many sports, she sang, danced, and showed off to get attention. Even before she could talk clearly, she had performed in public by singing to the customers in her father's department store.

The Shores were the only Jewish family in Winchester, and they had to face the usual anti-Semitic prejudices of the time and place. As a girl, Shore once saw a Ku Klux Klan parade going down a street, the Klansmen hiding behind hoods and sheets. She began to realize that she, as a "different" person, had to work harder than others for success. That feeling was intensified then and later by her sensitivity about her illness and about what she regarded as her physical unattractiveness at the time.

At the age of six she moved with her family to Nashville. Her mother, Anna, who was an aspiring opera singer, encouraged her to sing, though Shore preferred popular music. She took ukulele lessons and accompanied herself on that instrument while she sang everywhere she went, including the public swimming pool, where she serenaded the lifeguards.

At Hume-Fogg High School in Nashville, she was a cheerleader and acted and sang in various schol productions. She was voted the Best All-around Girl of her class.

On the advice of her family (except her mother, who had died when Shore was in high school), Shore enrolled at Vanderbilt University as a sociology major. However, she continued to pursue her interest in music, singing at school assemblies and in student musicals.

In her sophomore year at Vanderbilt, she got a job singing on a local radio show called *Rhythm and Romance*, billing herself as Fannye Rose Shore. The theme song of the show was "Dinah," which she sang not in the usual fast tempo but in a slow, personal manner. Radio was a perfect medium for Shore, who could sing her heart out without worrying about her physical imperfections. While experimenting with different distances from, and qualities conveyed over, the microphone, she became one of the pioneers in modern microphone techniques.

After graduating from college in 1938, Shore moved to New York City. She began to sing at WNEW, a local radio station. With her were the young unknowns Dennis Day, Frankie Laine, and Frank Sinatra, the last with whom Shore had a sometimes bitter rivalry. From her first appearance at WNEW, she called herself Dinah Shore because she had sung "Dinah" at her audition and the people at the station had referred to her as "the 'Dinah' girl." (In 1944 she legally changed her first name from Frances to Dinah.)

In 1939 she was given her own radio series, *The Dinah Shore Show*, which ran for the next three years at fifteen minutes per program. But she first began to acquire a national following when she spent two months in 1940 performing on the radio show *The Chamber Music Society of Lower Basin Street*.

She left that series for an even better position—a regular spot on Eddie Cantor's weekly radio show *Time to Smile*—and one that brought her lasting fame. Cantor taught Shore to relax and enjoy singing, which in turn brought more pleasure to the audience.

She rapidly became the top female blues singer in the country and the undisputed queen of the juke boxes. Among her early recording hits were "Yes, My Darling Daughter" (1940), "Memphis Blues" (1940), "Jim" (1941), "Body and Soul" (1941), and "Blues in the Night" (1942).

In 1942 her radio series, *The Dinah Shore Show*, was lengthened from fifteen to thirty minutes per program. The show continued to run for another five years.

In the summer of 1943, she hosted the radio show *Paul Whiteman Presents*. During World War II, she became a favorite with troops, traveling many thousands of miles to entertain at camps and hospitals.

In the early 1940s Shore was signed to a movie contract by Warner Bros. to begin her movie career. To initiate her new career as a film actress, the studio completely remade her appearance. Her black hair was bleached honey-blonde. She had plastic surgery to shorten and reconstruct her

Dinah Shore

nose, as well as massive dental work. The studio's makeup department gave her a makeover.

Soon after that, in 1943, she married the actor George Montgomery. They both had all-American images, and both lived quieter lives than did most of the Hollywood elite. Theirs was called "Hollywood's most successful marriage." They had one child of their own (Melissa) and adopted another (John, known as Jody). After the birth of her daughter, in 1948, Shore had no desire to return to work, but Montgomery prodded her into resuming her career.

Shore made her film debut in *Thank Your Lucky Stars* (1943). She also appeared in *Up in Arms* (1944), *Follow the Boys* (1944), *Belle of the Yukon*

(1945), *Till the Clouds Roll By* (1946), and *Aaron Slick from Punkin Crick* (1952). Her voice was featured in two Disney feature-length animated films: *Make Mine Music* (1946) and *Fun and Fancy Free* (1947).

Shore was never comfortable or particularly successful in movies, largely because of the types of roles that she was given. Meanwhile, however, she continued to sparkle on radio and on recordings. After the war, she performed on her own radio show and on other broadcasts. Among her record hits were "Shoofly Pie and Apple Pan Dowdy" (1946), "Buttons and Bows" (1948), "Dear Hearts and Gentle People" (1949), "Whatever Lola Wants" (1955), "Love and Marriage" (1955), "Chantez-Chantez" (1957), and "Fascination" (1957).

Shore was also much more successful on TV. She became enormously popular by hosting the musical-variety series *The Dinah Shore Show* (1951–57), a fifteen-minute program. During its last season, she also hosted specials sponsored by Chevrolet. Those specials became the genesis of her next musical-variety series, the one-hour programs known as *The Dinah Shore Chevy Show* (1957–62 and sometimes listed as 1956–63). She ended each show with the Chevrolet jingle that became her trademark. After this series ended, she hosted more specials sponsored by Chevy.

While Shore's career was flourishing in the 1950s, Montgomery's was stagnating. In 1958 he, too, entered TV, in a series called *Cimarron City*. Shore allowed him to plug the series on her own show, but *Cimarron City* failed anyway. The different states of their respective careers caused tension in the family. Shore and Montgomery drifted apart for a few years and then divorced in 1962.

In 1963 she married Maurice Smith, a building contractor whom she had met at a tennis match in Palm Springs, California. They divorced the following year.

Having left her TV series in 1962, Shore spent the rest of the 1960s performing at benefits, in nightclubs, and on TV specials. Then she returned to TV on a regular basis, with a variety-talk series entitled *Dinah's Place* (1970–74).

On one of her TV shows in 1971 she met the actor Burt Reynolds. They soon developed one of the most talked-about love affairs in entertainment history. The relationship ended in 1975.

In the late 1970s Shore returned to films. In *Oh, God!* (1977) she appeared as herself, hosting her TV show. In *Death on the Freeway* (TV, 1979) she gave a straight dramatic performance.

Meanwhile, she continued her TV work by hosting the talk shows *Dinah!* (1974–79) and *Dinah! And Friends* (1979–84).

She also hosted her own annual golf tournament in California. In 1984 it became the highest paying tournament on the LPGA tour.

In 1986 Shore acted in TV commercials for Glendale Federal Savings and Oreo cookies. In 1987 she sang with a jazz group on a tour of the United States and Japan. She then hosted what would be her final talk show, the cable-TV series *A Conversation with Dinah* (1989–91).

Shore died in Beverly Hills, California, on February 24, 1994.

SELECTED PERFORMANCES:

FILMS

Thank Your Lucky Stars (1943)
Up in Arms (1944)
Follow the Boys (1944)
Belle of the Yukon (1945)
Till the Clouds Roll By (1946)
Make Mine Music (animated, voice-only, 1946)
Fun and Fancy Free (animated, voice-only, 1947)
Aaron Slick from Punkin Crick (1952)
Oh, God! (1977)
Death on the Freeway (TV, 1979)

RADIO

The Dinah Shore Show (1939-47)
The Chamber Music Society of Lower Basin Street (1940)
Time to Smile (or *The Eddie Cantor Show*, 1940–43, 1948)
Paul Whiteman Presents (1943)
Call for Music (1948)

TV

The Dinah Shore Show (1951–57)
The Dinah Shore Chevy Show (1957–62)
Dinah's Place (197–74)
Dinah! (1974–79)
Dinah and Her New Best Friends (1976)
Dinah! and Friends (1979–84)
A Conversation with Dinah (1989–91)

Sylvia Sidney

Fragile Heroine of 1930s Films

———◄○►———

Sylvia Sidney was best known for playing fragile urban heroines in classic movies of the 1930s. But she also earned a reputation as a versatile stage actress and, in her later years, as a skillful character actress in films.

◄○►

Sylvia Sidney was born in New York City on August 8, 1910. Her original name was Sophia Kosow.

She studied acting at the American Theater Guild school, and starred in the title role of the school's graduation play, *Prunella* (1926). Soon, she made her professional debut by appearing in *The Challenge of Youth* (1926) in Washington, D.C. In early 1927 she gave her first Broadway performance, succeeding Grace Durkin as Anita in *The Squall*. Over the next few years she was busy in a number of New York City stage productions.

Sidney made her film debut with an appearance in *Thru Different Eyes* (1929). During the 1930s she gained considerable fame as a sweet, fragile "slum" girl in such films as *Street Scene* (1931) and *Dead End* (1937).

Tiring of being typecast in movies, Sidney began to spend more time on the stage again. She toured as Eliza in *Pygmalion* in 1938 and had the role of Stella Goodman in a New York City production of *The Gentle People* in 1939. In 1943 she appeared in the Ben Hecht and Kurt Weill Jewish pageant *We Will Never Die*, which was staged at Madison Square Garden. She also performed in *Jane Eyre* (1943), *The Two Mrs. Carrolls* (1949), and other plays.

From 1958 to 1959 Sidney toured the United States in the title role of *Auntie Mame*. She then portrayed Mrs. Kolowitz in *Enter Laughing* (1963) and showed her ability to handle roles in eighteenth-century classics by playing Mrs. Malaprop in Sheridan's *The Rivals* (1965) and Mrs. Hardcastle in Goldsmith's *She Stoops to Conquer* (1968). Later, she appeared in the comedy *Arsenic and Old Lace* (1974).

Meanwhile, in the 1950s Sidney began to make guest appearances on TV programs. Eventually, she acted in *The Defenders; My Three Sons; Playhouse Ninety; Trapper John, M.D.;* and many other TV series. In 1963 she performed in the Yom Kippur special *In the Last Place*.

After reaching middle age, Sidney became interested in acting in motion pictures again. In *Behind the High Wall* (1956), she played a wife torn between her sense of justice and her loyalty to her husband, a prison warden who allows an innocent man to be convicted of murder.

She was highly praised for her portrayal of the impatient mother in *Summer Wishes, Winter Dreams* (1973). In *Raid on Entebbe* (TV, 1977), a film based on a true story, she played Dora Bloch, one of a planeload of people kidnapped by terrorists and imprisoned at the Entebbe Airport in Uganda. In *Siege* (TV, 1978) she was a senior citizen terrorized by young hoodlums. In *Damien: Omen II* (1978), she was the first to sense something evil in young Damien.

Even after turning seventy, Sidney continued to act. She appeared, for example, in the plays *Vieux Carré* (1981) and *Sabrina Fair* (1981), and in the movies *The Shadow Box* (TV, 1980) and

Sylvia Sidney

Sylvia Sidney

Finnegan Begin Again (TV, 1985). In 1986 she had a regular role in the sentimental TV series *Morningstar/Eveningstar*, which focused on the continuing usefulness of the elderly. Her later films included *Beetlejuice* (1988) and *Mars Attacks!* (1996).

One of her favorite activities outside acting was needlepoint. She published two books on that subject (1968, 1975).

Sidney's first marriage, from 1935 to 1936, was to the well-known publisher Bennet Cerf. In 1938 she married the actor Luther Adler, with whom she had a son, Jacob. That marriage ended in the late 1940s, and soon afterward she wedded Carlton Alsop. They were divorced in the early 1950s.

Sidney died in new York City on July 1, 1999.

SELECTED PERFORMANCES:

STAGE

Prunella (1926)
The Challenge of Youth (1926)
The Squall (1927)

Crime (1927)
Mirrors (1928)
The Breaks (1928)
Gods of the Lightning (1928)
Nice Women (1929)
Cross Roads (1929)
Many a Slip (1930)
Bad Girl (1930)
To Quito and Back (1937)
Pygmalion (1938, 1942)
The Gentle People (1939)
Accent on Youth (1941)
Angel Street (1942)
Jane Eyre (1943)
We Will Never Die (1943)
Joan of Lorraine (1947)
Kind Lady (1948)
O Mistress Mine (1948)
The Two Mrs. Carrolls (1949)
Goodbye, My Fancy (1950)
The Fourposter (1952)
A Very Special Baby (1956)
Auntie Mame (1958)
The Dark at the Top of the Stairs (1960)
Enter Laughing (1963)
All My Pretty Little Ones (1964)
Damn You, Scarlett O'Hara (1964)
The Rivals (1965)
The Little Foxes (1966)
She Stoops to Conquer (1968)
Come Blow Your Horn (1968)
Cabaret (1970)
Butterflies Are Free (1972)
Suddenly Last Summer (1973)
A Family and a Fortune (1974)
Arsenic and Old Lace (1974)
Me Jack, You Jill (1976)
Vieux Carré (1981)
Sabrina Fair (1981)
Morning at Seven (1981)

FILMS

Thru Different Eyes (1929)
City Streets (1931)
Confessions of a Co-ed (1931)
An American Tragedy (1931)
Street Scene (1931)
Merrily We Go to Hell (1932)
Madame Butterfly (1932)
Pick Up (1933)
Jennie Gerhardt (1933)

Good Dame (1934)
Thirty Day Princess (1934)
Behold My Wife (1935)
Accent on Youth (1935)
Mary Burns, Fugitive (1935)
The Trail of the Lonesome Pine (1936)
Fury (1936)
You Only Live Once (1937)
The Woman Alone (1937)
Dead End (1937)
You and Me (1938)
One Third of a Nation (1939)
The Wagons Roll at Night (1941)
Blood on the Sun (1945)
The Searching Wind (1946)
Mr. Ace (1946)
Love from a Stranger (1947)
Les Misérables (1952)
Violent Saturday (1955)
Behind the High Wall (1956)
Do Not Fold, Spindle, or Mutilate (TV, 1971)
Summer Wishes, Winter Dreams (1973)
The Secret Night Caller (TV, 1975)
Winner Take All (TV, 1975)
Death at Love House (TV, 1976)
Raid on Entebbe (TV, 1977)
Snowbeast (TV, 1977)
I Never Promised You a Rose Garden (1977)
Damien: Omen II (1978)
Siege (TV, 1978)
F.D.R.: The Last Year (TV, 1980)
The Shadow Box (TV, 1980)
The Gossip Columnist (TV, 1980)
A Small Killing (TV, 1981)
Having It All (TV, 1982)
Order of Death (1983)
Finnegan Begin Again (TV, 1985)
Pals (TV, 1987)
Beetlejuice (1988)

Sylvia Sidney

Used People (1992)
Mars Attacks! (1996)

TV

Morningstar/Eveningstar (1986)
Fantasy Island (1998)

Phil Silvers

Hilarious Manipulator

Phil Silvers delighted in portraying fast-talking swindlers and manipulators, through whom he satirized the haste and deception that characterize so much of modern materialistic civilization. He reached the peak of his popularity as an actor during his four seasons (1955–59) as Master Sergeant Ernie Bilko in the TV sitcom *You'll Never Get Rich* (later known as *The Phil Silvers Show* or *Sergeant Bilko*). By then Silvers had already paid his dues by performing for many years in vaudeville, burlesque, nightclubs, musical comedies, and films.

Phil Silvers was born of Russian immigrant parents in New York City, on May 11, 1911. (The year is so given in his autobiography, though many sources continue to list 1912.) His original name was Philip Silver. He added an *s* to his surname because several other performers named Silvers had already become successful in show business, such as Lou Silvers (Al Jolson's conductor) and Sid Silvers (Phil Baker's heckler).

Before Silvers had reached the age of five, he was already singing at family weddings and bar mitzvahs. Soon, however, he was initiated into the violent street life of his native Brownsville, a section of Brooklyn, New York. When he was eight, he sang at a stag coming-out-of-jail party for a local hoodlum named Little Doggie; in the middle of the number, a man was shot to death at the boy's feet. Young Silvers himself became a gang member and committed petty crimes.

It was through show business that Phil Silvers was able to turn his life around. At a Brooklyn silent-movie house, the Supreme Theater, he got a job singing for the audience whenever the film broke, which happened quite often. His pay was simply free admission.

Silvers began to frequent Brooklyn's Bushwick Theater, where he could study the routines of vaudeville stars such as Sophie Tucker. With material that he learned at the Bushwick, he sang one night at a sleazy beer hall and then a number of times at variety shows performed by children.

In 1923, while singing for a group of his friends on the beach at Coney Island, he was spotted by the great entertainer Gus Edwards. Known as the Star Maker, Edwards had for years staged a series of popular vaudeville revues featuring children. He discovered Eddie Cantor, George Jessel, and many other youngsters who later became show-business superstars.

At the age of twelve Silvers hit the big time by appearing with Edwards's troupe at the famed Palace Theater in New York City. He went on to perform in Edwards's acts in several other cities, but within a few months the boy's voice began to change, and he was out of work. By then he had already dropped out of high school, and his immediate future looked bleak. In desperation, he convinced his parents that he needed to have his tonsils removed, secretly hoping that the operation would restore his pure child's voice. It did not.

When Silvers was fourteen, however, he got a job playing a juvenile in a comedy routine with the experienced vaudevillians Joe Morris and Flo Campbell. He stayed with the act for six years.

After he left, he continued to work in vaudeville for a short time, briefly worked on the borscht circuit, and then entered burlesque, where he performed in obscurity for seven years (1932–39). One of his early burlesque partners was Jack Albertson, who later became a renowned straight actor.

In 1939 Silvers was asked to play a small role in the Broadway musical comedy *Yokel Boy*. One of the leading members of the cast was Jack Pearl, a once-popular Dutch-dialect comedian. When Pearl left the show, Silvers replaced him. Pearl's role as a Dutch-dialect film director was rewritten to make Silvers a sharp Hollywood press agent who speaks New Yorkese. The role thus created, Punko Parks, became the prototype for the kind of comic character that Silvers played to perfection many times during the rest of his career: the aggressive, smiling manipulator.

Later that year Silvers signed a contract with a Hollywood film studio. At first, however, the movie executive did not know what to do with him. Silvers miserably failed his initial screen test when he was miscast as an English vicar for the film *Pride and Prejudice*. He had a funny bit part in *Babes in Arms*, but it was cut out. Meanwhile, he performed in a nightclub act with Rags Ragland, with whom he had worked in burlesque.

In the early 1940s, Silvers's studio began to cast him in comic roles that were well-suited to his talents. His films during this period included *Tom, Dick, and Harry* (1941); *My Gal Sal* (1942); *Cover Girl* (1944); and *Four Jills in a Jeep* (1944).

On the set of the film *Something for the Boys* (1944), Silvers met and began to court Jo-Carroll Dennison, who was Miss America of 1942 and who had a bit part in the movie. Her patron, an elderly state senator in her native Texas, offered to set up an annuity of $100,000 for her if she did not marry "that Jew." Refusing the offer, she married Silvers in 1945.

In the late 1940s, Silvers worked principally in nightclubs. He also performed in the Broadway musical *High Button Shoes* (1947).

Phil Silvers

During those years he traveled a great deal. His wife, who was childless, increasingly felt left out of his life. They separated amicably and divorced in 1950.

In 1951 Silvers made a tremendous impression in the Broadway musical comedy *Top Banana* as Jerry Biffle, a burlesque comic whose whole life centers on getting laughs at any cost. Silvers modeled his performance of the role after the real-life comedian Milton Berle.

During the mid-1950s Silvers became a television star. He had already had some experience in TV by hosting the variety series *Welcome Aboard* (1948) and *The Arrow Show* (1948–49), but he hit pay dirt with *You'll Never Get Rich* (1955-59). In that series he played the role of Master Sergeant Ernie Bilko, the manipulator par excellence. By the end of its four-season run, the comedy series had been renamed *The Phil Silvers Show*; it was later syndicated as *Sergeant Bilko*.

Soon after Silvers started working on *You'll Never Get Rich*, he met Evelyn Patrick, another beauty-contest winner (Miss Florida). Patrick also worked on TV, notably as the Revlon girl on the quiz show *The $64,000 Question*. In 1956 they were married. They had five children, all daughters: Tracey, Nancey, Cathy, Candy, and Laury. Ten years later, however, this marriage, too, ended in divorce.

In the 1960s Silvers had another TV series: *The New Phil Silvers Show* (1963-64), in which he played the factory foreman and con artist Harry Grafton. He also performed in the stage musical *Do Re Mi* (1960) and appeared in a number of movies, including *It's a Mad, Mad, Mad, Mad World* (1963) and *A Guide for the Married Man* (1967).

Silvers was offered the lead in the Broadway musical *A Funny Thing Happened on the Way to the Forum* (1962), based on ancient Roman comedies by Plautus. Feeling that the work was "too artsy," however, he turned down the role. Later, he changed his mind and played the secondary role of Lycus, the procurer, in the filmed version (1966). In a 1972 revival of the play, he took the starring role of Pseudolus, the conniving slave.

An admitted neurotic and a compulsive gambler, Silvers went through many years of torment both professionally (worrying about his performances) and personally (losing his wives). Eventually, relying on his work and on his daughters and friends, he developed the confidence and courage to face life afresh. "I've gone back to people—I don't see how I can withdraw into my cocoon again," he wrote in his autobiography, *This Laugh Is on Me: The Phil Silvers Story* (with Robert Saffron, 1973).

In 1974 Silvers suffered a stroke, and for a time he had to reduce his activities. Among his later performances were roles in the movies *Won Ton Ton, the Dog Who Saved Hollywood* (1976); *The Cheap Detective* (1978); and *Goldie and the Boxer* (TV, 1979).

Silvers died at his apartment in the Century City section of Los Angeles on November 1, 1985. At his funeral, Milton Berle delivered the eulogy.

SELECTED PERFORMANCES:

STAGE

Yokel Boy (1939)
High Button Shoes (1947)
Top Banana (1951)
Do Re Mi (1960)
A Funny Thing Happened on the Way to the Forum (1972)

FILMS

Tom, Dick and Harry (1941)
You're in the Army Now (1941)
All through the Night (1942)
Roxie Hart (1942)
My Gal Sal (1942)
Just off Broadway (1942)
Footlight Serenade (1942)
Coney Island (1943)
A Lady Takes a Chance (1943)
Cover Girl (1944)
Four Jills in a Jeep (1944)
Take It or Leave It (1944)
Something for the Boys (1944)
A Thousand and One Nights (1945)
Don Juan Quilligan (1945)
If I'm Lucky (1946)
Summer Stock (1950)
Top Banana (1954)
Lucky Me (1954)
Forty Pounds of Trouble (1963)
It's a Mad, Mad, Mad, Mad World (1963)
A Funny Thing Happened on the Way to the Forum (1966)
A Guide for the Married Man (1967)
Follow That Camel (1967)
Buona Sera, Mrs. Campbell (1969)
The Boatniks (1970)
The Strongest Man in the World (1975)
Won Ton Ton, the Dog Who Saved Hollywood (1976)
The Night They Took Miss Beautiful (TV, 1977)
The Cheap Detective (1978)
Goldie and the Boxer (TV, 1979)

TV

Welcome Aboard (1948)
The Arrow Show (1948–49)
You'll Never Get Rich (or *The Phil Silvers Show*, 1955–59; syndicated as *Sergeant Bilko*)
The New Phil Silvers Show (1963–64)

Susan Strasberg

First Actress to Play Anne Frank

An acting prodigy, Susan Strasberg became a professional actress while she was still in her teens. She played the title role in the original Broadway production of *The Diary of Anne Frank* (1955). Later, after overcoming an identity crisis as an adult, she settled into a fine career as a well-rounded actress.

Susan Strasberg was born in New York City, on May 22, 1938. She was raised in a theatrical milieu. Her father was the great director and teacher Lee Strasberg, later the artistic director of the famed Actors Studio. Her mother was the actress and acting coach Paula Strasberg (née Miller).

Strasberg made her stage debut when she was only fifteen, in an off-Broadway production of *Maya* (1953), playing the small role of Fifine, a young, innocent waif destined to become a street-walker. She then appeared in the TV plays "The Duchess and the Smugs" (1953) on the *Omnibus* series and "Catch a Falling Star" (1953) on *Goodyear Playhouse*. In 1954 she played Juliet in "Romeo and Juliet" on *Kraft Theater*.

At that time Strasberg was still a student at the High School of Performing Arts in New York City. Later, she studied at the Actors Studio. Her private acting coach was her mother.

In 1954 Strasberg appeared as a regular in the TV series *The Marriage*. She then guest-starred on many other TV shows.

Strasberg made her film debut in *The Cobweb* (1955), in which she played a hypersensitive, para-noid teenager. Then in *Picnic* (1955), she gave an outstanding performance as a rebellious girl struggling to emerge from tomboyishness into maturity.

The highlight of young Strasberg's early career was her performance in the original Broadway production of *The Diary of Anne Frank* (1955). With her portrayal of Anne Frank, Strasberg became, at seventeen, the youngest actress ever to star on Broadway.

During the next decade, Strasberg continued to perform on the stage, on TV, and in films. Her stage work included *Time Remembered* (1957) and *The Lady of the Camellias* (1963). She made guest appearances on *Dr. Kildare* (1963) and other TV series. Among her movies were *Stage Struck* (1958), *Hemingway's Adventures of a Young Man* (1962), and *Disorder* (1964).

But Strasberg's career had clearly slowed down. As she later explained in her strikingly honest autobiography, *Bittersweet* (1980), she had become "trapped in a welter of guilt, self-pity, fear, and doubt." She seemed to be running away from the success that she had earned perhaps too early and too easily.

Strasberg's emotional difficulties were caused by unsuccessful relationships with her family and the men in her life. She had an ambivalent relationship with her father, whose preoccupation with his students left him little time for her. She faced years of hostility from her mother, who tried to fulfill her own acting ambitions through her daughter. Susan also suffered from her feelings of rivalry with her surrogate sister Marilyn Monroe, whom the elder Strasbergs befriended and

Susan Strasberg

tormented herself wondering if Jenny's condition had been caused by her drug use.

But with great courage and determination, Strasberg pulled her life together. She ended the marriage with Jones. She provided the love and strength to help her child through corrective heart surgery. And, aided by psychotherapy, she resolved her identity crisis, finally coming out from the shadows of her parents to genuinely perceive herself as an individual.

Strasberg kept working, even in the unhappy late 1960s and early 1970s. She appeared in the movies *The Trip* (1967); *Chubasco* (with Christopher Jones, 1968); *Marcus Welby, M.D.* (TV, 1969); *Frankenstein* (TV, 1973); and others. She also guest-starred on TV programs and had a regular role on the series *Toma* (1973-74).

Strasberg matured as an actress in the years following her recovery. She has appeared in made-for-TV movies, playing Sarah Levy in *The Immigrants* (TV, 1978) and Ida Cohen in *Beggarman, Thief* (TV, 1979); toured Ohio and Florida in the one-person show *A Woman's Rites* (1982-83); and had roles in the theatrical films *The Delta Force* (1986) and *The Runnin' Kind* (1989). She gave a memorable performance as Helene Schweitzer, wife of the famed musician, theologian, and missionary physician Dr. Albert Schweitzer, in the biopic *The Light in the Jungle* (or *Schweitzer*, produced in 1990, shown in film festivals in 1991, and released on home video in the United States in 1992).

In the early 1990s Strasberg published another memoir: *Marilyn and Me: Sisters, Rivals, Friends* (1992). She also followed in her father's footsteps as a teacher of acting.

Strasberg died in New York City on January 21, 1999.

coached. In addition, young Strasberg was scarred by a reckless love affair with the married actor Richard Burton, with whom she had appeared in *Time Remembered*. In 1965 she wedded the actor Christopher (real name, William Frank) Jones, with whom she had a short, stormy marriage.

In the late 1960s Strasberg's emotional and psychological decline reached its nadir. Her mother died. Her brother, John, nearly killed himself while under the influence of the drug LSD. Her husband beat her and led her into the use of drugs, including LSD. And her daughter, Jennifer, was born with a seriously defective heart. Strasberg

SELECTED PERFORMANCES:

STAGE

Maya (1953)
The Diary of Anne Frank (1955)
Time Remembered (1957)
Shadow of a Gunman (1958)
The Time of Your Life (1958)

Caesar and Cleopatra (1959)
The Lady of the Camellias (1963)
A Woman's Rites (1982-83)

FILMS

The Cobweb (1955)
Picnic (1955)
Stage Struck (1958)
Kapo (1960)
Scream of Fear (1961)
Hemingway's Adventures of a Young Man
   (1962)
Disorder (1964)
McGuire, Go Home! (1966)
The Trip (1967)
The Brotherhood (1968)
Chubasco (1968)
The Name of the Game is Kill! (1968)
Psych-out (1968)
Marcus Welby, M.D. (TV, 1969)
Hauser's Memory (TV, 1970)
Mr. and Mrs. Bo Jo Jones (TV, 1971)
Frankenstein (TV, 1973)
Toma (TV, 1973)
SST—Death Flight (TV, 1977)
Rollercoaster (1977)
The Manitou (1978)
The Immigrants (TV, 1978)
Beggarman, Thief (TV, 1979)
In Praise of Older Women (1979)
Mazes and Monsters (TV, 1982)
The Delta Force (1986)
The Runnin' Kind (1989)
The Returning (1991, produced in 1983)
The Light in the Jungle (or *Schweitzer*; U.S., 1992;
   produced, 1990)

TV

The Marriage (1954)
Toma (1973–74)

Susan Strasberg

Barbra Streisand

Barbra Streisand, one of the most electric entertainers of her time, has made her mark as both a singer and an actress.

B arbra Streisand was born in New York City, on April 24, 1942. Her original name was Barbara Joan Streisand.

The death of her father, when she was only fifteen months old, had an extremely important effect on the formation of her personality. She felt deprived yet special: "It's like someone being blind; they hear better. With me, I felt more, I sensed more—I wanted more."

She was also self-conscious about being awkward and not particularly attractive. She had few close friends. While growing up in Brooklyn, she had a tense relationship with her stepfather, who married into the household when she was seven and who left at about the time that she started high school. Moreover, her practical mother had little sympathy for the girl's restless nature and impractical dreams of future glory in show business.

To escape her unhappy life, young Streisand spent as much time as possible in the local movie theater. Sometimes, she hid under her seat or in the ladies' room to avoid being shooed out with the other children after each Saturday matinee. She watched the films over and over again and dreamed of becoming an actress.

In her early teens she plunged into the world of real acting by going to the Malden Bridge Playhouse in upstate New York to try out for work in summer stock. She appeared on the stage only a few times, but afterwards, she was totally committed to a career in show business.

Eager to get her career under way, she studied extra hard to graduate six months early, in January 1959, from Erasmus Hall High School. Streisand soon moved from Brooklyn to Manhattan, where she enrolled in acting classes and went to theater auditions, without much success. Then some of her friends heard her sing and encouraged her to concentrate on a vocal career. Thus, she entered, as a singer, a talent contest held at the Lion, a Greenwich Village nightclub. She won the contest and got a short-term job at the club. It was during that time, June 1960, she decided to drop the middle *a* from her first name.

Streisand then became a regular performer at the Bon Soir nightclub. While working at the Lion and the Bon Soir, she began to conceive of singing as a form of acting. That insight led her to select unusual or seldom-heard songs and to perform them with unique interpretations that displayed an incredible range and depth of emotion. One of her selections was a song from a Disney cartoon of the 1930s: "Who's Afraid of the Big Bad Wolf?" Usually performed as a light and playful ditty, the song was transformed by Streisand into a surrealistic yet childlike lament. Her performances at the Bon Soir made a tremendous impact on audiences, and her stint there has become legendary.

In 1961 Streisand became a regular guest on *PM East*, Mike Wallace's late-night TV show. She also performed in the off-Broadway revue *Another Evening with Harry Stoones* and moved up from the Bon Soir to the Blue Angel nightclub. Additionally, she landed her first significant role in a Broadway play. The show, which opened in New York City in March 1962, was a musical entitled *I Can Get It for You Wholesale*. Streisand's acting (a comedic part as a shy secretary) and singing (especially her self-revealing solo, "Miss Marmelstein") stole the show.

The male lead in *I Can Get It for You Wholesale* was Elliott Gould, who later became a well-known dramatic actor. Streisand and Gould married in 1963, had one child (Jason), and then, after a long separation, divorced in 1971.

After her success in *I Can Get It for You Wholesale*, Streisand got work at major nightclubs and on TV. A memorable and truly historic TV program resulted from Streisand's appearance on one of Judy Garland's TV shows in 1963, during which the two stars sang together and praised each other's gifts. In May 1963 Streisand was invited to the White House to sing for President Kennedy.

In 1963 she also issued her first album: *The Barbra Streisand Album*. She released a number of other albums in the 1960s, including *People* (1965), *Color Me Barbra* (1966), and *What about Today* (1967).

In 1964 Streisand gave an unforgettable performance as the legendary performer Fanny Brice in the Broadway musical *Funny Girl*. In 1968 she reprised her performance in the filmed version of the show. Her sensitive portrayal of the tragedienne behind Brice's mask of comedy and her rendition of the song "People" were electric. That same quality of intense excitement has characterized most of her work, both as a singer and as an actress, throughout her career.

During the next decade, Streisand appeared in the movie musicals *Hello, Dolly!* (1969); *On a Clear Day You Can See Forever* (1970); *Funny Lady* (1975, a sequel to *Funny Girl*); and *A Star Is Born* (1976). Her nonmusical pictures included *The Owl and the Pussycat* (1970), *Up the Sandbox* (1972), *The Way We Were* (1973), and *The Main Event* (1979).

During the early 1970s Streisand began to broaden the stylistic range of her singing. Formerly,

Barbra Streisand

concentrating on a nonrock ballad style and singing standards and special material, she had succeeded Judy Garland as the queen of theatrical and torch songs. Now, however, she expanded her repertory and stylistic versatility to include various kinds of rock and soft-rock songs along with her previous material. Her album *Stony End* (1971) was the first to show her new style. *The Way We Were* (1974) contains rock and nonrock ballads. *Lazy Afternoon* (1975) features exclusively nonrock songs, while *Streisand Superman* (1977) is one of her most thoroughly contemporary pop-rock albums. However, she rightly remains principally identified with the artistically rich and musically sophisticated genre of theatrical songs, as she stunningly proved in *The Broadway Album* (1985).

Streisand spent much of her time during the late 1970s and early 1980s working on the movie *Yentl*

(1983). Based on a short story (whose movie rights she purchased in 1968) by Isaac Bashevis Singer, the film is set in a turn-of-the-century Polish ghetto and focuses on a young woman, Yentl (played by Streisand), who masquerades as a male so that she can study to become a rabbi. When she falls in love with a young man, she cannot reveal her feelings without exposing her true identity. Thus, she expresses her deepest emotions only to herself, by singing dramatic songs as interior monologues. Besides starring and singing in *Yentl*, Streisand coscripted, produced, and directed the movie—an unprecedented accomplishment for a woman in the history of major motion pictures.

The making of *Yentl* was a very deep personal experience for Streisand. She has said, "I made the commitment to *Yentl* when I read the first four words of the story, 'After her father's death . . .'" Those four words brought back memories of the death of Streisand's own father, Emanuel Streisand, who held a Ph.D. in education and who taught English, history, and psychology at a Brooklyn high school. Because she had had an unhappy relationship with her stepfather, Streisand continually sought to bring her real father back into her life through her art.

In the movie, Yentl's father secretly teaches her the Talmud, a study traditionally forbidden to women. When her father dies, she disguises herself as a man so that she can continue her studies in honor of her father. Streisand saw her own father in Yentl's, since both men were intellectual and religious Jews. She also saw herself in Yentl, since each had lost her father, had tried to keep him spiritually involved in her life, and had become enmeshed in a battle with the male establishment while trying to find her own identity. Streisand made the film as a memorial to her father: "*Yentl* gave me the chance to create the father I never had."

While researching for *Yentl*, Streisand sought the advice of rabbis. The rabbi of a Venice, California, synagogue refused her offer of payment for his help, but he said that he would be glad to teach her son, Jason Emanuel (named after her father) Gould, for his bar mitzvah. In gratitude, she has given much financial support to the Pacific Jewish Center's new day school, which became the Emanuel Streisand School.

In preparation for *Yentl*, Streisand studied Hebrew and the Talmud (studies that also made her feel closer to her devout father). During the same period, she donated a large sum to an institute for Jewish intellectual research and, in 1981, gave $500,000 to the cardiology department at UCLA, which thereupon established a cardiology charity in Emanuel Streisand's name.

Streisand remained active in film and in music throughout the 1990s. She directed and starred in *The Prince of Tides* (1991), in which her son, Jason, also had a role. In 1994 she went on her first concert tour in nearly thirty years. She then directed and starred in *The Mirror Has Two Faces* (1996) and released the album *Higher Ground* (1997). At the 1998 Grammy Awards, she performed "Tell Him" in a duet with Celine Dion.

In the summer of 1998, Streisand married the actor James Brolin.

SELECTED PERFORMANCES:

STAGE

Teahouse of the August Moon (1957)
The Desk Set (1957)
Tobacco Road (1957)
The Boy Friend (1957)
Picnic (1957)
Driftwood (1959)
Separate Tables (1959)
The Insect Comedy (1960)
Another Evening with Harry Stoones (1961)
I Can Get It for You Wholesale (1962)
Funny Girl (1964)

FILMS

Funny Girl (1968)
Hello, Dolly! (1969)
On a Clear Day You Can See Forever (1970)
The Owl and the Pussycat (1970)
What's Up, Doc? (1972)
Up the Sandbox (1972)
The Way We Were (1973)
For Pete's Sake (1974)
Funny Lady (1975)
A Star Is Born (1976)
The Main Event (1979)
All Night Long (1981)
Yentl (1983)
Nuts (1987)
The Prince of Tides (1991)
The Mirror Has Two Faces (1996)

Elizabeth Taylor

Last of the Studio Stars

Elizabeth Taylor is widely regarded as the last great star to come out of the old Hollywood studio system. She spent much of her childhood at the MGM lot, absorbing the techniques of acting and the ambience of stardom.

Elizabeth Rosemond Taylor was born of non-Jewish parents in London, England, on February 27, 1932. Her parents, Francis and Sara Taylor, both American nationals, were in England to run an art gallery for Francis's multimillionaire uncle. In 1939, to avoid the growing World War II hostilities in Europe, the family returned to the United States and settled in Los Angeles, California, where Francis opened his own art gallery.

Elizabeth's star-struck mother enrolled the girl in a dancing class with the daughters of many movie executives. Soon, Elizabeth was offered screen tests, not only by the parents of a child in the dancing class but also by a patron in Francis's art gallery. The auditions soon led to a contract with Universal Pictures, and Elizabeth's career became the passion of Sara's life.

After playing a small role in Universal's *There's One Born Every Minute* (1942), young Taylor moved to MGM, where she remained for many years (though her services were occasionally lent to other studios). She became totally immersed in being a movie star. Her formal education consisted only of the inadequate tutoring that she received in the little schoolhouse set up for young actors at the MGM studio. She was, however, able to write a book called *Nibbles and Me* (1945), about her pet chipmunk.

After playing a few minor roles notably in *Jane Eyre* (1944), Taylor was given a leading role, opposite Mickey Rooney in *National Velvet* (1944). In her next film, *Courage of Lassie* (1946), she received top billing for the first time. She then had the lead role in the film *Cynthia* (1947).

For the next few years she was cast in secondary roles as a pretty but sometimes spoiled teenager, as in *Little Women* (1949). Her first adult role was as the screen wife of Robert Taylor (no relation) in the forgettable film *The Conspirator* (1950). She played Spencer Tracy's daughter in the popular movie *Father of the Bride* (1950).

Taylor first began to see moviemaking as an art when she made *A Place in the Sun* (1951) with George Stevens (the director) and Montgomery Clift (her costar). But she continued to get shallow roles until she was cast as an Easterner fighting Texas primitivism in *Giant* (1956), costarring Rock Hudson and James Dean. In that film Taylor had to age thirty years, from a young bride to a grandmother. Then, in *Raintree County* (1957), again with Clift, she played a young woman who becomes mentally ill. In the filmed version of Tennessee Williams's play *Cat on a Hot Tin Roof* (1958), she played a seductive wife trying to get her homosexual husband to impregnate her. In the film version of Williams's gothic horror story *Suddenly Last Summer* (1959), she played a young woman who becomes hysterical and incoherent after witnessing the murder and cannibalistic devouring of her homosexual cousin. In *Butterfield 8* (1960) she played a prostitute.

By then she had reached the top of her profession, becoming the last of the glamorous studio-cultivated stars. She was America's biggest box-office attraction and the highest-paid actress in the world. Her acting ability was (and continues to be) disparaged by some. But her screen presence, her ability to make the screen sizzle, was undeniable.

Among her most important films in the late 1960s were *Cleopatra* (1963), in the title role; *Who's Afraid of Virginia Woolf?* (1966), as the drunken, venomous wife of a college professor; and Shakespeare's *The Taming of the Shrew* (1967), as Katherina.

In the 1970s memorable roles were harder for her to come by. She played four parts in *The Blue Bird* (1976), the first Soviet-American coproduction in film history. In the filmed version of Steven Sondheim's musical *A Little Night Music* (1977), Taylor identified closely with her role as the aging actress.

Throughout her career Taylor has had probably the most widely publicized personal life in Hollywood history. She gave her own version of her life in the book *Elizabeth Taylor* (1964). Her extravagances (particularly her love of diamonds), her recurring weight problems, and her numerous bouts with a variety of accidents and illnesses have been followed by the press for years.

Taylor's ailments have included back problems, bursitis, ulcers, amoebic dysentery, and acute bronchitis. In 1961 a case of pneumonia almost killed her, and once she nearly choked to death on a chicken bone. She has had over thirty operations.

Most dramatic of all have been her innumerable love affairs and her eight (to date) marriages (two of which were to one man). Taylor's first marriage, in 1950, was to Conrad Nicholson (known as Nicky) Hilton, Jr., heir to the Hilton Hotel corporation. MGM purposely released *Father of the Bride* (in which she played the bride) just one month after the wedding ceremony to capitalize on the attending publicity. But within a year, the marriage broke up.

In 1952 she wedded the British matinee idol Michael Wilding. They had two sons, Christopher and Michael, before separating in 1956 and divorcing in 1957.

In 1957 Taylor married Mike Todd (originally Avrom Hirsch Goldbogen), a producer. They had one daughter, Elizabeth (or Liza), before he died in a plane crash in 1958. While married to Todd, who was a Jew, Taylor wanted to convert to his faith. But he convinced her that such an important step should be preceded by lengthy consideration.

After his death she was comforted by one of his best friends, the singer Eddie Fisher, also a Jew. The comforting soon turned into a romance, though he was already married to the actress Debbie Reynolds. The triangle made headlines for weeks, most Americans regarding Reynolds as an innocent victim and Taylor as a home wrecker. Capitalizing on the scandal, MGM released *Cat on a Hot Tin Roof*, featuring Taylor as a seductress, at the height of the public interest in the affair. During that period, in 1959, Taylor formally converted to the Jewish faith, adopting the name Elisheba Rachel.

Shortly afterward, in 1959, she married Fisher, who had obtained a divorce from Reynolds. Taylor and Fisher adopted a German daughter, Maria. They starred together in *Butterfield 8* (Taylor insisted that studio executives give Fisher an important role in the film).

In the early 1960s Taylor began a widely publicized romance with Richard Burton, her costar (as Mark Antony) in *Cleopatra*. In 1964, immediately after divorcing Fisher, she married Burton, who legally adopted Maria. They had a stormy ten-year marriage, during which they made numerous movies together, including *The V.I.P.s* (1963); *The Sandpiper* (1965); *Who's Afraid of Virginia Woolf; The Taming of the Shrew, Doctor Faustus* (1967); *Hammersmith Is Out* (1972); and *Divorce His/Divorce Hers* (TV, 1973). In 1974 they divorced. The following year they remarried, but in 1976 they split up again.

In that same year, 1976, over one hundred Jewish airplane passengers were being held hostage at the Entebbe Airport in Uganda. Taylor privately communicated to Israeli officials that she would be willing to go to Uganda to negotiate with the hijackers and even to offer herself as a hostage for the release of others. However, on July 4, 1976, Israeli commandos stormed the airport and rescued the hostages. Taylor later had a role in a film based on the event, entitled *Victory at Entebbe* (TV, 1976). She played an Israeli who pleads with her government to negotiate with the terrorists, her daughter being one of the hostages.

Through the years Taylor has supported many Jewish and Israeli causes. As a result, her films have been banned in some Arab countries.

Taylor was married for the seventh time late in 1976. Her new husband was John Warner, who was elected to the United States Senate as a Republican from Virginia in 1978. They divorced in 1982.

In January 1983 Taylor was slightly injured in an auto accident in Tel Aviv. While in Israel on a private tour, she visited Prime Minister Menachem Begin.

In April 1983 Taylor and Burton reunited, at least professionally, to appear in the Broadway play *Private Lives*. She missed a number of performances, reportedly because of bronchitis and laryngitis.

In December of that year, Taylor entered the Betty Ford Center in California to cure herself of addictions to alcohol, sleeping pills, and painkillers. She checked out in January, 1984.

In 1985 Taylor helped to raise funds to fight AIDS. At that time, her good friend Rock Hudson was dying of the disease. In 1991 she founded the Elizabeth Taylor AIDS Foundation.

Meanwhile, she continued her acting career. She narrated the Holocaust documentary *Genocide* (1982), portrayed the gossip columnist Louella Parsons in *Malice in Wonderland* (TV, 1985), was a fading movie queen trying to stage a comeback in *There Must Be a Pony* (TV, 1986), and appeared in *Sweet Bird of Youth* (TV, 1989). In the 1990s she had a role in the movie *The Flintstones* (1994), appeared as herself in an episode of the TV sitcom *Roseanne* (1996), and participated in a number of TV specials, including *Happy Birthday, Elizabeth: A Celebration of Life* (1997).

During those years, her personal life continued its tumultuous course. In 1991 she married the construction worker Larry Fortensky, her seventh husband. Again, the marriage did not work out,

Elizabeth Taylor

and they divorced in 1996. In early 1998 Taylor fell and suffered a painful compression fracture of the back, requiring her to spend months in a back brace.

However, those years also produced many well-earned honors for her. In 1993 Taylor received the Life Achievement Award from the American Film Institute, and in 1998 she was given a similar award from the Screen Actors Guild.

SELECTED PERFORMANCES:

STAGE

The Little Foxes (1981)
Private Lives (1983)

FILMS

There's One Born Every Minute (1942*)*
Lassie Come Home (1943)
Jane Eyre (1944)
The White Cliffs of Dover (1944)
National Velvet (1944)
Courage of Lassie (1946)
Cynthia (1947)
Life with Father (1947)
A Date with Judy (1948)
Julia Misbehaves (1948)
Little Women (1949)
The Conspirator (1950)
The Big Hangover (1950)
Father of the Bride (1950)
Father's Little Dividend (1951)
A Place in the Sun (1951)
Callaway Went Thataway (1951)
Love Is Better Than Ever (1952)
Ivanhoe (1952)
The Girl Who Had Everything (1953)
Rhapsody (1954)
Elephant Walk (1954)
Beau Brummell (1954)
The Last Time I Saw Paris (1954)
Giant (1956)
Raintree County (1957)
Cat on a Hot Tin Roof (1958)

Suddenly Last Summer (1959)
Butterfield 8 (1960)
Cleopatra (1963)
The V.I.P.s (1963)
The Sandpiper (1965)
Who's Afraid of Virginia Woolf? (1966)
The Taming of the Shrew (1967)
Doctor Faustus (1967)
Reflections in a Golden Eye (1967)
The Comedians (1967)
Boom! (1968)
Secret Ceremony (1968)
The Only Game in Town (1970)
Under Milk Wood (1972)
Z and Co. (1972, G.B.; U.S., *X Y and Zee*)
Hammersmith Is Out (1972)
Divorce His/Divorce Hers (TV, 1973)
Night Watch (1973)
Ash Wednesday (1973)
The Blue Bird (1976)
Victory at Entebbe (TV, 1976)
A Little Night Music (1977)
Winter Kills (1979)
The Mirror Crack'd (1980)
Genocide (narrator, 1982)
Between Friends (TV, 1983)
North and South (TV, 1985)
Malice in Wonderland (TV, 1985)
There Must Be a Pony (TV, 1986)
Poker Alice (TV, 1987)
Il Giovane Toscanini (1988, It.; U.S., *Young Toscanini*)
Sweet Bird of Youth (TV, 1989)
The Flintstones (1994)

Sophie Tucker

Last of the Red-Hot Mamas

Sophie Tucker was one of the great musical-variety artists of her time. Her signature song was "I'm the Last of the Red-Hot Mamas."

Sophie Tucker was born in Poland on January 13, 1884. Her mother was en route to the United States when she gave birth to her. The family's name at the time was Kalish. Earlier, however, Sophie's father had run away from his military service and had fled to the United States. Along the way, he made friends with an Italian, Charles Abuza. When Abuza died, Kalish, in fear of being caught by the Russian police, took the dead man's name and papers. Arriving in Boston, he got a job and sent for his pregnant wife. Thus, when the baby girl reached America, she became Sophie, or Sophia (originally Sonia), Abuza.

In 1892 the Abuzas moved from Boston to Hartford, Connecticut, where they opened a restaurant. Sophie hated working in the restaurant. But one day she began to sing popular songs to help bring in customers. Theater people who frequented the restaurant inspired and encouraged Sophie to enter show business.

She began to appear in local amateur shows. At first, however, she was shy because of her weight (145 pounds at the age of thirteen), and she restricted herself to playing the piano accompaniment (with one finger) for her younger sister, Anna, who sang. "Gradually," Sophie later wrote in her autobiography, *Some of These Days* (1945), "at the concerts I began to hear calls for 'the fat girl.' . . . Then I would jump up from the piano

stool, forgetting all about my size, and work to get all the laughs I could get." She concluded that "maybe in show business size didn't matter if you could sing and could make people laugh."

Sophie begged her parents to let her leave town so that she could begin a career in show business, but they refused. After graduating from high school, she stayed with the restaurant until 1903, when she married Louis Tuck, a local beer-wagon driver. Louis, however, could not support Sophie and their son, Bert, and the Tucks soon separated.

In 1906, not long after her separation from Tuck, Sophie left her son to be raised by her family, with her financial support, while she went to New York City to enter show business under the name Sophie Tucker. She found jobs scarce and often had to literally sing for her supper at restaurants.

Late in 1906 she entered an amateur show, and when the manager saw her he told an associate, according to Tucker's autobiography, "This on'e so big and ugly the crowd in front will razz her. Better get some cork and black her up." At that time the use of blackface was still common among white entertainers, but it was usually a matter of choice. Tucker, already insecure about her own appearance, was led to believe that she needed blackface as a disguise. Though she hated blackface, she put it on for her performance in the amateur show, where her robust singing style was very successful.

In December 1906 tucker made her professional New York City debut, again in blackface, at the Music Hall. She played in various vaudeville theaters for the next couple of years, and in 1908 she joined a traveling burlesque show. One

Sophie Tucker

day the luggage with her makeup failed to arrive, and she soon discovered to her pleasant surprise that the audience loved her just as she was. She never used blackface again.

In 1909 she was signed to appear on Broadway in Florenz Ziegfeld's annual *Follies*. But the female stars of the revue became jealous of her talent, and she was fired before she could appear during the show's New York City run.

Returning to vaudeville, Tucker soon became a major star, specializing in belting out ragtime songs. She also developed a distinctive stage personality in which her large dimensions became an asset, as in her humorous double-entendre singing of the song "Nobody Loves a Fat Girl, but Oh, How a Fat Girl Can Love."

In 1911 Tucker appeared in two musical comedies in Chicago, and while she was there she introduced "Some of These Days," which became her trademark song. In 1914 she appeared at the Palace Theater in New York City, the most prestigious house in vaudeville.

Also in 1914 she married her pianist, Frank Westphal, in Chicago. However, the marraige soon began to fail. After setting Frank up in a garage business, Sophie went on with her career alone. They were divorced in 1919.

During World War I the fashion in popular music changed from ragtime to jazz. Tucker organized her own little band, called the Five Kings of Syncopation, and billed herself as the Queen of Jazz.

After her father's death in 1915, Tucker began to incorporate sad, sentimental ballads into her performances. She also began to dramatize songs by introducing them with skits and monlogues that intensified the emotional impact. By 1920 she had polished her act into its final form: a booming voice, a dramatic and emotional presentation, a suggestive kind of humor, and a repertoire of songs ranging from lively jazz to tearjerking ballads.

In December 1916 Tucker, with the Five Kings of Syncopation, opened at Reisenweber's New York City restaurant, where the group stayed for five years. During that time she also appeared elsewhere, as in the Broadway show *Hello, Alexander* (1919).

In 1922, shortly after Tucker and her jazz group broke up, she made the first of many tours in England, where she immediately became a huge success and where she remained extremely popular throughout the rest of her career. While she was there, she appeared in the London stage production of *Round in Fifty* (1922). But her proudest moment during her first trip to England was when London's Jewish population gave her a tremendous reception at the Rivoli Theater in Whitechapel.

Back in the United States, she made a two-year vaudeville tour. In 1925 she introduced "My Yiddishe Momme" (or "My Yiddisha Mama"), which became one of the songs with which she was most closely identified.

In 1928, at the Palace Theater, Tucker introduced the song "I'm the Last of the Red-hot Mamas." From that time forward she was billed as the last of the Red-hot Mamas.

Also in 1928 she married Al Lackey, a fan who had become her personal manager. It was another short-lived marriage, and they were divorced in 1933.

Though successful in England, Tucker had difficulty on the Continent because of the language barrier. Nonetheless, her rendition of "My Yiddishe Momme" became very popular in Vienna, and she was invited to broadcast the song over the Berlin radio in 1931. However, after Hitler came to power, her existing records were smashed and further sales of her recordings were banned.

In the early 1930s, when American vaudeville was rapidly dying out, Tucker successfully made the transition to nightclubs, where she remained a headliner for the rest of her life.

She also worked on Broadway in the musical shows *Leave It to Me* (1938) and *High Kickers* (1941), in the latter of which she portrayed herself.

Her energetic performances enlivened the film musicals Honky Tonk (1929), Broadway Melody of 1938 (1937), and Follow the Boys (1944). In 1937 she took acting lessons from Laura Hope Crews and performed a nonmusical role in the movie *Thoroughbreds Don't Cry* (1937).

Tucker also made numerous guest appearances on radio. Later she was a hit on TV, notably on Ed Sullivan's variety show.

But Tucker always preferred live theater to films, radio, and TV. "I couldn't even say 'hell' or 'damn,'" she complained about radio, "and nothing, honey, is more expressive that the way I say 'hell' or 'damn.'"

In England, however, music halls continued the tradition of uninhibited live variety shaows, and Tucker performed there frequently. Her 1934 tour of England was climaxed by her command performance for King George V.

By the late 1930s Tucker was already being referred to as an American "institution." Particularly with her explosive live performances, she maintained her popularity for over fifty years.

Tucker's personal life, however, was troubled by the fact that though she always wanted to be home with her family, her career often required her to travel. In marriage, she had to face the inner conflict of simultaneously wanting a strong man and wanting independence. She became the provider and leader in each of her three marriages.

Tucker was a giving person, being involved with much fund-raising and philanthropy. In 1945 she established the Sophie Tucker Foundation, and ten years later she endowed a chair in the theater arts at Brandeis University. Also an activist, she helped to organize the American Federation of Actors (later absorbed into the American Guild of Variety Artists, a division of Actors' Equity), which elected her president in 1938.

Even late in life Tucker held her audience. In the 1950s she appealed to the new generation with her self-effacing humor: "I'm the 3-D Mama with the Big Wide Screen." In 1962 she gave another command performance in London. In 1963 she was the subject of the Broadway musical play *Sophie*.

In late 1965, at nearly eighty-two years of age, she made a successful appearance in the Latin Quarter of New York City. Tucker died a few months later in the same city on February 9, 1966.

SELECTED PERFORMANCES:

STAGE

Merry Mary (1911)
Louisiana Lou (1911)
Hello, Alexander (1919)
Tick-Tack-Toe (1920)
Round in Fifty (1922)
Earl Carroll Vanities of 1924 (1924)
Gay Paree (1927)
Follow a Star (1930)
Leave It to Me (1938)
High Kickers (1941)

FILMS

Honky Tonk (1929)
Broadway Melody of 1938 (1937)
Thoroughbreds Don't Cry (1937)
Follow the Boys (1944)
Sensations of 1945 (1944)

Erich von Stroheim

The Man You Love to Hate

Erich von Stroheim was one of the great silent-movie directors. He also had an illustrious career as an actor. He played mainly villains, and in his early years, he was often billed as "the man you love to hate."

E rich von Stroheim was born in Vienna, Austria, on September 22, 1885. As an adult he claimed that his original name was Erich Oswald Hans Carl Maria Stroheim von Nordenwald and that his parents were members of the Catholic aristocracy in Austria. But shortly after his death, it was discovered that his parents were Jewish and that his real name was Erich Oswald Stroheim.

Little is known about von Stroheim's childhood, as many of his stories about his early years have proven to be false. It is known, however, that he arrived in the United States in November 1909.

Settling at first in New York City, von Stroheim took odd jobs for the next few years. In 1912 a job as a traveling salesman took him to San Francisco, where he met Margaret Knox. They married in 1913. She helped him perfect his English and collaborated with him in writing stories and plays. They were divorced in 1914.

Continuing with odd jobs, he went to Lake Tahoe and then to Los Angeles. From a group of extras, he was selected by the producer-director D. W. Griffith to play the small part of a black Confederate soldier in *The Birth of a Nation* (1915). Over the next few years, von Stroheim performed as a bit player in many other pictures, such as Griffith's *Intolerance* (1916). He was usually type-

cast as a brutal Prussian soldier and was promoted as "the man you love to hate." He continued to play principally villainous roles throughout the rest of his career.

In 1917 von Stroheim married May Jones, a theatrical costume designer. They had one son, Erich. Later that year they were divorced. In 1919 he married Valerie Germonprez, with whom he had his son Josef.

In *Blind Husbands* (1919), which he wrote, directed, and starred in, von Stroheim played an Austrian lieutenant attempting to seduce the wife of an American doctor. In *Foolish Wives* (1922), which he directed, he played a ruthless seducer preying on wealthy, idle women. It was banned in some American cities.

Von Stroheim next wrote and began to direct *Merry-Go-Round*, a film about prewar Vienna. But the costs of the filming became so great that Irving Thalberg, the young production chief at Universal, fired von Stroheim. The film was completed in 1923 by Rupert Julian, who, in fact, followed his predecessor's shooting script.

Moving over to the Goldwyn Studio (soon to become Metro-Goldwyn-Mayer, or MGM), von Stroheim prepared an adaptation of Frank Norris's novel *McTeague* and filmed it as *Greed*. Intent on making the movie a naturalistic epic, he shot it on locations in San Francisco, Oakland, and the Mojave Desert. The result was a forty-two reel picture that ran for nine hours. He suggested that it be released in two or three parts. The studio, rejecting that plan, slashed the film down to ten reels and released it in 1924. *Greed* is now regarded as a masterpiece.

though later shown in Europe and South America).

In 1928 Joseph P. Kennedy (father of John F. Kennedy) engaged von Stroheim to write and direct a movie starring Gloria Swanson. In the film, *Queen Kelly*, von Stroheim deliberately restored scenes that had been eliminated from the script at the urging of the Hays censorship office. He also made *Queen Kelly* as a silent film even though talkies had been invented in 1927. Those factors caused Kennedy and Swanson to halt the production before it was finished. Swanson later released the first half of the film abroad.

The last and only sound movie that von Stroheim directed was *Walking down Broadway*, but his 1933 work was judged unmarketable by Fox studio officials and was never released, though a few scenes were incorporated into *Hello, Sister* (1933).

Von Stroheim was one of the great creative directors in the history of the cinema, a master of realism and surrealism. Sergei Eisenstein called him "The Director." But because of his extravagances and his independence, producers gave up on him.

Rejected as a director, von Stroheim returned to acting. He played a schizophrenic music-hall ventriloquist in *The Great Gabbo* (1929), a treacherous German diplomat in *Friends and Lovers* (1931), a fanatically realistic movie director in *The Lost Squadron* (1932), and a sadistic writer in *As You Desire Me* (1932).

Soon, however, he was unable to get roles in major films. In 1934 he became a wardrobe consultant at MGM. The following year he went bankrupt and joined the MGM story department, where he worked on several scripts. During that time he also wrote a successful novel, *Paprika* (1935).

In 1936 he moved to Paris, where he appeared in a number of popular films. Most notable was his role as the disabled aristocratic German military officer in *La Grand Illusion* (1937, released in America as *Grand Illusion* in 1938).

The outbreak of World War II in Europe caused von Stroheim to return to Hollywood, where he was now in demand as an actor because of his success in France. He appeared in many films during the war, including *I Was an Adventuress* (1940) and *So Ends Our Night* (1941). His finest perfor-

Erich von Stroheim

He then directed his own adaptation of Franz Lehar's operetta *The Merry Widow* (1925). It was a tremendous success, and in 1926 American critics voted von Stroheim the best director of the year. Also in 1926 he became a naturalized American citizen.

Leaving MGM, von Stroheim made his next film for an independent producer, Pat Powers. He wrote, directed, and starred in the picture, entitled *The Wedding March*, another film about pre-World War I Vienna. Because the filming was taking too long, the producer stopped the project before completion. The footage was divided by others into two movies: *The Wedding March* (1928) and *Honeymoon* (unreleased in the United States,

mance during that time was as the German general Rommel in *Five Graves to Cairo* (1943). In *The North Star* (1943) he had the role of a cold-blooded Nazi doctor who performs fiendish medical experiments on prisoners of war. In *The Great Flamarion* (1945) von Stroheim played a trick-shot artist who falls in love with the wife of his assistant and then, during a performance, "accidentally" kills the man.

From early 1941 to late 1942, he toured in the comedy *Arsenic and Old Lace*. He then replaced Boris Karloff in the Broadway production of the play. In 1945 von Stroheim returned to France. He made several films there, including *La Danse de Mort* ("The Dance of Death," 1947).

Von Stroheim made his last appearance in an American film in *Sunset Boulevard* (1950). He portrayed a director who has become the butler of a former movie queen (played by Gloria Swanson).

In the early 1950s von Stroheim acted in French films, notably *Napoléon* (1954), in which he portrayed Beethoven. He also devoted much time to writing scenarios (still hoping to have a chance to direct again) and novels, including *Les Feux de Saint-Jean* ("The Fires of Saint Joan"; volume 1, 1951; volume 2, 1954). He was preparing to write his memoirs when he died in Naurepas, Seine-et-Oise, France, on May 12, 1957.

SELECTED PERFORMANCES:

STAGE

Arsenic and Old Lace (1941)

FILMS

The Birth of a Nation (1915)
Ghosts (1915)
Old Heidelberg (1915)
The Social Secretary (1916)

Intolerance (1916)
His Picture in the Papers (1916)
Panathea (1917)
Sylvia of the Secret Service (1917)
For France (1917)
The Unbeliever (1918)
The Hun Within (1918)
In Again, Out Again (1918)
Hearts of the World (1918)
The Heart of Humanity (1918)
Blind Husbands (1919)
Foolish Wives (1922)
The Wedding March (1928)
The Great Gabbo (1929)
Three Faces East (1930)
Friends and Lovers (1931)
The Lost Squadron (1932)
As You Desire Me (1932)
Crimson Romance (1934)
Fugitive Road (1934)
The Crime of Dr. Crespi (1935)
Martha Richard, au Service de la France ("Martha Richard, in the Service of France," 1936)
La Grande Illusion (1937)
Ultimatum (1938)
Tempéte sur Paris (1939, Fr.; U.S., *Thunder over Paris*)
I Was an Adventuress (1940)
So Ends Our Night (1941)
Five Graves to Cairo (1943)
The North Star (1943)
The Lady and the Monster (1944)
Storm over Lisbon (1944)
The Great Flamarion (1945)
The Mask of Dijon (1946)
La Danse de Mort ("The Death Dance" 1947)
Portrait d'un Assassin ("Portrait of an Assassin," 1949)
Sunset Boulevard (1950)
Napoléon (1954, Fr.)

Eli Wallach

Master of Method Acting

Eli Wallach was an original member of the famed Actors Studio in New York City, where he learned the Method technique of acting. He has since become one of the most highly respected Method actors on the stage, in film, and on TV.

E li Wallach was born in New York City, on December 7, 1915. He grew up in a predominantly Italian neighborhood in Brooklyn, where he acted in plays at school. At a local boys' club he portrayed the old man in *Fiat Lux* (1930).

After graduating from Erasmus Hall High School (1932), he attended the University of Texas, where he had the title role in *Liliom* (1936). He then got a master's degree in education at the City College of the City University of New York (1938).

Deciding against a career in education, Wallach studied acting under Sanford Meisner at the Neighborhood Playhouse School of the Theater in New York City. His studies were interrupted by World War II, during which he served in the army medical corps (1941-45).

Returning to civilian life, Wallach began to appear in plays, making his Broadway debut as the crew chief in *Skydrift* (1945). In 1946 he played Cromwell in *Henry VIII* and the coward in *Androcles and the Lion*.

In 1947 Wallach became a charter member of the Actors Studio in New York City. There, under Lee Strasberg, he became a master of Method acting, a dramatic technique by which an actor seeks close personal identification with the character being portrayed.

In 1948 Wallach married the actress Anne Jackson, whom he had met when they were doing off-Broadway work together. They had three children: Peter, Roberta, and Katherine.

Meanwhile, though working fairly steadily, Wallach was unsatisfied with the progress of his career. He even put in an application to become a postman.

Then, in early 1949, the producer Joshua Logan asked Wallach to replace Ted Kazanoff as Stefanowski in the fabulously successful Broadway production of *Mister Roberts*. That role finally gave him the showcase necessary for advancing his career.

In 1951 Wallach gave a critically acclaimed performance as Mangiacavallo, the passionate truck driver in Tennessee Williams's *The Rose Tattoo*. He then turned down the juicy role of Maggio (eventually played by Frank Sinatra) in the film *From Here to Eternity* so that he could appear in Williams's next play, *Camino Real* (1953). Though the play was not successful, Wallach's performance as Kilroy was hailed by critics.

Since then Wallach appeared in many plays, frequently with his wife. They acted together in *Major Barbara* (1956); *Rhinoceros* (1961); *The Typists and The Tiger* (as a double bill, 1963); *Luv* (1964); *The Waltz of the Toreadors* (1973); *The Diary of Anne Frank* (1978), with their two daughters; *Twice around the Park* (1982); *The Nest of the Wood Grouse* (1984); *In Persons* (1993); and *The Flowering Peach* (1994).

Wallach made his film debut in *Baby Doll*

Eli Wallach and Anne Jackson

(1956), as the sly and terrifying seducer. Later, he played a wide variety of leading and supporting roles, both villainous and sympathetic, in a number of movies, including *The Misfits* (1961), *Lord Jim* (1965), *The Tiger Makes Out* (1967), *Cinderella Liberty* (1973), *Skokie* (TV, 1981), and *The Wall* (TV, 1982), a film about the desperate attempt of the Waraw Jews' to defend themselves against the Nazis in April 1943. In *Sam's Son* (1984), an autobiographical film directed and written by Michael Landon, Wallach sensitively conveyed the humiliations and hopes of Sam, the hero's father. Anne Jackson appeared in the movie as Sam's wife.

Wallach has made TV commercials and appeared on many TV programs. He gave masterful performances as Vincent Danzig, head of a Mafia family, in *Our Family Honor* (1985-86). He also guest-starred in a 1986 episode of *Highway to Heaven*.

In the late 1980s and throughout the 1990s, he remained busy in films. He added zest to *Tough Guys* (1986); *The Godfather, Part III* (1990); *Vendetta: Secrets of a Mafia Bride* (TV, 1991); *Teamster Boss:*

The Jackie Presser Story (TV, 1992); and *The Associate* (1996).

Wallach is widely regarded as a consummate craftsman and is renowned for the passion that he puts into his performances.

SELECTED PERFORMANCES:

STAGE

Fiat Lux (1930)
Liliom (1936)
The Bo Tree (1939)
Skydrift (1945)
Henry VIII (1946)
Androcles and the Lion (1946)
Yellow Jack (1947)
Alice in Wonderland (1947)
Antony and Cleopatra (1947)
Mister Roberts (1949)
The Lady from the Sea (1950)
The Rose Tattoo (1951)
Camino Real (1953)

The Scarecrow (1953)
Mademoiselle Colombe (1954)
The Teahouse of the August Moon (1954)
Major Barbara (1956)
The Chairs (1958)
The Cold Wind and the Warm (1958)
Rhinoceros (1961)
Brecht on Brecht (1961)
The Typists (1963)
The Tiger (1963)
Luv (1964)
Staircase (1968)
Promenade, All! (1971)
The Waltz of the Toreadors (1973)
Saturday, Sunday, Monday (1974)
Absent Friends (1977)
The Diary of Anne Frank (1978)
Every Good Boy Deserves Favour (1979)
Twice around the Park (1982)
The Nest of the Wood Grouse (1984)
The Price (1992)
In Persons (1993)
The Flowering Peach (1994)

FILMS

Baby Doll (1956)
Seven Thieves (1960)
The Magnificent Seven (1960)
The Misfits (1961)
Hemingway's Adventures of a Young Man (1962)
Act One (1963)
How the West Was Won (1963)
The Victors (1963)
Kisses for My President (1964)
The Moon-Spinners (1964)
Genghis Khan (1965)
Lord Jim (1965)
How to Steal a Million (1966)
The Poppy Is Also a Flower (1966)
The Good, the Bad, and the Ugly (1967)
The Tiger Makes Out (1967)
How to Save a Marriage—and Ruin Your Life
    (1968)
A Lovely Way to Die (1968)
New York City—the Most (1968)
Ace High (1969)
The Brain (1969)

Mackenna's Gold (1969)
The Angel Levine (1970)
The People Next Door (1970)
Zigzag (1970)
Cinderella Liberty (1973)
A Cold Night's Death (TV, 1973)
Indict and Convict (TV, 1974)
Crazy Joe (1974)
Nasty Habits (1977)
The Domino Principle (1977)
The Deep (1977)
Seventh Avenue (TV, 1977)
The Pirate (TV, 1978)
Girlfriends (1978)
Movie Movie (1978)
The Adventures of Gerard (1978)
Circle of Iron (1979)
Firepower (1979)
Winter Kills (1979)
The Hunter (1980)
Fugitive Family (TV, 1980)
The Pride of Jesse Hallam (TV, 1981)
Skokie (TV, 1981)
The Wall (TV, 1982)
The Executioner's Song (TV, 1982)
Anatomy of an Illness (TV, 1984)
Sam's Son (1984)
Murder: By Reason of Insanity (TV, 1985)
Christopher Columbus (TV, 1985)
Tough Guys (1986)
Something in Common (TV, 1986)
Nuts (1987)
The Two Jakes (1990)
The Godfather, Part III (1990)
Vendetta: Secrets of a Mafia Bride (TV, 1991)
Article 99 (1992)
Mistress (1992)
Night and the City (1992)
Legacy of Lies (TV, 1992)
Teamster Boss: The Jackie Presser Story (TV, 1992)
Vendetta 2: The New Mafia (TV, 1993)
The Associate (1996)
Two Much (1996)

TV

Our Family Honor (1985–86)

Lotus Weinstock

Split Personality

Lotus Weinstock was a comedienne who based much of her humor on the conflicting aspects of her personality (what she called her "split personality"). Originally named Marlene Weinstock, she replaced her first name with "Lotus" to stand for her spiritual aspirations, while she retained "Weinstock" to reflect her earthy, Jewish realism. "The Lotus in me wants to be totally free," she said. "Weinstock will settle for a discount."

—◦—

Both of her were born in Philadelphia, Pennsylvania, on January 29, 1943. She studied dance at the Philadelphia Academy of Music and theater arts at Emerson College in Boston. Weinstock left college to join a musical-comedy repertory company. Later she studied dancing and acting in New York City, where she became a hostess at the legendary Bitter End, joined a comedy act billed as the Turtles, and then performed a solo stand-up comedy act in Greenwich Village in the early 1960s.

Her life and career changed when she moved to the West Coast. There she met the uninhibited comedian Lenny Bruce, who became her mentor and fiancé. His death in 1966 prevented their marriage, but from him she learned to provoke thought as well as laughter in her comedy act. "Lenny was the turning point of my life," she later recalled. "Never again would I play beneath my intelligence or be anything less than honest onstage."

During the 1970s her career moved steadily forward. She became a regular on the nightclub circuit and began to appear on TV talk shows, such as Merv Griffin's.

Weinstock told audiences about her "split personality" and about the problems it presented in raising her daughter, Lily Haydn. (About her husband, Weinstock said, "I was married to him for eighteen years. He was married to me for three. Possibly.") As Lotus, she was confident that the child would be guided by the "One Presence and Power," but as Weinstock, a typical Jewish-American mother, she constantly worried.

Weinstock also tackled a wide range of important topical issues. Combining astrology with the hotly debated issue of school busing, she made this whimsical suggestion: "Too many Geminis at one school? Bus them! Let them mingle with a Taurus or a Sag! Get to know the other half of the zodiac!" She never hurt or ridiculed people. Her jokes were carefully designed to make people laugh and think. Among the other subjects she explored were sex, health food, gun control, marijuana, cancer cures, and extrasensory perception. She gathered many of her stories into the book *The Lotus Position* (1982).

In 1988 Weinstock dealt with her anxiety over her daughter's impending departure for college by writing a two-person comedy play, Molly and Maze, which they performed together in Beverly Hills, California. When Lily graduated four years later, they celebrated by performing the same play in San Diego.

In Weinstock's later years, she not only continued her comedy career but also branched out into straight acting roles, as in an episode of the TV

Lotus Weinstock

dramatic series *L.A. Law*. She also appeared in the documentary film *Wisecracks* (1992).

Her interests extended far beyond her career. She served, for example, as president of the board of directors of the private Sheenway School and Culture Center in the Watts section of Los Angeles.

Lotus Weinstock died in Hollywood, Los Angeles, California, on August 31, 1997. She left behind a special legacy through her thoughtful humor, perhaps summed up in one of her own quips: "Remember, angels can fly because they take themselves lightly."

SELECTED PERFORMANCES:

STAGE

Molly and Maze (1988, 1992)

FILM

Wisecracks (1992)

Jesse White

Comic Character Actor

Jesse White was a dependable character actor in both comic and dramatic roles. But his most characteristic role was that of a comically nervous, cigar-chewing heavy.

Jesse White was born in Buffalo, New York, on January 3, 1919. His original name was Jesse Marc Weidenfeld.

He moved with his family to Akron, Ohio, as a youngster. There he made his stage debut, as the court jester, in *Mary of Scotland* (1934). After graduating from high school, White worked odd jobs and performed in small-time productions of plays. White got his first big break when he played a Nazi soldier in a touring production of *The Moon Is Down* in 1942. That year he also married Cecelia Kahn, with whom he had two daughters, Carole and Janet.

White then moved to New York City, where he appeared in numerous plays over the next few years. He played a vacuum-cleaner salesman in *Sons and Soldiers* (1943). He also played Duane Wilson, the mental-hospital attendant, in the comedy-fantasy *Harvey* (1944), and had the role of Harry Brock (succeeding Paul Douglas) in the comedy *Born Yesterday* (1949).

White also began to make guest appearances on TV during its early years. He acted, for example, in plays on the *Chevrolet Theater* (1945) and *Ford Theater* (1947).

White made his movie debut when he repeated his role for the filmed version of *Harvey* (1950). White quickly became a popular character actor in movies, such as *Bedtime for Bonzo* (1951), *Death of a Salesman* (1951), *Million Dollar Mermaid* (1952), *The Bad Seed* (1956), and *Marjorie Morningstar* (1958). White's later movies included *It's a Mad, Mad, Mad, Mad World* (1963); *Pajama Party* (1964); *The Reluctant Astronaut* (1967); *The Cat from Outer Space* (1978); and *Matinee* (1993).

He also became a familiar figure on TV as a regular on the comedy series *Private Secretary* (1953-57, syndicated as *Susie*), *Make Room for Daddy* (or *The Danny Thomas Show*, 1954-57), and *The Ann Sothern Show* (1959-61). Later, he frequently appeared as a guest performer on many shows, including *Seinfeld* (1996).

After moving to films and TV, White continued to return occasionally to the stage, appearing in *Will Success Spoil Rock Hunter?* (1956), *Guys and Dolls* (1959), and *Show Boat* (1963). He replaced John McGiver as the mayor in *The Front Page* in 1969, and he once again played Wilson in revivals of *Harvey* in 1970 and 1971.

In 1967 White became the TV spokesman for Maytag Company. For many years young people knew him principally as the "lonely" Maytag repairman in TV commercials, the sales ploy being that Maytag appliances are so reliable that no one ever goes to him for help.

White was very positive about his experiences as an actor. "At age seven," White once said, "I knew what I wanted in life—to bring a little laughter and joy to the world. I've been blessed twice—to be able to do the thing I know and do best and to make a decent and respectable living at it. I have had a good life in show business and feel sorry for people who are not in it."

Jesse White

Jesse White

White died in Los Angeles, California, on January 9, 1997.

SELECTED PERFORMANCES:

STAGE

Mary of Scotland (1934)
The Moon Is Down (1942)
Sons and Soldiers (1943)
My Dear Public (1943)
Unexpected Honeymoon (1943)
Mrs. Kimball Presents (1944)
Helen Goes to Troy (1944)
Harvey (1944, 1970, 1971)
The Cradle Will Rock (1947)
A Month in the Country (1948)
Red Gloves (1948)
Goodnight Ladies (1949)
Born Yesterday (1949)
Will Success Spoil Rock Hunter? (1956)
A Hole in the Head (1957)
Guys and Dolls (1959)
Kiss Me, Kate (1960, 1965)

Show Boat (1963)
Stubborn Ernie (1964)
Kelly (1965)
The Front Page (1969)

FILMS

Harvey (1950)
Bedtime for Bonzo (1951)
Francis Goes to the Races (1951)
Callaway Went Thataway (1951)
Death of a Salesman (1951)
The Girl in White (1952)
Million Dollar Mermaid (1952)
Forever Female (1954)
Hell's Half Acre (1954)
Witness to *Murder* (1954)
Not as a Stranger (1955)
The Come On (1956)
Back from Eternity (1956)
The Bad Seed (1956)
Designing Woman (1957)
Marjorie Morningstar (1958)
The Rise and Fall of Legs Diamond (1960)
The Big Night (1960)
A Fever in the Blood (1961)
On the Double (1961)
The Right Approach (1961)
Tomboy and the Champ (1961)
It's Only Money (1962)
Sail a Crooked Ship (1962)
It's a Mad, Mad, Mad, Mad World (1963)
The Yellow Canary (1963)
A House Is Not a Home (1964)
Looking for Love (1964)
Pajama Party (1964)
Dear Brigitte (1965)
The Ghost in the Invisible Bikini (1966)
The Reluctant Astronaut (1967)
The Spirit Is Willing (1967)
Bless the Beasts and Children (1971)
New Girl in Town (1977)
The Cat from Outer Space (1978)
Monster in the Closet (1987)
Matinee (1993)

TV

Private Secretary (1953–57, syndicated as *Susie*)
Make Room for Daddy (or *The Danny Thomas Show*, 1954–57)
The Ann Sothern Show (1959–61)
Devlin (animated, voice only, 1974-76)

Gene Wilder

Deadpan Comic Actor

————◄○►————

Gene Wilder has developed a unique style as a comic actor: he wears a deadpan expression at all times, even when he is engaging in the most madcap behavior. That contrast reflects the real man. "My quiet exterior used to be a mask for hysteria," he says. "After seven years of analysis, it just became a habit."

Wilder is one of the truly outstanding comic actors in contemporary motion pictures. He likes to draw humor from characters who are essentially sad, perhaps reflecting his early experiences in creating comedy for his invalid mother. His performances in Mel Brooks's frenetic films *The Producers* (1967), *Blazing Saddles* (1974), and *Young Frankenstein* (1974) are comic gems.

◄○►

Gene Wilder was born in Milwaukee, Wisconsin, on June 11, 1935. His original name was Jerome Silberman.

When he was six years old, his mother had a heart attack that left her a partial invalid. He used to cheer her up by improvising comedy skits, thus developing an early awareness of the coexistence of laughter and pain.

Wilder's parents sent him to the Black Fox Military Institute in Los Angeles. "I was the only Jew in school," he later said, "and I got either beaten up or insulted every day." He soon returned to his native city, where he began acting lessons in 1947 and made his first stage appearance, as Balthazar in *Romeo and Juliet* at the Milwaukee Playhouse, in 1948.

After graduating from Washington High School in 1951, Wilder enrolled at the University of Iowa. While he was there, he acted in student plays and worked in summer stock. He graduated with a B.A. degree in 1955. He then studied voice, judo, fencing, and gymnastics at the Old Vic Theater School in Bristol, England (1955–56).

Returning to America, Wilder was drafted for two years of service in the army (1956-58). He was assigned to Valley Forge Hospital in Pennsylvania, and he requested a position in the neuropsychiatric ward because he felt that the experience would be helpful in his acting studies. On weekends he went to drama classes at the Herbert Berghof Studio in New York City.

In 1961 he joined the Actors Studio, where he began to study with the famed Lee Strasberg. That year he also made his off-Broadway debut, in the comedy *Roots*, and his Broadway debut, as the confused valet in *The Complaisant Lover*. By then he had changed his name to Gene Wilder.

While playing in *Mother Courage and Her Children* (1963), Wilder met Mel Brooks, who called for the show's star, Ann Bancroft, every evening. Brooks promised to give the young actor a role in a movie someday.

Wilder honed his dramatic and comedic skills in several more plays. One of them was *One Flew over the Cuckoo's Nest* (1963), which was set in a mental hospital, giving him a chance to draw on his experiences in the neuropsychiatric ward at Valley Forge Hospital.

During the early 1960s Wilder also made some guest appearances on TV series, such as *The De-*

fenders. On the *Eternal Light* series, he acted in "Home for Passover" (1966).

Wilder made his film debut in *Bonnie and Clyde* (1967), in which he played a neurotic undertaker kidnapped by a gang of outlaws. Then, Brooks, keeping his promise, gave Wilder an important role in his first film, *The Producers* (1967). Wilder portrayed the neurotic accountant Leo Bloom, who is drawn into a wild scheme by a crooked producer (played by Zero Mostel). Wilder next starred in several movies in which his comic acting far outshone the scripts, *Start the Revolution without Me* (1970) and *Willy Wonka and the Chocolate Factory* (1971).

But when he began working once again with Brooks, comic magic resulted. For example, in *Blazing Saddles* (1974), a spoof of Hollywood westerns, Wilder portrayed a brazen alcoholic gunslinger. In *Young Frankenstein* (1974), a gothic-horror parody whose script he cowrote with Brooks, Wilder played the title role, a brain surgeon who tries to live down the scandal of his infamous ancestor but who finally succumbs to the temptation to follow in his forebear's footsteps.

Encouraged by his successful collaboration on *Young Frankenstein*, Wilder began to write and direct, the movies that he starred in. Following Brooks's lead, he constructed spoofs of well-known film genres. First was *The Adventure of Sherlock Holmes' Smarter Brother* (1975), a parody of the Holmes detective movies. *The World's Greatest Lover* (1977), which he also produced, was a takeoff on the Rudolph Valentino romantic films of the 1920s. In *Skippy* (1981) Wilder spoofed sex comedies, the hero (Wilder) going so far as to sign himself into a mental hospital to overcome a sex problem.

Among the other movies he appeared in were *The Frisco Kid* (1979), a comedy about an Orthodox rabbi (Wilder) traveling from Poland to San Francisco in 1850; *Stir Crazy* (1980); *Hanky Panky* (1982); *The Woman in Red* (1984); *Haunted Honeymoon* (1986); *See No Evil, Hear No Evil* (1989); and *Another You* (1991).

In the mid-1990s he starred in a TV sitcom,

Gene Wilder

Something Wilder (1994-95). He played Gene Bergman, an older father who, with his wife, tries to raise four-year-old twins.

Wilder has been married four times. In 1960 he wedded the actress Mary Mercier, who appeared with him in *Roots*. After divorcing her he married Mary Joan Schutz in 1967. He also adopted Schutz's daughter, Katherine, from a previous marriage. In 1974 Wilder's second marriage ended in divorce. In 1984 he married the actress Gilda Radner, who appeared with him in *Hanky Panky* (1982), *The Woman in Red* (1984), and *Haunted Honeymoon* (1986). Radner died of cancer in 1989, and in her memory he cofounded Gilda's Club, a cancer support center in Manhattan. In 1991 Wilder married Karen Boyer.

SELECTED PERFORMANCES:

STAGE

Roots (1961)
The Complaisant Lover (1961)
Mother Courage and Her Children (1963)
One Flew over the Cuckoo's Nest (1963)
Dynamite Tonight (1964)
The White House (1964)
Luv (1966)

FILMS

Bonnie and Clyde (1967)
The Producers (1967)
Quackser Fortune Has a Cousin in the Bronx (1970)
Start the Revolution without Me (1970)
Willy Wonka and the Chocolate Factory (1971)
Thursday's Game (TV, 1974)
Rhinoceros (1974)

Blazing Saddles (1974)
The Little Prince (1974)
Young Frankenstein (1974)
The Adventure of Sherlock Holmes' Smarter Brother (1975)
Silver Streak (1976)
The World's Greatest Lover (1977)
The Frisco Kid (1979)
Stir Crazy (1980)
Skippy (1981)
Hanky Panky (1982)
The Woman in Red (1984)
Haunted Honeymoon (1986)
See No Evil, Hear No Evil (1989)
Funny about Love (1990)
Another You (1991)
Alice in Wonderland (TV, 1999)

TV

Something Wilder (1994-95)

Debra Winger

Intense Actress

Debra Winger is one of the most highly respected contemporary actresses. Unlike many actresses of her generation, who quickly become famous on the basis of publicity and physical beauty and then lacked the motivation to develop the big talents to go with their big names, Winger has gained the respect of critics and audiences solely through her genuine gift for bringing passion and intensity to her performances.

Debra Winger was born in Cleveland, Ohio, on May 16, 1955. Her full name was Mary Debra Winger. As a small child, she moved with her parents to Van Nuys, California.

After graduating from high school in 1971, Winger briefly visited Europe and then went to Israel to live and work on a kibbutz. She also applied for Israeli citizenship. But after three months of rigorous military training with the Israeli army, she changed her mind.

Returning to the United States, Winger studied sociology and criminology at California State University in Northridge. However, while working in her spare time at Magic Mountain amusement park, she was thrown from a moving truck. As a result, she developed a cerebral hemorrhage that almost killed her, and for several months she was partly paralyzed and was blind in one eye.

That experience gave Winger a new perspective on life, and she decided to pursue an acting career. To that end, she dropped out of college and studied acting for three years with the actor

Michael V. Gazzo. During that time she also acted with a repertory company in the San Fernando Valley.

Soon, Winger began to appear on TV. She made commercials for McDonald's, Metropolitan Life Insurance, and other companies. She also appeared in guest roles on TV series, such as *Wonder Woman*, and acted in the movie *Special Olympics* (TV, 1978).

Winger's first role in a theatrical film was a small part in *Thank God It's Friday* (1978). But she first attracted major attention with her small role as Melanie, an American student in Paris, in the comedy *French Postcards* (1979).

Winger became a full-fledged star with her performance as the female lead, the tough but sweet Sissy, in the blue-collar romantic melodrama *Urban Cowboy* (1980). She prepared for her part with a vigorous exercise routine so that she could ride a mechanical bucking bull in a bar.

Winger then gave several performances that established her as one of the most talented film actresses of her generation. In *Cannery Row* (1982) she played a reluctant bordello girl. In *An Officer and a Gentleman* (1982) she was a sexy but sensitive Polish-American paper-mill worker. In *Terms of Endearment* (1983) she portrayed an ill-starred daughter caught in a volatile relationship with her overly possessive mother. In *Mike's Murder* (1984) she played a young woman drawn into the sleazy world of the Los Angeles drug culture. In *Legal Eagles* (1986) she extended her range by giving an excellent performance as a young attorney.

Versatility marked her later performances as well. She played an FBI agent investigating the killing of a controversial radio personality in *Betrayed* (1988), a mentally and emotionally dysfunctional person in *A Dangerous Woman* (1993), and a woman prematurely dying of cancer with dignity in *Shadowlands* (1993). Her other films included *Black Widow* (1987), *Leap of Faith* (1992), and Billy Crystal's comedy *Forget Paris* (1995).

Winger's most noticeable physical characteristic is her gravelly voice, which can be strangely touching. In the movie *E.T.* (1982), her voice was one of two that were electronically mixed to create the sound of the extraterrestrial creature.

Winger married the actor Timothy Hutton in 1986. They had one child, Emmanuel Noah, before divorcing.

SELECTED PERFORMANCES:

FILMS

Special Olympics (TV, 1978)
Thank God It's Friday (1978)
French Postcards (1979)
Urban Cowboy (1980)
Cannery Row (1982)
An Officer and a Gentleman (1982)
Terms of Endearment (1983)
Mike's Murder (1984)
Legal Eagles (1986)
Black Widow (1987)
Betrayed (1988)
The Sheltering Sky (1990)
Leap of Faith (1992)
A Dangerous Woman (1993)
Shadowlands (1993)
Wilder Napalm (1993)
Forget Paris (1995)

Debra Winger

Henry Winkler

Fonzie

Henry Winkler, a versatile actor, a director, and a producer, is best known for portraying one of the most beloved characters in TV history: Fonzie in the sitcom *Happy Days* (1974–84).

Henry Franklin Winkler was born in New York City, on October 30, 1945. His parents had grown up and married in Germany, moved to Amsterdam in 1938, and immigrated to the United States in 1939. Many of their relatives who stayed in Germany perished in Nazi concentration camps.

While growing up in New York City, Winkler appeared in many school dramatic productions. After graduating from McBurney, a private boys' school in Manhattan, he attended Emerson College (1963–67) in Boston. There he performed in theater productions for both Emerson and nearby Harvard.

Having earned his B.A. degree at Emerson, Winkler went to Yale for postgraduate study. While at the Yale School of Drama (1967-70), he became one of the founders of the New Haven Free Theater (1968). He graduated from Yale with an M.F.A. in 1970 and then spent one year (1970-71) with the Yale Repertory Theater.

Moving to New York City, Winkler appeared in some TV commercials and performed in a revue called *Off the Wall* (1972). Late in 1972 his career took off when he got a role in the movie *The Lords of Flatbush*, a lighthearted film about a group of teenagers in 1957. The picture was filmed in New York City and released in 1974.

By the time the movie hit the theaters, Winkler had already moved to Hollywood and established himself as a TV actor. That year he won a leading role in a new TV series, *Happy Days* (1974-84), a nostalgic look at high-school life in late-1950s Milwaukee, Wisconsin. In that series he created one of the most popular characters in TV history, Arthur ("Fonzie" or "the Fonz") Fonzarelli, the respected know-it-all high-school dropout who works as an auto mechanic and dominates everyone around him; yet when the chips are down, he continually shows an underlying softheartedness.

Winkler has had difficulty finding roles that would help the public see him as more than just Fonzie. But he is a well trained actor who has given fine performances in a variety of films, including the drama *Heroes* (1977), as a demented Vietnam veteran; the comedy *The One and Only* (1978), as a would-be actor who tries to become famous by wrestling on TV; the sentimental drama *An American Christmas Carol* (TV, 1979), as a Scrooge-like character in Depression-era New Hampshire; and the comedy *Night Shift* (1982), as a milquetoast morgue supervisor who becomes a pimp. Among his later movies were *Absolute Strangers* (TV, 1991), *Scream* (1996), and *National Lampoon's Dad's Week Off* (1997).

A man of great personal depth and integrity, Winkler has used his Fonzie-based fame as a means to do good. He has been chairman of the Toys for Tots and honorary chairman of the Epilepsy Foundation.

Since the early 1980s, Winkler has devoted much of his time to producing, directing, and writing. He served as coexecutive producer of the

Henry Winkler

made-for-TV movies *Starlight: The Plane That Couldn't Land* (TV, 1983) and *When Your Lover Leaves* (TV, 1983); executive producer of the *MacGyver* TV series (1985-92); and director of the TV series *Clueless* (1996-98). He and the singer-songwriter David Capri wrote *Happy Days: The Musical* (1998).

In 1978 Winkler married Stacey Weitzman. They had a daughter, Zoe.

SELECTED PERFORMANCES:

STAGE

The Bacchae (1969)
Don Juan (1970)
Three Philip Roth Stories (1970)
Cops and Horrors (1970)
The Revenger's Tragedy (1970)
Off the Wall (1972)
Incident at Vichy (1973)

FILMS

The Lords of Flatbush (1974)
Katherine (TV, 1975)
Heroes (1977)
The One and Only (1978)
An American Christmas Carol (TV, 1979)
Night Shift (1982)
Absolute Strangers (TV, 1991)
The Only Way Out (TV, 1993)
One Christmas (TV, 1994)
Scream (1996)
National Lampoon's Dad's Week Off (1997)
The Waterboy (1998)

TV

Happy Days (1974-84)
The Fonz and the Happy Days Gang (animated, voice only, 1980-82)
Monty (1994)

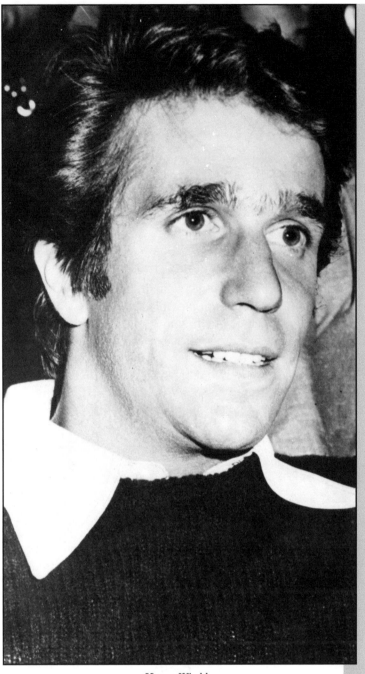

Henry Winkler

Shelley Winters

Young Innocent and Mature Meanie

Shelley Winters has had, in effect, two careers in motion pictures. In her early films, she played gentle, vulnerable young women, while later she specialized in portraying some of the meanest females ever put on the screen. Remarkably, she excelled equally in both types of roles.

Shelley Winters was born in Saint Louis, Missouri, on August 18, 1922. Her original name was Shirley Schrift. Her mother sang at the Saint Louis Municipal Opera, and Shirley developed an early interest in show business.

As a small child, she moved with her parents to the borough of Brooklyn in New York City. In her early teens, she entered a number of beauty contests, winning some. She also participated in many theatrical productions at school and elsewhere. In her senior year at Thomas Jefferson High School, she sang in the school's production of Gilbert and Sullivan's operetta *The Mikado*.

A few months before she would have graduated from high school, she dropped out and began to work as a model in New York City's garment district. Then, she studied acting at the New Theater School and worked in a variety of show-business jobs.

By then, still in her teens, she had adopted the stage name Shelley (the name of her favorite poet) Winter (her mother's maiden name). Later, in Hollywood, her studio added an *s* to her last name.

In 1941 Winters began to appear on the New York City stage. She played her first important role in the Broadway operetta *Rosalinda* (1942). She then had the role of Ado Annie Carney (alternating with two other actresses) in the original Broadway run of the Rodgers and Hammerstein musical *Oklahoma!* (1943).

Soon afterwards she was signed to a Hollywood movie contract. After appearing in a few minor roles she gave a powerful performance in *A Double Life* (1948), as a waitress strangled by a deranged actor (played by Ronald Colman).

Her best early roles were in a similar vein, that is, a young, innocent woman victimized by her own vulnerability. In *He Ran All the Way* (1951), for example, her character becomes romantically involved with a doomed criminal (played by John Garfield). In *A Place in the Sun* (1951) she was a factory worker who becomes pregnant by her boyfriend (played by Montgomery Clift), is deserted by him, and then tries so hard to pressure him into marriage that he drowns her (or allows her to drown) because of his love for a beautiful girl (played by Elizabeth Taylor). In *The Night of the Hunter* (1955), her character is murdered in a particularly gruesome manner.

In 1952 Winters married the Italian actor Vittorio Gassman (it was her second marriage—in 1942 she married Mack Mayer, a textile salesman, whom she divorced in 1948). It was a stormy, sometimes violent, marriage. They had one child, Vittoria, before divorcing in 1954.

In the mid-1950s Winters took some time off from making films to work on the stage. She appeared, for example, in *Girls of Summer* (1956).

During that time, in 1957, she married the Italian-American actor Anthony Franciosa. They divorced in 1960.

Returning to movies in the late 1950s, she developed a completely different image—plump, matronly, sometimes rowdy, and often downright evil. She played her first "mature" role in *The Diary of Anne Frank* (1959), as the most self-centered of the Jews hiding in the Amsterdam attic.

In *A Patch of Blue* (1965), she played a bitchy whore who wants to turn her blind daughter into a prostitute. In *Bloody Mama* (1970) she was the matriarch of a gang of violent hoods. Winters portrayed mentally unbalanced women in the horror tales *What's the Matter with Helen?* (1971) and *Who Slew Auntie Roo?* (1972). In *The Devil's Daughter* (TV, 1973), she was Satan's vessel. And she made an effectively revolting hag in *The Magician of Lublin* (1979).

During that time Winters was also active as a writer. Her stage work *One-Night Stands of a Noisy Passenger* (consisting of three short plays) began a New York City run near the end of December 1970. In 1980 she came out with her widely publicized and highly controversial autobiography of her early years, *Shelley: Also Known as Shirley*, in which she tells about her romances with Marlon Brando, Errol Flynn, Burt Lancaster, and many others. She soon became a frequent guest on TV talk shows.

While Winters accepted numerous meanie roles, she nevertheless remained more than capable of handling other kinds of characters. She played Minnie Marx, the Marx Brothers' mother, in the Broadway musical *Minnie's Boys* (1970). Winters appeared in the comedy film *Over the Brooklyn Bridge* (1984), and in *Alice in Wonderland* (TV, 1985), she portrayed the Dodo Bird. Her other films in the 1980s included *The Delta Force* (1986) and *The Purple People Eater* (1988).

In the 1990s Winters entered her seventies but remained incredibly active. Besides teaching master classes at the Actors Studio in Los Angeles, she continued to work regularly in films, including *Touch of a Stranger* (1990), *The Pickle* (1993), *Jury Duty* (1995), *The Portrait of a Lady* (1996), and *Gideon's Web* (1998). In August 1998 she received

Shelley Winters

a lifetime achievement award at the Hollywood Film Festival.

SELECTED PERFORMANCES:

STAGE

Meet the People (1941)
The Night before Christmas (1941)
Rosalinda (1942)
Oklahoma! (1943)
The Merry Widow (1946)
Born Yesterday (1950)
A Streetcar Named Desire (1952)
A Hatful of Rain (1955)
Girls of Summer (1956)

A Piece of Blue Sky (1959)
Two for the Seesaw (1960)
The Country Girl (1961)
A View from the Bridge (1961)
The Night of the Iguana (1961)
Cages (1963, 1975)
Under the Weather (1966)
Minnie's Boys (1970)
The Effect of Gamma Rays on Man-in-the-Moon Marigolds (1973)
Kennedy's Children (1976)

FILMS

Knickerbocker Holiday (1944)
A Double Life (1948)
Larceny (1948)
Cry of the City (1948)
Take One False Step (1949)
The Great Gatsby (1949)
Johnny Stool Pigeon (1949)
South Sea Sinner (1950)
Winchester '73 (1950)
Frenchie (1951)
He Ran All the Way (1951)
A Place in the Sun (1951)
Behave Yourself! (1951)
Phone Call from a Stranger (1952)
Meet Danny Wilson (1952)
Untamed Frontier (1952)
My Man and I (1952)
Saskatchewan (1954)
Executive Suite (1954)
Playgirl (1954)
Mambo (1955)
I Am a Camera (1955)
The Night of the Hunter (1955)
The Big Knife (1955)
I Died a Thousand Times (1955)
The Treasure of Pancho Villa (1955)
Cash on Delivery (1956)
The Diary of Anne Frank (1959)
Odds against Tomorrow (1959)
Let No Man Write My Epitaph (1960)
The Young Savages (1961)
The Chapman Report (1962)
Lolita (1962)
The Balcony (1963)
Wives and Lovers (1963)
A House Is Not a Home (1964)
The Greatest Story Ever Told (1965)
A Patch of Blue (1965)

Time of Indifference (1965)
Alfie (1966)
Harper (1966)
Enter Laughing (1967)
The Scalphunters (1968)
Wild in the Streets (1968)
Buona Sera, Mrs. Campbell (1969)
The Mad Room (1969)
Bloody Mama (1970)
Flap (1970)
How Do I Love Thee? (1970)
What's the Matter with Helen? (1971)
Revenge (TV, 1971)
A Death of Innocence (TV, 1971)
The Adventures of Nick Carter (TV, 1972)
Who Slew Auntie Roo? (1972)
The Poseidon Adventure (1972)
Blume in Love (1973)
Cleopatra Jones (1973)
The Devil's Daughter (TV, 1973)
Big Rose (TV, 1974)
The Sex Symbol (TV, 1974)
Next Stop, Greenwich Village (1976)
The Tenant (1976)
Diamonds (1976)
The Three Sisters (1977)
Tentacles (1977)
Pete's Dragon (1977)
King of the Gypsies (1978)
The Initiation of Sarah (TV, 1978)
Elvis (TV, 1979)
The French Atlantic Affair (TV, 1979)
City on Fire (1979)
The Magician of Lublin (1979)
S.O.B. (1981)
Over the Brooklyn Bridge (1984)
Alice in Wonderland (TV, 1985)
Déjà Vu (1985)
The Delta Force (1986)
The Purple People Eater (1988)
An Unremarkable Life (1989)
Touch of a Stranger (1990)
Stepping Out (1991)
Superstar: The Life and Times of Andy Warhol (1991)
The Pickle (1993)
The Silence of the Hams (1995)
Jury Duty (1995)
The Portrait of a Lady (1996)
Mrs. Munck (1996)
Heavy (1996)
Gideon's Web (1998)

Joseph Wiseman

Dr. No

Joseph Wiseman played villains in many films. His most memorable role was perhaps that of the title character in *Dr. No* (1963). But he has always been capable of portraying the gentlest of men as well, as he has often proved on the stage.

Joseph Wiseman was born in Montreal, Canada, on May 15, 1918. As a child he moved to New York City, where he graduated from John Adams High School (1935) in Ozone Park and then briefly attended the City College of the City University of New York.

He began his professional acting career by appearing in three stage productions in Saugerties, New York, during the summer of 1936. He made his New York City debut when he played a Union soldier in *Abe Lincoln in Illinois* (1938).

Over the next decade, Wiseman developed a reputation as a fine character actor on the stage. Among the plays that he appeared in were *The Three Sisters* (1939), *Journey to Jerusalem* (1940), *Antony and Cleopatra* (1947), and *Detective Story* (1949).

In 1943 Wiseman married Nell Kinard, with whom he had a son and a daughter. That marriage ended in divorce, and he later wedded Pearl Lang.

Wiseman made his film debut with a role as a moody Italian unionist in *With These Hands* (1950). He then gave an impressive performance as a tough criminal in the filmed version of *Detective Story* (1951).

Because of his gaunt, severe appearance, he was frequently cast as a sinister villain in movies. In *Viva Zapata!* (1952), for example, he played a ruthless manipulator in revolutionary Mexico. And in the James Bond spy thriller *Dr. No* (1963), Wiseman had the title role as a mad scientist.

Meanwhile, he also began to appear on TV. He acted in "Darkness at Noon" (1955) on *Producers' Showcase* and in many other plays telecast on anthology series during TV's golden age. During the 1950s he frequently performed on TV's *Frontiers of Faith*; later, he made memorable guest appearances on drama series, such as *The Untouchables* (1965) and *Twilight Zone* (1966).

Wiseman also continued to work on the stage, where he was allowed a wide range of roles. For example, he played the gentle Mr. Frank in *The Diary of Anne Frank* (1958). He portrayed the saintly Thomas Beckett in *Murder in the Cathedral* (1966), the Rabbi in *The Madness of God* (1974), and the evil Tadeus in *The Golem* (1984).

In the movie *The Apprenticeship of Duddy Kravitz* (1974), Wiseman had the role of Uncle Benjy, a rich Jewish socialist. In *Buck Rogers* (1979) he was Draco, the tyrannical king of Draconia. Among his other films were *The Valachi Papers* (1972), *Masada* (TV, 1981), *Rage of Angels* (TV, 1983), and *Seize the Day* (TV, 1986).

In the TV series *Crime Story* (1986-88) Wiseman played the mobster Manny Weisbrod. At the age of seventy-six, he gave a well-received performance as the Oldest Living Bolshevik in the New York City stage production of *Reds Scared* (1994).

Joseph Wiseman

SELECTED PERFORMANCES:

STAGE

The Milky Way (1936)
Abe Lincoln in Illinois (1938)
The Three Sisters (1939)
The Grass Is Always Greener (1939)
Journey to Jerusalem (1940)
Candle in the Wind (1941)
The Three Sisters (1942)
The Barber Had Two Sons (1943)
Storm Operation (1944)
Joan of Lorraine (1946)
Antony and Cleopatra (1947)
Detective Story (1949)
That Lady (1949)
King Lear (1950)
Golden Boy (1952)
The Lark (1955)
Susan and the Stranger (1956)

The Duchess of Malfi (1957)
The Diary of Anne Frank (1958)
The Queen and the Rebels (1959)
Turn On the Night (1961)
Naked (1963)
Marco Millions (1964)
Incident at Vichy (1964)
Murder in the Cathedral (1966)
In the Matter of J. Robert Oppenheimer (1968)
Uncle Vanya (1969)
The Madness of God (1974)
Balyasnikov (1977)
The Lesson (1978)
The Golem (1984)
The Tenth Man (1989)
Reds Scared (1994)

FILMS

With These Hands (1950)
Detective Story (1951)
Viva Zapata! (1952)
Les Misérables (1952)
The Silver Chalice (1954)
The Prodigal (1955)
Three Brave Men (1957)
The Garment Jungle (1957)
The Unforgiven (1960)
The Happy Thieves (1961)
Dr. No (1963)
The Outsider (TV, 1967)
Bye Bye Braverman (1968)
The Counterfeit Killer (1968)
The Night They Raided Minsky's (1968)
Stiletto (1969)
The Mask of Sheba (TV, 1970)
Lawman (1971)
The Valachi Papers (1972)
Pursuit (TV, 1972)
Men of the Dragon (TV, 1974)
QB VII (TV, 1974)
The Apprenticeship of Duddy Kravitz (1974)
Murder at the World Series (TV, 1977)
The Betsy (1978)
Buck Rogers (1979)
Masada (TV, 1981)
Rage of Angels (TV, 1983)
Seize the Day (TV, 1986)
Lady Monster (TV, 1988)

TV

Crime Story (1986-88)

Ed Wynn

Perfect Fool

Ed Wynn, more than any other stage comedian, made himself up to resemble the traditional image of a circus clown. He whitened his face, grease-painted his eyebrows, put on horn-rimmed glasses, emphasized his prominent nose and red-lipped mouth, covered his pear-shaped frame with zany hats and misfit clothes, and wore oversized flopping shoes.

Wynn said he was a "method comedian"—that is, one for whom the material was secondary to his method of delivering it. His style was his comedy. By the time he created his show *The Perfect Fool* (1921), his style and stage persona were fully formed. From 1921 on, he billed himself as the *Perfect Fool*.

His trademarks included a lisp, a squeaky voice, a high-pitched giggle, fluttering hands, and a constant look of surprise and wonderment. Wynn loved wordplay. He introduced his ball-juggling routine by asking the orchestra conductor to "play something in a jugular vein." As a showboat impresario he said, "I bred my cast upon the waters." His celebrated exit line was "I'll be back in a flash with more trash." his character was also known for his preposterous inventions, including an eleven-foot pole "to use on people you wouldn't touch with a ten-foot pole" and a pianocycle, a combination piano and tricycle that he pedaled around the stage while a girl sat on the piano and sang.

Ed Wynn was born in Philadelphia, Pennsylvania, on November 9, 1886. His original name was Isaiah Edwin Leopold.

His father, a moderately prosperous manufacturer and retailer of women's hats, had come from Bohemia, while his mother had been born of Sephardic Jews in Turkey. As soon as the boy could walk, he was putting on ladies' hats and making his father's customers laugh.

Young Leopold desperately wanted to become a professional comedian, but his parents objected. Hence, in the summer of 1902, at the age of fifteen, he ran away from home and joined a repertory company as a backstage helper and occasional onstage player. Soon, however, the company went bankrupt and he returned home.

After selling hats for a while, he ran away again. To avoid embarrassing his father, he formed a stage name by splitting the two syllables of his middle name: Edwin became Ed Wynn.

In 1903 he began his long, successful vaudeville career. For a while he teamed up with Jack Lewis (they billed themselves as Win and Lose), but Wynn worked principally on his own as one of the top vaudeville comedians of his time.

In 1910 he made his Broadway debut in the short-lived musical *The Deacon and the Lady*. But it was through the *Ziegfeld Follies of 1914* that Wynn became a Broadway star. In the 1915 edition of the Follies, Wynn was in the show with W. C. Fields. During the latter's famous pool-table act, the audience kept laughing at the wrong times. At last

Ed Wynn (right) and Keenan Wynn (left)

ing *The Perfect Fool* on an East Coast station in 1922. In his first radio series, *The Fire Chief* (1932-35), he introduced the technique of combining his comedy with the sponsor's commercial messages. He also starred in *Happy Land* (1944-45), as King Bubbles, ruler of a mythical kingdom of happiness. His shows were popular, but Wynn was essentially a visual comedian, working in costume even for his radio broadcasts.

The arrival of television in the late 1940s gave him a much more appropriate medium. He hosted the independent variety program *The Ed Wynn Show* (1949-50) and then a similarly titled program (1950-51) on a rotating basis with other shows as part of the *Four-Star Revue* series. However, by the mid-1950s his brand of vaudeville humor had become dated. He feared that his career was over.

Then, in 1956, Wynn surprised everyone by performing a straight dramatic role in the movie *The Great Man*, in which he delivered a prolonged monologue on the phoniness of the "great" man. However, by the time *The Great Man* was released in early 1957, he had already performed a larger and more important dramatic role in Rod Serling's TV play "Requiem for a Heavyweight" (1956) on the *Playhouse Ninety* anthology series. It was a live telecast (a frightening prospect even for experienced dramatic actors), but Wynn, playing the faithful trainer of a broken-down boxer, came through beautifully.

In the 1958 to 1959 TV season he starred in *The Ed Wynn Show*, a situation comedy with him as a widower and retired businessman.

During the rest of his career, he concentrated on being a film actor, in both dramatic and come-

Fields discovered Wynn under the table-comically catching flies. The two great comedians did not speak to each other for several years, but peace was eventually restored.

Wynn went on to perform in many Broadway shows, including *Ed Wynn Carnival* (1920); *The Perfect Fool* (1921); *The Laugh Parade* (1931); and *Laugh, Town, Laugh* (1942). Besides clowning in his Broadway and vaudeville shows, he often had a hand in producing, directing, and writing books and lyrics and composing music for them.

Wynn was the first performer to broadcast a full-length comedy show to a radio audience, perform-

dic roles. Among his serious parts were roles in *The Diary of Anne Frank* (1959), as one of the Jews hiding from the Nazis, and *The Greatest Story Ever Told* (1965), as Old Aram, a blind man whose sight is restored. On the light side, he played a fairy godfather in *Cinderfella* (1960) and numerous other roles in Disney movies, such as the fire chief in *The AbsentMinded Professor* (1961), the toymaker in *Babes in Toyland* (1961), Uncle Albert (who floats to the ceiling whenever he laughs—and he can't stop laughing!) in *Mary Poppins* (1964), and Rufus (the 1,100-year-old gnome king) in *The Gnome-Mobile* (1967).

Wynn was married three times. In 1914 he wedded actress Hilda Keenan, daughter of the Irish-American actor Frank Keenan. She was a staunch Catholic. Their son, Keenan, became a well-known character actor and performed with his father a number of times, as in *The Great Man, Requiem for a Heavyweight,*: and *The AbsentMinded Professor.*

In 1937 Wynn divorced Hilda and married Frieda Mierse, a showgirl. That marriage ended in divorce in 1939.

His final marriage, to Dorothy Nesbitt, began in 1946. it was dissolved in 1955.

Wynn died in Beverly Hills, California, on June 19, 1966

SELECTED PERFORMANCES:

STAGE

The Deacon and the Lady (1910)
Ziegfeld Follies of 1914 (1914)
Ziegfeld Follies of 1915 (1915)
The Passing Show of 1916 (1916)
Doing Our Bit (1917)
Over the Top (1918)
Sometime (1918)
Ed Wynn Carnival (1920)

The Perfect Fool (1921)
The Grab Bag (1924)
Manhattan Mary (1927)
Simple Simon (1930)
The Laugh Parade (1931)
Hooray for What! (1937)
Boys and Girls Together (1940)
Laugh, Town, Laugh (1942)
Big Time (1948)

FILMS

Rubber Heels (1927)
Follow the Leader 1930)
The Chief (1933)
Stage Door Canteen (1943)
The Great Man (1957)
Marjorie Morningstar (1958)
The Diary of Anne Frank (1959)
Cinderfella (1960)
The AbsentMinded Professor (1961)
Babes in Toyland (1961)
Son of Flubber (1963)
Sound of Laughter (1963)
Mary Poppins (1964)
The Patsy (1964)
Dear Brigitte (1965)
The Greatest Story Ever Told (1965)
That Darn Cat (1965)
Those Calloways (1965)
The Daydreamer (1966)
The Gnome-Mobile (1967)

RADIO

The Fire Chief (1932-35)
Happy Island (1944-45)

TV

The Ed Wynn Show (1949-50)
The Ed Wynn Show (1950-51, part of *Four-Star Revue*)
The Ed Wynn Show (1958-59)

Thumbnail Sketches

a

ADAMS, JOEY (originally Joseph Abramowitz: born January 6, 1911, in New York City, New York). Comedian. After becoming a leading vaudeville and nightclub entertainer, he turned his attention to writing humorous books.

ADLER, CELIA (born 1890; died January 31, 1979, in New York City, New York). Yiddish stage actress. Daughter of Jacob Adler and half sister of Frances, Jay, Luther, and Stella Adler. Celia was often referred to as the First Lady of the Yiddish Theater.

ADLER, FRANCES (born 1891 in New York City, New York; died December 13, 1964, in New York City, New York). Yiddish stage actress. Daughter of Jacob and Sara Adler; sister of Jay, Luther, and Stella Adler; and half sister of Celia Adler.

ADLER, JACOB P(AVLOVITCH) (born February 12, 1855, in Odessa, the Ukraine; died March 31, 1926, in New York City, New York). Yiddish stage actor. He began his stage career in Russia and then immigrated to the United States in 1887. Striving toward lofty artistic goals rather than quick commercial success, he became the most respected actor in the American Yiddish theater. His Yiddish performances as Shylock in Shakespeare's *The Merchant of Venice* were so impressive that he was engaged to appear in Broadway productions of the play in 1903 and 1905, speaking the part in Yiddish while the other players used English. Adler's three marriages produced many children who became well-known actors and actresses. With his first wife, the stage actress Sophia Oberlander, Adler had his son Abram. With his second wife, the stage actress Dinah Shtettin, Adler had his daughter Celia. With his third wife, the stage actress Sara Heine (nee Levitzky), Adler had five children, Frances, Jay, Julia, Luther, and Stella.

ADLER, JAY (born 1896; died September 24, 1978, in Woodland Hills, California). Character actor. Son of Jacob and Sara Adler; brother of Frances, Luther, and Stella Adler; and half brother of Celia Adler. Jay began on the stage, but soon he became a film actor, appearing in films such as *The Juggler* (1953), *Lust for Life* (1956), and *The Family Jewels* (1965).

ADLER, SARA (originally Sara Levitzky: born 1858 in Odessa, the Ukraine; died April 28, 1953, in New York City, New York). Yiddish stage actress. Wife of Jacob Adler and mother of Frances, Jay, Luther, and Stella Adler. Sara joined a Yiddish acting troupe in Russia and married its manager, Maurice Heine. In 1884 she immigrated to the United States and began to work in the American Yiddish theater. In 1890 she divorced Heine to marry Jacob Adler. She appeared in hundreds of plays, and her performances as Katusha Maslova in Tolstoy's *Resurrection* established her as the greatest Yiddish actress of her time.

ADLER, STELLA (born February 10, 1902 [some sources give 1901], in New York City, New York; died December 21, 1992, in Los Angeles, California). Stage actress. Daughter of Jacob and Sara Adler; sister of Frances, Jay, and Luther Adler; and half sister of Celia Adler. Stella began in her father's Yiddish theater

troupe and later alternated between Yiddish and English plays. A highlight of her Broadway work was her performance as Bessie Berger, the harassed matriarch of a financially troubled Jewish family, in *Awake and Sing!* (1935). Using the stage name Stella Ardler, she made her film debut in *Love on Toast* (1938). Under her real name, she appeared in the movies *Shadow of the Thin Man* (1941) and *My Girl Tisa* (1948). She was also an outstanding acting teacher; one of her students was Marlon Brando.

AIMÉE, ANOUK (originally Francoise Dreyfus; later Francoise Sorya, after her mother's name, Genevieve Sorya [née Durand]; born April 27, 1932, in Paris, France). Leading lady of films in various languages. Notable roles include those of a nymphomaniac in *La Dolce Vita* ("The Sweet Life," 1960), a prostitute in *Lola* (1961), and a lover in *Un Homme et une Femme* ("A Man and a Woman," 1966).

ALCALAY, MOSCU (born September 10, 1931, in Bucharest, Romania). Stage actor. He began his stage career in Bucharest and then moved to Israel in 1962. A regular performer at the Habimah Theater, he has also acted with the Cameri company.

ALITURUS (or Alityros; lived in the first century). Roman actor. A special favorite of the emperor Nero.

ALLEN, MARTY (born March 23, 1922, in Pittsburgh, Pennsylvania). Comedian and comedy character actor with a mournful nasal voice, a mass of black hair, and large frightened eyes. He worked in a comedy duo with Steve Rossi for several years until they amicably broke up in 1968. Allen then worked solo in nightclubs and on TV game shows until 1983, when he and Rossi reunited. Allen's film appearances included a role in *Murder Can Hurt You!* (TV, 1980).

AMSTERDAM, MOREY (born December 14, 1908 [some sources give 1914], in Chicago Illinois; died October 28, 1996, in Los Angeles, California). Comedian and character actor. He was a panelist on the TV game show *Stop Me If You've Heard This One*, the first series to be telecast with a live studio audience (beginning locally in Los Angeles in 1945; network,

1948–49). He then hosted his own variety series, *The Morey Amsterdam Show* (network, 1948–50; later New York City only). Amsterdam is best remembered, however, for his role as the wisecracker on the situation-comedy series *The Dick Van Dyke Show* (1961–66). He also appeared in some movies, including *Beach Party* (1963) and *Sooner or Later* (TV, 1979).

ARQUETTE, PATRICIA (born April 8, 1968, in Chicago, Illinois). Leading lady. Her films include *True Romance* (1993), *Betrayed by Love* (TV, 1994), *Beyond Rangoon* (1995), and *Lost Highway* (1997). Sister of Rosanna Arquette. Their paternal grandfather was the non-Jewish humorist Cliff Arquette (under the stage name Charlie Weaver), and their father is Lewis Arquette, an actor known for his role on TV's *The Waltons*. Patricia and Rosanna's mother is Jewish.

ARQUETTE, ROSANNA (born August 10, 1959, in New York City, New York). Leading lady. Her films include *More American Graffiti* (1979), *Desperately Seeking Susan* (1985), *Pulp Fiction* (1994), and *Liar* (1997). Sister of Patricia Arquette.

ASHEROFF, MISHA (or Misha Asherov; born March 28, 1924, in Samarkand, the Soviet Union). At the age of ten, he moved to Palestine, where he became an important actor with the Habimah Theater. He won the Habimah Prize in 1957 and the Kinor David in 1968. Asheroff has also worked in Israeli film productions and coproductions, including *Raq Lo b'Shabbat* (1965; U.S., *Impossible on Saturday*) and *Shlosha Yamim ve-Yeled* (1966; U.S., *Not Mine to Love* or *Three Days and a Child*).

BALIN, INA (originally Ina Rosenberg; born November 12, 1937, in New York City, New York; died June 20, 1990, in New Haven, Connecticut). Leading lady. She appeared on the New York City stage in *Compulsion* (1957) and *A Majority of One* (1959); in the films *The Patsy* (1964), *The Don Is Dead* (1973), and *The Comeback Trail* (1982); and on TV as a guest star on *Barnaby Jones, Bonanza, Run for Your Life,* and other series.

BANNER, JOHN (born January 28, 1910, in Stanislau, Poland; died January 28, 1973, in Vienna, Austria). He worked on European stages before arriving in the United States in 1938. Often playing fiery Europeans, Banner became a reliable character actor in English-language movies, such as *The Fallen Sparrow* (1943), *The Juggler* (1953), and *Operation Eichmann* (1961). He became familiar to American TV audiences as the bumbling Sergeant Hans Schultz in the comedy series *Hogan's Heroes* (1965–71).

BAR, SHIMON (born October 26, 1927, in Romania). Actor and singer permanently associated with Tel Aviv's Cameri Theater.

BARA, THEDA (originally Theodosia Goodman; born July 20, probably 1885, in Cincinnati, Ohio; died April 7, 1955, in Los Angeles, California). Actress who became the first star created by Hollywood publicity, the screen's first sex symbol, and the most celebrated vamp of silent films. In her first movie, *A Fool There Was* (1915), she created the popular catchphrase "Kiss me, my fool!" Hollywood publicity claimed that the name Theda Bara was an anagram for Arab Death, but in fact, Theda was merely a shortened form of Theodosia, and Bara was derived from the middle name of her maternal grandfather.

BAUR, HARRY (born 1881 in Paris, France; died April 1943 in Paris, France). Known in France as the King of the Character Actors. Baur gave a memorable performance as a withdrawn father in *Poil de Carotte* (literally, "Carrot Hair"; idiomatically, "The Redhead" or "Carrot Top"; 1932). He played Jean Valjean in *Les Misérables* ("The Miserable Ones," 1933), Porphyria in *Crime et Chatiment* ("Crime and Punishment," 1935), and Rasputin in *La Tragedie Imperiale* ("The Imperial Tragedy," 1938). Among his other films, many of them costume dramas, were *Le Golem* ("The Golem," 1936) and *Mollenard* (1938). In May 1942 he was arrested by the Gestapo in Berlin, charged with forging a certificate of Aryan ancestry. He was tortured for several months. Shortly after his release, he died in Paris.

BAYES, NORA (originally Dora Goldberg; born about 1880, perhaps in Milwaukee, Wisconsin; died March 19, 1928, in New York City, New York). Singing actress. She was one of the most popular vaudeville and musical-comedy stars of the period 1900 to 1925. In 1907 Bayes starred in the very first edition of *Ziegfeld's Follies*. She helped Jack Norworth (her husband) to compose the melody for the song "Shine On, Harvest Moon" (lyrics, Norworth), which she introduced in the *Follies of 1908* and which became her trademark.

BELZER, RICHARD (born August 4, 1944, in Bridgeport, Connecticut). Comedian and character actor. He began his career as an insult comedian but later became an actor. He appeared in the film comedy *The Wrong Guys* (1988) and in the TV drama series *Homicide: Life on the Street* (1993–).

BEN-AMI, JACOB (originally Jacob Shtchirin; born November 23, 1890, in Minsk, Russia; died July 22, 1977, in New York City, New York). Stage actor. In his early twenties, he immigrated to the United States, where he alternated between Yiddish-language and English-language plays. One critic called Ben-Ami "the knight of the Yiddish intelligentsia." In a rare film appearance, he gave an outstanding performance in the leading role of the Yiddish movie (with English subtitles) *The Wandering Jew* (1933). His most successful English-language stage role was that of the grandfather in *The Tenth Man* (1959).

BEREGI, OSCAR (or Oszkar Beregi; born 1875 in Hungary; died October 18, 1965, in Los Angeles, California). Stage actor; famous in Hungary for his Shakespearean roles. Later in his career, he moved to the United States and appeared in some films. Oscar Beregi, Jr., his son, acted in many movies, including *Young Frankenstein* (1974).

BERG, GERTRUDE (née Edelstein; born October 3, 1899, in New York City, New York; died September 14, 1966, in New York City, New York). Character actress. She became famous by playing the lovable Jewish housewife Molly Goldberg on the radio series *The Rise of the Goldbergs*, later called simply *The Goldbergs* (1929–34, 1937–45, 1949–50), often referred to as the earliest soap opera. Berg also appeared as Molly in the Broadway play *Me and Molly* (1948), in the TV series *The Goldbergs* (1949–55), and in the movie *Molly* (1951). Later, Berg was praised for her performance as a middle-aged Jewish woman who finds romance with a Japanese man in the play *A Majority of One* (1959).

BERGNER, ELISABETH (born August 22, 1900, in Vienna, Austria; died May 12, 1986, in London, England). Leading lady of fragile beauty and sensitive acting. After attaining success in German-language stage and film productions, she moved to England in the early 1930s, later working in the United States as well. She gave remarkable performances in the plays *The Two Mrs. Carrolls* (1943) and *The Duchess of Malfi* (1946). Bergner's most memorable film performances were in *Catherine the Great* (1934) and *Escape Me Never* (1935). Her later appearances included a part in the movie *Cry of the Banshee* (1970).

BERLINGER, WARREN (born August 31, 1937, in New York City, New York). Chubby character actor. He began his New York City stage career as a juvenile, in *Annie Get Your Gun* (1946). His later performances included roles in the stage work *Blue Denim* (1958), the TV comedy series *The Joey Bishop Show* (1961–62), and the films *Teenage Rebel* (1956), *Blue Denim* (1959), *Thunder Alley* (1967), *The Magician of Lublin* (1979), *The Other Woman* (TV, 1983), and *The November Conspiracy* (1997). He often played innocents, especially in his youth.

BERMAN, SHELLEY (originally Sheldon Berman; born February 3, 1926, in Chicago, Illinois). Comedian and character actor. A popular performer in nightclubs, he also became the first comedian to appear at Carnegie Hall. Berman acted in several films, including *The Best Man* (1964), *Divorce American Style* (1967), and *Motorama* (1993). On the stage he portrayed Oscar Madison in *The Odd Couple* (1966), the biblical Noah in *Two by Two* (1972), Meyer Rothschild in *The Rothschilds* (1973), and other roles.

BERNARDI, HERSCHEL (born October 30, 1923 in New York City, New York; died May 9, 1986, in Los Angeles, California). Character actor. As a child he was a star in the New York City Yiddish theater and appeared in the Yiddish film *Green Fields* (1937). Later, he performed in a production of *The World of Sholom Aleichem* (1953), made his Broadway debut by appearing in *Bajour* (1964), starred as Tevye in *Fiddler on the Roof* (1965, 1981), and had the title role in *Zorba* (1968). On TV he played Lieu-

tenant Jacoby in the popular crime-drama series *Peter Gunn* (1958–61) and the title character in the comedy series *Arnie* (1970–72). He also worked on famous TV commercials, lending his voice to the Charlie the Tuna ads and providing the Jolly Green Giant's deep, reverberating "Ho-ho-ho!" His films included *Irma La Douce* (1963) and *The Front* (1976).

BERNHARD, SANDRA (born June 6, 1955, in Flint, Michigan). Comedienne and actress. She is known for her coarse but vulnerable comic style. Her acting credits include roles in the films *The King of Comedy* (1983) and *Wrongfully Accused* (1998).

BERNHARDT, SARAH (born October 22 or 23, 1844, in Paris, France; died March 26, 1923, in Paris, France). Leading lady, known as the Divine Sarah. Accounts of her birth date and original name vary because she was the illegitimate offspring of a Jewish courtesan and a non-Jewish man named Bernard or Bernhardt, and her birth certificate was not made out until she was eleven years old. Different sources record her original given name(s) as Rosine, Henriette Rosine, Sarah-Marie-Henriette, and variants of those possibilities. Touring frequently and performing mostly French plays and Shakespeare, she dominated world stages for nearly sixty years. She was renowned for her acting prowess, emotional range, perfect diction, clear voice (like a "golden bell"), and flair for self-publicity (some dubbed her Sarah Barnum). Bernhardt was the first great actress to appear in films, such as *La Dame aux Camelias* ("The Lady of the Camelias," 1912) and *Jeanne Dore* (1917). She also recorded some dramatic recitations. In 1905 she injured her right leg, and in 1914 it was amputated; using an artificial leg, she continued to act for the rest of her life.

BERNSTEIN-COHEN, MIRIAM (born December 14, 1895, in Kishinev, Russia; died July 4, 1991, in Tel Aviv, Israel). Stage actress. She was the daughter of the renowned Russian Zionist leader Jacob Bernstein-Kogan (or Cohen). She earned a medical degree in Russia and served in the Red Army. From 1917 to 1921, she acted on the Russian stage. In 1921 she moved to Palestine and became one of the pioneers in the Hebrew theater there. She appeared with many companies, including the Habimah and the Cameri. In 1969 Bernstein-Cohen won the Tel Aviv Municipal Prize for her work in *Harp of David*. She earned international acclaim for her outstanding performance in the Israeli film *Neither by Day nor by Night* (1972). In 1975 she won the Israel Prize for her lifetime achievements.

BERTONOFF, YEHOSHUA (born 1879 in Russia; died 1971 in Israel). Stage actor. He performed in Russian and Yiddish plays before moving to Palestine in 1927. Later, he became one of the Habimah Theater's most popular actors. He specialized in playing folk and patriarchal characters, as in *Tevye the Milkman* (1943). Deborah Bertonoff, his daughter, became a renowned dancer.

BISHOP, JOEY (originally Joseph Abraham Gottlieb; born February 3, 1918, in New York City, New York). Comedian and character actor. He worked as a comedian in nightclubs and on TV, and he starred in the TV series *The Joey Bishop Show* (situation comedy, 1961–65; variety, 1967–69). Bishop had roles in several films, including *The Naked and the Dead* (1958), *Sergeants Three* (1962), *The Delta Force* (1986), and *Mad Dog Time* (1996).

BLANC, MEL(VIN) (born May 30, 1908, in San Francisco, California; died July 10, 1989, in Los Angeles, California). The voice of cartoon characters Bugs Bunny, Daffy Duck, Porky Pig, Tweety Pie, Sylvester, Woody Woodpecker, Yosemite Sam, and many others.

BLONDELL, JOAN (full name, Rose Joan Blondell; born August 30, 1909, in New York City, New York; died December 25, 1979, in Santa Monica, California). One of the great wisecracking blondes in film history. Her movies included *Dames* (1934), *A Tree Grows in Brooklyn* (1945), and *The Blue Veil* (1951). She also gave memorable performances as Lottie Hatfield, the owner of a logging camp saloon, in the TV series *Here Come the Brides* (1968–70).

BOCHNER, LLOYD (born July 29, 1924, in Canada). He appeared in New York City productions of Shakespeare plays in the 1950s; he had a role in the TV series *Hong Kong* (1960–61); acted in the movies *Drums of Africa* (1963), *The Man in the Glass Booth* (1975), *The Golden Gate Murders* (TV, 1979), *The Lonely Lady* (1983), and many others; and

played Cecil Colby in the TV series *Dynasty* (1981–82). He is a frequent guest star on TV drama series.

BOND, STEVE (originally Shlomo Goldberg; born 1953 in Haifa, Israel). Leading man. He arrived in the United States when he was twelve. He is best known for playing the role of Jimmy Lee Holt in the daytime TV serial *General Hospital*.

BOOSLER, ELAYNE (born August 13, 1952, in New York City, New York). Comedienne widely regarded as the principal forerunner of the new breed of women comics who address topical issues from a woman's point of view without being self-demeaning or pandering to men.

BOSLEY, TOM (originally THOMAS BOSLEY; born October 1, 1927, in Chicago, Illinois). Character actor. After years of struggling, he won critical acclaim for his Broadway performance as New York City's Mayor La Guardia in *Fiorello!* (1959). However, he was not offered other good stage roles after that, so he became a film and TV actor. He appeared in *Love with the Proper Stranger* (1963), *The World of Henry Orient* (1964), *Who Is the Black Dahlia?* (TV, 1975), *The Bastard* (TV, 1978), and *The Jesse Owens Story* (TV, 1984), and many other films. He is best known for playing the role of Howard Cunningham in the TV comedy series *Happy Days* (1974–84). He also played Sheriff Amos Tupper in *Murder, She Wrote* (1984–88) and the title character in *Father Dowling Mysteries* (1989–91).

BRAND, OSCAR (born February 7, 1920, in Winnipeg, Canada). Folk singer and TV and radio personality. He has hosted many TV and radio shows in Canada and the United States, notably the New York City radio program *Folksong Festival*.

BRENNER, DAVID (born February 4, 1945 [according to published sources, though the actual year may be as much as a decade earlier], in Philadelphia, Pennsylvania). Comedian. One of the most successful humorists of his generation. He has frequently guest-hosted the TV talk-variety program *The Tonight Show*. During the 1986 to 1987 season, he hosted his own late-night series, *Nightlife*.

BROOKS, GERALDINE (originally Geraldine Strook; born October 29, 1925, in New York City, New York; died June 19, 1977, in Riverhead, New York). Intense leading lady. She made her biggest impact in a few 1940s movies, including *Possessed* (1947) and *The Reckless Moment* (1949). In her later years, she frequently guest-starred in TV series, such as *Ben Casey* and *The Fugitive*.

BROTHERS, JOYCE (née Bauer; born 1928 in New York City, New York). TV and radio personality. In 1955 she won the grand prize on the popular TV game show *The $64,000 Question*; her subject was boxing. Later, Brothers, a popular psychologist, hosted several TV talk-show series and appeared as a guest on many others.

BROWN, GEORGIA (originally Lillian Claire Laizer Getel Klot; born October 21, 1933, in London, England). Singer-actress. She appeared in the stage musicals *The Threepenny Opera* (London, 1956; New York City, 1957) and *Oliver!* (London, 1960; New York City, 1963). Among her films were *The Fixer* (1968) and *The Bawdy Adventures of Tom Jones* (1976).

BULOFF, JOSEPH (born December 6, 1899 [some sources give 1907], in Vilnius, Lithuania; died February 27, 1985, in New York City, New York). Character actor. He performed with a Yiddish theater troupe in Europe (1918–28) and then immigrated to the United States to join the Yiddish Art Theater. Buloff eventually produced, directed, and acted in hundreds of plays in several languages—including English, Russian, and Yiddish—in North and South America, Europe, and Israel. He became famous for playing the role of the peddler in the original Broadway production of *Oklahoma!* (1943). During the 1960s and 1970s, he was a mainstay in the imperiled Yiddish theater. In the Broadway Show *The Price* (1979), he displayed his flair for comedy. He also appeared in movies, such as *Somebody up There Likes Me* (1956) and *Running Out* (TV, 1983).

BURSTEIN, MICHAEL (or Mordecai Burstein; born 1945 in New York City, New York). Actor-singer. Michael moved to Israel in 1954 with his parents, the entertainers Pesach and Lillian Burstein. He appeared many times with his parents in their hit musical comedy *The Megilla*. He became a popular Israeli singer and performer in plays and movies, starring, for example, in the Israeli musical-comedy film *Shnei Kuni Lemel* (1965; U.S., *The Flying Matchmaker*).

BURSTEIN, PESACH (born 1897 in Warsaw, Poland; died April 6, 1986, in New York City, New York). Yiddish actor. He joined a wandering Yiddish troupe when he was just a boy. In 1924 he was engaged by Thomashefsky's Yiddish company in New York City. There, he met the Yiddish actress Lillian Lux, whom he married in 1940 and with whom he organized a theatrical company in Brooklyn. In 1954 they moved to Israel. The Bursteins were especially successful with their performances of the musical comedy *The Megilla*, in which they were joined by their son, Michael. Pesach appeared in the Israeli musical-comedy film *Shnei Kuni Lemel* (1965; U.S., *The Flying Matchmaker*). He issued about three hundred recordings, which made him one of the most famous and beloved personalities in the Yiddish-speaking world. In 1985 he was among the first ten recipients of the Goldie Awards, bestowed by the Congress of Jewish Culture to individuals for their lifetime achievements. In Burstein's later years, he lived in both New York City and Tel Aviv.

C

CARLISLE, KITTY (originally CAtherine Conn; early in her career also known by her mother's surname, Holtzman, and later by her married name, Kitty Carlisle Hart, [her husband was the playwright Moss Hart, who died in 1961]; born September 3, 1914, in New Orleans, Louisiana). Singing actress and TV personality. In the 1930s she performed in musicals and operettas on the New York City stage, such as *White Horse Inn* (1936), and appeared in a few movies, notably the classic Marx Brothers film *A Night at the Opera* (1935). She scored her biggest acting success by playing the mother who admits to having had premarital sex in the stage comedy *Anniversary Waltz* (1954). A few years later, she began a twenty-year run as a panelist on the TV game show *To Tell the Truth*. In recent years she has led cultural organizations and been a guest lecturer.

CAROLY, FELIX (born March 3, 1933, in Iasi, Romania). Stage actor. He was active in the Romanian classical theater. In Israel he has worked as a stage actor and director. Caroly has also appeared as a pantomimist on Israeli TV.

CARTER, JACK (originally Jack Chakrin; born June 24, 1923, in New York City, New York). Comedian and character actor. A successful stand-up comedian on TV and in nightclubs, he is also a fine actor in both dramatic and comedic roles. His films included *The Horizontal Lieutenant* (1962), *The Family Rico* (TV, 1972), *History of the World, Part I* (1981), and *In the Heat of Passion* (1992).

CARTER, NELL (or Nell-Ruth Carter; originally Nell Hardy; born September 13, 1948, in Birmingham, Alabama). Actress best known for her Tony Award-winning performance in the Broadway musical Ain't Misbehavin' (1978) and her role as Nell Harper in the TV sitcom *Gimme a Break!* (1981–87). An African-American convert to Judaism.

CLARY, ROBERT (originally Robert Widerman; born March 1, 1926, in Paris, France). Character actor. He appeared on the New York City stage, including in *New Faces of 1952* (1952), and in films, including *The Hindenburg* (1975). But he is probably best known as Corporal Louis LeBeau, a French prisoner, in the TV comedy series *Hogan's Heroes* (1965–71). Clary is a volunteer in an outreach program of the Simon Wiesenthal Center, teaching high-school students about the Nazi extermination of European Jewry.

COHEN, MYRON (born 1902 in Grodno, Russian-ruled Poland; died March 10, 1986, in Nyack, New York). Comedian. Brought to the United States when he was a child, Cohen later worked for many years as a textile salesman in New York City, where he told jokes to amuse his customers. Though he had no foreign accent in his ordinary speech, he told his stories with imitations of the eastern European dialects of his colleagues in the garment district. In his forties he finally became a professional comedian, usually working in a Yiddish dialect but sometimes using Irish or Italian accent. When dialect comedy went out of fashion, Cohen maintained his popularity because of his low-key manner, his inoffensive material, his unique delivery, and his universal appeal.

COREY, IRWIN ("PROFESSOR") (born January 29, 1912, in New York City, New York). Comedian famous for his double-talk. Wearing an overlarge frock coat and a mop of flying hair, he gives "lectures" that turn into social and political satire.

CROSBY, NORM (full name, Norman Lawrence Crosby; born September 15, 1927, in Boston, Massachusetts). Comedian. Besides appearing regularly in theaters, nightclubs, and concert halls, he has frequently worked on TV. His style is based on the use of malapropisms, such as *"puberty"* for *"poverty"* in the line "President Johnson declared war on puberty."

D

DALE, CHARLIE. *See* Smith and Dale.

DAMON, STUART (originally Suart Zonis; born February 5, 1937, in New York City, New York). Leading man. He appeared on Broadway in *From A to Z* (1960), *The Boys from Syracuse* (1963), and *Do I Hear a Waltz?* (1965). His other work included the TV series *The Adventurer* (1972) and the film *Fantasies* (TV, 1982).

DANA, BILL (originally William Szathmary; born October 5, 1924, in Quincy, Massachusetts). Comedian and character actor. He is best known for his portrayal of the comical character Jose Jimenez on TV in the late 1950s and early 1960s, especially on Steve Allen's variety show and Danny Thomas's comedy series. Dana continued to play the character in his own comedy series, *The Bill Dana Show* (1963–65). In 1970 pressure from Latin-Americans caused him to drop Jose. Later, he played a variety of roles on TV and in movies, such as *The Snoop Sisters* (TV, 1972), *The Nude Bomb* (1980), and *Lena's Holiday* (1991).

DARVAS, LILI (born April 10, 1902, in Budapest, Hungary; died July 22, 1974, in New York City, New York). Leading lady. She was a major figure on the European stage from the early 1920s until 1938, when she moved to the United States and began a long, active career in the theater and on TV. Darvas appeared in a handful of movies, notably as the dying mother in the Hungarian film *Szerelem* ("Love," 1971).

DIAMOND, SELMA (born 1921 in London, Ontario, Canada; died May 13, 1985, in Los Angeles, California). Comedy actress and writer. She wrote for Milton Berle, Sid Caesar, and other TV personalities in the 1950s. Later she became an actress. Her most prominent characteristic was her gravelly voice. She is best remembered as Selma Hacker, the sardonic court officer, in the TV sitcom *Night Court* (1984–85).

DONATH, LUDWIG (born March 6, 1900, in Vienna, Austria; died September 29, 1967, in New York City, New York). Stage and film actor. He appeared on the stages of major European cities before moving to the United States in the 1930s. American productions in which he appeared included *The Dybbuk* (1954). He became a fine character actor in American films. In *The Strange Death of Adolf Hitler* (1943), he played a dual role, as Hitler and as Hitler's double, Franz Huber. Donath portrayed Al Jolson's father, a cantor, in *The Jolson Story* (1946) and *Jolson Sings Again* (1949). His other films included *Sirocco* (1951) and *Torn Curtain* (1966).

DRESCHER, FRAN (born September 30, 1957, in New York City, New York). Actress best known for her role as Fran Fine in the TV sitcom *The Nanny* (1993–99).

EDELMAN, HERB (born November 5, 1933, in New York City, New York; died July 21, 1996, in Woodland Hills, Los Angeles, California). Bald, lanky character actor, usually in comic roles. He made his New York City stage debut in *Barefoot in the Park* (1963). Among his films were *The Odd Couple* (1968), *The Front Page* (1974), *On the Right Track* (1981), and *Cracking Up* (1983, originally released as *Smorgasbord*). He was a frequent guest star on TV, notably, in the late 1980s and early 1990s, in occasional appearances as Stanley Zbornak, Dorothy's ex-husband, in the sitcom *The Golden Girls*.

EPSTEIN, ALVIN (born May 14, 1925, in New York City, New York). Stage actor and mime. He

was a resident member of the Habimah Theater in Tel Aviv (1953–55). In New York City and elsewhere in the United States, he has appeared in many plays, including *Waiting for Godot* (1956), *The Passion of Josef D.* (1964), and *The Possessed* (1974).

F

FELDSHUH, TOVAH (born December 27, 1952 [or 1953], in New York City, New York). Leading lady. She made her Broadway debut by performing in the musical *Cyrano de Bergerac* (1973). Later, she starred in *Yentl* (1974) and other theatrical productions. Her films included *Holocaust* (TV, 1978); *Beggerman, Thief* (TV, 1979); *Daniel* (1983); *Citizen Cohn* (TV, 1992); and *Comfortably Numb* (1995).

FIELDS, LEW. *See* Weber and Fields.

FIELDS, TOTIE (originally Sophie Feldman; born May 7, 1930, in Hartford, Connecticut; died August 2, 1978, in Las Vegas, Nevada). Comedienne. Performing in nightclubs and on TV, she had the gift of being able to laugh at herself.

FIERSTEIN, HARVEY (born June 6, 1954, in New York City, New York). Actor and playwright. He became famous by writing and starring in the seriocomic play *Torch Song Trilogy* (1981), which explores the homosexual experience in universal terms. His later work included an appearance in the film *Kull the Conqueror* (1997).

FINKEL, SHIMON (born December 8, 1905, in Grodno, Russian-ruled Poland). Stage actor. He began to appear on the Polish stage when he was a boy. Later, he joined a Yiddish troupe. In 1922 he went to Berlin, and in 1924 he settled in Palestine. A few years later, he joined the Habimah Theater. Finkel became one of the company's most important actors, starring in many productions, such as *Hamlet* (1946, winning the Jewish Agency Prize), *Peer Gynt* (1952), *King Lear* (1957, Tel Aviv Prize), and *Touch of the Poet* (1960, Gnessin Prize). He also served as the Habimah's artistic director from 1961 to 1962 and from 1970 to 1975. In 1969 he was awarded the Israel Prize for his lifetime accomplishments. In 1980 he directed and acted in a highly acclaimed production of *Between Two Worlds* (a musical adaptation of *The Dybbuk*), which opened New York City's Yiddish National Theater. Finkel has published many books about the Israeli theater, including *Onstage and Backstage* (1968), *Margin of the Bill* (1976), *Chana Rovina* (1978), and *Sparks* (1985).

FISHER, EDDIE (originally Edwin Fisher; born August 10, 1928, in Philadelphia, Pennsylvania). The popular singer acted in a few movies, including *Bundle of Joy* (1956) and *Butterfield 8* (1960).

FLANAGAN, BUD (originally Chaim Reeven Weintrop; anglicized on birth certificate as Robert Winthrop; born October 14, 1896, in London, England; died October 20, 1968, in London, England). Comedian. He chose his stage name as an act of revenge against a sergeant-major named Flanagan who had made the aspiring comedian's life miserable in the artillery during World War I. In 1926 Flanagan teamed up with Chesney Allen, and they became immensely successful music-hall performers, Allen's patient dignity contrasting with Flanagan's hilarious roguery. In many of their shows, they worked as part of a group known as the Crazy Gang, of which the undisputed leader was Flanagan. Flanagan and Allen also appeared in movies, such as *Underneath the Arches* (1937) and *Here Comes the Sun* (1945). In 1945 Allen retired and Flanagan went on alone, working in his last Crazy Gang show in 1959.

FOSTER, PHIL (originally Fivel Feldman; born March 29, 1914, in New York City, New York; died July 8, 1985, in Rancho Mirage, California). Comedian and actor. Though he began as a stand-up comedian, he is best remembered for his role as the gruff but kindhearted Frank DeFazio in the TV comedy series *Laverne and Shirley* (1976–83).

FRYE, DAVID (originally David Shapiro; born 1934 in New York City, New York). Impressionist and comedian. For a brief period in the 1970s, he was at the top of his profession. He was best known for his impersonations of politicians, especially Richard Nixon, with whom Frye felt an empathy because, according to the comedian, both men were neurotic. In his nightclub work today, he imitates William F. Buckley, Billy Graham, and other personalities.

FUNT, ALLEN (born September 16, 1914, in New York City, New York; died September 5, 1999, in Big Sur, California). TV personality. In 1947 he created a radio program called *Candid Microphone*. It was made into a very popular TV series, *Candid Camera*, which Funt hosted off and on in various formats for many years.

g

GABEL, MARTIN (born June 19, 1912, in Philadelphia, Pennsylvania; died May 22, 1986, in New York City, New York). Character actor. His stage appearances included roles in *Dead End* (1935), *Will Success Spoil Rock Hunter?* (1955); and *Big Fish, Little Fish* (1961). Among his films were *M* (1951); *Marnie* (1964); *The Front Page* (1974), as Dr. Eggelhofer; and *The First Deadly Sin* (1980). He often appeared with his wife, Arlene Francis, on TV's *What's My Line?*

GELLER, URI (born December 20, 1946, in Tel Aviv, Palestine). Entertainer. Geller's act, which he performs in many parts of the world, features demonstrations of clairvoyance, telepathy, and psychokinesis—or the power of mind over matter.

GETTY, ESTELLE (originally Estelle Scher; born July 25, 1923, in New York City, New York). Character actress. In her youth she worked as an actress in the Yiddish theater and as a stand-up comedienne on the borscht circuit. After leaving the theater and spending many years as a housewife and mother, she gradually returned to the stage, notably as the Jewish mother in the off-off-Broadway play *Torch Song Trilogy* (1981). From 1985 to 1992, she played the role of Sophia in the popular TV comedy series *The Golden Girls*, for which Getty used makeup to age herself twenty years. Later, she played the same role in the sitcoms *The Golden Palace* (1992–93) and *Empty Nest* (1993–95).

GNESSIN, MENAHEM (born 1882 in Russia; died 1952 in Israel). Stage actor. He moved from the Ukraine to Palestine in 1903. In 1907 he founded the Amateur Dramatic Arts Company for producing plays in Hebrew. In 1912 he returned to Russia and, in Moscow, helped Nahum Zemach to organize a group that became a forerunner of the Habimah Theater, which Zemach created there in 1917. Gnessin worked on his own in various cities until 1928, when he joined the Habimah in Palestine. He became one of the company's most important actors.

GOLDSTEIN, JENNIE (born 1897 in New York City, New York; died February 9, 1960, in New York City, New York). Stage actress. At the age of six, she began acting in the Yiddish theater, where she eventually became the leading tragedienne of her time. Later, she starred in English-language plays, including *Camino Real* (1953).

GRAHAM, VIRGINIA (originally Virginia Komiss; born July 4, 1912, in Chicago, Illinois). TV and radio personality. She hosted the TV talk show *Girl Talk* (1962–69) and the TV talk-variety series *The Virginia Graham Show* (1970–72).

GREENE, SHECKY (originally Sheldon Greenfield; born April 8, 1926, in Chicago, Illinois). Comedian and character actor. He has performed in nightclubs since 1947 and on TV since 1953. His films included *Splash* (1984).

GRODIN, CHARLES (born April 21, 1935, in Pittsburgh, Pennsylvania). Actor and TV talk-show host. His acting credits include roles in the films *The Heartbreak Kid* (1972), *Midnight Run* (1988), and *Beethoven* (1992). In the mid-1990s, he hosted his own talk show on the cable TV network CNBC.

H

HAAS, HUGO (born February 19, 1903, in Brno, Moravia; died December 1, 1968, in Vienna, Austria). Character actor. He appeared in Czech films from the mid-1920s until the late 1930s, when he immigrated to the United States. His early American movies included *A Bell for Adano* (1945) and *Casbah* (1948). Later, he wrote, directed, and starred in low-budget melodramas, such as *Lizzie* (1957).

HALL, MONTY (originally Monty Halparin; born August 25, 1925, in Winnipeg, Canada). Host of TV's *Let's Make a Deal* (1963–76).

HARAREET, HAYA (or Haya Hararit; born 1931 in Haifa, Palestine). She worked at the Cameri Theater and appeared in Israel's first important feature film, *Hill 24 Doesn't Answer* (1955). In 1959 she achieved international stardom with her performance in the American epic *Ben Hur*. Later, she starred in a number of European and American movies, including *The Secret Partner* (1961) and *The Interns* (1962).

HELD, ANNA (born probably March 18, 1865, in Warsaw, Poland; died August 12, 1918, in New York City, New York). Singing actress, known for her coquettish manner. She claimed to have been born a Catholic in Paris, France; her death record stated her year of birth as 1877, while obituaries listed the year as 1873. But much evidence indicates that she came from Jewish parents, and according to the Institute for Jewish Research, she was born in Warsaw in 1865. Held began her career by performing in the Yiddish theater in London. Later, she became one of London's top music-hall comediennes. In the late 1890s, she was hired by the American impresario Florenz Ziegfeld, and she moved to the United States. She married Ziegfeld and performed in American musical comedies. Held and Ziegfeld separated in 1908 and divorced in 1913. In her later years, she performed in vaudeville.

HILL, STEVEN (originally Solomon Berg; born 1924 in Seattle, Washington). Character actor. His stage work included *A Flag Is Born* (1946) and *Mister Roberts* (1948). Among his films were *A Child Is Waiting* (1963) and *Rich and Famous* (1981).

HIRSCH, JUDD (born March 15, 1935, in New York City, New York). Leading man. He has appeared in many New York City plays, such as *Below the Belt* (1996) and *A Thousand Clowns* (1996), and in some films, including *Ordinary People* (1980) and *Betrayal of Trust* (TV, 1994). But he is best known as Alex Rieger, a career cabdriver, in the TV comedy series *Taxi* (1978–83).

HIRSCH, ROBERT PAUL (born July 26, 1925, in L'Isle-Adam, France). Character actor. He distinguished himself for many years as a comic actor and mime in Paris at the Comedie-Francaise. Hirsch also appeared in some movies, notably the French-Israeli fantasy film *Pas Question le Samedi* (1965; Israeli title, *Raq Lo b'Shabbat*; American title, *Impossible on Saturday*); Hirsch played eight roles in the film.

HOWARD, WILLIE (originally William Levkowitz; born April 13, 1886, in Neustadt, Silesia; died January 12, 1949, in New York City, New York). Vaudeville and Broadway revue comic known for the plaintive quality of his confused-little-man persona. He was a master of dialect, combining his usual Yiddish accent with French, Spanish, Scottish, and other idioms. A fine singer, he got laughs with his celebrated opera take-offs and with his impressions of leading performers of the day, including Charlie Chaplin and Eddie Cantor.

I

INGELS, MARTY (originally Marty Ingerman; born March 9, 1936, in New York City, New York). Comedian and character actor. He was Arch Fenster in the TV comedy series *I'm Dickens—He's Fenster* (1962–63), and he had roles in the movies *The Ladies' Man* (1961) and *If It's Tuesday, This Must Be Belgium* (1969). Later, he quit performing to become a theatrical agent and producer.

J

JACOBI, LOU (born December 28, 1913, in Toronto, Canada). Character actor. He worked on the stage in Toronto and London before making his Broadway debut, as Mr. Van Daan in *The Diary of Anne Frank* (1955), a role that he repeated in the filmed version of the story (1959). His other movies included *Irma La Douce* (1963), *Cotton Comes to Harlem* (1970), *Lucky Star* (1982), and *Isaac Littlefeathers* (1984). He is an expert performer of comic roles, as he proved when he guest-starred in a couple of hilarious episodes of the TV series *Too Close for Comfort* and several shows on the *Barney Miller* series.

JAFFE, CARL (born 1902 in Germany; died April 12, 1974, in London, England). Aristocratic-looking character actor. He fled Hitler's Germany and later appeared in many British and American films, including *The Life and Death of Colonel Blimp* (1943) and *The Roman Spring of Mrs. Stone* (1961).

JAMES, SID (born May 8, 1913, in Johannesburg, South Africa; died April 26, 1976, in Sunderland, England). Crumple-faced comedy character actor. In 1946 he settled in England, where he worked extensively on TV. He also appeared in many British films, including *The Lavender Hill Mob* (1951). James was featured in most of the Carry On series of movies, such as *Carry On, Constable* (1961); *Carry On, Cabby* (1967); and *Carry On, Matron* (1972).

JESSEL, GEORGE (born April 3, 1898, in New York City, New York; died May 24, 1981, in Los Angeles, California). Entertainer. He was a child singer in vaudeville, where he performed as one of Gus Edwards's famous troupe of juveniles. A highlight of his adult stage career was his starring role in the original Broadway production of *The Jazz Singer* (1925). He also acted in silent movies, including *The Other Man's Wife* (1919). But after making the mistake of turning down a role in the filmed version of *The Jazz Singer*, he had only a sporadic career as an actor, including appearances in the films *Four Jills in a Jeep* (1944) and *The Busy Body* (1967). He also worked as a producer. In his later years, he became famous for making melodramatic speeches at funerals, banquets, and fund-raising affairs for Israel and other causes. Jessel came to be known as the Toastmaster General of the United States.

K

KALICH, BERTHA (surname also spelled Kalish or Kalisch; born May 17 [sometimes given as September 8], 1874 [sometimes given as 1872], in Lemberg, Galicia; died April 18, 1939, in New York City, New York). Stage actress. She began her career in Europe and then, in 1894, immigrated to the United States, where she became a leading lady in the Yiddish theater and later in English-language Broadway plays as well. Kalich was at her best in highly emotional plays, such as *The East Side Ghetto*. Her greatest role was as the Jewish woman whose marriage to a Russian nobleman leads to tragedy in *The Kreutzer Sonata* (Yiddish, 1902; English, 1906).

KAMEN, MILT (born March 5, 1921, in Hurleyville, New York; died February 24, 1977, in Beverly Hills, California). Comedian and character actor. He worked as a stand-up comedian in nightclubs; appeared on TV game and variety programs, such as *To Tell the Truth* and *The Tonight Show*; and acted on the stage, as in *The Passion of Josef D.* (1964), and in films, including *W. C. Fields and Me* (1976).

KAMINSKA, IDA (born September 4, 1899, in Odessa, the Ukraine; died May 21, 1980, in New York City, New York). Character actress. From the late 1940s until the late 1960s, she directed the Jewish State Theater of Poland. She became internationally famous for playing the aged Jewish shopkeeper facing deportation in the Czech film *Obchod na Korze* (1965; released in the United States as *The Shop on Main Street*, also known as *The Shop on High Street*). In the late 1960s, she immigrated to the United States. Kaminska was widely known as the Queen of the Yiddish Theater.

KAPLAN, GABE (born March 31, 1945, in New York City, New York). Originally a nightclub comedian, Kaplan recorded the comedy album *Holes and Mellow Rolls* (1974). He is best known for playing Gabe Kotter on the TV comedy series *Welcome Back, Kotter* (1975–79). His few movies included *Fast Break* (1979). In 1983 he began years of touring in the one-man show *Groucho*.

KAPLAN, MARVIN (born January 24, 1924 or 1927, in New York City, New York). Comedy character actor of owlish appearance. His films included *The Reformer and the Redhead* (1950), *Angels in the Outfield* (1951), *Wake Me When It's Over* (1960), *The Nutty Professor* (1963), *The Great Race* (1965), and *Delirious* (1991). On TV he was in the comedy series *Meet Millie* (1952–56); and in the late 1970s and early 1980s he played Henry, the telephone repairman, in the comedy series *Alice*.

KATCH, KURT (originally Kurt Isserkac; born January 28, 1896, in Grodno, Russian-ruled Poland; died August 14, 1958, in Los Angeles, California). Bald character actor. He settled in Hollywood in the early 1940s. His films included *Watch on the Rhine* (1943), *The Mask of Dimitrios* (1944), and *Song of Love* (1947).

KATZ, MICKEY (originally Meyer Myron Katz; born June 15, 1909, in Cleveland, Ohio; died April 30, 1985, in Los Angeles, California). Comedian and musician. Father of entertainer Joel Grey. For many years Katz toured and starred in an English-Yiddish stage revue called *Borscht Capades*, which he also coproduced.

KAUFMAN, ANDY (born January 17, 1949, in New York City, New York; died May 16, 1984, in Los Angeles, California). Comedian and comic actor. His offbeat stage act included two unforgettable characterizations: Tony Clifton, an untalented but arrogant singer, and the obnoxious

Intergender World Wrestling Champion, who challenged women to wrestling matches. Kaufman acted in several films, including *In God We Tru$t: Gimme That Prime Time Religion* (1980). However, he is best remembered for his appearance on the TV series: *Saturday Night Live* (1975–82) and, for his performance as the gentle Latka Gravas, *Taxi* (1978–83).

KAYE, STUBBY (born November 11, 1918, in New York City, New York; died December 14, 1997, in Rancho Mirage, California). Chubby comic actor and singer. He began as a vaudeville comedian and later became successful on Broadway as Nicely-Nicely Johnson in *Guys and Dolls* (1950) and as Marryin' Sam in *Li'l Abner* (1956). Kaye also appeared in the filmed versions of those musical plays (1955 and 1959, respectively). He had regular roles in the TV comedy series *Love and Marriage* (1959–60) and *My Sister Eileen* (1960–61). Other works in which he appeared included the play *The Ritz* (1975) and the movies *Forty Pounds of Trouble* (1963), *Cat Ballou* (1965), *Goldie and the Boxer Go to Hollywood* (TV, 1981), and *Ellis Island* (TV, 1984).

KEITEL, HARVEY (born May 13, 1939, in New York City, New York). Character actor. He worked briefly on Broadway before becoming a film actor. His film roles have tended to be seedy streetwise characters: in *Mean Streets* (1973) he was a petty hood, in *Taxi Driver* (1976) a pimp, in *The Border* (1982) an unscrupulous guard, and in *Order of Death* (1983) a cop on the take. Among his many later motion pictures were *Bugsy* (1991), *Pulp Fiction* (1994), *Fairy Tale: A True Story* (1997), and *Shadrach* (1998).

KESSLER, DAVID (born probably 1859 in Kishinev, Russia; died May 14, 1920, in New York City, New York). Yiddish stage actor.

KING, ALAN (originally Irwin Alan Kniberg [also reported as Kinberg and Kingberg]; born December 26, 1927, in New York City, New York). Comedian and character actor. Working with a cigar in hand, he has become a top nightclub and TV comedian. He is sometimes called "an aggressive Jack Benny." He gently lampoons just about everyone and everything. King has acted in plays, such as *Applause* (1970), and in movies, including *Hit the Deck* (1955); *Bye Bye Braverman* (1968); *I, the Jury* (1982); *Enemies, a Love Story* (1989), as a rabbi; and *Night and the City* (1992).

KLEIN, ROBERT (born February 8, 1942, in New York City, New York). Comedian and character actor. As a stand-up comedian, he has performed on TV and in theaters. He has also acted on Broadway, as in *The Apple Tree* (1966) and *The Sisters Rosensweig* (1992), and in movies, such as *Your Place or Mine* (TV, 1983) and *Mixed Nuts* (1994).

KOSSOFF, DAVID (born November 24, 1919, in London, England). Character actor. He appeared in *The World of Sholom Aleichem* (1955), *Come Blow Your Horn* (1962), and other plays. His films included *A Kid for Two Farthings* (1956), *The Bespoke Overcoat* (1956), *Freud* (1962), and *The Private Life of Sherlock Holmes* (1970). Since 1970 he has performed a solo stage act called *As According to Kossoff*.

KRUSCHEN, JACK (born March 20, 1922, in Winnipeg, Canada). Character actor, often in comedies. He was one of the earliest performers on TV, appearing on an experimental Los Angeles station in 1939. His stage work included *I Can Get It for You Wholesale* (1962). Among his many films were *The War of the Worlds* (1953), *Money from Home* (1954), *The Apartment* (1960), *The Unsinkable Molly Brown* (1964), *Sunburn* (1979), *Dark Mirrors* (TV, 1984), and *'Til There Was You* (1997).

ℒ

LANCET-FRYE, BATIA (born 1922 in Hungary). When she was two years old, she was taken to Palestine. In the mid-1940s, she helped to found the Cameri Theater, of which she has been a permanent member ever since. She was named Actress of the Year (1956–57) for her title role in Lorca's *Yerma*. In 1959 she won the Klausner Prize for her performance as Eliza Gant in *Look Homeward, Angel*. Lancet-Frye has also appeared in Israeli films.

LAVIN, LINDA (born October 15, 1937, in Portland, Maine). Actress best known for her title role in the TV sitcom *Alice* (1976–85). She was universally praised for her performance in Neil Simon's play *Broadway Bound* (1986). Her other credits include roles in the TV movie *For the Future: The Irvine Fertility Scandal* (TV, 1996) and the play *The Diary of Anne Frank* (1997).

LEDERER, FRANCIS (originally Frantisek Lederer; born November 6, 1906, in Prague, Bohemia). Leading man. After getting stage and screen experience in Europe, he moved to the United States in the early 1930s. His stage roles included Joe Bonaparte in *Golden Boy* (1937) and Mr. Frank in *The Diary of Anne Frank* (1958). He also acted in films, including *Confessions of a Nazi Spy* (1939).

LEE, MICHELE (originally Michele Lee Dusick; born June 24, 1942, in Los Angeles, California). Leading lady. She appeared in the stage musical *How to Succeed in Business without Really Trying* (1961) and later repeated her performance for the filmed version (1967). Her other movies included *The Comic* (1969), *Bud and Lou* (TV, 1978), *A Letter to Three Wives* (TV, 1985), and *Color Me Perfect* (TV, 1996). She played Karen Fairgate, later Karen Fairgate MacKenzie, on the TV drama series *Knots Landing* (1979–93).

LEE, PINKY (originally Pincus Leff; born 1916 in Saint Paul, Minnesota; died April 3, 1993, in Mission Viejo, California). Comedian. A wild sight-gag performer, Lee began in vaudeville. But he reached the peak of his popularity by cohosting the TV variety show *Those Two* (1951–53) and especially by hosting the children's TV series *The Pinky Lee Show* (1954–56).

LENYA, LOTTE (originally Karoline Blamauer; born October 18, 1898, in Vienna, Austria; died November 27, 1981, in New York City, New York). Known principally for her performances in the stage musicals of her first husband, Kurt Weill. She also worked as a dramatic actress, notably as a cynical procuress in the film *The Roman Spring of Mrs. Stone* (1961).

LEONARD, JACK E. (Originally Leonard Lebitsky; born April 24, 1911, in Chicago, Illinois; died May 10, 1973, in New York City, New York). Comedian, known as Fat Jack. A predecessor of Don Rickles as an insult comedian, he worked in nightclubs and on TV. Leonard appeared in a few movies, including *The Disorderly Orderly* (1964) and *The Fat Spy* (1966).

LEONARD, SHELDON (originally Sheldon Leonard Bershad; born February 22, 1907, in New York City, New York; died January 10, 1997, in Beverly Hills, California). Character actor. He acted on Broadway during the 1930s and then moved to Hollywood, where he acted in films, frequently playing comic gangsters. His films included *Another Thin Man* (1939); *Lucky Jordan* (1943); *It's a Wonderful Life* (1946); *Stop, You're Killing Me* (1952); *Guys and Dolls* (1955); and *Pocketful of Miracles* (1961). He had a regular role on the TV comedy series *The Danny Thomas Show* (1957–64). In his later years, Leonard worked mainly as a TV producer and director, though he occasionally returned to the front of the cameras, as in the movie *The Islander* (TV, 1978).

LEONTOVICH, EUGENIE (born March 21, 1900, in Moscow, Russia; died April 3, 1993, in New York City, New York). Character actress. She appeared on the Moscow stage until the 1917 revolution, after which she stayed in Paris and other European cities, finally settling in the United States in 1922. She acted in some films, including *Four Sons* (1940) and *The Rains of Ranchipur* (1955). But her principal work was on the stage, notably as the Dowager Empress in *Anastasia* (1954). Her other stage roles included Sarah Bernhardt in *Fires of Spring* (1929), Mr. Pepys in *And So to Bed* (1945), and the title part in *Anna K* (1972).

LEVANT, OSCAR (born December 27, 1906, in Pittsburgh, Pennsylvania; died August 14, 1972, in Beverly Hills, California). Pianist who appeared as a wisecracking supporting actor in several films, including *Rhythm on the River* (1940), *Rhapsody in Blue* (1945), *Humoresque* (1946), and *An American in Paris* (1951). In the 1950s he was a panelist on many TV shows, where he displayed his cynicism and neuroses.

LEVENSON, SAM (born December 28, 1911, in New York City, New York; died August 27, 1980, in New York City, New York). Comedian. In his nightclub and TV monologues, he stressed the happy side of being poor in the old days. For many years he was a witty panelist on TV game shows, such as *To Tell the Truth*.

LEWIS, JOE E. (originally Joseph Klewan; early stage name, Joe Lewis; he inserted the middle initial, which stood for nothing, to avoid confusion with the boxer Joe Louis; born January 12, 1902, in New York City, New York; died

June 4, 1971, in New York City). Nightclub comedian long esteemed by his peers for his ability to build successful routines with mediocre material through the sheer force of his timing, delivery, and personality.

LEWIS, RICHARD (born June 29, 1947 [some sources give 1948 or 1949] in Brooklyn, New York City, New York [some sources give Englewood, New Jersey]). Comedian and comic actor. His stand-up performances are rooted in an extreme—and extremely funny—form of neuroticism. He starred in the TV sitcom *Anything but Love* (1989–92) and had roles in some movies, including *Robin Hood: Men in Tights* (1993).

LEWIS, SHARI (originally Shari Hurwitz; born January 17, 1934, in New York City, New York; died August 2, 1998, in Los Angeles, California). Puppeteer and ventriloquist. She hosted several TV series, including *The Shari Lewis Show* (1960–63), on which she entertained children with her puppets Charlie Horse, Hush Puppy, and Lamb Chop. Later, she appeared in Las Vegas, worked as an actress, wrote dozens of books, and hosted the children's TV shows *Shari at Six* (G.B., 1968–76), *Lamb Chop's Play-Along* (1992–96), and *The Charlie Horse Music Pizza* (1998).

LEWIS, TED (originally Theodore Leopold Friedman; born June 6, 1891, in Circleville, Ohio; died August 25, 1971, in New York City, New York). Entertainer, clarinetist, and bandleader. Working in burlesque, vaudeville, and nightclubs, he became famous for his vocal renditions of the song "Me and My Shadow" and for his expression "Is everybody happy?" He also appeared in a few movies, including *Is Everybody Happy?* (1929) and *Follow the Boys* (1944).

LIGHT, JUDITH (born February 9, 1949, in Trenton, New Jersey). Leading lady. She played Karen in the daytime TV serial *One Life to Live* (1977–82); had the role of Angela in the prime-time TV sitcom *Who's the Boss?* (1984–92); and appeared in many TV movies, such as *Betrayal of Trust* (TV, 1994).

LINDER, MAX (originally Gabriel-Maximilien Leuvielle; born 1883 in Cavenne, Bordeaux, France; died November 1, 1925, in Paris, France). Comic actor. He was a major star of French silent films and became the first internationally famous actor, influencing Chaplin and others. Linder also made a few Hollywood films, including *Three Must-Get-Theres* (1922). He and his wife committed double suicide by taking drugs and slashing their wrists.

LION, LEON M. (born March 12, 1879, in London, England; died March 28, 1947, in Brighton, England). Stage actor. He was well known for his performances in Galsworthy plays.

LOEB, PHILIP (born 1894 in Philadelphia, Pennsylvania; died September 1, 1955, in New York City, New York). Comic character actor. He appeared in many plays on the New York City stage before becoming famous for playing Jake in the radio and TV comedy series *The Goldbergs* in the late 1940s and early 1950s. His movies included *Room Service* (1938) and *Molly* (1951). Blacklisted during the McCarthy-era witch-hunts, Loeb committed suicide by taking an overdose of sedatives.

LOUISE, TINA (originally Tina Blacker; born February 11, 1934 or 1937, in New York City, New York). Leading lady. She is best known for her role as Ginger Grant, the beautiful movie actress, on the TV comedy series *Gilligan's Island* (1964–67). But she also appeared in many films, including *God's Little Acre* (1958), *Armored Command* (1961), *For Those Who Think Young* (1964), *Advice to the Lovelorn* (TV, 1981), and *Johnny Suede* (1992).

m

MANN, HANK (originally David Liebermann; born 1887 in New York City, New York; died November 25, 1971, in South Pasadena, California). Supporting actor in silent movies. One of the original Keystone Kops, he also played in many Chaplin films, notably *City Lights* (1931) and *Modern Times* (1936). His few talkies included Chaplin's *The Great Dictator* (1940).

MANNHEIM, LUCIE (born April 30, 1895, near Berlin, Germany; died July 28, 1978, in Braunlage, West Germany). Character actress. Before the rise of Nazism, she was an important stage actress in Berlin. One of her best roles was that of Nora in Ibsen's *A Doll's House*. Later, she worked in England and America. She played the mysterious victim in Hitchcock's classic film *Thirty-Nine Steps* (1935). Her

other movies included *So Little Time* (1953) and *Bunny Lake Is Missing* (1965).

MARCEAU, MARCEL (originally Marcel Mangel; born March 22, 1923, in Strasbourg, France). The world's greatest mime, particularly beloved for his character Bip, the sad, white-faced clown he created in 1947. Marceau has performed in dozens of countries, language being no barrier for the enjoyment of his silent skits. Among his short pantomimes, which run the gamut from playfulness to profundity, are *Bip at a Society Party*, *Bip Hunts Butterfly*, *The Cage*, and *The Creation of the World*. His full-length "mimodramas" include *The Overcoat*, which was filmed (1951), as were several of his other works. Despite the physical demands of his work, he has continued to perform in his senior years, touring the United States, for example, in 1998, when he was seventy-five years old.

MARCH, HAL (originally Harold Mendelson; born April 22, 1920, in San Francisco, California; died January 19, 1970, in Los Angeles, California). Comic character actor. He is best remembered for hosting *The $64,000 Question* (1955–58), the first prime-time big-money TV game show. But he also appeared on the stage, as in *Come Blow Your Horn* (1961), and in some films, such as *My Sister Eileen* (1955) and *Send Me No Flowers* (1964).

MARGOLIN, JANET (born 1943 in New York City, New York; died December 17, 1993, in Los Angeles, California). Dark-haired, attractive leading lady. She successfully played a mentally disturbed girl on the New York City stage in *Daughter of Silence* (1961). As a result, she was hired to play the schizophrenic female lead in the movie *David and Lisa* (1962). Margolin was later a frequent guest on TV series. She also appeared in the Woody Allen films *Take the Money and Run* (1969) and *Annie Hall* (1977), and she starred in the movie *The Plutonium Incident* (TV, 1980).

MARTIN, ROSS (originally Martin Rosenblatt; born March 22, 1920, in Grodek, Poland; died July 3, 1981, near San Diego, California). Character actor. Martin came to America when he was a baby. He was best known for his role as an underground intelligence agent in the TV adventure series *The Wild, Wild West* (1965–69). His films included *The Great Race* (1965) and *I Married Wyatt Earp* (TV, 1983). Martin was a master of disguise.

MARTIN, TONY (originally Alvin Morris; born December 25, 1913, in Oakland, California). The popular singer acted in many musical films, including *Ali Baba Goes to Town* (1937), *The Big Store* (1941), *Till the Clouds Roll By* (1946), and *Casbah* (1948).

MAY, ELAINE (originally Elaine Berlin; born April 21, 1932, in Philadelphia, Pennsylvania). Comedienne and character actress. As a teenager she married and divorced Marvin May, whose surname she kept for professional use. In the late 1950s, she and Mike Nichols performed, prepared, and improvised comedy skits in nightclubs and on TV. Later, on her own, she distinguished herself as an actress in several movies, including *Luv* (1967), *A New Leaf* (1971), and *In the Spirit* (1990). She costarred with Nichols in a stage production of the powerful drama *Who's Afraid of Virginia Woolf?* (1980). May is also active as a writer and director. She scripted *Tootsie* (1982), wrote and directed *Ishtar* (1987), and provided the script for *The Birdcage* (1996), which was directed by Nichols.

MEISNER, SANFORD (born August 31, 1905, in New York City, New York; died February 2, 1997, in Sherman Oaks, Los Angeles, California). Actor, director, and acting teacher. He studied and successfully performed with the Theater Guild (1924–31) and the Group Theater (1931–41). But he became most famous as a teacher, principally at the Neighborhood Playhouse School of the Theater in Manhattan. His students included Gregory Peck, Tony Randall, Steve McQueen, Grace Kelly, Peter Falk, and Joanne Woodward.

MENKEN, ADAH ISAACS (originally Adah Bertha Theodore; born 1835 in Chartrain, near New Orleans, Louisiana; died August 10, 1868, in Paris, France). Leading lady. Her origins are shrouded in mystery. Apparently she was raised as a Catholic, but she converted to Judaism in 1857, having married a Jew named (Alexander) Isaac Menken in 1856. Later, she divorced him, but she lived the rest of her life, and was buried, as a Jew. For her stage name, she blended her and her husband's names: Adah Isaacs (adding an s for euphony) Menken. After struggling as an actress for a few years, she was offered the title role in *Mazeppa*, a melodrama based on Byron's poem. Menken first played the role in 1861 and thereafter appeared in almost no other plays. But with just that one role she became famous in America and in Europe. She shocked Victorian Age audiences with a costume that exposed her thighs. And at the climax of the play, she absolutely astounded them by appearing nude (actually wearing flesh-colored tights and a small loin cloth), being strapped to a horse, and being sent on a wild ride into the hills. Menken was popularly referred to as the Naked Lady.

MERON, HANNA (or Channa Marron; original surname, Maierzak; born November 22, 1923, in Berlin, Germany). She appeared as a child actress on the German stage and in the Fritz Lang classic film *M* (1931). In 1933 she moved to Palestine. From 1940 to 1945, she served in the British armed forces. In the mid-1940s, she joined the newly founded Cameri Theater, and in the following years, she was a major factor in some of its greatest successes. She had a special flair for modern sophisticated comedy, though she also excelled in dramatic roles, such as the lead in Ibsen's *Hedda Gabler*. In 1970 Meron lost a leg as a result of an Arab terrorist attack on Israeli airplane passengers in Munich. After she recovered, she resumed her stage career in Israel.

MIKHOELS, SOLOMON (originally Solomon Vovsi; born 1890 in Dvinsk, Russia; died January 13, 1948, in Minsk, the Soviet Union). Yiddish stage actor. One of the original members of the State Jewish Theater in Moscow, he became famous for his performance in Aleichem's *Agents* (1921). After several years as the company's leading actor, he took over its directorship in 1928. He was especially renowned for his tragic and tragicomic roles. One of his greatest achievements was his interpretation of the title role in a Yiddish version of Shakespeare's *King Lear* (1935). After World War II, when Jewish refugees were trying to settle or resettle in the Soviet Union, Mikhoels served as their spokesman with Soviet authorities. He was brutally murdered by the Soviet secret police, who, with the personal aid of Stalin, covered up the deed to look like an auto accident. Mikhoels' death was the first step in Stalin's attempt to liquidate all Jewish intellectuals and cultural institutions in the Soviet Union. In 1962 a Tel Aviv square was named after Mikhoels.

MILLER, MARTIN (originally Rudolph Muller; born 1899 in Kremisier, Moravia; died August 26, 1969, in Austria). Character actor. He worked principally in Vienna and Berlin until moving to London in the late 1930s. He sometimes performed in the United States as well. Miller acted in some plays but he is best known for his performances in such films as *Exodus* (1960), *The Phantom of the Opera*

(1962), and *The Pink Panther* (1964). He was noted for his portrayals of elderly Jews.

MIROSLAVA (full name, Miroslava Stern; born February 26, 1926, in Prague, Czechoslovakia; died March 10, 1955, in Mexico City, Mexico). Popular leading lady in Mexico from the mid-1940s until her death, of suicide by poisoning. She also made a few English-language films, notably *The Brave Bulls* (1951).

MOGULESKO, SIGMUND (originally Zelig Mogulesko; born December 16, 1858, in Kaloraush, Bessarabia; died February 4, 1914, in New York City, New York). Yiddish stage actor. In 1886 he settled in New York City, where he became the premier Yiddish comedian of his time.

MOODY, RON (originally Ronald Moodnick; born January 8, 1924, in Hornsey, London, England). Versatile character comedian. A master of disguise, he is most famous for playing the villain Fagin in both the stage (1960) and screen versions of the musical *Oliver!* His other stage work included *Move Along Sideways* (1991), *Streets of Dublin* (1992), and *Bertie* (1993). Among his later films were the Mel Brooks comedy *The Twelve Chairs* (1970), the black comedy *Wrong Is Right* (1982), *A Ghost in Monte Carlo* (TV, 1990), and *A Kid in King Arthur's Court* (1995).

MORRIS, HOWARD (born September 4, 1919, in New York City, New York). Comic character actor. He was a regular on the TV variety series *Your Show of Shows* (1950–54) and *Caesar's Hour* (1954–57) and on the TV sitcom series *The Andy Griffith Show* (1960–68). His films included *The Nutty Professor* (1963), *Don't Drink the Water* (1969), *Splash* (1984), *Return to Mayberry* (TV, 1986), *Life Stinks* (1991), and *Boogie Nights* (1997). Morris is also a director.

MOSCOVITCH, MAURICE (original surname Maaskoff or Masskoff; born November 23, 1871, in Odessa, the Ukraine; died June 18, 1940, in Los Angeles, California). Character actor. In 1893 he arrived in the United States, where he appeared in Yiddish and English plays. His films included *Winterset* (1936) and *The Great Dictator* (1940).

MUNSHIN, JULES (born February 22, 1915, in New York City, New York; died February 19, 1970, in New York City, New York). Rubber-limbed musical-comedy performer. His stage work included *Call Me Mister* (1946). Among his films were *Easter Parade* (1948), *On the Town* (1949), and *Silk Stockings* (1957).

MURRAY, JAN (originally Murray Janofsky; born October 4, 1917, in New York City, New York). Comedian and character actor. He is an excellent nightclub performer, though he is best known as host of several TV game shows. Murray had roles in *The Busy Body* (1967); *Which Way to the Front?* (1970); *History of the World, Part I* (1981); and other films.

MYERSON, BESS (born July 16, 1924, in New York City, New York). TV personality. Miss America of 1945, Myerson later became a fixture on TV, where she helped to host the game show *The Big Payoff* (1951–59), served as a panelist on *I've Got a Secret* (1958–68), and appeared on other programs. In 1983 she became cultural-affairs commissioner of New York City.

n

NAZIMOVA (full name, Alla Nazimova; original surname, Leventon; in her early years, in Russia, she used the surname Alexandrovna; later, in America, Nazimova; during her lifetime, many sources gave her family name as Nazimoff; born June 4, 1878 [sometimes given as 1879], in Yalta, Crimea, Russia; died July 13, 1945, in Los Angeles, California). Dark-featured, intense leading lady. She performed on the Russian stage until czarist censors prohibited her from acting in the Zionist play *The Chosen People*. Leaving Russia, she acted in that work in Berlin and London before settling in the United States, where she debuted by giving a New York City performance, in Russian, as Lia in *The Chosen People*. Beginning in 1906 she acted in English-language plays or translations of plays, most effectively in those of Ibsen. She was highly praised for her interpretation of the role of Christine Mannon, the murderous wife, in the original production of O'Neill's *Mourning Becomes Electra* (1931). Nazimova also starred in silent movies, including *War Brides* (1916), *Camille* (1921), and *A Doll's House* (1922).

Later, she became a successful motion-picture character actress. She played an aging Polish countess in *In Our Time* (1944) and also appeared in *Escape* (1940), *Blood and Sand* (1941), and *The Bridge of San Luis Rey* (1944).

NEILSON, JULIA (born June 12, 1868, in London, England; died May 27, 1957, in London, England). Stage actress. Daughter of a Jewish mother and non-Jewish father. She was a famous leading lady in London and in touring productions during the period 1900 to 1929, especially in romantic costume comedies.

NEWMAN, BARRY (born November 7, 1938, in Boston, Massachusetts). Leading man. He starred in the title role of the TV crime-drama series *Petrocelli* (1974–76). His films included *Pretty Boy Floyd* (1960), *Vanishing Point* (1971), *Second Sight: A Love Story* (TV, 1984), and *My Two Loves* (TV, 1986).

NEWMAN, PHYLLIS (born March 19, 1935, in Jersey City, New Jersey). Actress and TV personality. She performed in the New York City stage revue *I Feel Wonderful* (1954) and the movie *Picnic* (1956). Beginning in the late 1950s, she made regular appearances on TV game and talk shows. She also acted on the stage play *The Prisoner of Second Avenue* (1971) and the films *To Find a Man* (1972) and *The Beautician and the Beast* (1997). In 1999 she was acclaimed for her performance as the lead character in the off-Broadway revival of *A Majority of One* by Leonard Spiegelgass.

NICHOLS, MIKE (originally Michael Igor Peschkowsky; born November 6, 1931, in Berlin, Germany). Comedian and character actor. In his youth he and Elaine May performed prepared and improvised comedy skits in nightclubs, on TV, and in the Broadway show *An Evening with Mike Nichols and Elaine May* (1960). Later, he became a successful film director. His films include *The Odd Couple* (1965), and *The Graduate* (1967). In 1980 he and May reunited to star in a stage production of the explosive drama *Who's Afraid of Virginia Woolf?* He also directed the film *The Birdcage* (1996), which was scripted by May.

PARKS, LARRY (originally Samuel Lawrence Klausman Parks; born December 13, 1914, in Olathe, Kansas; died April 13, 1975, in Studio City, California). Leading man. After several years in B movies, he suddenly became a star with his portrayal of Al Jolson in *The Jolson Story* (1946) and *Jolson Sings Again* (1949). His career was ruined in 1951 when he admitted before the House Un-American Activities Committee that he had been a member of the Communist Party from 1941 to 1945. After that, he did a small amount of nightclub and theater work; appeared in a few movies, such as *Freud* (1962); and then entered the real-estate business.

PEERCE, JAN (originally Jacob Pincus Perelmuth; born June 3, 1904, in New York City, New York; died December 15, 1984, in New Rochelle, New York). Great opera tenor who sang in several films and had a straight dramatic role in the movie *Goodbye, Columbus* (1969). In the 1970s Peerce performed the role of Tevye in *Fiddler on the Roof*, both on Broadway and on tour.

PELEG, ALEXANDER (born May 25, 1938, in Bucharest, Romania). He moved to Israel in 1952 and has been a member of the Habimah Theater since 1963. He gave excellent performances in the plays *The Castle* and *Who's Afraid of Virginia Woolf?* He has also performed the one-man shows *A Way of Life* and *Flowers for a White Mouse*.

PICHEL, IRVING (born June 24, 1891, in Pittsburgh, Pennsylvania; died July 13, 1954, in Los Angeles, California). Character actor. He appeared in *An American Tragedy* (1931), *Oliver Twist* (1933), *Juarez* (1939), *Martin Luther* (1953), and many other films. Pichel was also an important movie director. He was blacklisted for a time during the McCarthy era.

PORAT, ORNA (originally Orna Placek; born June 6, 1924, in Cologne, Germany). She has long been associated with Israel's Cameri Theater. In 1965 she cofounded the Cameri Children's Theater, of which she became the director. In 1970 she became the artistic director of the Theater for Youth and Children. Porat has performed in plays in Europe and Israel. She is well known for her performances in classic plays by Euripides, Shakespeare, and George Bernard Shaw. In the mid-1980s she gave a strong performance in the Israeli film *When Night Falls*.

PREMINGER, OTTO (born December 5, 1906, in Vienna, Austria; died April 23, 1986, in New York City, New York). A major film director, he also acted in a few movies, notably as the German commandant of a World War II prisoner-of-war camp in *Stalag 17* (1953).

Q

QUESTEL, MAE (born September 13, 1908, in New York City, New York; died January 4, 1998, in New York City). Supporting actress in Broadway plays, such as *A Majority of One* (1959), and in films, including *Funny Girl* (1968). She was best known, however, as the voice of the cartoon characters Betty Boop and Olive Oyl.

R

RACHEL (originally Elisabeth Felix; born February 28, 1821, in Mumpf, Switzerland; died January 3, 1858, in Le Cannet, France). Leading lady. A world-famous star at the Comedie-Francaise in Paris, she played tragic roles in plays by Racine, Corneille, and others. In 1855 she made an American tour.

RADNER, GILDA (born June 28, 1946, near Detroit, Michigan; died May 20, 1989, in Los Angeles, California). Comic actress. She rose to stardom through her daffy sketches on the TV comedy-variety series *Saturday Night Live* (1975–80) and appeared in several movies, including *The Woman in Red* (1984) and *Haunted Honeymoon* (1986), both of which featured her husband, Gene Wilder.

REEVE, ADA (born March 3, 1874, in London, England; died September 25, 1966, in London, England). Character actress. She was a popular music-hall and musical-comedy performer in the late 1800s and early 1900s. Later, she acted in plays, such as *The Shop at Sly Corner* (1945), and in some movies, including *They Came to a City* (1944) and *The Passionate Stranger* (1957, G.B.; U.S., *A Novel Affair*). At the age of ninety, she was still appearing on TV.

REINER, CARL (born March 20, 1922, in New York City, New York). Comic actor. He played roles on the TV variety series *Your Show of Shows* (1950–54) and *Caesar's Hour* (1954–57) and on the TV comedy series *The Dick Van Dyke Show* (1961–66). His films included *It's a Mad, Mad, Mad, Mad World* (1963); *The Russians Are Coming, the Russians Are Coming* (1966); *The End* (1978); *Skokie* (TV, 1981); *Dead Men Don't Wear Plaid* (1982); and *Fatal Instinct* (1993). He played straight man to Mel Brooks's two-thousand-year-old man on their celebrated series of comedy recordings. For many years he has also been active as a writer, producer, and director. He is the father of the comic actor Rob Reiner, who played Mike ("Meathead") Stivic on the TV comedy series *All in the Family* (1971–78).

RITZ BROTHERS. Family of comedians consisting of AL (originally Alfred; born August 27, 1901, in Newark, New Jersey; died December 22, 1965, in New Orleans, Louisiana), Jimmy (originally Samuel; born October 22, 1904 [or October 5, 1903], in Newark, New Jersey; died November 17, 1985, in Los Angeles, California), and Harry (born May 22, 1906 [or 1907/ 1908], in Newark, New Jersey; died March 29, 1986, in San Diego, California). Their original surname was Joachim. They took their zany slapstick humor to vaudeville and then appeared in a number of movies in the late 1930s and early 1940s, including *On the Avenue* (1937), *The Goldwyn Follies* (1938), *The Three Musketeers* (1939), and *Behind the Eight Ball* (1942). Later, they appeared in nightclubs and on TV until Al's death, after which Jim and Harry semiretired. They made a cameo appearance in the film *Won Ton Ton, the Dog Who Saved Hollywood* (1976). Harry, the team's leader, greatly influenced other comedians: he encouraged Milton Berle to wear dresses on TV, he introduced the scat singing later imitated by Danny Kaye, and he employed some mannerisms that were adopted by Jerry Lewis.

ROBBINS, JEROME (originally Jerome Rabinowitz; born October 11, 1918, in New York City, New York; died July 29, 1998, in New York City, New York). Dancer, choreographer, and director who was unique in the world of American dance because he was equally successful in ballet and on Broadway. He choreographed the ballets *Fancy Free* (1944), *Dybbuk Variations* (1974), and *Glass Pieces* (1983), among others. His masterpiece was *West Side Story* (1957), a landmark in extending the expressive range, and organic function, of dances in Broadway musicals. He also choreographed the Broadway hits *The King and I* (1951) and *Fiddler on the Roof* (1964).

ROSENBLOOM, MAXIE ("SLAPSY [or SLAPSY] MAXIE") (born September 6, 1904, in New York City, New York; died March 6, 1976, in South Pasadena, California). Comic character actor. An ex-boxer, he appeared in many films, often as a gangster or a punch-drunk fighter. His movies included *Nothing Sacred* (1937), *Louisiana Purchase* (1941), *Hollywood or Bust* (1956), and *Cottonpickin' Chickenpickers* (1967).

ROTH, LILLIAN (born December 13, 1910, in Boston, Massachusetts; died May 12, 1980, in New York City, New York). Singing actress. She entered show business when she was a small child and soon, she became a major star on Broadway. She appeared in the 1928 and 1931 editions of the *Earl Carroll Vanities*, and in the movies *The Love Parade* (1929), *Animal Crackers* (1930), *Madam Satan* (1930), and *Take a Chance* (1933). But then her career collapsed for nearly two decades as she struggled against alcoholism and mental illness. In her book *I'll Cry Tomorrow* (with Mike Connolly and Gerold Frank, 1954), she movingly told the story of her return to a healthy life and an active career. The book was turned into a powerful 1955 movie. In 1958 she came out with another autobiographical book, *Beyond My Worth*. Among her later performances were an appearance in the Broadway musical *I Can Get It for You Wholesale* (1962) and a small but effective role as a lonely Jewish widow in the movie *Boardwalk* (1979).

ROVINA, HANNA (born 1888 in Minsk, Russia; died 1980 in Israel). Stage actress. In 1917 she helped Nahum Zemach to found the Habimah Theater in Moscow. The company's first great success was the Hebrew version of Ansky's *The Dybbuk* (1922), in which Rovina starred as Leah, a role that she subsequently played many times. Another important role in her career was that of the mother of the Messiah

in *The Eternal Jew* (1925 and many other times thereafter). She and the company appeared in Palestine in 1928 and then, after a European tour, permanently settled in the Holy Land in 1931. Possessing great beauty and dignity, Rovina made an excellent classical heroine, as in Euripides's *Medea*. Later in her career, she played matronly roles, as in Brecht's *Mother Courage*.

RUBIN, BENNY (born February 2, 1899, in Boston, Massachusetts; died June 15, 1986, in Los Angeles, California). Bug-eyed, rubber-faced comedian and comic actor. In his early years he starred as a comic dialectician in vaudeville and as a film actor, notably in *Sammy Skies* (1930). Later he played supporting roles on radio and TV, including many appearances on Jack Benny's shows in both media. He also acted in the films *Here Comes Mr. Jordan* (1941) and *The Patsy* (1964).

RUBINSTEIN, IDA (full name, Ida Lvovna Rubinstein; born about 1885 in Saint Petersburg, Russia; died September 20, 1960, in Vence, France). Dancer who starred in the first production of the Ballets Russes in Paris (1909) and who commissioned some of the twentieth century's most important ballets, including Ravel's *La Valse* (composed 1919–20, performed 1928) and Stravinsky's *Persephone* (1934).

S

SAHL, MORT (born May 11, 1927, in Montreal, Canada). Comedian and character actor. As a sardonic political-satire comedian, he peaked in popularity in the early 1960s. He also acted in several films, including *All the Young Men* (1960) and *Inside the Third Reich* (TV, 1982).

SALES, SOUPY (originally Milton Supman; born January 8, 1926, in Franklinton, North Carolina). Comedian and comic character actor. He acquired his nickname, Soupy, from his childhood playmates, who created it by altering his family name, Supman. For a brief time, early in his career he used the surname Hines (from which came the erroneous story that his nickname was derived by punning "Hines" with "Heinz", the name of a well-known food-processing company). Sales hosted many local and national youth-oriented shows featuring jokes, puppets (including White Fang and Black Tooth), and pies in the face. He had local shows in Detroit (1953), Los Angeles (late 1950s), and New York City (1964); later his work was syndicated. But he reached the peak of his popularity when *The Soupy Sales Show* was nationally telecast from 1959 to 1962. Sales acted in a few movies, including *Birds Do It* (1966).

SANDLER, ADAM (born September 9, 1966, in Brooklyn, New York). Comedian and comic actor. He performed regularly on TV's *Saturday Night Live* (1991–95) and then turned to films, appearing in *Billy Madison* (1995), *Happy Gilmore* (1996), and *The Waterboy* (1998).

SATZ, LUDWIG (born 1891 in Lemberg, Galicia; died August 31, 1944, in New York City, New York). Yiddish comedian. He appeared in the first Yiddish film made with sound: *His Wife's Lover* (1932).

SCHACHT, AL (full name, Alexander Schacht; born November 12, 1892, in New York City, New York; died July 14, 1984, in Waterbury, Connecticut). The Clown Prince of Baseball, who entertained fans in ballparks for over fifty years.

SCHILDKRAUT, RUDOLF (born 1865 in Constantinople, Turkey; died July 15, 1930, in Los Angeles, California). Leading man. Father of the actor Joseph Schildkraut. Rudolf had successful stage careers in both Germany and the United States, performing in German, English, and Yiddish. He became famous for playing the Shakespearean roles of Shylock and King Lear. Schildkraut also acted in some silent films, such as *Proud Heart* (1925) and *Christina* (1929).

SCHLAMME, MARTHA (originally Martha Haftel; born about 1925 in Vienna, Austria; died October 6, 1985, in Jamestown, New York). Singing actress. Her first marriage was to a man named Hans Schlamme, whose surname she kept for professional use even after their union ended in annulment. In her concert appearances, she sang Jewish and other folksongs. She also acted in plays by Shakespeare and Sholom Aleichem. Schlamme made her Broadway debut in the musical *Fiddler on the Roof* (1968).

SCHREIBER, AVERY (born April 9, 1935, in Chicago, Illinois). Comedian and comic character actor. Early in his career, he worked with Jack Burns. Schreiber had a role on the TV comedy series *My Mother the Car* (1965–66), cohosted the TV variety series *The Burns and Schreiber Comedy Hour* (1973), appeared regularly on the TV variety series *Sha Na Na* (1977–78), and performed as a guest on many other TV shows, particularly in skits featuring him as a New York City cabdriver. His stage work included roles in New York City productions of *Dreyfus in Rehearsal* (1974) and *Welcome to the Club* (1989), and he appeared in numerous movies, such as *Don't Drink the Water* (1969), *The Last Remake of Beau Geste* (1977), *Robin Hood: Men in Tights* (1993), and *The Lay of the Land* (1997).

SCHWARTZ, MAURICE (originally Avrom Moishe Schwartz; born June 15, 1889, in Sudilkov, the Ukraine; died May 10, 1960, in Tel Aviv, Israel). Yiddish stage actor. In the early 1900s, he immigrated to the United States, where he directed and acted in over 150 plays in his Yiddish Art Theater. Among his most admired performances were those as Shylock in Shakespeare's *The Merchant of Venice* and as an aging Hasidic rabbi in *Yoshe Kalb*. Some of his stage performances were filmed for limited circulation. He also appeared in the Hollywood film *Salome* (1953). Schwartz died while on tour in Israel.

SEGAL, SHMUEL (born 1924 in Poland). At the age of ten, he moved to Palestine. With Shmuel Rodensky he formed a famous artistic partnership known as the Shmuliks. Segal has also performed in one-man shows on both the stage and the radio, and he has issued recordings in Hebrew and Yiddish.

SHAWN, DICK (originally Richard Schulefand; born December 1, 1929, in Buffalo, New York; died April 17, 1987, in San Diego, California). Comedian and character actor. He had roles in many plays such as *I'm Solomon* (1968) and *The World of Sholom Aleichem* (1976). His films included *Wake Me When It's Over* (1960); *It's a Mad, Mad, Mad, Mad World* (1963); *The Producers* (1967); *Fast Friends* (TV, 1979); and *Angel* (1984).

SHEAN, AL (originally, Adolf Schoenberg or Schonberg; born May 12, 1868, in Dornum, Germany; died August 12, 1949, in New York City, New York). Comedian and character actor. He and Ed Gallagher formed one of vaudeville's most popular comedy teams (1910–12, 1920–25). In 1921 they first performed their famous song "Mr. Gallagher and Mr. Shean." Shean also worked on his own in vaudeville and in Broadway musical comedies. Later in his career, he played character roles in films such as *San Francisco* (1936), *The Prisoner of Zenda* (1937), and *Atlantic City* (1944). He was an uncle of the Marx Brothers comedy team, their mother, Minnie, being Shean's sister.

SHERMAN, ALLAN (originally Allan Copelon; born November 30, 1924, in Chicago, Illinois; died November 20, 1973, in Los Angeles, California). Comedian. After beginning as a writer, he became a performer and issued the album *My Son, the Folksinger* (1962), a folksong travesty in Jewish style. He had his greatest success with his rendition of the song "Hello, Muddah; Hello, Fadduh" (on his album *My Son, the Nut*, 1963), in which he applied comical lyrics to a melody called "Dance of the Hours" from Ponchielli's 1876 opera *La Gioconda*.

SHORE, SAMMY (originally Samuel Semelah; born 1925 in Chicago, Illinois). For many years the most sought-after warm-up comedian in show business. He has opened shows for such stars as Elvis Presley and Sammy Davis, Jr.

SHUSTER, FRANK. *See* Wayne and Shuster.

SIDNEY, GEORGE (originally Sammy Greenfield; born March 18, 1876, in New York City, New York; died April 29, 1945, in Los Angeles, California). Leading vaudeville comedian. Later, he became a fine comic actor in films, particularly as Abe Potash in *Potash and Perlmutter* (1923) and as Jacob Cohen in *The Cohens and the Kellys* (1926). Both films generated sequels starring Sidney, such as *In Hollywood with Potash and Perlmutter* (1924) and *The Cohens and the Kellys in Trouble* (1933).

SKULNIK, MENASHA (born May 15, 1892, in Warsaw, Poland; died June 4, 1970, in New York City, New York). Comedian. After working on the European Yiddish stage, he immigrated to the United States and performed as a leading member

of the Yiddish Art Theater (1930–50). His English-language work included roles in the TV series *Menasha the Magnificent* (1950) and *The Goldbergs* (1953). He also performed on Broadway, notably as Noah in *The Flowering Peach* (1954). Skulnik was a sad-looking comedian, famous for his ludicrous shrugs.

SMIRNOFF, YAKOV (originally Yakov Pokhis; born January 24, 1951, in Odessa, the Soviet Union). Comedian who became a naturalized American citizen in 1986. He bases his humor on jokes that confirm Russian stereotypes and poke fun at American customs and language.

SMITH AND DALE. Comedy team consisting of Joe Smith (originally Joseph Sultzer; born February 16, 1884, in New York City, New York; died February 22, 1981, in Englewood, New Jersey) and Charlie Dale (originally Charles Marks; born September 6, 1881, in New York City, New York; died November 16, 1971, in Teaneck, New Jersey). Famous in vaudeville, they also appeared in some movies, including *Manhattan Parade* (1931) and *Two Tickets to Broadway* (1951). Smith got the punch lines, while Dale was the deadpan straight man.

STANG, ARNOLD (born September 28, 1925, in Chelsea, Massachusetts). Comic character actor, known for his hilariously weak chin. In the 1950s he was a regular on Milton Berle's TV variety shows. Stang also appeared regularly on the TV comedy series *The Goldbergs* (1954–55) and occasionally on the TV comedy series *December Bride* (1954–59). His films included *The Man with the Golden Arm* (1955), *The Wonderful World of the Brothers Grimm* (1962), *Hercules in New York* (1970), *Raggedy Ann and Andy* (1977), and *Dennis the Menace* (1993).

STEINBERG, DAVID (born August 9, 1942, in Winnipeg, Canada). Comedian and character actor. An excellent stand-up comedian, he has performed on many top TV talk and variety shows. He acted in the films *The End* (1978) and *Something Short of Paradise* (1979). Steinberg has also directed films, such as *Going Berserk* (1983), and episodes of TV sitcoms, including *Newhart*, *The Golden Girls*, and *Seinfeld*.

STEWART, ELAINE (originally Elsy Steinberg; born May 31, 1929, in Montclair, New Jersey). Beautiful leading lady and supporting actress. Her films included *The Bad and the Beautiful* (1952), *Brigadoon* (1954), *The Tattered Dress* (1957), and *The Rise and Fall of Legs Diamond* (1960).

STILLER, JERRY (born June 8, 1927, in New York City, New York). Comic actor best known for his stage and TV two-character comedy sketches with his wife, Anne Meara. His acting credits include roles in the theatrical film *Airport* 1975 (1974), the Broadway play *Hurlyburly* (1984), and the TV movie *Seize the Day* (TV, 1986).

STORCH, LARRY (originally Lawrence Storch; born January 8, 1923, in New York City, New York). Comic character actor. He began as a nightclub comedian and impressionist and then appeared in a few Broadway productions in the 1950s. He is best known, however, for his work on TV, especially in the comedy series *F Troop* (1965–67). His films included *Captain Newman, M.D.* (1963); *The Great Race* (1965); *The Adventures of Huckleberry Finn* (TV, 1981); and *I Don't Buy Kisses Anymore* (1922).

STRASBERG, LEE (born November 17, 1901, in Budanov, Austria-Hungary; died February 17, 1982, in New York City, New York). Character actor, as in the films *The Godfather, Part II* (1974) and *Skokie* (TV, 1981). Better known as artistic director of the Actors Studio in New York City (1948–82), where his pupils included Marlon Brando, Julie Harris, and many other major acting talents.

STRAUSS, PETER (born February 20, 1947, in Croton-on-Hudson, New York). Leading man. He is best known for his appearances in TV movies and miniseries, such as *Attack on Terror: The FBI versus the Ku Klux Klan* (TV, 1975); *Rich Man, Poor Man* (TV, 1976); *Masada* (TV, 1981); *Heart of Steel* (TV, 1983); *Kane and Abel* (TV, 1985); *Under Siege* (TV, 1986); and *Texas Justice* (TV, 1995).

STRAUSS, ROBERT (full name, Henry Robert Strauss; born November 8, 1913, in New York City, New York; died February 20, 1975, in New York City, New York). Character actor. Strauss often played comic heavies. His stage work included *Detective Story* (1949). He is best remembered for his role as Animal in the movie *Stalag 17* (1953). Among his other films were *Sailor Beware* (1952), *The Seven Year Itch* (1955), and *The Family Jewels* (1965).

SUSSKIND, DAVID (born December 19, 1920, in New York City, New York; found dead February 22, 1987, in New York City, New York). Host of a provocative TV talk show from 1958 to 1986, originally called *Open End*, later *The David Susskind Show*. Also an important producer.

T

TAMIRIS, HELEN (originally Helen Becker; born April 23, 1903, in New York City, New York; died August 24, 1966, in New York City, New York). One of the founders of modern dance, and of that group, the one most accomplished in ballet and the one most committed to presenting social themes in her performances.

TAYLOR, KENT (originally Louis Weiss; born May 11, 1907, in Nashua, Iowa; died April 11, 1987, in Los Angeles, California). Suave leading man. Among his best pictures were *Death Takes a Holiday* (1934), *Ramona* (1936), *I'm Still Alive* (1940), and *Playgirl* (1954). He also appeared on TV, notably in the title role of the popular mystery series *Boston Blackie* (1951–53). His later movies were low-budget horror pictures, such as *The Crawling Hand* (1963), and melodramas, including *Hell's Bloody Devils* (1970), in which he played a neo-Nazi leader.

TAYLOR, RENEE (originally Renee Wexler; born March 19, 1935, in New York City, New York). Actress and playwright. She has appeared in plays such as *The Rehearsal* (1952) and *The Third Ear* (1964), and in movies, including *The Errand Boy* (1961), *The Producers* (1967), and *Delirious* (1991). Taylor frequently cowrites scripts and costars with her husband, Joseph Bologna. Their films together include *Made for Each Other* (1971) and *Woman of the Year* (TV, 1976).

TEOMI, ODED (born 1937 in Tel Aviv, Palestine). Israeli stage and film actor. He has acted at Israel's principal theaters, including the Ohel, the Zavit, the Cameri, and the Habimah. He has also appeared in many Israeli films, including *Hem Hayu Eser* (1960; U.S., *They Were Ten*).

THOMASHEFSKY, BESSIE (originally Brukhe Baumfeld-kaufman; born 1873 in Kiev, Ukraine; died July 6, 1962, in Los Angeles, California). Yiddish actress and comedienne. She arrived in the United States in 1883, married Boris Thomashefsky in 1891, and became the star of his Yiddish theater troupe in New York City. Her acting range included classics, such as *Hamlet*, and contemporary plays that explored women's rights themes, such as *Jennie Runs for Mayor*. She also excelled at musical comedy, becoming a model for Fanny Brice and Molly Picon. In 1922 she separated from Boris Thomashefsky, and in 1930 she retired.

THOMASHEFSKY, BORIS (born May 12, 1868, in Kiev, the Ukraine; died July 9, 1939, in New York City, New York). Actor, playwright, producer, and impresario. In 1881 he immigrated to the United States. With his first wife, Bessie Kaufman (Baumfeld-Kaufman), he became one of the founders of the American Yiddish theater. He reverently staged Yiddish versions of the classics, such as works by Shakespeare and Goethe. However, possessing a flamboyant personality, he preferred to act in farces, musical comedies, and light romantic works. His second wife, Regina Zuckerberg, was, like Bessie, an actress.

THREE STOOGES. Comedy team initially consisting of Moe Howard (originally Moses Horwitz; born June 19, 1897, in New York City, New York; died May 4, 1975, in Los Angeles, California), his brother Shemp Howard (originally Samuel Horwitz; born March 17, 1900, in New York City, New York; died November 22, 1955, in Los Angeles, California), and Larry Fine (originally Louis Fineburg; born October 5, 1911, in Philadelphia, Pennsylvania; died January 24, 1975, in Woodland Hills, California). They worked in vaudeville with Ted Healy in an act called Ted Healy and His Stooges. In 1930 they began making films (for a short period, Healy appeared with them). In the early 1930s, Shemp left the team, and he was replaced by his brother Curly Howard (originally Jerome Lester Horwitz; born 1906 in New York City, New York; died January 19, 1952, in San Gabriel, California). While Shemp was on his own, he appeared in many films, notably the W. C. Fields comedy classic *The Bank Dick* (1940). When Curly retired in 1947 because of ill health, Shemp returned to the team. After Shemp's death in 1955, he was replaced by others for the last decade of the team's existence. Making numerous short films and a few features, the Three Stooges became world famous for their slapstick clowning in the old burlesque-vaudeville tradition.

TOMACK, SID (born 1907 in New York City, New York; died November 12, 1962, in Palm Springs, California). Character actor with a rich Brooklyn accent. Tomack appeared in many movies, including *A Double Life* (1948), *Force of Evil* (1948), and *Sail a Crooked Ship* (1962). He was a familiar face on early TV series, playing Jim Gillis, Riley's neighbor, in the first version of *The Life of Riley* (1949–50); Al, the con man, in *My Friend Irma* (1952–53); and Knobby Walsh, the boxing manager, in *The Joe Palooka Story* (syndicated 1954).

TOPOL (full name, Chaim [or Haim] Topol; born September 9, 1935, in Tel Aviv, Palestine.) He acquired his first acting experience when he performed with the Israeli army entertainment unit in the 1950s. Later, he acted in plays at the Haifa Municipal Theater. He also appeared in Israeli movies, including *Sallah Shabati* (1964; U.S., *Sallah*) and *Roman be'Hemschechim* (U.S., *Serial*). His British and American films include *Cast a Giant Shadow* (1966), *Before Winter Comes* (1969), *Fiddler on the Roof* (1971), *Flash Gordon* (1980), and *The Winds of War* (TV, 1983). He has often starred in stage productions of the musical *Fiddler on the Roof*, notably in London in 1967 and from 1994 to 1995 and in New York City in 1989.

V

VIGODA, ABE (born February 24, 1921, in New York City, New York). Character actor. He is best known as Sergeant Phil Fish in the TV comedy series *Barney Miller* (1975–77), a role that he continued in his own series, *Fish* (1977–78). Vigoda labored for many years as a fairly obscure stage actor appearing in New York City productions of *Richard II*

(1961), *The Man in the Glass Booth* (1968), and other plays. He first attracted major attention with his role as a loyal but dull-witted gangster in the movie *The Godfather* (1972). His later work included the films *The Cheap Detective* (1978) and *Gridlock* (TV, 1980), a New York City revival of the classic stage comedy *Arsenic and Old Lace* (1986), and the movie *Good Burger* (1997).

VOSKOVEC, GEORGE (originally Jiri Voskovec; born June 19, 1905, in Sazava, Bohemia; died July 1, 1981, in Pearblossom, California). Excellent character actor. He became immensely famous in Czechoslovakia as part of the comedy team Voskovec and (Jan) Werich, performing satiric revues and plays aimed at Hitler and Nazism. In 1939 the Nazi onslaught forced him out of his homeland, and he moved to the United States. After World War II, he returned to Czechoslovakia, where he proceeded to aim his satire at the new regime— the Communists. Again, he was expelled from his native land, finally settling permanently in America in the early 1950s. Voskovec turned to straight dramatic acting and became one of the best character actors of his time on both the stage and the screen. He was especially fond of Chekhov and Shakespeare, making his New York City debut in *The Tempest* (1945). Voskovec played Mr. Frank in a London production of *The Diary of Anne Frank* (1956). He also appeared in the plays *The Love of Four Colonels* (1953), *Brecht on Brecht* (1961), and *Cabaret* (1968). Among his films were *The World is Ours* (1939), *Twelve Angry Men* (1957), *The Spy Who Came In from the Cold* (1965), *The Iceman Cometh* (1973), and *Barbarosa* (1982).

W

WALBROOK, ANTON (originally Adolf Anton Wilhelm Wohlbruck; born November 19, 1900, in Vienna, Austria; died August 9, 1967, in Munich, West Germany). Elegant leading man. Descended from a long line of circus clowns, he broke family tradition by entering the legitimate German-language theater. He was also a popular romantic star in German-language movies, such as *Maskerade* ("Masquerade," 1934). In the late 1930s, he moved to England, where he appeared in the plays *Design for Living* (1939), *Watch on the Rhine* (1942), and other plays, including the musical *Call Me Madam* (1953), and others. But he is best known for acting in a number of well-known movies. In *Victoria the Great* (1937), he played the misunderstood Prince Albert; in

Dangerous Moonlight (1941, G.B.; U.S., *Suicide Squadron*), a romantic flyer-pianist playing the *Warsaw Concerto*; in *The Life and Death of Colonel Blimp* (1943), a "good German"; in *The Red Shoes* (1948), a sinister ballet impresario; *Wien Tanzt* (1951, Austria; U.S., *Vienna Waltzes*), as the composer Johann Strauss, Sr.; and *I Accuse!* (1958), as Major Esterhazy, the spy whose acts brought about the persecution of the Jewish officer Alfred Dreyfus.

WARFIELD, DAVID (originally David Wollfeld; born November 28, 1866, in San Francisco, California; died June 27, 1951, in New York City, New York). Stage actor. While he played only a handful of roles over and over again, he came to be regarded as the greatest American actor of the first quarter of the twentieth century. In the 1890s he played comic Jewish characters in burlesque theaters. He became a celebrity when, at the turn of the century, the famed producer David Belasco signed him to play Simon Levi, a Lower East Side peddler, in *The Auctioneer*. Perhaps Warfield's greatest role was as Anton von Barwig, a man who searches for his long-lost daughter, in *The Music Master*. That play and Warfield's other principal vehicles were produced by Belasco.

WAYNE AND SHUSTER. Comedy team consisting of Johnny Wayne (original surname, Weingarten; born 1918 in Toronto, Canada) and Frank Shuster (born 1916 in Toronto, Canada). Working on radio and TV, they became perhaps the only internationally famous performers based almost solely in Canada.

WEBER AND FIELDS. Comedy team consisting of Joe Weber (full name, Joseph Morris Weber; born August 11, 1867, in New York City, New York; died May 10, 1942, in Los Angeles, California) and Lew Fields (originally Lewis Maurice Schanfield; born January 1, 1867, in New York City, New York; died July 20, 1941, in Los Angeles, California). They teamed up as children and developed a German-Yiddish dialect act. At the turn of the century, they were top burlesque comedians. They also appeared in vaudeville, musical comedies, and movies, including *Friendly Enemies* (1925).

WEINER, MARC (born 1952 in Far Rockaway, New York). Comedian whose popularity was a major factor in the growth of comedy clubs in the 1980s. In the 1990s his Nickelodeon series, *Weinerville*, won him a large following.

WELCH, JOE (originally Joseph Wolinski; born May 15, 1873, in New York City, New York; died July 15, 1918, in Westport, Connecticut). The prototype Jewish vaudeville comedian, imitated by hundreds of later dialect comics.

WEST, BILLY (originally Roy B. Weissberg; born September 21, 1893, in Russia; died July 21, 1975, in Hollywood, California). Vaudeville and silent-screen comedy star. His films included *His Waiting Career* (1916), *His Day Out* (1917), *The Rogue* (1918), and *Lucky Fool* (1927).

American parents were there on an extended honeymoon, he grew up in Brooklyn. Known as the King of the One-Liners, he could tell 250 jokes in a forty-five-minute appearance. The one for which he was best known was "Take my wife—please!" For decades he gave about two hundred performances a year, not only in nightclubs and on TV but also at sales meetings, trade shows, college campuses, and even bar mitzvahs.

Y

YADIN, YOSEPH (or Joseph/Yosef/Yossi Yadin; original surname, Sukenik; born June 7, 1920, in Jerusalem, Palestine). He was a cofounder of the Cameri Theater, where he had leading roles in many plays, such as *Kasablan* and *Of Mice and Men*. Yadin appeared in Israel's first important feature film, *Hill 24 Doesn't Answer* (1955). He also acted in the European movies *Four in a Jeep* (1951) and *Stop Train 349* (1964), the Canadian picture *Lies My Father Told Me* (1975), and other films. Son of Eleazar Sukenik, the archaeologist who identified the antiquity of the Dead Sea Scrolls, and brother of the Israeli army general and archaeologist Yigael Yadin.

YOUNGMAN, HENNY (originally Henry Youngman; born March 16 [some sources give January 12], 1906, in Liverpool, England; died February 24, 1998, in New York City, New York). Comedian and character actor. Born in England while his

Z

ZEMACH, BENJAMIN (born 1902 in Russian-controlled Poland; died June 18, 1997, in Jerusalem, Israel). Dancer and choreographer who specialized in Jewish themes. He was a modern-dance pioneer who began his career at the famed Habimah Theater in Moscow (founded by his brother, Nahum Zemach) and later worked in the United States and Israel.

ZIMBALIST, EFREM, JR. (born November 30, 1918, in New York City, New York). Leading man. He starred in the TV detective series *77 Sunset Strip* (1958–64) and the TV crime-drama series *The F.B.I.* (1965–74). His stage work included *Hedda Gabler* (1948). Among his films were *The Chapman Report* (1962), *Airport 1975* (1974), and *Shooting Stars* (TV, 1983). He is the son of the violinist Efrem Zimbalist, Sr., and the singer Alma Gluck.

Index

Index

About the Author

Darryl Lyman has composed music for piano, voice, and chamber ensembles. He is the author of *Great Jewish Families* (1997), *Jewish Heroes and Heroines: Their Unique Achievements* (1996), *The Jewish Comedy Catalog* (1989, revised 1996), *Great Jews on Stage and Screen* (1987, revised 1994), and *From Simple Sounds to Symphonies* (1982). He contributed film reviews to *Magill's Cinema Annual* (1989, 1990) and coedited *Fifty Golden Years of Oscar* (1979), the official history of the Academy of Motion Picture Arts and Sciences. Among his other books are many language studies: *Civil War Quotations* (1995); *Civil War Wordbook* (1994), which was nominated for the prestigious Lincoln Prize at Gettysburg College; *Dictionary of Animal Words and Phrases* (1994); and, as coauthor, *Essential English* (1981), a college textbook. His shorter works have appeared in various periodicals, including *Newsday* and *Jack and Jill*.